THE
PASSION
OF
Isis and Osiris
A UNION OF TWO SOULS

JEAN HOUSTON

BALLANTINE/WELLSPRING

New York

For my beloved husband, Robert E. L. Masters, an untiring explorer of the experience of the ancient Egyptian mysteries and the dimensions of human consciousness. His reconstruction of the powerful and strangely beautiful magic of the goddess Sekhmet also illumines the sacred ways of the goddess Isis and the god Osiris.

CONTENTS

ACKNOWLEDGMENTS

It is with pleasure and profound gratitude that I acknowledge those friends and associates who have worked closely with me in seminars dealing with the material presented in this book: Sarah Dubin-Vaughn, Robert Gass, Frank Hayes, Michael Houlihan, Lynne Larsen, Derek Lawley, Gay Luce, Judith Morley, and Robin Van Doren.

I am also deeply grateful to those who helped so generously in the preparation of the final manuscript. Elisabeth Rothenberger devoted much time and care to the transcribing and organizing of the transcripts of the Isis and Osiris seminar.

Normandi Ellis, a poet and heiress of the Egyptian mysteries, provided a forum for dialogue on the multilayered meanings of the myth, offered suggestions, and emerged as an Isis in the editing, development, and birthing of the book. Her masterful poetic rendering of the tale of the passion of Isis and Osiris given here in Part 1 is as much a gift to scholarship as it is to literature.

My editor for the first draft of this book, Marie Glynn, offered unstintingly of her fine eye and keen mind in the preparation of the early manuscript. Cheryl D. Woodruff, at Ballantine, one of the world's great editors, guided this work from embryonic protobook to the finished version. Her rich understanding of the issues inherent in my presentation of the story, her immense store of knowledge, and her psychological acuity were critical to bringing the cultural richness of ancient Egypt to life. Finally, my close associate Peggy Nash Rubin lent the ear of a classical actress tuned to cadences of text meant to be spoken aloud. I am grateful also to Scott Frey for his wonderful "hieroglyphic" drawings.

This book is the result of my nearly half-century immersion in the culture and lore of Egypt. As a young child I was taken regularly to visit the Egyptian sections of the museums in the various cities where my family lived. I can still remember my dad carrying me on his shoulders and saying as we rounded the corner of one Egyptian room, "Hot dog, Jeanie! Mummies!" Then at ten I saved my lunch money to be able to buy Gardiner's *Egyptian Grammar* and painfully taught myself to read hieroglyphs.

At Columbia University, I went on to teach courses in the Department of Religion on the archaeology and culture of ancient Egypt. My husband-to-be, Robert Masters, and I did our courting in the Egyptian section of New York City's Metropolitan Museum of Art.

I later attended a number of archaeological digs at the temples of Luxor and Karnak in Egypt, and eventually Robert and I acquired a large collection of Egyptian antiquities. Over the years I have also led a number of groups to the region. The fact that Robert sometimes thinks that he's the reincarnation of Rameses II (and behaves accordingly) adds to my Egyptophilic cast of mind. So the book grows out of a daily life that is still in ancient Egypt.

The Transforming Myth Series

When I was ten years old I read a book that primed the deepest imaginings of my childhood. It sent me off on adventures more appropriate to myths and fairy tales than to the America of the early 1950s. When I was twenty I read the book again, and it seized the now metaphysical focus of my mind and leavened it with the eternal stories of the human soul. It filled my thoughts with the gruesome, gorgeous, awesome, living patterns that can quicken, destroy, or transform the human endeavor at all times and any place along life's turnings.

Recently, after many years of exploring the vastness of the human condition and its possibilities, I read the book again. My reading this time was impelled by what I have come to sense as the nature and nearness of the "possible human." By that I mean our nascent selves who are yearning to make actual that which is still, for most of us, only potential—the vast untapped possibilities of mind, body, and spirit that reside in every one of us.

The wider use of the self has been the dream for millennia, but only in our time do we have access to the findings of many cultures as well as scientific studies concerning the nature and variety of this potential. Now there is an almost desperate sense of need for this possible human in us all to help create the possible society and the possible world if we are to survive our own personal and planetary odyssey and come safely home to the sanctuary of the soul.

The title of the book that so inspired my life and work is *The Hero with a Thousand Faces* by Joseph Campbell. Campbell became a luminous spokesman for myth, ritual, and symbol, famed for evoking and writing about the timeless images and stories that form the loom upon which our humanity is woven. I was privileged to have known and worked with him over the course of the last twenty years of his life. His great genius was to discover that

> throughout the inhabited world, in all times and under every circumstance, the myths of man have flourished; and they have been the living inspiration of whatever else may have appeared out of the activities of the human body and mind. It would not be too much to say that the myth is

the secret opening through which the inexhaustible energies of the cosmos pour into human cultural manifestation. Religions, philosophies, arts, the social forms of primitive and historic man, prime discoveries in science and technology, the very dreams that blister sleep, boil up from the basic magic ring of myth.

The wonder is that the characteristic efficacy to touch and inspire deep creative centers dwells in the smallest nursery fairy tale—as the flavor of the ocean is contained in a droplet or the whole mystery of life within the egg of a flea. For the symbols of mythology are not manufactured, they cannot be ordered, invented, or permanently suppressed. They are spontaneous productions of the psyche, and each bears within it, undamaged, the germ power of its source.[1]

The Nature of Myth

When a society is in a state of breakdown and breakthrough—what I have called whole system transition—it often requires a new alignment that only myth can bring. It is the mythologically wise community that finds ways to mediate and so refocus the shadow sides of self and society.

In its Jungian usage, "shadow" refers to the repressed and disavowed aspects of self. When these same shadow qualities are recognized and reconciled, there is often a movement to greater maturity and depth of personality. Since time immemorial, myth and mythic knowing have served to balance shadow and light in individuals and in cultures, which has helped to prevent the exaltation of certain archetypal themes that, if played out unchecked and unorchestrated, could destroy the world.

Never has this mythic knowing been more needed than today, when our shadows are lengthened by a nuclear sun that is threatening to lead us into a world of endless night. Thus, it is imperative that we understand the functions of mediation and integration that myth can provide for past, present, and future societies.

Joseph Campbell observed how mythology serves four major psychological and social functions in any given civilization:

1. Myth provides a bridging between one's local consciousness and the *mysterium tremendum et fascinans* of the universe—the sheer vast, overwhelming environment of Being. It reconciles local, historical space-time with the transcendent realms and the eternal forms.
2. Myth renders an interpretive total image of this relationship. In artistic and religious form, it provides a "revelation to waking consciousness of the powers of its own sustaining source."[2]
3. Myth empowers the moral order and brings about both a shaping of and a conciliation between individuals and the requirements of their differing climates, geography, cultures, and social groups.[3]

For those societies in which the local mythology still works, there is "the experience both of accord with the social order and of harmony with the universe." However, most of us are several times removed from that harmony, by virtue of the effects of industrialization on our lives, which includes the shattering of natural rhythms. Thus we find ourselves longing for that storied universe we were once so intimately a part of, that realm of nature and deep belonging.

Myth assures us that the universe fits together, even though we may live in towering glass houses and get our dogma from editorials. But when the mythological symbols no longer work, there is a pervading sense of alienation from society, often followed by a desperate quest to replace the lost meaning of the once-powerful myths. The shadow aspect of this can be the willingness to comply with totalitarian regimes when all else fails. Or it can mean returning to a kind of fundamentalism that reduces consciousness to a limiting though comforting notion of the way things work.

4. The fourth and most important function of the myth is to "foster the centering and unfolding of the individual in integrity," with himself (the microcosm); his culture (the mesocosm); the universe (the macrocosm); and finally with the pan-cosmic unity, ultimate creative Mystery which is "both beyond and within himself and all things."[4]

As Campbell also noted, since the beginning of the Industrial Revolution, these fascinations have pulled our focus away from the mystery of life. This has severely limited our awareness of the world of spirit and left us in a coma of forgetfulness. We have lost our capacity to tap into the greening power of the symbolic and mythic resources of humankind. Gods, myths, and metaphors are abandoned, then blamed for being dead.

Yet myth still beckons us like a strange and beautiful country seen through the mist, only to retreat again when we have approached too near. Myth remains closer than breathing, nearer than our hands and feet. Mythic tales serve as source patterns originating in our very being. While they appear to exist solely in the transpersonal realm, they are the key to our personal and historical existence. These primal patterns unfold in our daily lives as culture, religion, art, architecture, drama, ritual, epic, social customs, even mental disorders. Myth waters our every conscious act. It is the very sea of the unconscious.

As Joseph Campbell wrote, "The latest incarnation of Oedipus, the continued romance of Beauty and the Beast, stand this afternoon on the corner of Forty-second Street and Fifth Avenue, waiting for the light to change."[5] Is it any wonder, then, that our most popular television shows and movies brim mythically with thinly disguised high-tech scenarios rooted in the oldest stories in the world?

Myth has a more universal formulation than fairy tales; it speaks to the codings of the deep unconscious. Embedded in the psyche itself, myth engages the depths because it expresses the mind of creation. Myth not only excites our understanding, it evokes our own passionate creativity. How often, in the midst of a creative moment, have you felt your horizons expanding to mythic proportions? Suddenly, you know yourself to be a creator, a celebrant of the Mass of the world, a willing participant in the restorying of life with all its possibilities.

A myth is something that never was but is always happening. Mythic themes are rampant in modern life. In the Middle East we find dragon kings snorting fire from the latest unnatural weaponry to protect their black gold from pale corporate princes. Drugs seep into the veins of those who could be heroes, rendering them as pathetic as those in ancient tales who were lured to sip the poisoned brew of mad magicians or were frozen into immobility at the sight of the Gorgon's writhing snakes. Then there are the money mad—individuals and countries alike—who are endlessly driven to seek the elusive Grail of material success because they have lost their inner spirit and can only look outward for identity and meaning.

In all the dramatic, soul-threatening, even world-threatening action of these present-day reflections of ancient myths, one thing becomes very clear: these modern participants have not studied and lived the myth deeply enough to understand its true purposes. They have not realized that in the myth a force of wisdom heals and restores the wounded ones.

Suggestions, warnings, and genuine guidance are encoded in myth that we would be foolish to ignore. Sometimes modern sensibilities demand that we change the story, or add to it, or make substitutions as we enact our own versions of the world's many myths. But we deny much of life's juiciness when we fail to embrace as fully as possible the inexhaustible richness of the classic myth.

Mythic Archetypes: In the Natural World

Myths are filled with archetypes, and archetypes are about derivations. The word itself refers to the "first types" or "primal patterns" from which people derive their sense of essence and existence. Earlier peoples saw archetypes in nature and in the starry heavens—in the sun, the moon, the earth, the vast oceans—implicitly understanding that they had descended from these primal entities.

Everyone and everything derives from the stars, those fiery generators of the primary elements of beingness. The sediments of the earth make up our cells, and the briny oceans flow through our veins and tissues. Our ancestors storied this deep knowing into tales of the community of nature: the marriage of heaven and earth; the churning of the ocean to create the nectar of life; the action of the wind upon the waters to bring form out of chaos.

The biophysical assault made upon the planet by our plundering industrial economies is polluting and depleting the major life-giving archetypes and architects of our existence: air, water, and soil. Mind declares war on Nature in the name of progress; as a consequence, we lose our ability to tell Her stories. We have become autistic, as nonmythic, nonstoried folk always do when they lose the ability to communicate with their own inner life.

If words fail, perhaps we can see images with fresh eyes—images with the potential to remind us of Nature as a sustaining and refreshing spiritual source. For example, seeing the image of the whole Earth from space never fails to jolt us out of our stupor. As we look back at this living planet and see the immense power of the image of our Mother Earth, floating alive and luminescent in the vast ocean of space, our feeling of partnership with Her is quickened.

Yet rich and vivid as Gaia's presence is for us, we are now venturing out through space and time into the macrocosm of galaxies upon galaxies, investigating quantum fields and primal cosmic forces. At the same time, our imaginations and technologies are allowing us to spiral into the microcosm, toward subatomic infinities where we find the universe in miniature. We marvel anew at the ancient alchemical dictum of Hermes Trismegistus: "As above, so below; as below, so above." We study and reflect upon these miracles and mysteries, hoping to fathom the vastness expanding in both directions, as well as the fragile balancing point between them where we exist.

This awareness is a fabulous gift. But it comes with provisos. For today, our vision of the possible human must include all present knowledge, plus all previous visions of time and space and natural phenomena, as well as those of tribe, race, and social class. What a responsibility! It requires us to reexamine and honor the archetypes, which contain all human possibilities and which are emerging once again to be freshly considered, explored, played out, and transfigured.

Mythic Archetypes: In the Inner Soul

Quintessentially, archetypes are about relationship. They are the connectiveness for the way things evolve, grow, relate, and become more complex, until they are integrated into the essence of simplicity. It may be easier to understand archetypes in psychological terms. Standard interpretations describe them as the primary forms and constellations of energy that govern the psyche or that inner self we call the soul.

Carl Jung, the great Swiss psychoanalyst, observed that when archetypes are repressed—whether within one person or in an entire society—all kinds of alienation occur, and we are cut off from Nature, self, society, and Spirit. The consequences of this alienation can be seen wherever to-day's mechanistic view of the world has infected modern life with what the American philosopher Lawrence Cahoone calls "the three pernicious dichotomies": the split between subject and object (mind and body, in-ner and outer), the split between individuals and their relationships, and the split between the world of human culture and the natural realm of biophysical processes.[6]

Archetypal structures are always available, but when they're perceived through the lens of alienated cultures and consciousness, they appear as warped, even demonic versions of what they truly are, and their energy becomes brutalized. For example, we've seen how Hitler's Germany re-fashioned Teutonic and Scandinavian myths and archetypes for its own alienated purposes. This certainly explains the valid fear throughout Eu-rope and Russia today concerning a reunified and rearmed Germany Will the reunification of Germany activate the old archetypes?

Archetypes, in their finest sense, bridge Spirit and Nature, mind and Na-ture, and self and universe. They are always within us, the essential ele-ments of the structure of our psyches. Without them, we would live in a gray, two-dimensional world. That is why, even when archetypes are re-pressed, they bleed through into other realms of human experience: into dreams, religious knowings, visions, artwork, ritual, love—and madness.

Sometimes the archetypes come in their archaic forms of gods, demons and rituals of earlier cultures. But always they ask to be seen in new and fresh ways. They ask to be regrown. Whenever they move into our aware-ness, both personally and collectively, mythic archetypes announce a time of change and deepening. This is what I deeply believe is happening all over the globe today.

Seeking the Soul of the World

In this time of whole system transition, the Soul of the World, the *an-ima mundi*, is emerging. It seems to be with us through all the things and events of the world. Speaking through myths, it enlarges our percep tions of the deeper story that is unfolding in our time. Myth does no ground our experience; rather, it opens the questions of life to culturall imaginative reflection and movement.

When we work with a mythical figure, or a historical being who through time and legend has been rendered mythical, we come to see the experience of our own lives reflected and ennobled within the stor of that great life. For example, in the journey of this book, we becom Isis and Osiris. Gradually we discover that their stories are our own sto ries, that they are the amplified rhythms of our own lives. After becom ing Isis, we return to our own life enhanced. We find ourselves saying, "I too, have the strength of Isis, her depth, capacity, wisdom, and purpose. I will prevail."

Sacred Psychology: Becoming the Myth

When myths are actively pursued—as they will be in our journey with Isis and Osiris—they can lead us from the personal-particular, our own concerns, the frustrations of our everyday lives, to the personal-universal, with its capacity to broaden the context of our lives and our vision and to integrate these new understandings within us.

This is one of the basic practices of what I call "sacred psychology." In this journey of transformation, as we participate in these symbolic dramas, we form a powerful sense of identity with the mythic character, often called the hero or heroine. This mythic being then assumes an aspect of ourselves writ large. Symbolic happenings begin to appear in our lives that bear undisguised relevance not only for our own existence but also for the remaking of society.

A myth is always about soulmaking. It tells the journey of the heroic soul as it travels from an outmoded existence to the amplified life of the Kingdom. In times of breakdown and breakthrough—such as the period we're living through now—legends arise of new heroes and heroines. These new stories show us the noble journey we must take in search of the possible human, both within ourselves and in others. For it is only when we have discovered this possibility that we can create the possible society and, in T. S. Eliot's great phrase from his poem "Ash-Wednesday," "redeem the time."

In becoming heroes and heroines, we undertake the extraordinary task of dying to our current, local selves and being reborn to our eternal selves. We then continue to travel deeper still until we reach the eternal place of sourcing and resourcing.

There are two great works for us as heroes and heroines to perform. The first is to withdraw from everyday life and open ourselves to the inner creative life through which lies our only means of reaching the Source. The second is to return to everyday life, carrying the knowledge we have gained in the depths and putting it to use to redeem time and society.

For the first work, we journey within to seek the great patterns and stories, the forgotten magic and knowings of earlier or even deeper phases of our existence, down to the seedings of evolution to come, to the structures within the self that remain unfulfilled and unfinished. These are our hidden heroic potentials, which in myth often appear as secret helpers. We must view these forgotten or neglected potentials for living the larger life as deep codings of the Source—the

Infinite within. By uncovering them, by having the courage to cleanse, purify, and prepare our soul for the difficult task of becoming an instrument through which the Source may play its great music, we become part of the energy, raising consciousness to its next level of possibility.

The Three Realms of Sacred Psychology

Another way we may express this revelation is to say: "I prevail because I become a part of a larger life altogether, the life of the psyche." For it is not psyche that exists in us, but we who exist in psyche, just as the larger life of psyche exists within the realm of God. This view of existence is another essential tenet of sacred psychology.

The many traditions of sacred psychology tend to map three major realms of experience:

1. The realm of the historic and factual (This Is Me).
2. The realm of the mythic and symbolic (We Are).
3. The realm of the unitive, the source level of being (I Am).

Each realm seems to have its own reality. And while each is reflected within us, each exists independently of us as well. We are not the only center of reality. We do not singularly create all we behold and experience, as some psychologies have suggested. Neither, however, can we escape from any part of experience, existence, or reality, for all are woven together. Our challenge now is to become fully aware, fully conscious cocreators in all three realms—the factual, the mythic, and the unitive.

THIS IS ME

The first and certainly most familiar realm, the This Is Me reality, refers to ordinary, everyday existence—our biography. It is bound and limited by geographical space and calendrical time. When we operate in this realm, we are guided by habit, personal conditioning, and cultural patterns. Our joint reality is structured by the definitions of gender, physical characteristics, name, local identity, profession, family, and other relationships and affiliations, all of which cease to exist when we die. Yet many of us yearn for the self from "Someplace Else."

WE ARE

This is the residence of symbols, guiding archetypes, and myths. Durative and enduring in a world beyond time and space, as well as thoroughly transhistorical, the We Are realm functions as the contact point for sacred time and space.

What we call gods are actually encodings of particular energy patterns from the We Are realm seen with certain qualities and moods to help us relate to them more readily. This is the place where the self joins its larger possibilities, often perceived as gods and goddesses. We may feel inspired by an especially loving resonance with particular beings who have been elevated to godhood, identifying with both their numinous power and their storied humanity.

Myths and archetypes communicate from the poetic level of mind and thought, allowing Nature to speak to the imagining soul rather than just presenting us with scientific laws and probabilities. Indeed, evidence exists that, in certain states of consciousness, the mind-brain system appears to move into a larger wave resonance, which may itself be nested in a continuum of mind beyond the field of the experiencing body. When we meet myths and archetypes in this state, we can speak directly to the inner imaginal realm where mind, nature, and spirit converge, and our highest potentialities become available to us.

A sense of relationship with an archetype, especially one that is experienced as a spiritual partner, the Beloved of the Soul, amplifies the deeper aspects of the self. This relationship disengages us for a while from the demands and demeanings of our local, ego-focused personalities and allows us to view our personal concerns from a universal perspective.

I AM

This realm exists beyond and within the other two. The I Am is the realm of Being itself, pure potency, love, the very stuff of reality. This is the realm many of us know as God. This does not mean "the gods," for they live in the We Are, but rather the One, God as the Unity of Being.

Growing the Gods

Today, what we refer to as "the gods" come down to us as the imaginative products of earlier historical ages—Greek, Roman, Egyptian, Germanic, Native American, Middle Eastern. They are numinous borderline personalities. Embedded in earlier myths and ways of being, they serve as vehicles through which we may understand our strengths, as well as our weaknesses. They grant us perspective into the ways in which certain behavioral patterns dominate our life.

Part of the emergence of an archetypal spirituality and mythology is our ongoing story of permitting the gods their own growth. Only then can they be seen as the ones who allow us to rise to them as copartners in creation. The divine-human partnership has thus become the leading archetypal image for our time. This archetype of partnership is a once and future image, one that mystics and poets have known to be true. In the words of the poet Rainer Maria Rilke: "We are the bees of the invisible. We madly gather the honey of the visible to store it in the great golden hive of the invisible."[7]

Perhaps the whole purpose of evolution is to develop cocreators who can help transform the potentialities existing in matter and ideas into new forms, richer meanings, and high art. In such an all-encompassing relationship, we have a feeling of participation in the totality and vigor, the creativity and generosity of divine life. The seed within, which held and nurtured the divine spark, is now fully grown.

This shift from the personal-particular to the personal-universal may well be a deep and essential requirement for an emerging planetary society. Otherwise, locked into our own experience and culture, we will have neither the passion for the possible nor the moral energy to cocreate with both the divine and those of different cultures and beliefs a world that works. We are now in the process of learning to see with our souls—combining our life's experience with our deepest archetypal knowings.

This movement into the greater life is what awaits us as we grow in our partnership with the "neters," or the gods, of ancient Egypt, especially with the divine-human pair of Isis and Osiris. By participating in the story of Isis and Osiris, their contentions with their brother and rival Seth, and the long journey to kingship of their son Horus, we will be expanding our perceptions, our understandings, our creativity—the very limits of our being. And we shall return from our journeys in the depth realms to our own homeplace, our own inner Egypt, renewed, reborn, rededicated to the full potentialities of life.

HOW TO USE THIS BOOK

This is a book to be lived through and done, not just read and considered. It provides an experiential journey into a myth and mystery that has engaged the human spirit for over five thousand years.

The story of Isis and Osiris predates even written history. Its roots lie in Africa, and its branches extend toward Asia, the Near East, the Mediterranean, and Europe. It finds its way into the Old Testament of the Hebrews and into the Greco-Roman tale *The Golden Ass* by the Roman writer Lucius Apuleius. It resonates throughout the works of William Shakespeare, James Joyce, and Thomas Mann. And it embellishes the human drama of the birth, teachings, and death of Jesus.

The study of the mysteries requires a courage and a willingness to participate in a powerful adventure of the soul that is at once both universal and intensely personal. Through the exploration of the drama of Isis and Osiris, as recorded by Plutarch and other writers of Greco-Roman times, along with certain ancient Egyptian inscriptions in stone and papyrus texts, we embark on a journey in which we join the personal themes of our own life with those of the universal reality informing the Egyptian myth. In pursuing the mystery play of Isis and Osiris with its themes of love and loss, death and rebirth, revenge and reconciliation, we meet ourselves writ large.

When we actively enter into them, these great journeys of the soul lead us away from the frustrations of the personal-particular to the fulfillment of the personal-universal. We no longer see ourselves as separate and isolated in our sorrows, regrets, or burdens. Because myth is a communal as well as an individual experience, it broadens the context of our lives and provides more universal formulations for meaning to our journeys. It gives substance and value to our common daily experience. Gradually we discover that these ancient stories are our own. After having been Isis and Osiris, we come back to our own lives with our energies and abilities enhanced.

Since theater and symbolic enactment provide so fundamental and effective a context for human learning and growth, sacred psychology teaches mythic stories using drama. By engaging us as participants, actors, and playwrights in profound stories of growth, challenge, wounding, and transformation, as well as involving ourselves in processes that extend our own perceptual and conceptual capacities, we live this larger story dramatically. This in turn creates the conditions and impetus we need for extraordinary growth.

However, one should be cautioned against perceiving these mythic journeys as interesting esoteric diversions. These myths of transformation include the immensely potent themes of wounding and betrayal, suffering and loss, the yearning and search for the Divine Beloved.

By probing the tragic dimensions of our own wounding for its deeper story, as well as by raising it to a mythic level, we discover ways to heal and resolve those areas in our lives that have kept us caught in static anguish. Thus each chapter in Part 3 is a partial retelling of the myth accompanied by processes and practices that have the effect of quite literally reweaving the tapestry of our own individual and collective humanness. In participating in these stories, we initiate a quickening in our own journey, a deepening of our own path.

Mindfulness is the appropriate attitude with which to approach the soul. In such mindful states of ritual enactment, we make ourselves receptive to a knowing, inspiriting, and evolving that might otherwise take years of questing to achieve.

The conditions listed below are part of an appropriate spiritual pilgrimage. They may seem difficult, even impossible, to fulfill at this point in your journey. But as you go along, you will find that they are a natural outcome of your travels. These conditions are:

1. Communion with people who have completed their transformations or are well on the way to it. Often, speaking with the Higher Self of a respected friend is helpful.
2. If possible, visiting sacred sites where intensive spiritual transformation has occurred and where the area is charged with *baraka*, or the illuminating spirit. If you are unable to do this, you might consider surrounding yourself with images of such powerful sacred sites as the pyramids of Giza and the contemplative island of Philae, or reproductions of the wall art found in the ancient tombs.
3. Help from teachers who have made contact with the Source. If you work through the processes within a group, your teachers will often be other group members.
4. Special rituals and initiatory ceremonies in which a transmission from the gods is made.
5. Help from a deep, unaccountable source—often the god or goddess within. The pilgrimage we are making is one of traveling inward among ideas, influences, and archetypes on a subtle plane by movement of inward attention.[1]

Those who wish to experience these mysteries must devote careful attention to the preparation and conducting of each session. The sections that follow are guidelines for this mythic journey.

Instructions for Solo Journeyers

The role of the solo journeyer is an honorable one in this myth. Isis traveled to Byblos alone in search of her lost love. Osiris entered the depths of the underworld alone to confront his ultimate self. Wherever we are, the divine spirit is always within us, within each grain of sand, each breath of wind.

The solo journeyer is charged with the sacred task of meeting the divine within by calling on aid from the Light that dwells within all things. Every one of us who engages in communion with the soul travels alone. But we are able to manifest this divine spark outwardly by calling on the gods to assist us, just as Isis called upon Thoth for the words of power when her child lay ill and dying in the papyrus swamps. The power and guidance of the gods—the ancient neters—is ours today, simply for the asking.

If you travel this mythic journey alone, it is important not to rush through the exercises outlined in this book or to skip any of them. Also, allow ample time for meditation on the experiences. The wonderful thing about solo journeying is that you can adjust your pace as needed. In certain spots that resonate with issues and experiences in your own life you may wish to linger and deepen your experience.

When Isis journeyed through Egypt attempting to find the lost parts of Osiris, she was joined by her spiritual companion and sister, Nephthys. Try to find a like-minded companion outside your community, perhaps a trusted friend in a distant city. This person will be your personal Nephthys. With this companion of the heart you can celebrate your transformations, the remembered parts of your lost self, your own birth as the divine child. Your friend may wish to journey with you in spirit on a given day and time and share his or her own journey in return.

Or you may wish to participate in dreams—in the Night Mystery School. In this way those who are involved in group journeys can hold you and your sacred space in mind during the times in which they meet. In your dreams, then, you may travel between Anubis and Anpu, the sacred jackal guardians. To the west stands Anubis, the guardian of the mysteries, his arms outstretched to escort you safely through the portal of sleep, dream, and the underworld. To the east stands Anpu, ready to assist you through your transformation and lead you safely to the Light on the other side.

It is very important to create a sacred space for each ritual you do. If possible, establish a separate room. Here, you can consecrate the space as the ancients consecrated the earth at their temple sites. Bless the heavenly goddess Nut, the Mother Creator, the god Geb, the Father Creator, and invoke the guardianship of the Egyptian angels of the four directions: Isis (the north), Neith (the east), Nephthys (the south), and Selket (the west).

As the divine spirits of the Egyptian gods and goddesses become more clear to you on your journey, you may wish to find images of the neters with whom you feel a strong affinity and place these in your sacred space. Specific objects that call to mind one or another of the neters can also be placed in this space—for example, a flute and a drum to signify the dancing goddess Hathor; a jug of water to recall the Nile god Hapi; or a bit of lace to remind you of Neith, the goddess of weaving. Or you may simply wish to place natural objects from the surrounding environment in your private temple. Along your journey you will begin to feel more comfortable with the divinity within a rock, a tree limb, a flower, or whatever object speaks to you.

Imbue your space with sacredness and make the commitment to journey at holy times, perhaps the same time each day. You may choose to work at dawn or at dusk, those magical, transformative hours in which the inner and outer worlds meet, or any period that seems a convenient and consistent time in which to work. You may want to coincide these sacred intensives with the festival calendar of Egypt, which appears in Appendix E.

You also may want to tape the scripts for the exercises given in Parts 2 and 3. In this way, you can concentrate on your spiritual work without being interrupted by reading from the book. Be sure not to use an overly dramatic voice when you record, though, or you'll end up not trusting the person on the tape. For those processes that require a partner or a third person, you can imagine such a person or neter being present. Then conduct a dialogue with the imagined presence either in journal writing or by actually playing his or her part.

Your process will deepen the more often you hear and live within the story of Isis and Osiris. You may wish to spend some time reading aloud on tape sections of the myth and some of the hymns to the gods and goddesses. Give yourself permission to read the story passionately, for it is the story of the passion that drives every human being to the depths of the soul.

A tape series I have made utilizes most of the lectures and processes in this book; they are drawn from an actual seminar on this material. You may also wish to listen to audio recordings from the Book of the Dead. These tapes are listed among the source materials at the end of this book.

Before continuing on to Part 1, read through the following information on the group process and on journal keeping so you can glean all the necessary information about your journey.

Journeying with a Group

The soul journey embedded in this book is equally available to solo journeyers and to groups. If you choose to form a group to do this work, then you and the other members will be making your ways from your individual worlds into the common world of Egypt. Each of you will begin to embody those sacred men and women who were called by the ancients "the companions of Horus."

This community may take any form: family, friends, colleagues, students, clients, parishioners, and so forth. As the impact of the spiritual experiences described in this book can be made either trivial or profound, it is crucial that the sacred intention of the group and its members be clear from the beginning. The group should consist only of those who freely choose to participate and who feel strongly motivated to do so.

In general, the exercises outlined here should be undertaken by intelligent, resourceful people who are mature enough to have had sufficient life experience to appreciate the psychological and spiritual scope of the divine-human drama they will be invited to enact.

A note of caution must be added. Some of these exercises are physically and psychically demanding. General good health may be considered a prerequisite, especially when undergoing processes designed to restructure—at times to jump-start—and rebuild the body's subtle energy systems. You should be careful not to exceed your own natural limits and physical capacity. Sometimes less is more. The ancient magi preferred to pass on sacred traditions directly from teacher to student so that any problems that arose could be resolved. This is why a supportive community of attentive companions is invaluable. Dialogues with your Higher Self or with the neters may also prove very helpful.

People in community stimulate, support, and evoke each other's highest qualities. Working in groups also helps to eradicate the tyranny of the dominant perception. Having companions helps us to see that our different beliefs and perspectives are enriching. As we recognize the enormous variety and richness of the realm of the sacred in others, we stand in awe before the abundance of life.

Practicing the mysteries of Isis and Osiris in a group also helps us bypass another insidious human failing—the potential for sloth. Self-discipline and good intentions have a way of evaporating without some consistent external commitment.

And there's a third important consideration. We live in a critical time in human history; never before has the ultimatum "Grow or die" threatened us more. I believe that working in groups creates transformational synergy, that we can travel faster together than alone. Through the evocation of one another we expand the base of our concern, developing an enhanced relationship to our planet and intensifying our recognition of its needs as well as our willingness to respond creatively to those needs.

Thus, in working within a group, you should try to involve people who, in their faith in the future of humanity and the planet, are willing to act together with constancy and caring to develop and extend the presence of the sacred in daily life. Narcissists, psychic exhibitionists, and "poor me's" may offer more challenge and distraction than you need.

THE ORGANIZATION OF THE GROUP

The group of covoyagers for the Isis and Osiris mysteries should number no fewer than five and no more than twenty-five. It is helpful if there is an uneven number of participants, since some of the experiences are performed in pairs while one member of the group acts as a guide.

At its initial meeting the group should assign members to take responsibility for obtaining and preparing the setting or settings (indoors or out) for each of the mysteries. This includes providing appropriate music and record, tape, or CD players, art supplies, musical instruments, and other materials, as well as bringing food for closing celebrations after each session. During the sessions there should be no intrusions. The setting is to be treated as a sacred space.

Each session is built around a particular sequence from the Egyptian story. Before the group undertakes its journey, all members should be familiar with the myth and the background material provided in Parts 1 and 2, as well as such general information as the names and qualities of the gods, which can be found in the appendixes. The text should be read in such a way that the participants can dialogue with it, taking note of images and ideas that emerge so that these may feed the group discussion. See the section on keeping a journal that follows.

The group discussion of the readings of the text should be the subject of the first part of the meeting in order to explore the meaning of its content in the lives and understanding of the members of the group. The purpose of the text is to evoke a depth reflection—it is not an occasion for theological argument. You don't need to engage in research or critical debate; you need only to concern yourself with how the myth of Isis and Osiris unfolds in your own life.

However, let me offer the following caveat. In re-creating the myth of Isis and Osiris, I am aware that we do not have precise knowledge of how it was performed in either ancient Egypt or later in the Greco-Roman period. Although portions of the texts of the popular drama as it was produced during the Osiris festival in Abydos four thousand years ago still exist, the deeper mysteries were unrecorded.

My presentation here is to be viewed only as a series of mysteries to be encountered and danced and dreamed as a living metaphor of human transformation. So, I'd like to gently warn you not to become too preoccupied with the details of historical or esoteric purity. This is not what the Isis and Osiris journey is about. Some participants will agree with the perspectives offered here, others will not. Try to leave it at that.

After the discussion ends, there should be a break of at least fifteen minutes before the group comes back together to share the mystery of the particular stage of the Isis and Osiris journey that has been reached. A good way to do this is to leave the space in which the discussion was held and reenter it later as a sacred space—silently, with full awareness of a commitment to making the journey meaningful.

The members of the group should then spend some time centering themselves and bringing their own consciousness to an awareness of the experience about to be undertaken. As you do this, you should make an internal commitment to take responsibility for yourself, while at the same time being respectful of the needs of others and of the group as a whole.

THE GUIDE

The role of the guide is critical. Those who guide the Isis and Osiris mysteries may find themselves essentially playing the role of Anubis, the jackal-headed god who escorts, initiates, and assists souls in their transition and becoming, the being who crosses from this realm into the next. This role may be held by one person, or it may be shared among the members of the group.

In any case, the guide needs to be thoroughly familiar with the material, attentive to the timing of the group, and respectful of the experience of everyone in the group. The guide is not to interpret the experience of others but rather to trust the process and the enormous individual variations that are possible. The job of the guide is to be understood by everyone as assisting and enabling, not leading.

The role of guide is an ancient one. It reached one of its most accomplished forms in the role of the hierophant (sacred observer and revealer) of the ancient mysteries. In this tradition the guide is the midwife of the soul, the evocator of growth and transformation. This means that whoever plays the role of guide invests it with Higher Self.

The guide needs to have the capacity to be both a part of the experience and an observer of the journey of the other travelers. The scripts and suggested events described here are not cast in stone. They would gain much from any suggestions and additions of the group and the guide.

In addition, the guide needs to have read the process material aloud several times before the group meeting, sensing the nature of the journey and allowing his or her voice and timing to reflect that experience. The voice must not be intrusive, yet it must remain clear and in relation to the experience. Wherever music is called for, the guide must rehearse with the music in order to integrate voice, sound, and timing of the process, always knowing, however, that timing can shift according to the needs and experience of the group.

Finally, the guide may want to have one or more "soul catchers" present. These are members of the group selected because of their capacity to be sensitive to the needs of others. Thus, even while going through the experiences themselves, they will have a part of their consciousness available to help others should this be required. It must be stated, however, that part of helping others may be knowing when to leave them alone and not intrude unnecessarily on their experiences. Guides who have not made the journey alone may enjoy having a soul catcher guide them through the experience once the group journey has ended.

Treading Gently

In working with this material, it is most important that members of the group refrain from acting as therapists or theologians. Professional therapists and theologians may find this very difficult, but it is imperative that they practice their profession only during regular working hours.

Comments I have heard, despite repeated pleas to refrain from making them, have included "You really are blocked," "I can see some enormous anger stored up there," and even "You clearly are spiritually immature." Such remarks are inappropriate here, even if they seem accurate and you intend them to be helpful. Accepting people for who and where they are in the present moment is critical to the practice of sacred psychology. Each person is perfectly capable of interpreting his or her own experience and can invite the comments of others if desired.

One of the great advantages of sacred psychology is that it invites participants to move into high witness, to tap into forgotten wisdom, and to practice nonobtrusive spiritual intimacy with others. One is always in a place to see the other as God-in-hiding, and to be so seen.

Many of the processes given in this book allow for the practice of a deep empathy. This connection can be maintained in a variety of ways— the gentle holding of your partner's hand while she or he is describing an experience or reflections; eye-to-eye contact whenever appropriate; and, above all, careful and compassionate listening, knowing when to speak out of your deepest wisdom and when to maintain silence, communicating understanding and respect through your eyes or gestures alone.

Sharing the powerful experiences and reflections that emerge from the processes of this book, especially when done by a group, requires people to enter into a state of mutual trust. Be very careful not to overstep anyone's boundaries. And refrain from interpreting someone else's experience, or from offering advice. Also, after the sharing it's often a good and satisfying thing to express words of appreciation to each other for the trust given. One might say, for example, "I'm honored that you shared your experience so deeply with me."

Keep in mind that there is no such thing as doing any exercise wrong. This is a journey of the soul. Each person will have his or her unique way of approaching it. In fact, whenever possible, do the exercise differently, or add other ideas or images or actions to enhance your process. And whatever else you do, throw self-criticism away. For one thing, it's not the style of the gods you're invoking.

Keeping a Journal

After the session is over, take some time out to reflect and to write down your experience. Your understanding of sacred psychology as well as the journey of Isis and Osiris will deepen as you keep a journal, recording your experiences in retellings, drawings, musings, dreams, quotes, questions, dialogues, and whatever else asks to be written down. Keeping a journal engages you in the most fascinating kind of conversation there is—dialogues with the divine beings who inhabit the sacred barge of the transformative self.

You may wish to decorate your journal. For example, you might look for appropriate images for the map of your very own Egypt of the soul as you enter your own sacred sites of Abydos, Memphis, Byblos, and Thebes. This is your passage to the mythic homeland to which the gods longed to return. Remember that during your spiritual journey, you are always somewhere on the map; the thing is to make a conscious record of your soul's footsteps.

The *ba* (bird, or soul), as the Egyptians knew it, is always journeying in the spirit realm, flying off and gleaning the secrets of the gods. While the *aufu* (you, your physical body) is busy cooking dinner for the hungry *ka* (the desire nature), for instance, the *ba* is communing with the gods on the nature of the life cycle.

Keeping a journal allows you to tap into your multilayered spiritual nature. It helps your *ba* nature, or soul, to commune with the gods. It helps you to keep track of your *haidit*, or shadow. And it allows you to recount your flashes of brilliance through the *khu*, or divine wisdom. Pay close attention to these inner whisperings. They bring you messages for your life today.

Through the process of writing, through the process of uncovering and creating your personal myths, you reconnect in a deeper way with sacred space and time. As the writing teacher Natalie Goldberg has said, it takes a while for experience to "compost" and enter consciousness.[2] Through the act of writing our life stories we approach our deepest selves in body, mind, and spirit. How deep our healing will be, how great our transformation, depends on how deep we can go in our own writing to remember our joys and sorrows, to tap our fears, and to speak to our longings and desires for life's possibilities.

Writing is completely Osirian. Isis gathers the dismembered parts of the slain Osiris to make him whole, to heal him, to rebirth him. Re-member yourself. Bring in through your writing your own scattered pieces and make yourself whole. And after you've gathered your parts, you will find that you have made something beautiful. As you re-create, as you transform, you rebirth your own beautiful new self in the process. You'll find that the writing will shape you as much as you try to shape the writing.

Watch your dreams. Keep an accurate record of your internal and external nighttime activity. The neters appear to us now in the realm of dream. Some dreams are precognitive, others are spiritual gifts; some are shadow dances from the unconscious, others are out-of-body, astral experiences; some are past lives, present lives, or future lives. The dream time knows no boundary in the time/space continuum.

Whenever a dream occurs, write it down immediately upon waking. Don't wait for the coffee to perk or you'll forget it. Not only do dreams tell us where we've been, but they provide the symbols and soul clues for where we're going. If possible, pay attention as well to those random images and thoughts that wander in and out of consciousness just as you're drifting off to sleep. These twilight images are also messages from the psyche.

The god Horus was said to have received his spiritual charge by contacting his father, Osiris, through a dream. The pharaoh Thutmose IV was said to have fallen asleep between the paws of the Sphinx, who spoke to him in a dream and foretold his rise to kingship.

The ancient Egyptians ritually spent the night within the temples of the gods to receive healing dreams. They believed the goddess Isis was in charge of sending dreams. Before falling asleep, ask her for the dream you need, by saying:

O mighty, powerful Isis, goddess of love, mother of all children, keeper of all time, look upon me, thy child, with love and compassion. May the sands of time be turned that I may see, that I may live in worlds before and beyond. Show unto me that which I should see. Great Isis, grant me peace of mind so that I may hear the quiet, still voice of the gods and so do the will of the divine. Reveal to me that which is true for me to know and steer me gently toward the path of Light.

DIALOGUING WITH THE NETERS

Actively engage your dreams and visions by writing about them, by dialoguing with the people and powers and images that appear to you. You might find a particularly charged symbol appearing, such as a stone or a leaf. Go out and find an object that solidifies the dream image for you and keep it with you in your sacred space.

You may also find that in your dreams and visions you are put in contact with your ancestors and friends who have passed on. "People come and go in life," says the essayist Patricia Hampl, "but they never leave your dreams. Once they're in your subconscious, they are immortal."[3] Your dreaming and meditation on them keeps them alive and feeds their spirits. That is the function of the ritual of remembering the dead. In turn, they invest your dreams with numinous power.

You may find that, as you progress through the journal exercises, one particular aspect of your life keeps appearing over and over again. This means that you may be working on solving a dilemma or deciphering the answer to a spiritual question. To keep yourself on track, you might want to pick several blank pages at random farther on in your journal and in red ink write down the question that keeps coming up. When you come across that page again, that's the signal to spend some time meditating and writing on the subject. You'll find that your responses to the question deepen as you move through your journey.

Actively dialogue with the gods and goddesses, your Higher Self, your lower self, your child self, and your self-to-be. Your journal dialogues may take the form of an interview, where you ask the questions and the neter or other self provides the answers. Or you may decide to engage two or more neters at the same time and let them talk with each other, in which case your dialogue may begin to look more like a play. You can also dialogue with people, events, works, your whole body or parts of it, the earth, your emotions, yourself younger or older, your symbols, and anything else you can think of.

Dialoguing may seem unnatural at first, but just relax. The main thing is not to censor yourself. Where silence enters in, allow the silence. When your dialogue is complete, exit gracefully, thanking the other for its time and words.

USE YOUR JOURNAL TO PRAY

Make your prayers passionate and public. You might even want to transcribe your prayers on a piece of transparent paper and paste them in the eastern window of your house for a while. Allow the sun to shine on them and infuse them with light and life. It may look a little strange to your neighbors, but you'll feel wonderful when you get up early in the morning and see the sun shining through your prayers. Anything and everything will feel possible.

WRITING EXERCISES

In this book you will find timed writing exercises. They're there to assist you in deepening your own experience. By all means, write whatever comes up for you, but do the exercises as well. Work for ten minutes *only* on each exercise. Although it may not seem long enough, it's ample time. Timed writing forces you to say what you need to say straight out, rather than backing into what you mean. It keeps you honest. If something important comes up, the best tactic is to meet it head on. You'll find that by writing as fast as you can for ten minutes and ten minutes only, your writing will become deeper. Soon you'll be surprising yourself with what you know and can say in a short period of time.

For the purpose of this journey—the journey of your lifetime—you will want to keep a journal and record your thoughts there. Begin this journal with an appropriate invocation of your own or a quote from a favorite poem, prayer, or essay.

It doesn't matter what kind of journal you choose to use. It may be pocket-size so you can carry it with you. Or it may be a five-subject notebook that allows you to keep your dreams and other topics separate. Or it may be a loose-leaf three-ring binder so you can move the pages into any order you wish. All that matters is that the journal is comfortable for you, that all entries are dated, and that it is bound in some fashion so you can keep it all together.

Above all, remember to remember. Work actively in your journal. If possible, go beyond these written exercises and develop some of your own. Maintain the heartful notion of the ritual and the spiritual aspects of daily life. The journal is your alchemical stone, your record of transformation.

Of Time and the Mysteries

The entire Isis and Osiris journey is comprised of fourteen processes that involve the participant in activities designed to stimulate the physical, emotional, intellectual, and intuitive parts of the self. The fourteen processes coincide with the fourteen scattered parts of the broken body of Osiris and are symbolic of the processes an individual goes through in reclaiming and reuniting the broken, scattered parts of a lifetime.

These processes can be performed over different time periods. It can take as long as twelve weekends or be as short as two very long days, although some people feel this latter period is too compact and intense. Others, however, have discovered this condensed sequence to be extremely powerful because of the immediate continuity it provides for all the states in the mysteries of the Isis and Osiris journey. I have found it best to incorporate the discussion and experiences of this book over a three- or four-day period, such as over a long weekend.

The journey through ancient Egypt provides for rich treasures of esoteric and exoteric knowledge. One digs in the sands and finds intriguing shards of forgotten lore. Without a guide, however, it is almost impossible to understand what it is you are seeing. Therefore a guidebook and background material will be found in the appendixes. These contain the following:

Appendix A: Alphabetical list of neters. This list provides the names, characteristics, cult sites, and potent lyrical hymns to major and most minor gods and goddesses of ancient Egypt. This appendix can serve as your guide to the world of Spirit.

Appendix B: Glossary of words, phrases, and place names. Here you will find not only the definitions of ancient Egyptian words used in the text but also the meanings of philosophical, theological, and psychological terms. Here, too, are descriptions of the main sites of ancient Egypt.

Appendix C: Map of ancient Egypt. With this you will never get lost.

Appendix D: Historical overview. This provides a quick summary and sense of the pattern of four thousand years of Egyptian history and development. Nearly every major pharaoh is listed, his reign described, the battles fought, the glories won. A general time line is given to help you trace events.

Appendix E: Festival calendar. This is a key document, for in it you will come to realize that nearly every day the ancient Egyptians celebrated their knowledge of the gods.

This book is intended as an introduction to the mythic journey of transformation. You may also want to consult my book *The Hero and the Goddess: The Odyssey as Mystery and Initiation* (New York: Ballantine Books, 1992).

A bibliography and a list of suggested musical selections are given at the end of this book. The music may be played in the background when reading aloud the processes. The recordings have been identified as to whether they are suitable for meditation, ritual, or celebration. The use of both the bibliography and musical selections will enhance your understanding and experience of the journey of Isis and Osiris.

PART ONE

The Myth of
Isis and Osiris

I

Heaven and Earth:
The Marriage of Isis and Osiris

HYMN TO OSIRIS
The doors of perception open; what was hidden has been revealed. It is myself I see and a thousand colors swirling in liquid light. . . . I have come home. I have entered humanhood, bound to rocks and plants, men and women, rivers and sky. I shall be with you in this and other worlds. . . . All these things am I, portents, images, signs. Though apart, I am a part of you. . . . You and I together are a single creation. . . . May we come and go in and out of heaven through the gates of starlight. As the houses of earth fill with dancing and song, so filled are the houses of heaven. I come in truth. I sail a long river and row back again. It is joy to breathe under the stars. I am the sojourner destined to walk a thousand years until I arrive at myself.

from *Awakening Osiris*
by Normandi Ellis

Like Homer's Odyssey, *the myth of Isis and Osiris originally penetrated the human psyche by means of the spoken word. Under the stars, through subtle whisperings in the dark, the words of the tale twine and shush like serpents traversing the golden sands of time, leaving a trail that disappears then reappears suddenly elsewhere. This is a tale passed from one teller to the next, rolling off the tongue in enchanted circles, only to be rediscovered in dreams.*

Perhaps the full knowing of such a story comes only after years of meditation. After long hours of sitting cross-legged in the temples, inhaling the perfumes of cinnabar and storax while staring at the hieroglyphs chiseled on the walls. Perhaps it is a tale inscribed in our DNA, encoded in the genetic memory. Perhaps it is a tale we imbibe as infants at our mother's breasts.

This tale of life, love, and transformation is as ancient as the soul. But it is only one of a multitude of Egyptian myths. Unlike Homer's Odyssey, *the complete story was never written down by its indigenous storytellers. It was recorded and popularized by the Greeks some three thousand years after its* first allusion, but the allusions are to a complex tale more ancient than written language. The appearance of the myth of Isis and Osiris predates known civilization. Who knows for how many eons the story was told or how often the telling changed over many thousands of years. What we have are remnants, divergent versions, bits of mummy cloth out of which we attempt to reconstruct a living, breathing tale.

Because the versions of the tale are divergent, contradictory, and complex, the possibility of accuracy does not exist. We are interested in telling truths, and in Egypt—where the hieroglyph for truth is a rolled scroll tied with string and many grains of corn—the truth is both multitudinous and ultimately unknowable. Here, then, is one of the stories of Isis and Osiris as retold by Normandi Ellis. It is a revisionist's tale, an attempt to unite matriarchal myths with patriarchal stories. My part in this retelling was to serve as Ellis's evocateur, her Thoth, helping her to enter states of consciousness in which she found herself living in the myth, and to emerge again with the precious words of this once and future story.

The story begins, as does Genesis, with the spoken word. The creation of the universe arises from the desire of a lonely god to know companionship. Ironically, the longed-for other is but a part of himself. All life on earth and all the gods in heaven are aspects of this one supreme god. In most cultures, father is sky and mother is earth, but the ancient Egyptian inversion of Mother Sky and Father Earth shows a long tradition of matriarchal culture. This was a culture based on astrological signs that mark time in twenty-eight-day lunar cycles, coincident with the menstrual flow.

The story of Isis and Osiris really begins with their conception and their siblings' conception in the belly of Nut, the great heavenly goddess. Theirs is a tale of passion, of love and sorrow. It is a story of betrayal and forgiveness. It is the remembrance of love lost and found and lost again, a tale of the jealousy of brothers, the pain of death, and the transformative joy that arises unexpectedly from the bitter fruit of the sorrows. Osiris loses his life and gains the heavens. Isis loses her husband and later gains a child. Even as Isis mourns the loss of partnership with her beloved Osiris, she finds the strength to discover her own unique individuality.

And so the tale begins . . .

In the Womb of Nut

In the beginning there was the Great He/She: Atum. Complete. Whole. Perfect. And lonely. Passion without form. Atum was everything and nothing—an ourobouric serpent biting its tail, a cosmic dervish (atom/Atum) whirring in the void, or perhaps nothing more than Spirit. There was neither height nor depth, neither past nor future. All was eternal darkness. A hot breath, a long sigh, moved across the primordial waters of Chaos. Lonely and isolated in His/Her perfection, the divine being desired companionship with an Other, with the possibilities of selves that existed within the one Self. Therefore, the Word was spoken, a breathing of the vowels of a divine name: Atum or Om or Yod-He-Vav-He—all the single name of the Self.

Said Atum, "These arms arise from the waters of nothingness; from Nun I uplift myself, the gods." And there came into being every god, the lesser and the greater. And on every side there was magic (Heka) and wisdom (Hu) and knowledge (Sia) and truth (Ma'at). Said Atum, "I am the creator of myself, in that I gave myself my Self according to my desire and in accordance with that which lived in my heart. Thus the heart and the will form the Word that becomes the Great Becoming."

From this union of self with Self, Atum, the Great He/She, begat two tawny lion-headed children. Shu, the son, became the practical, the mind, the god of air. Tefnut, the daughter, became the passionate, the emotional, the goddess of moisture. He was yesterday, she was tomorrow. Together they settled in the sand upon their haunches. Like golden-eyed sphinxes they gazed in opposite directions, their tails entwined, guarding the entrances to the world. And they begat two children, who were Heaven and Earth.

The daughter, named Nut, was dawn and dusk, the beautiful, ethereal body of Heaven. The son, named Geb, was the passionate life force of the Earth, which lay below. They were a pair of divine lovers; whatever emotion passed through Geb passed also through Nut. What mattered to Heaven mattered to Earth. What mattered to Earth mattered to Heaven. The two lay together as one in an embrace as long as eternity. Geb inclined himself ever toward his wife, the sky, rising up as a hill, a mountain, or pyramid toward that which he adored. In the same way, Nut, covered in shimmering stars, bent over to hover above Earth, her beloved. Therefore it was said, "As above, so below; as below, so above"—meaning that what happens here matters there, what happens there matters here. And so between the two of them there existed space, in which children might be born.

Because of the love of Earth and Heaven for each other, there dwelt in the body of Mother Sky a thousand souls, which were the stars and planets, who called out to each other like sparks of fire in the darkened heavens. Nut bore Geb a pair of sons who emerged red and round from her vulva during the hours of dawn and dusk. One she named Ra, the golden child and noble Sun. The other she named Thoth, the silvery orb of Moon. These two brilliant children crept out of their mother's womb and crawled upon her belly, circling ever round and round her. As Sun and Moon they measured the cycles, and because of them there existed time, in which other children might be born.

The two children, golden and silver orbs, shone forth their light upon their parents so that at last Nut and Geb could see the splendor of each other's bodies, which before they had only touched and felt. Now there appeared before their eyes a vision of woman and man—the changeable, dreamy blue nature of Nut, the sky, and the verdant, green growth of trees and plants, the solid valleys and hills of the body of Geb. Just as quickly Nut became pregnant again and her belly swelled with the presence of her expected children.

As her excitement about her pregnancy grew, so grew the irritation of her firstborn, Ra. Jealous of his mother's love, he, who by birthright was heir to the kingdoms of his Mother Heaven and his Father Earth, devised a way to separate his parents. Relying upon the strength of Grandfather Shu, he commanded the god of air to uplift Nut. Now she found herself removed ever farther from her beloved, able always to see him, but unable to touch him except at the edges of the horizon, where her fingers and toes brushed Earth.

Said Ra, "I who invented night and day . . . I who measure the length of years and months, decree that no other child shall be born on any day of my year. Furthermore, I shall create children of my own, flesh of my flesh, for I have no need of a wife."

Meanwhile, the cries of the increasingly pregnant Nut rang throughout the edges of the universe. Skies rained, stars darkened, and Earth's bones quivered. The planets stood still. Heaven shrieked and Earth trembled. Nut bellowed and moaned like a great cow whose udders are too full of milk. Her belly grew rounder and rounder. Day by day her breasts swelled, her thighs strained, and her arms ached. Yet she could not be delivered of her children, whom she loved as much as life itself but who now became an unbearable burden to her.

Ignoring the clamor all around him, Ra withdrew and gave himself over to the pleasures of his own hand. All alone he gave birth to a multitude of children, men and women whom he named the "Remit," likewise called humanity. They were as seeds fallen to the ground, and like the seeds of all earthly life they were both good and evil. Blown to the far corners of the world, they took root, prospered, and grew wild as weeds. They could not be contained.

Meanwhile eons had passed. It is impossible to tell how long Ra's brothers and sisters, as yet unborn, still lived in shadow in the womb of Nut. Dreaming red dreams, they turned in the dark. They sucked their thumbs, rocking to the beat of their mother's heart. Her body sang the thrum of Africa, the dark rumble of thunder, the syncopation of the universe. Boom, boom. Boom, boom. They followed the pulse of these ancestral drums. Brothers and sisters, they danced blindly with the light of their own becoming, mad with the spirit incarnate, pounding fists and feet against Earth and Sky, which were the limits of Nut's nurturing belly. She groaned, then bellowed a sweet, lowing song.

Dressed in the bone-white clothes of spirit, they danced; and the first three ages passed. Their turnings brought no hurry. They ripened like figs on the branches of eternity. They grew into their bodies. Their mother sang as she knitted the web of flesh, binding their fates, tying knots, stitching time to space, spinning the whole cloth of their stories. She imagined the bronzed skin of their bodies, the perfect curve of their hips, the amber light in their eyes, the faces of incarnation. Her children rocked and listened. Boom, boom. Boom, boom. Boom, boom. My heart, my mother. My heart, my mother. Boom, boom. As above, so below.

There was Osiris, brother, son, father, husband, watcher in the dark. There was Isis, woman, wife, widow, dancer, goddess of desire, mother of a god. There was Horus, whom the mortals called Hero, the divine son of a divine couple, twice-born, once in Heaven and once on Earth. There was Nephthys, lady of the house, mistress of the shadows. There was Seth, warrior and rebel.

Woe to he who forgets the divine names. Banished from heaven is she who mocks the neters with smiles. Isis, Osiris, and their brothers and sister slept nine ages inside the Great She, mother Nut, daughter of air, blue stone of heaven, cerulean primordial water. Her children were as swollen planets sailing in and out of clouds, each turn in the womb accompanied by the flute and bird song of distant stars. Say the word—their secret names—and they become the pattern of all future becoming.

The ages passed. And again the ages passed. The children grew tall, beauteous, full of desire. Brother married sister: Seth and Nephthys; Isis, Queen of Heaven and Earth, and Osiris, Lord on Earth and in the realm of dreams. He was a handsome man—dark and almond-eyed, muscular, his backbone straight; she his dark-haired, blue-eyed, passionate sister. Together they lay four ages, eight thousand years. (But what is time to lovers?) Draped in the blue linen of sky they lay, wrapped in embraces, inhaling each other's breath. Oh, the scent of ambergris and musk! Breast to breast they lay, feeling one body with its thousand longings. Skin to skin. Lip to lip. He entered her. She licked salty tears from beneath the curve of his chin. They lay so long that a·world sprang from his lips, then swallowed itself, and with the next breath was reborn. Ages passed in but a moment.

Said she, "I'd know the dark, loamy smell of his beard anywhere. I'd know by touch any single strand of hair on his head, the ripple of his ribs, the bulb of his phallus. He is as much a part of me as my own skin."

Man and woman, they were one destiny. Eons passed while she lay in the crook of his arm. Time's thread wove in and out, pulled along by the silver crescent of Moon. There Isis learned the sacred vowels, the breathings caught in the rapture of his hands. In deep rivers of passion, then soaring birdlike to the heights, amid great waves of light, the two lovers imagined, then counted and named the greater and lesser constellations. They gave their names to the stars.

Ages passed while the five children lay in the dark moon of their mother, waiting to be born. It was not necessary to speak, for they knew each other's thoughts, dreamed each other's dreams. So great was their attunement that a whole world rose out of their dreaming. Images streamed beneath their eyelids and bubbled out of the ground: sandals for feet, staffs for hands, honeyed cakes for the tongue, the scent of ambergris for the perfume of their breaths. The sigh of one brother rippled across them all, as a wind stirs the branches of a sycamore.

But in the outer world, things fractured. Waves of light bent into ten thousand directions. Forms took shape, breathed, walked on land. A ball of flame roared across the sky, scorching the land, burning the belly of the heavens, frightening animals, and blinding men. Women fell face-down upon the ground. The savanna lands withered; the elephant, the giraffe, and the baboon withdrew into the darkest parts of the world. Grains shriveled on their hollowed stalks. Shamans slaughtered lambs, oxen, birds, chieftains, children. Holy dancers entwined themselves in asps, chanting, "Great Mother! What sin have we committed that you must torture us with such bright contempt?"

Nut, Mother Sky, gave forth no answer but the panting of the hot wind and the rustle of dried papyrus stalks. The labor of Heaven was long and arduous. Her lament became the soured waters of Earth. Once-verdant fields turned to dust. Strange birds nested in the marshes of the Nile. Crocodiles devoured the fish. And the river shrank in its banks every day. Brothers sat with their backs to each other; young boys killed their old fathers. The Sun roared through the world, searing, blinding. It was not day, for there was no night.

It was Ra, the bright Sun, who lived and no one else.

"Am I not perfect?" he said. "Am I not unlike anything you have ever seen?" His hot breath seared the yellow sand, dried the lakes to salt. "Always and always essentially myself, I do not tire myself with evolutions and becomings. Am I not glorious as I am, my face burning bright as metal? Self-made am I. I had no mother. Self-created, an eternity of magnificent selves. See, there are no golden others like me. Fall down, man. I am your master."

After a time even the children of Nut understood that something was wrong. They pressed their ears to Heaven's belly, heard the mother's sick moaning, heard the voice of Ra.

"What filth our older brother speaks," shouted Seth. "He professes to be The God. He denies even the ripe womb of our mother."

Nephthys trembled like a dim star at dawn. "Sixteen thousand years have passed! Do you not hear our mother groaning while we sleep? She is heavy with our becoming. She shivers and shakes and cries out, 'Let my children be born! Release me from my belly's burden!' But Ra pretends not to hear."

Said Horus, "It is Ra who imprisons us here. He has written a decree:

In no day of his year shall we be born. He has ordered some invisible god to uplift Nut. And the god himself now strains beneath the weight. How she suffers, and we feel that suffering, imprisoned as we are in her belly, separated as is she from what she loves."

"Bastard Sun!" shouted Seth, waving his staff. "Could I but see him face-to-face, I'd poke out his eye. I'd ... I'd ..." The unborn god was a dark storm. His rage shattered even the dreams of the dead. "Turn about, turn about," he cried. "Turn about, oh sleepers, in this haunted place, which you know not, but which I know utterly." Beneath his sandals the red dirt spawned snakes.

In sympathy, Isis and Osiris threw their arms about him. They whispered words of comfort in order to stay his spell, but he cast them off, as if they were ropes binding him. "If you are not against Ra," he shouted, "then you stand against me. Now and forever. The damage is done. Sorrow follows us for all time. But with my last breath, I shall fight."

With this, he withdrew to nurse his rage in silence, to sit apart and mutter, sharpening the end of his staff into a sword. By his mad rage were the gods, brothers and sisters, disjoined. Even Osiris felt his heart harden and cleave like an ancient stone. He stood apart from Isis, lost in his own dark musings. Nephthys reached out to Seth, touching his face, bathing his feet in her tears. He spurned her, and she stood weeping, not knowing what to do.

And so the last age passed, a lifetime in the dark, pulsing womb, long seasons of disparate silences that words could not mend. Thoth, the god of the Moon, stood apart. He saw the sickness of Nut, his Mother Sky; he saw the bereavement of Geb, his abandoned Father Earth. He heard the mutterings of the unborn, and he knew what it was to be hidden from the world by the Sun's powerful light.

The Birth of the Gods

No other way to birth Nut's children could be found, no way to release the mother's burden, except that moments of time be stolen from the grain heap of eternity, except that the glistening sweat that dripped from Heaven's forehead be captured in the cup of form. Here was a great sacrifice. Where the unborn children grew beautiful and suffered not from the ravages of time in the womb of their mother, now they must be born in time. Time became the net that was needed to catch them in their descent from Heaven. Time would hold them and bind them to the eternally shifting forms of light and dark, night and day, until the ends of all things.

And, being of like mind, the children of Mother Sky agreed. "Isis, Osiris, Seth, Nephthys, and Horus must be born," they said in unison.

Thus it was that somewhere in Heaven or on Earth, the subtle and cunning Moon, Thoth, played endless rounds of checkers with his arrogant brother, Ra, the Sun, letting Ra win the majority of the games. Yet Thoth was such a clever gamesman that over a period of time he slowly won from Ra several small parts of the god's golden light. Furious at having been deceived, Ra beat his hands on the gaming table, and the Earth shook. The Moon god gathered his winnings.

"You are bright, brother Ra," Thoth said. "But greed hinders your brilliance. Let's make a deal. I have, by my own reckoning, won five days of your light. These days shall be returned to you, on the condition that the children of Nut be born, one child for each day I have taken."

Ra banged his hands and feet together, but at length he finally agreed. Then the five sky-born gods and goddesses of Heaven gathered at the edge of the great abyss, drawing lots to see who should be born first. Osiris. Horus. Seth. Isis. Nephthys. Osiris agreed to go forth first and make peace with Ra, to join forces with the Sun in reviving the land, in returning the river Nile to abundance. Seth complained that he wanted to be firstborn to go out and do battle with the Sun on the first day.

"The lots are cast as they are cast," said Horus. "There are those of us who would prefer not to be born at all. It is an endless striving, full of unfulfilled desire, and regret. But this is the way of our becoming. The law of gods and goddesses is unfaltering."

Isis placed her hand in the hand of Osiris and they left the others. She lay down once more with her husband and bound her soul to his with a silver cord. "In three days we meet again, my brother," she said. "Let the way be opened unto you. May I gaze again on your face and form in three days, and we shall pass eternity thereafter together." Brushing his lips against the palms of her hands, Osiris took leave of her.

With a sigh from Mother Sky and a rush of amniotic waters, the first god-man was born complete with his seven souls—his intelligence, his names, his heart, his shadow, his flesh, his beatific body, his double. Because he was the first to see the world as a divine god-man, the great mother gave him the most beautiful eyes. His was a quiet strength, a subtle knowing. He fell out of Heaven and into time, and where his feet first touched the ground there rushed up a green field of wheat. Wherever he passed, the dry rocks cleaved and water flowed to the ground.

Then Horus was born. But he clung to the belly of the Sky—a hawk of gold whose clawed feet never pressed against Earth. Keen were his eyes and wide his vision. To the ends of the universe he flew and back again. From the heights he observed how the laws of Heaven and Earth were formed, how deep the night, how bright the noon, how cool the shade, how beautiful the dusk and dawn.

Then Seth, malformed by his rage, was born with the head of an ass. He was hideous to behold, his noble heart hardened into a lump of iron. On the day of Seth's birth, Ra sent forth a whirling red and ocher windstorm, full of fury and sand. And Seth raised his fist in defiance against the Sky. He changed himself into an asp and slithered away into the crevice of some desert rock to wait out the storm.

Three days had passed in the red orb of time. Isis held Nephthys. They wept for their husbands—only three days, yet it seemed they had been separated from their lovers for a lifetime. "Sister," cried Nephthys. "Your sorrows are mine. I feel in my own bosom the sobs that shake you to the core. Hold my hand. Let us comfort each other in the darkness, two swallows skimming the sky at dusk."

"Beloved," said Isis, "heart of my heart. You and I will spend our lives together. Your children will be my children, my children will be yours. We shall be mothers of the world. We shall be as two kites soaring at dawn, rejoicing in our good fortune."

On the fourth day, the sudden windstorm ceased. Then Isis passed through the portal of time, leaving Nephthys alone awaiting deliverance from the darkness. In the eastern sky shone the yellow orb of a gentle Sun; in the western sky hung a hot, white star, which was the fiery soul of the goddess herself, held between the horns of the pale, white Moon.

At the divine birth of the beautiful one, there came not a moan from the lips of Mother Sky, but a song like that of a lark. Said Nut, "I am mother of the gods; and you, my daughter, shall be mother of the world. And Nephthys who awaits yet shall be your twin soul. As I have given birth to you, my children, you have given birth to me. You have molded me, you have shaped me, you have created me in the image of your mother." Then a breeze like the caress of a woman's hand wrapped itself around the world.

On the fifth day the goddess Nephthys was born amid a shroud of mystery. She hid her light in the way that the Sun often hides the face of the Moon by day, or in the way that some faint stars can be seen only at night when viewed from the corner of the eye. It is said that on the evening of her birth wolves howled and frogs, gulping air, leaped from the depths of the river. And it was said that she carried truth with her into the land of Egypt, but her kind of truth could be glimpsed only in dreams.

Perhaps Nephthys so often sat apart on Earth because she was the last born. In green gardens of light Isis sang her woman songs of becoming, while by night Nephthys sang her songs of unbearable sorrow. Gods and goddesses remember their becomings, their births, their lives in the womb. From these patterns was the world made, and the gods called their land Kemet.

The Rule of the Gods on Earth

Holy light streamed forth from Heaven's height in rays that touched the bewildered faces of barbarians. When the gods first stepped down to Earth, the baboons of Egypt raised their palms and scorpions scurrying across the sands lay still. Nut's children stood in the golden light dressed in fine white linen, alive with morning song that caused even the dead to stir and awakened the deepest sleepers. The gods' faces glowed white with heat. Chicks pipped in their eggs; cattle became immediately pregnant. Fish leaped in the river, their scales flashing in sunlight. Trees grew heavy with figs and dates, the vines heavier with dark purple grapes. Barley sprang up, and emmer, and wheat. Great green waves of water gushed forth from the distant mountains to water the fields that would feed the people of Egypt.

The hidden gods decreed that Osiris, the firstborn, should be given the black lands of Egypt that lay on either side of the river Nile and the seven streams of water that fanned out in the shape of a lotus at the opening of the delta. In this small strip of black, thick, rich mud grew the golden grains of emmer and the red grains of barley. Here, the animals knelt to drink; here, the women gathered, hand in hand, to birth their children in the shelter of reed huts. Here, they scattered seeds and awaited a harvest.

To Seth was given all the red land as far as the eye could see. On these lands antelope leaped across the sparse vegetation, wild dogs padded across the cool sand by moonlight, and wild boars rooted among the rocks. Here, the men banded together, bathing themselves in the red blood of the hunt. Here, they covered their heads in animal skins and hid from the blowing sand. In the land of Seth, men learned isolation, hunger, survival, loneliness.

Isis took the hand of Osiris. She called him husband, he called her sister; she called herself the god's wife. Together, they built a house chased with gold, its ceilings of lapis lazuli, its walls of silver, its floors of sycamore, its doors of copper. The house of the gods was a splendid sight set high amid orchards on a golden hill, its alabaster walls gleaming at dusk and dawn. "One day," Osiris said, "Egypt's children will dwell in just such a house of eternity."

Together they took what the land offered them and used it—the rich soil, the fertilizing waters, the seeds. They gathered the animals into herds; they tilled the soil and planted the emmer, the pumpkin, the onion. They trained the grapevines to the trellises.

The women of Kemet gathered at the edge of the river to watch the goddess Isis, her hands plucking reeds, weaving baskets to gather the fruits of the field, holding the flour ground fine as sand and baked into steaming cakes. She taught them how to weave reed baskets, pluck cotton, spin and weave cloth, plait hair. She showed them the lilies pressed into fragrant oils, the malachite crushed to fine green powder, the kohl that defined her beautiful eyes.

By day Osiris showed the strong young men and women how to harness the cow and guide the plow. The land broken up fell on either side of the blade into deep black furrows. The children followed behind

Osiris, dropping grains of wheat. He stomped the grape, he brewed the barley. By night he taught his people the song of his mother, the music of Heaven, the breath shivering and playing across reed pipes to the heartbeat of the drum and the quiver of strings upon the lyre.

Isis rattled the gourds. She shook the sistrum in soft shushing sounds like papyrus sandals dancing across the sand. She taught the women to dance, to move their arms as a breeze stirring leaves, to bow their backs and leap like cats under the dark of the Moon, to glide quick as light and shimmering as fishes. She taught them the names of the stars, the hidden souls of the beloved gods and goddesses. She gave them chants, hymns, and praises. She gave them the counting of the full, waning, and waxing moons, the honor accorded to the horns of the mother, the knowledge of herbs and their own bodies' cycles in time.

The dancing sistrum frightened the snakes and kept the scorpions at bay, but the men who had stood on the edges of the desert with Seth drew near to watch the women dancing under moonlight by the fire. They saw the gleam of those golden bodies, the breasts fragrant and plump as twin fruits. Then the hunters threw down their spears to return to their own women and children, to rest and celebrate in the houses of comfort.

Seth grew angry, provoking his band of hunters into driving a herd of wild boars through Osiris's greening fields. But this was still early in the history of man, and Seth was nothing more than a nuisance as yet, a little sand flea biting the heel of Osiris. He waited, biding his time until the moment was right. Then he swore to himself that he would take the throne from his brother.

Many times Osiris left his house to travel throughout Egypt, teaching the secrets of the soil and the blissful fruits of the garden. But always vigilant Isis remained behind, keeping a watchful eye over the village in her husband's absence.

The men who had returned to their homes began to build houses of brick and boats of papyrus. They wove nets and cast them into the river, bringing home abundant fishes. They ferried their boats to the villages on the far bank, bringing gifts of wine, pots of clay, perfumes and incense, bright feathers and shells, beads of malachite, carnelian, and gold. They made children and their villages grew strong. Osiris and Isis ferried up and down the Nile, teaching their people the holy, peaceful ways of communion with each other and the divine. They gave them laws, the gift of Ma'at, the way of truth laid down in the primordial era by the great gods.

The people called Osiris their king.

The women admired the stitches in the hem of the goddess's dress with its seams so delicate, so fine. And Isis admired their plump, pink, healthy children laid in her arms at the moment of birth. She breathed upon them, she sucked the mucus from their lungs, she counted and unfurled their tiny fingers. She read each child's fate in the cracks of the birthing bricks on which the mother had squatted during birth. There she read the blessings of fruitfulness. But each time she sighed, wanting a child of her own.

The Birth of Anubis

Already nearing her twenty-eighth year, the goddess Isis still had not borne a child. Although her sister Nephthys had already become a mother, Nephthys had given her child away. It was a child conceived by deception; it was not Seth's own.

As it happened Seth's rage drew him more and more away from the comfort of his wife. He left Nephthys too much alone. Each night she stole into the palace garden of Isis and Osiris to be near her siblings for comfort, to listen in the dark to the beautiful songs and laughter drifting like petals in water over the garden wall, to see the house aglow, lit by fragrant burning oil in alabaster bowls. She sat at the edge of the garden closest to the palace beneath Isis's window in order to smell her sister's perfume, to revel in the deep-throated music of her brother's voice, to hear them exchange their vows of love, their whispers, their cries, their silences.

"If only I were as beautiful as she," Nephthys thought, "perhaps Seth would love me, too."

Day by day she practiced becoming more and more the twin of Isis. She bade her maidservant to plait her long black hair in many small braids. She perfumed her hair with lotus oil, her skin with cinnabar. Her lips and cheeks she painted with pomegranate juice; her eyes she outlined in kohl and she brushed the lids with malachite. About her throat she wore a golden necklace with beads of blue lapis and carnelian. On her feet she wore white sandals, on her body fine linen. Her waist she girdled with red belts and a buckle of green jasper in the shape of the frog goddess Heket, guardian of the transformations. And when she went into the village, the women mistook her for Isis. They birthed their children into her hands. They heaped her baskets with honey, saffron, and cakes. They gave her a white goose in a reed cage for her supper. They held her hands and they kissed her cheek.

Still Seth did not stay home; he did not make love to his wife. The heart of Nephthys did not sing. Dressed like her sister, she found her way by the dark of the Moon alone to the palace garden to sit and weep and beat her breast, for her sorrows were many. It was there that Osiris discovered her, sitting sad and beautiful as he strolled about picking the small, pungent yellow flowers of the melilot. He wove them into a garland for his beloved's hair. His breath was taken away by her beauty.

"My wife, my sister," he said. "Why do you look so sad? Come to your husband. I will make you a happy woman."

He took her hand, and Nephthys did not protest. She did not cry out, she did not turn from his embrace. And when he called her name, "Isis," she did not betray herself. Her heart was made glad by the love of Osiris. She fell asleep in the garden with the garland of flowers in her hair, and he went into the house to bring out the lyre and play the music of her dreaming. But before he returned, the goddess Nephthys awoke and ran home. She entered the house and went straightway to her room.

Seth said, "Where have you been? And what are those flowers in your hair?"

Nephthys said nothing.

"The melilot grows only in the garden of Osiris."

She nodded and he scowled, closing the door.

Isis surprised Osiris in the palace as he was playing his lyre. "Have you had good dreams?" he asked.

"Why should I be dreaming?" Isis asked.

Then Osiris saw that there were no melilot flowers in her hair. "Something terrible has happened," he said, and he turned his eyes from her and wept. The hardest knowledge of all to bear was that after lying with her so many years in the dark still he did not know the scent of his own wife.

The Moon waxed and waned. The belly of the goddess Nephthys grew hard and round, her robes more flowing to hide her shape. During the last three months she shut herself up in her room, begging the maidservant to send Seth and even her dear sister Isis away whenever they tried to visit her. Then one night beneath a full Moon Nephthys stole out of the palace and into the desert. There, squatting among the rocks and alone, amid the howling of wolves, she held her belly, moaned, and delivered the boy child in the sand. She could not bring him home, fearing that Seth would murder both her and her illegitimate child. So she left the boy there in the wilderness covered only in a blanket of golden melilot.

In the morning, the maidservant, bringing in the silver tray of milk and fruit for the new mother, saw the softness of Nephthys's belly, and hearing no cries of the new infant knew immediately what had happened. She ran to the river to find Isis. Here the goddess went early every morning amid the dew on the bank's edge to pick herbs for poultices and potents. Crying and begging for the goddess's mercy, the servant told Isis what had happened. And though the servant did not say, Isis in her mind's eye could see the child covered in golden melilot flowers and knew he was the son of Osiris—perhaps he would be the only son of her husband.

She cursed her own barrenness and wept, saying, "We must hurry now. A child lies naked and new in the wilderness. We must go to him

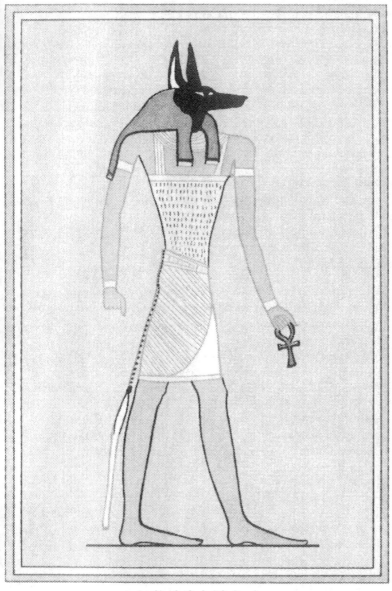

Anubis, the God of the Dead.

fleeter than light. Call the greyhounds; they alone can sniff out the birth-place of a god."

After much searching among the rocky cliff faces and dusty valleys, the child at last was found, red and squalling, lying in the sand and hidden amid crushed melilot flowers. The goddess bathed him in the river, anointed him with oils, protected him with birth charms, and carried him home wrapped in her own black linen skirt to the palace of his father, her husband.

One of her greyhounds, wild creatures of the desert she had tamed with bits of meat, had recently whelped four pups. She gave the child to the bitch to suckle, and the child prospered, growing strong and healthy with the instincts of his animal mother, her keen sense of smell and hearing, her reliance on instinct. He was part man, part animal, totally divine. Isis named the boy Anubis and taught him her magic—the art of seeing into the future and beyond to the land of the dead. He became her faithful attendant and guardian and called the royal couple Mother and Father. They called him Opener of the Way.

Isis bore her sorrow alone, keeping the knowledge of his maternity secret. Although Isis knew the truth, and Nephthys knew that she knew, neither sister said a word. The two of them raised the god as if they were his two mothers, and their mutual love for the child bound them ever more tightly together.

When challenged by Seth, Isis merely shrugged and replied, "Brother, when did I have time to tell you about my child? You've stayed gone these many months at a time—hunting, we presume." As for Osiris, there was nothing to be said after forgiveness. The terrible mistake of that one night was never mentioned again.

The Vengeance of Seth

Seth continued his brooding and spent much of his time in the desert, gathering his tribe of seventy-two companions. Among them was Aso, a dark Ethiopian queen, a beautiful sorceress whose power was said to be nearly as great as that of Isis. It was she whose shadow entered the dreams of Isis and Nephthys to discover the exact dimensions of Osiris's body.

One day Isis was called away to assist in the births of the women at Coptos. Nine moons before a beautiful man had passed through the city. Tall and handsome was he, the image of love. At dawn and dusk he sang as he played upon the lyre. By moonlight he held in his arms the beautiful women of Coptos. The cattle, the cats, the lions, the dogs, all the animals fell to mating. The stranger told no one his name, but by the praises the young girls sang of his strong arms, his deep voice, his good looks, Isis knew that the love god Min had passed through the city.

Now all of the young women were pregnant, all nearing the full and ready to birth the god's children at the same time. Isis tied her herbs and medicine in loose cloth bundles and hurried to the city, preparing to be gone for quite some time. Osiris sent Anubis with his wife to protect her from thieves along the road, but in their long absence the king grew lonely. He arranged to cheer himself with a party commemorating the twenty-eighth year of his arrival in Egypt.

Hearing of this party and knowing that Isis was away, Seth devised a plan. He fashioned a beautiful cedar box the size and shape of a man, overlaid it with leaves of gold, and ornamented it with a thousand gems of carnelian and turquoise. On the lid of the box appeared the face of the king in black and shining ebony, his lips carnelian, his eyes bright lapis and ivory. And inside the box, carved upon its inner lid, was the portrait of Nut, the gods' mother. Her body was painted deep blue as night and her belly was spangled with yellow stars. Her smile was tender, beckoning, comforting as a drink of cool water. One could almost hear the soft beat of her heart, the sound of her celestial singing. Over this jeweled box the Ethiopian queen Aso spoke her dark charms of eternity, sleep, and binding.

On the seventeenth day of the month of Athyr, with the sun in the sign of the Scorpion, the palace was lit with candles, fragrant with incense, and filled with good things to eat. The walls vibrated with the deep sound of the drums, reverberated with the music of lutes. Laughter and wine spilled over onto the shining silver floors. The aroma of roast duck permeated the rooms. Tables were heaped with green salads, cheeses, fruits of every kind, raisins, honey, and breads. All these were the gifts of the Earth Father, Geb, to his oldest son, Osiris, who had caused the Earth to bring forth such abundant harvest.

A messenger from Geb appeared, finding Osiris clothed in green and white linen, wearing white sandals on his feet, and seated on a golden throne in the shape of a lion. The scribe spoke: "The state of the year is good, Osiris—very good. I come with the congratulations of your father. No happiness rippled through the Earth until you came down. Now, wherever Osiris appears, there is an outflow of water—the rising of the flood, the fatting of the calves, and the ripening of the red juices of pomegranates and grapes. Because of you the world abides in abundance and peace. Blessed be the god Osiris."

Into the midst of this celebration strode the god Seth with his seventy-two companions dressed in animal skins and feathers, their faces painted black and white and red. Osiris embraced his wild-eyed younger brother, happy to see that Seth had laid aside their differences. He kissed Seth's cheeks and ordered more wine and beer brought up from the caches. The music began anew.

While the drinking and dancing continued in the palace, Seth brought in his present draped in white linen. Laughing, he threw back the covering and revealed the beautiful gold chest that glittered in the candlelight. Then Seth announced: "I shall give this trophy to whoever may lie in it and fit it exactly." The guests roared with delight. One by one they lay down inside the box, but it was much too large for a mortal woman or man. At last, Osiris stepped into it and lay down, and, of course, it fit him exactly.

The seventy-two conspirators ran toward the coffin, slammed the lid down upon the king and nailed it shut, then soldered the edges with molten lead. Osiris shouted and struggled, but the weight of the jeweled coffin lid was too great. The revelers, too, tried to save Osiris, but they were too weak with drink. Some of them died on the blades of the barbarians' spears; others ran from the palace screaming. The seventy-two, led by Seth, hoisted the box upon their shoulders, carried it down the hill, and heaved it with an enormous splash into the green river. The chest sank immediately to the bottom and bubbles broke the surface of the water. Then the currents of the Nile carried the coffin along toward the mouth of the river.

Seth stood upon the banks and shouted, "He drowns in his own waters. He is trapped in form, inert. He is cut down like his own stalks of wheat. Ever after his name shall be Still-Heart, ruler in the land of the dead." With a whoop of victory and a fist raised to the sky, Seth ran back up the hill and into the palace, where he drank Osiris's wine, ate his honey-eyed cakes, and ordered about and beat the servants of the dead king. Then, dirty and sweating, he fell asleep, content with himself in the soft, perfumed sheets of his brother's bed.

The Mourning of Isis

The first creatures to hear of the deed were the pans and satyrs, the half-men, half-beasts who lived in the desert wilderness, lifting their sharp noses to the wind to catch the scent of death. They ran howling through the darkened, moonless streets of the villages in a blind panic, heralds of doom and destruction, messengers who preceded the season of death. Hearing wild goats and dogs within the village, the women ran to their windows and shuttered them, then sat huddled in the darkness of their houses, covered in blankets and quivering with fear. The children woke with fitful dreams of drowned men, of sandstorms, of desolation. The men shouted the news in the streets, while the coffin of the dead king floated down the Nile, unseen.

In Coptos, Anubis first heard the howling of the dogs and intuited the news of Osiris's murder. When he told Isis, she grabbed the silver knife with which she had cut the umbilical cords of the new children of Coptos. She thought first of plunging it into her chest, then she tore at her long, thick, black braids and cut them off at the scalp. "My husband, Osiris, dead!" she cried. "Brother has murdered brother. Oh bitterest curse of the mother's womb, maw of life, lips curled in red death!" Fistful after fistful of sand she scooped up and poured over her head while the tears streamed down her breasts. "Why must we suffer? How much can we endure? Two brothers, damned for all time. And how I loved both of them."

With tears she sent Anubis away to protect and comfort Nephthys. Alone, dressed in the black rags of mourning, the goddess wandered, barefoot, disconsolate, up and down the muddy edges of the riverbank, peering into the sedge and papyrus clumps, walking dusty streets, wailing, seeking the coffin of Osiris. Although she had delivered their children, the village people no longer recognized her. Seeing the mad woman in black muttering to herself, moaning, weeping, raging, and covering her head in sand, the children screamed and the women ran away from her. Isis ran after them, grabbing at their fine clothes with her ragged fingernails. "Have you seen him? The king? Ensnared in the golden chest? Have you seen Osiris?" she pleaded.

"Go away! And take your evil eye with you," cried the village chiefs.

The women shouted at her, "A curse upon you, witch, and upon your mother and father!"

"A curse upon us all," responded Isis, wailing.

And she left the city weeping, carrying her shorn braids in a linen bag along the dusty roads, sand sticking to the soles of her bare feet. With each step she muttered to herself, "When I find my beloved, I shall open my sack of sorrow and cover him in my shorn hair, place the braids upon his chest, and hide him, the way I once covered him when I loved him, all pleasure hidden in a veil of hair perfumed with the essence of orange blossoms. And in the weaving of my braids, I shall reweave his dream, bring his body back in time anew, shining, radiant, a god-man made all god. My loss I offer up to life."

Weeks passed, and on Isis walked. Many days and nights she slept alone in the desert, shivering in the cold, surrounded by scorpions and watched over by wild dogs, who took pity on the half-mad goddess. The stars hid themselves from her view behind clouds, but the rains did not come. Wherever Isis went, she asked the villagers, "Have you seen my brother, Osiris? Has his coffin come this way? I lay with him in the womb of my mother. We lay together, he and I, skin to skin, lip to lip. How could I not know him again? I search. I walk up and down the river. Have you seen him?"

"Go away," the people said.

Weary, the goddess stretched herself out on the riverbank, an offering to a hungry crocodile, who was one of the secret companions of the power-hungry murderer Seth. The crocodile crawled to her and looked on the muddy, bedraggled form with a lazy, yellow eye. Trying to frighten her, he opened his mouth wide and showed her a row of bloody, jagged teeth stinking with the flesh of a freshly devoured hippopotamus. Isis closed her eyes, waiting for the prick of his teeth. But the crocodile felt pity and closed his mouth; he did not devour the goddess.

"Vile creature of the depths who dwells at the bottom of time," Isis cried. "Vile creature, writhing in the mud and slime of matter, if you will not devour me, then tell me, have you seen him? Has your thick, pink tongue tasted the skin of my brother, Osiris?"

The crocodile turned and sank back into the depths of the river.

Isis rose and walked on, more weary than before. Many more weeks passed. She fell to her knees and begged the merchants traveling down the road, "Have you seen him? Have you seen my brother?" The merchants hurried their asses and cattle by her.

"Out of the way, old hag," they said.

Isis wept. "What? Have I grown old, too?" She wandered all across the deserts of Egypt, into the swamps of the delta, and through villages she had never seen before. All the while she muttered to herself in a daze, "I am lost. He is lost. We are lost."

From out of a thicket of papyrus a great white cow stepped, parting the reeds with her curved horns. "I have seen him, your husband," the animal said. "He dwells with me now in the womb of time."

"Mother!" cried Isis. "Nut!" But the cow was gone. Behind a screen of papyrus stalks, she heard little children playing. She crept to their hiding place and watched the three girls place a doll into a cradle. No, not a doll and a cradle, but a man and a coffin! She approached them slowly, so as not to frighten them, but though she was wild and terrifying, still the children did not run. They were innocents, budding priestesses of the goddess, who knew many things they did not yet know they knew.

"Look!" cried one of the girls. "It is Isis!"

The goddess kissed them upon their foreheads. "What game do you play, child?" she asked. "What game is it with the man in the coffin?"

"It is only a dream that all three of us had. It is a secret game."

"Tell me," Isis cried.

In the dream, they said, the three of them had seen many men covered in animal skins throwing a golden and jeweled chest into the river. It floated along the canal outside their house. The children went down to the river's edge and the chest flew open. They saw that a man was drowning, and they were afraid. The man called to them. They tried to grab him, crying out, "We will save you!" But the coffin lid slammed closed, and the golden chest floated down to the mouth of the river near Tanis, where the waters carried it out to sea.

Isis in Byblos

Isis continued walking along the seacoast, past the Bitter Lakes, beyond the borders of Egypt, and through strange countries. Everywhere she went she asked the children if they had seen the coffin of Osiris, and the children pointed the way. At last she came to Byblos, on the coast of Syria, where the coffin was said to have drifted ashore. There, she was told, when the coffin first touched land a tamarisk tree sprang up suddenly, enclosing the jeweled chest in its trunk. Trapped once already inside his coffin, Osiris in the tree was now doubly ensnared.

Isis went to search for the tree, and at last she found it. She ran to the tamarisk but, because its trunk was so thick, she could not get her arms around it. Isis threw herself at the base of the tree and embraced its roots. "My husband!" she cried. "You are strong, you are mighty. The whole Earth bows before you. If I could leap into this tree's branches, I'd climb all the way up to the gods. There I would see the shining body of my husband, Osiris."

She caressed the tree trunk with her fingers, then beat her fists against the bark. "Brother, come out," she cried. "Awake!" A breeze moved through the tree branches. It seemed as if the leaves murmured. Osiris was listening. But trapped in the tree, he could do nothing. Several days passed. At length a Syrian king, named Malcander, and his army happened to pass by. The king so admired the height, width, and strength of the tamarisk that he ordered his men to chop it down.

"What a fine central pillar this tree will make for my house," he said.

"A curse upon you and your house!" cried Isis. "Do not touch the tree. In it resides the body of a god. My life, my husband. Cut not a single branch!"

But the king's men pulled her aside and drew out their copper axes. Metal rang against wood and the Osirian tree was felled, its branches cut, its leaves stripped. The heavy trunk was placed with great effort upon a sledge. Pulled by a team of white cows, the sledge carried the body of Osiris away across the fields. Isis, shocked and bereft once again, followed after them, wailing and tossing dirt upon her head. The sledge drew farther and farther away until she saw it no more, but followed only the hoofprints of the cattle and the sledge's tracks.

Outside the great walls of Byblos, Isis lost the trail of the sledge. Tired, ragged, and lost, she had never felt such desolation and despair. She stood a moment confused before the houses at the crossroads, then wandered through the streets and sat down wearily by a well.

The grief she had felt all this time suddenly overtook her, and the tears she had so long held back tracked down her dirty face. To none would she speak. The women at the well turned their backs to her and whispered. Their children gathered at the goddess's blistered feet and stared.

At last, the queen's handmaidens came to the well, young girls who giggled innocently and splashed each other with water. One of them accidentally splashed Isis and—wonder of wonders—the goddess laughed. It was as if she had awakened from a long dream. The handmaiden smiled shyly; Isis smiled.

"Come," Isis said, motioning the girl to sit between her knees. With her soft hands the goddess braided the handmaiden's hair. The divine fragrance of her breath on the girl's neck created a wondrous perfume. In turn, each girl sat eagerly at the knees of the goddess and allowed Isis to braid her hair.

When Queen Astarte saw the lovely plaits of her handmaidens' hair, when she had embraced them and inhaled the sweet smell of the perfume that had emanated from the goddess's breath, a longing for the unknown woman overcame her. The handmaidens told her what a sad sight the stranger had been, how hungry, poor, and lost.

"Go to her," Astarte said. "Bring her into our house. Perhaps she is the perfect one to nursemaid my new child."

When Isis came into the palace, she swooned at the sight of the tamarisk column, its wood carved into the beautiful faces of lions and gazelles and covered now in gold leaf. The tree had transformed itself into a divine shrine to Osiris. She felt as if she had come home, and she swore to herself that as long as the body of her husband remained in Syria she would not return to Egypt. She bathed, dressed in a clean, simple linen dress, and presented herself before the queen. Astarte saw the peace that descended upon her fitful baby as soon as Isis appeared, and she knew at once that this woman would be the perfect nurse for her new son.

Soon after Isis arrived, the queen's other children began to follow her wherever she went. Underfoot all day, they were like kittens scampering after a mother cat. Isis sang to them with a voice as clear and sweet as a bird's. She knew many songs and stories. In secret she taught them several spells for curing the sting of bees, for hypnotizing snakes, and for catching innumerable fish in their nets.

"Mother," they said to Astarte, "she smells so wonderful. She must be a goddess in hiding."

Isis came to love the children as well. It appeared to be her fate that she would always be the nursemaid of other women's children and never have a child of her own. But if that was so, she accepted it and loved them as much as if they were her own children. She wished no harm to befall them, and strove day and night to protect them from the dangers of wild animals, falls, and accidents.

Because the baby was young and there was still time for magic to work on his behalf, and because she understood in her own tortured soul the grief that the loss of a loved one causes, Isis determined to weave a spell of protection about the child, to create of this mortal little boy a living and eternal creature.

Rather than nursing him with his mother's milk, which was the milk of mortality, Isis gave the baby her own divine and immortal finger to suck instead. At night while the rest of the palace slept, Isis took the child and wrapped him in a protective spell by rubbing him with the skin of a salamander. Then she began to rid him of all that was mortal by laying him upon a bed of burning coals and incense and leaving him there for the night. This she did for twenty-one days, and with only one more week of magic left to do, the child would have been as shining and eternal as a night star.

Meanwhile, as the boy lay sleeping amid the flames, the goddess transformed herself into the likeness of a swallow. Spreading her wings, she fluttered about the pillar that contained the body of her dead husband. With her body disguised, she wailed, wept in secret, and called his name—the swallow dipping and spinning about the pillar, twittering mournfully. Yet the changeless pillar remained rigid, resolute, a moment in time now encased in an eternity, a soul trapped in matter, a god lost in form. The swallow shrieked and wailed.

Hearing the cries of the bird one night, Astarte awoke, thinking she had heard one of her children sobbing. On tiptoes she crept next to their beds and found them all asleep, smiling in dream—all of them except the baby, whose crib was empty. She stole into the great hall, hugging the walls and staying within the shadows until she reached the doorway. There, she saw the dark swallow—a bad omen, she thought—circling endlessly around the pillar. With another glance toward the hearth she spied her youngest child lying in a shroud of flames. She shrieked and her cry broke the spell. The child awoke and screamed, and the goddess flew down from the ceiling and scooped him out of the fire.

Isis stood now before Astarte in her true form—not as a swallow, not even as a simple nursemaid, but with her skin radiant, her eyes aflame, and her robes royal. Remembering her own true majesty, she revealed herself for the first time as she once had been—a living, breathing goddess.

"I am sorry for you," Isis said. "You came a week too soon. Had my spell continued the child would have become immortal as a god. As it is, he shall be merely talented, handsome, and beloved, but then goodness, beauty, and even talent are no salvation. One day, like all beloved men, he will die. Time will pass, and it will be as if he had never lived."

"Who are you?" Astarte blurted out.

"I am the goddess Isis, beloved queen of Egypt, golden daughter of my mother, Nut. And there, trapped eternal as death inside his coffin, lies my husband, Osiris. His coffin resides inside the pillar upholding your roof."

The goddess lowered her eyes because they were filling with tears. "Please, you have shown me only kindness, Astarte. You have restored me to myself at a time when I knew only great sorrow . . . Please, give me my husband. Lay him in my arms once more. I want only to take his body home."

Moved by her speech, King Malcander and Queen Astarte ordered their men to hew down the enormous pillar, to cut the overgrown wood away from the coffin. When at last the jeweled chest was revealed, Isis fell upon it and embraced it with such loud cries of anguish and despair that the younger daughter of Astarte and Malcander cried out in fright, slumped to the ground, and died.

The wood that had come from the tamarisk tree Isis wrapped in a linen cloth and anointed with her perfume of myrrh, orange blossoms, and lotus. Around the relic she built a small temple, a place of solace where all women who had lost husbands or children might come to weep and be comforted.

The elder son of Astarte, Maneros, held the goddess Isis in such esteem that he did not want her to leave. With his mother's permission, Isis took the boy with her. Together they placed the coffin of Osiris in a rowing ship and that morning set sail on the Phaedrus River. Because the early morning fostered a boisterous wind, the ship made little headway even after hours of rowing. Isis looked angrily over her shoulder at the river, and in the boat's wake the waters behind them dried, leaving only a dusty channel filled with rocks and boulders.

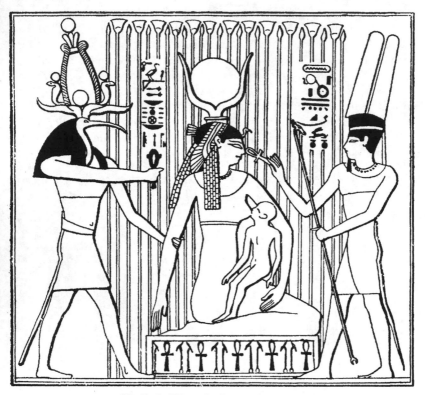

The birth of Horus in the papyrus swamps.

2

The Childhood of Horus

Believing herself to have the power to conquer death, Isis attempts to revivify the drowned Osiris. She does create life, but not the life she knew previously. The child that she conceives is born out of her deep longing, a kind of consolation for her lost husband.

Isis rejoices over the new life in her womb, but despair follows quickly when Seth finds the body of Osiris and does away with it once and for all by hacking it to pieces and casting it into the river. Isis attempts to gather all the parts of her slain husband and re-member him, to bring him back to fullness. Sadly, the symbol of his most creative powers is gone. His remembrance can occur only by holding sacred his memory through religious ritual; therefore, Isis establishes for him temples throughout Egypt. This done, in order for her life to continue on Earth, she must finally let go of Osiris by sending him into the land of the dead from which he can return to her only through dreams.

Now Osiris becomes lost in the neterworld and suffers like some sort of subterranean Job of the Old Testament. He sees that the other gods, even evildoers like Seth, will have an eternal place in the boat of the Sun god—all but Osiris, and he does not understand. He has lost his mission in life, has died to his former self, and is in a quandary to discover another reason for living. In the meantime, he discovers that Isis has conceived a child who will become heir to all of Egypt, taking the place of his father.

No sooner has Isis relinquished Osiris to the underworld than she is captured by Seth and imprisoned in his spinning mill. Now the goddess must undergo her own death-in-life and rebirth experience. She forgets for a moment that she is a goddess and the embodiment of the creative matrix. Instead, she sits and spins, and as she spins, the life within her womb grows. Although hidden in the womb, the child itself is reshaping Isis's world. At last, through the intervention of the goddesses of fate, Isis escapes from her prison.

When Isis gives birth to the child in the papyrus swamps, she is attended by a number of divine guardians. She recognizes the child Horus as the earthly embodiment of her heavenly brother, the first Horus, who was conceived along with Isis, Osiris, Seth, and Nephthys in the belly of their mother, Nut. Horus, she says, is twice-born.

Because Seth, like Herod in the Christ story, is trying to kill the holy child, Isis hides the newborn in the swamps. Horus grows up surrounded by loving goddesses; and even when his life is jeopardized by the evil powers of darkness, in the end a mother's love saves him. But there is only so much Isis herself can do to save the child. Seth has usurped the powers of Osiris. Egypt itself suffers from the loss of a gentle, true king.

When Horus is old enough to be left alone, and when Isis understands that her presence with him is more of a hindrance than a help, she places the child with her sister goddesses and goes off alone throughout Egypt. With a heavy heart she leaves, knowing that she must attend to other duties, duties that are even more demanding than raising her child. Finally, the goddess herself discovers the necessity for her independence.

With the magical conception of the inheritor child Horus, the future of Osiris's earthly realm is assured. Like Mary in the Christ story, the holy child is born of a virgin mother; that is, conceived by means of divine intervention. Unlike the Christ story, however, the gentle, nurturing Isis of the previous tale has journeyed to the borders of madness. In order to find herself, she must first lose herself. Motherhood not only is deep compassion and love; it often is a fury.

So the tale continues . . .

The Begetting of Horus

At last the boat set off on glassy seas, and while the oarsmen rowed by day, Isis sat silently by the coffin of Osiris. She neither wept nor cried out her rage, fearing that by such divine wrath she might yet again injure an innocent bystander. But by night when the others slept she threw herself on top of the coffin and wept bitterly, murmuring, "Brother, I am here. My fine barley maker, lyre player, joy maker, my dancer, my husband, speak. Look at me. It is I, Isis, your sister who loves you. How can you seem so far from me when you yet lie in my arms? I have searched the ends of the Earth for you. Simply to look upon you would be such happiness, yet your face is hidden, turned away from me. You hold yourself so separate and my heart is bitter. I scream to the heights of Heaven, to the depths of the sea. I call your name. Answer me, if you hear me. No woman or man alive loved you more than I. I am your sister, your favorite, your sweetness, your wife. Speak, Osiris, speak. I beg you."

But Osiris remained silent as his wooden coffin, distant as Egypt or the far-off stars. Hearing dreadful wails rising from the throat of Isis, Maneros crept to the edge of the boat to watch. Isis felt his staring eyes like an icy wind upon her back, and turning in great rage, her own eyes flashed red, burning coals to counter his ice. The frightened boy stumbled backward and fell over the edge of the boat with a small splash. The sleepy oarsmen, hearing nothing, rowed on through the night. Isis, again lost in sorrow and half-mad with grief, immediately forgot about the boy and threw herself anew on the coffin of her husband and wept. From her tears that dripped into the water sprang a thousand-petaled white lotus.

At last the boat came to shore in Abydos, land of the dead, land of dreams, land of desire. Osiris had returned to Egypt, but his kingdom lay in ruins. The beautiful palace he had built for Isis had been burned to the ground, reduced to ashes. The gardens lay barren, dry as bones. No ibis waded in the pools. No figs ripened on the branches. No children ran to the shore to greet him. How much time had passed since his death no one knows; joy seems so fleeting, sorrow so eternal.

The oarsmen turned the boat from the Nile up into a canal that ended in a grove of acacia trees. When Isis stepped to the ground with the body of Osiris, a spring of water erupted like some bittersweet memory from a crevice in the rocks. Isis paid the oarsmen with her necklaces and bracelets of gold, carnelian, and ebony. The boat turned and headed back to Byblos, leaving the goddess alone on the shore.

Her hair was covered with dust, her eyes filled with tears, her heart overflowed with grief. With bars of iron, curved ribs of the Earth, Isis pried open the jeweled coffin to gaze at length on the form of her beloved. The face of Osiris was black as death, passive, immobile, the eyes dreaming. Where is it that the dead go? Osiris knew: into a land of eternally rising barley; into an Island of Flame; into a land where rivers flow red and shining as blood in the veins, where shining souls sit birdlike in the tops of trees, where the arms of mothers embrace their sons. They go to a land where the words of dead men sit patiently as seeds held moist in the mouth. His dreams were dreams eternal as the dreams of stones. He saw fields of reeds, cattle lowing, hawks flying, children suckling. Inert, lifeless, waiting there in the dark, still of heart, the dead Osiris dreamed the dream of a god—the return of possibility.

Isis touched his eyes with her fingers; she anointed them with her tears. She gazed at herself reflected there in his face as if in two mirrors, and she read the story in his eyes of a man's love for his woman. She read the tale of his last thoughts: "Isis, Sister, Wife, Mother, Queen of Heaven and Earth." Her name was like a tongue of fire, a serpent rising—beautiful, graceful, enchanting, dreadful, terrible.

In her sorrow she began to dance, to weep, to spin, her feet raising great clouds of dust. She spun round and round. She keened. She sighed. Her arms became great feathered wings. Kitelike she fluttered above the corpse of Osiris, chanting, singing, crying, as she had done in Byblos, mad with the grief of separation even now as he lay in her arms, enchanted by the power and hunger of her love.

Isis danced and danced, while the heavens whirled about her. The great wheel of time stopped and rolled backward. Clouds of ether gathered overhead, tumbling black, white, and gray, filled with flashes of lightning. It was only in despair, in gloom, in her deepest grief, in the darkest clouds that the power of light sparked and forms merged. Separated by death from that which she loved, Isis was like some spirit desperate to return and resume form in the body. It was as if she were making life anew. A god blinked in the darkness. A god rose up, bright fire from the watery abyss. He and She. She and He. In the beginning the one became two, the self and the other, the selfsame Self. Now she cried, "Merge and merge and merge again. In the flesh, the two are made one."

As she sang her songs of love, the great gates of Heaven stood open, and the circling, unfaltering stars wheeled in the evening sky, weaving a new fate for Osiris, making for him the new crown of a king.

"Desire," she cried. "Flame. Flame. Passion of body and spirit. Earth, rise up; Heaven, descend. Flame. Flame in the heart of Isis inflame the body of Osiris. What sustenance is in my hand bring to his hand. Flame in the belly and navel. Breath. What is in my mouth bring to his mouth, the wind of my wings bring breath to his lungs. Desire, a flame. What is in my belly, be in his—seed of creation, spark of life, enter the we. Rise up, phallus of Osiris, and enter Isis. Rise up, milk in the breast of Isis, and nourish Osiris. Rise up. Rise up. Flame, enter truth. Rouse the Earth. Rouse Heaven. Rouse the hearts of Isis and Osiris."

Amid the hills distant lightning flashed. The words of Isis were the words of a sorceress. Truth and love are the divine powers. Her speech was as pure as her heart and mind, her tongue perfect, her love mighty. She who sought the lost one without ceasing, she who loved him without fail, she who traveled to the ends of the Earth in sorrow to find him and bring him home, brought life back into the lifeless. She filled him with the light of her own eyes. She breathed his breath for him.

An entire night passed as she lay with him, whispering endlessly, "Love. Light. Life. Power. Might. Blessed be thee." She raised him up. She drew him into her body. She gave him her essence, he gave her his. She made the heir. Osiris breathed the breath of Isis, perfume of pomegranates and honey. His eyes opened, closed. Eons passed. Magic happened.

At last, exhausted, the goddess fell upon the chest of Osiris and slept. She dreamed the dream of Osiris: from the blue egg of the world a hawk of gold was born, shining and blue-haired, with enormous wings that spanned the length of Egypt. She dreamed footprints of the hawk in the sand, footprints of the hawk in river mud. She dreamed a snake rising to heaven, grasped in the talons of the hawk. The gods placed a double crown upon the bird's head.

She woke to the crash of thunder, the forked tongues of lightning, torrents of rain descending. The thirsty Earth drank in Heaven's flood. Out on the desert she heard the confused sounds of jackals and wild dogs howling. Snakes rose up, slithered from their holes, slid along the banks this way and that, a jumble of creatures writhing in the hard silver rain. Nearby wild boars squealed; hippos bellowed, mired in the mud. The animals of Seth were all in a panic.

Isis felt the clot of blood and flesh in her womb. She knew and ran out into the rainstorm shouting, washing the dust from her hair, the rain streaming down her swollen breasts. A god of great power was to be born.

"I am I," she cried. "I am Isis, sister and wife of Osiris, mother of a god. How I wept for my husband, made a corpse by his brother. How I wept for my barren womb while I cared for the children of my sisters. How I bemoaned my fate. I weep no more. I carry the seed of Osiris. I will birth a god, the child who avenges his father, makes good the sorrows of his mother. The child in my womb is none other than Horus, my son, my brother, slayer of enemies. Twice-born, he emerged once in Heaven, and now on Earth. He shall be known as king of Egypt. Already he is known as the golden god in the hearts of the people. As he lives, so lives Osiris!"

With that, a mighty thunderbolt cleaved the sky and thick drops of rain descended, falling upon the shining form of Isis and the sleeping form of Osiris. From the god's lips, as if he had held the seeds of potentiality in his mouth, there sprang up green shoots of barley.

Now the storm grew fearsome and terrible, but Isis was filled with great happiness, overwhelmed with joy. She who had conceived a god and raised a storm determined now to raise the dead—the body of Osiris himself, already renewed and greening. But she needed time and she needed a guardian, a watchman, a helpmate. Hesitant to leave Osiris alone, Isis had little choice. Unable to battle Seth and his tribe by herself, she needed the help of Anubis and her sister, Nephthys.

When the storm had passed, a white orb full as a goddess's belly burst through the shredding clouds. Isis carried the body of her husband high into the moonlit hills, to a remote and desolate place far from the prying eyes of any villagers, away from the streams of water and the river. There she hid him in a desert cave and sealed the entrance with a boulder. She disguised the resting place of Osiris with a maze of rocks, a winding labyrinth of white stone walls. Then, with a kiss, she left him there for only one night while she rushed off to find Anubis and Nephthys.

The Dismemberment of Osiris

It happened that on that same night Seth himself was roaming the great red sandhills of Abydos, hunting the wild boar by moonlight. Armed with bow and arrows and accompanied by a pack of wild dogs, he paused upon the trail of the black boar who was snuffling along the rocks, stopping now and again to catch the scent of food, of barley growing somewhere amid those desert rocks.

Seth, too, paused, pricked up his ears, and sniffed the wind, catching the scent of wild pig. He moved as stealthily as darkness along the winding white-walled path, following his prey through a labyrinth of stone until he came to the sealed door of the cave.

Outside the entrance he spied the bits of jeweled and gilt wood left by Isis, and recognizing these as the coffin of Osiris, he became enraged. His face and limbs reddened with anger as he pried loose the boulder with his bow of iron, heaved aside the boulder, and entered the tomb. There he spied the body of Osiris lying upon a bed of stone, breathing, dreaming, nearly alive, surrounded by candles and draped in the shorn locks of the hair of Isis. Seth knelt slowly at his brother's side, stroked his face, and leaned over a moment to whisper in Osiris's left ear. Worms slithered from the lips of Seth.

"Sleep eternal, my brother, Still-Heart," he said, "Lord of Death, Chief of No Man, King of Abundant Sleep. The flesh rots and stinks. The intestines become fetid liquid. The bones of the body crumble away. The soul departs. Matter becomes chaos, a helpless mass. Fish and worms shall dine on thee. An end has been made of thee. Fear me now. I am Seth, Death Itself, the Heir of Egypt."

Osiris opened his eyes once, beheld Seth, and cried out, "Isis, come to me!" With a cry of rage and a thunderclap, Seth drew from his belt an Ethiopian knife. The sharp blade of obsidian he plunged into the chest of his awakened brother. Then the god Osiris closed his eyes, breathed no more, and died his second death.

In his pain and rage, Seth slashed the knife again and again across the body of Osiris. He cut the head from its body. He hacked off the arms and legs and penis. He disassembled the bones of his back. He quartered his brother like a slain animal and stuffed all the pieces in a leather sack, then carried the bits of the body down to the river and heaved them into the water.

The Nile ran red with the blood of Osiris, and the scattered bits of his body drifted away to wash ashore later on the riverbank—all but the phallus of Osiris, which floated on the water like a lotus bud on its stalk. The clotted blood of Osiris, mixed with the regenerative powers of the water, gave birth to a long-nosed oxyrhynchus fish. In turn, the fish, newborn and hungry, spied the bobbing phallus of Osiris. Because it seemed a tasty bit of flesh, the fish swallowed it, then sank immediately to the bottom of the river.

At the moment of his death, Isis, who had been sitting with Nephthys many miles away, heard the cry of her brother. The two women rushed out into the darkness, beheld the blood-red Moon, and gasped. A shadow had descended upon the face of the Moon. They watched in growing horror as bit by bit the Moon disappeared, eaten up by black shadow. When only a crescent of light remained, Isis was seized with the knowledge of her husband's fate. "That crescent of light is the leg of Osiris," she cried. "That blackened crescent is the knife of Seth," Nephthys answered. The goddesses fell to their knees with wails of grief and sent their anguished cries toward Heaven. Their sobs shattered stone.

Isis and Nephthys hurried to the river, led by Anubis, who knew the smell of his father and followed the trail of his blood. There on the banks of the Nile at Abydos, the goddess spied the severed head of her husband. She threw herself onto it, grasped it in her lap, and began weeping and kissing the blue lips of his mouth, speaking her words of power, breathing her breath into him, but there was no Osiris left to receive her sacred gift. A madness deep and dark descended upon her, a sorrow greater than any despair she had ever known.

"O helpless one!" she cried. "O god asleep! Osiris inert, who knows not the darkness of this place, I know it for him in my heart! I found him, dead, lying on his side. Awake! Rise up! Set the floodwaters in motion!"

Isis washed the head of Osiris in the water of the Nile. She bathed him in natron and niter; she perfumed his hair with frankincense, his lips with myrrh. She plunged her fingers between his teeth. "I open his mouth," she said, "that he may speak to me, that he may eat, that he may draw breath wherever he is." She sat singing softly as she offered the severed head a loaf of bread, a jug of wine, the milk of her breast. The god did not stir. His eyes remained open, passive, immobile.

"Oh, sister!" said Nephthys to Isis. "Here lies our brother Osiris, slain. Father of our children, a good and shining one. He shall be remembered. We shall lift up his head. We shall find his bones. We shall reassemble his limbs. Love shall put an end to all his woe, and he will suffer no more."

Isis rose, shook the sand from her feet, and shaved her head; she smeared herself with mud. And Nephthys joined her sister in the sorrowing. The two goddesses danced by the bank of the river around the severed head of Osiris. They shook the sistrum, they tore their dresses and beat their breasts. They keened and sighed like two birds, waving their arms. They rose above the body of Osiris on soaring wings.

Seeing the two sisters like hawks circling above the river through the bloody light of dawn, the people ran from their houses. When they saw that their king lay slain, they, too, began to beat their breasts, wave their hands in the air, shave their heads, and shout. They gathered palm branches from the trees and thrashed the air with them, crying, "A multitude of days, the innumerable leaves of this tree shall be the years of Osiris in the land of his mother."

Yet Isis was not willing to surrender Osiris unto death, at least not while his heir grew in her belly. In a nearby cave she, Anubis, and Nephthys hid the head of Osiris, determined to bring together all the mangled and missing parts of the god and to resurrect him. The tomb of Osiris became like the womb of his mother. His broken limbs and body would be gathered into Nut, Mother Sky, even as she gathered to herself the multitude of stars. By her great magic, Isis would restore her husband's divine rulership. But to revive a god, Isis needed to teach the people her rituals of magic.

By the side of the river where she had discovered him, the goddess built for her husband a place of honor. The eternal stones of the temple to Osiris stretched nearly up to Heaven. For the people she fashioned a body of wax and spices and wrapped it in the linen rags of her shredded dress. She gave this body to the village priests and they buried it. The spirit of the god entered into the eternal stones that bore the likeness of his face. At the feet of the statue the mourners laid garlands of onions, garlands of lotus, garlands of desert flowers. They prayed, they sang, they danced, they burned incense. The life of the people gave life to Osiris.

"Render him honors," Isis said. "He was the noblest man in Egypt, child of the sky, inheritor of the Earth. Remember him as I re-member him. Say his name. Osiris. Say his name. Unnefer, the beautiful one. Say his name. Khentamenti. Lord of hidden things. Bring him geese, raisin cakes, pomegranates, beer. Remember yourselves. Whether you live or die, you are an Osiris, too. He enters in and reappears through you. He decays in you; he grows in you, a god eternal as the growing emmer. Living or dead, he is like the barley. He is yesterday; he is tomorrow. He shall be born again and again. He shall be born within you. His body is the wheat in your bread, his blood the fluid of your wine. Osiris has entered Truth; he relies on Truth. Master of the god's ways, he emerges in Truth. Lord of Khemet, Lord of the Dead, Osiris lives. He has no limits."

So saying, the goddess left Abydos. Dressed now in mourning clothes of blue and gray, faces smeared with mud, Isis and Nephthys set sail in a sloop of bundled papyrus reeds. Anubis, dark as night and robed in panther skin, stood at the head of the boat, sniffing the breezes, searching out the missing pieces of his father. Unbeknownst to the goddess, the papyrus boat was being followed by a large, crooked-toothed crocodile, the same creature who once had encountered Isis on the riverbank. He had seen the fish devour the regenerative part of Osiris, and he felt pity for the goddess, knowing as he did (since he himself was a devourer, a monster of destruction) that all the parts of Osiris would never be found. Yet the crocodile followed the boat of Isis, protecting her from the followers of Seth while she gathered together the other body parts. The name of the crocodile was Sobek.

For twenty-eight days the trio sailed up and down the river gathering the fragments of Osiris's body. Wherever Isis found a piece—a foot, an arm, a leg, a thigh, his heart, bits of his backbone, his ears, his tongue, his jaws—she cried out with joy, "He lives! He rises up! The god is found anew!" Then her joy descended again into sorrow and she cried in loud lamentation, "He is dead. He is dead. Alas, the king is dead."

Nephthys wept with her sister, her own troubles weighing heavily upon her heart. It had been her husband, after all, who had slain the husband of her sister, her husband who had slain her brother. Yet she could not speak against him. Love and anger existed like twins in the same heart. It was her child, Anubis, who knew her not, who led the search for Osiris, who adored Isis, who called her mother. Nephthys's life was bitter, bitterer, bitterest.

In every city, by every riverbank where the body parts of Osiris were found, the goddesses cried with joy, were immediately consumed with grief, and in happiness and sorrow erected a new temple. Thus Isis protected the fragments of Osiris by confusing Seth as to the real burial site of the body.

The companions of Seth followed every movement of the two sisters, determined to find Osiris and corrupt him yet again. Therefore, Isis and Nephthys traveled throughout Egypt with their heads shaved, their faces concealed by beards, disguised as beggar men so that they might confuse the enemies of Osiris. Said Isis to Nephthys, "In my grief, I have found another kind of strength. I have turned myself into a man. Although I was a woman, I have become a man in order to make the name Osiris endure on Earth."

Osiris Rules the Underworld

When at last all the pieces had been found, except the phallus, Isis, Nephthys, and Anubis sailed back to Abydos in the middle of the night. No one saw them depart from the boat. No one saw them walk into the desert hills. None but the Moon god Thoth saw them enter the crypt of Osiris, and he descended from the sky. He who had pieced together the stolen hours to create the day of Osiris's birth would create the supernal time in which the god would live—an eternity in the land of gods, a life of blessing in the field of reeds, a land of quiet fire where Osiris would rule forever.

Because the fish had swallowed the phallus of Osiris, Isis fashioned another from cedar wood and gold. Over this she whispered the words of power, the words of passion, the words of remembrance so that in the next world Osiris might remember himself and give birth to all good things, to all growing plants, all children, all souls. With his hands as dark and rich as fertile soil, Anubis pieced together the broken body of his father. Isis and Nephthys swathed Osiris in linen bandages torn from their dresses. Thoth and Anubis knotted the cords.

"His body to Earth," said Thoth, "his soul to Sky."

The ground trembled. Heaven stirred. Nut descended and lay entirely upon the body of her son and embraced him. With her own divine hands she gathered him up, molded him into a living god, and took him into

her heart. "Osiris lives," she said. "Osiris did not die. Osiris was not anni-
hilated." Isis and Nephthys spread their arms and began to sing the song
of changing. They themselves transformed into hawks of gold; their
wings stirred fresh breezes. On these winds, Nut sailed back into Heaven,
enfolding the soul of Osiris. Then Geb yawned and took the mortal form
of his son into his own belly.

Dark were the ways, dark were the changes, dazzling the incarnations.
Osiris lived, a king of the living dead. In the belly of the world, he
dreamed and remembered us; yet he himself was lost and did not know
how much dreams mattered. God of myriad forms, none of which he
could see, he was splendor and madness. Terrible and mighty are the
powers of the dead. Visible, the wheel of eternity turns, sings in the mind,
among the beasts and fields. Invisible, Osiris joined himself to the Atum,
the serpent of nothing which is the beginning.

Osiris-Atum lived. Complete. Whole. Perfect. Lonely. Atoms whirred
in the void, all was darkness, passion without form. In the land of the
dead there was neither past nor future. No air. No light. No water. Only
void, emptiness, endless desert where width and depth lay unfathomable.
Dreamless, Osiris lay on a pillow of stone. He stirred, he moved, going
nowhere.

"Atum!" he cried. "What is this desolate place? The heart breaks. The
heart yearns. I thirst. I suffocate. The self I thought I was dies. How is it
that a man who loved a goddess, who cupped the lotus in his hand, who
inhaled her fragrance, can no longer exist?"

And a voice answered, "Be still, Still-Heart. Look now on Egypt without
its god, without form, without hope, without love, without its beginning
and without its end. Be still, Still-Heart. Yearn for the emptiness."

Osiris searched night's darkened stars and wept for himself and his shattered world. The great green river no longer flowed. Sand encroached on
the empty temples. Wild beasts stalked children playing in the street. Old
men wept with their heads in their hands. Wild asses trampled the shriveled shoots in a land beset by chaos. Isis and Nephthys shaved their heads.
Bare breasted as men they traveled from village to village, bringing herbs
for the sick, burying the dead; their eyes were glazed with sadness.

"I thirst," said Osiris. Atum brought the god water. "I cannot breathe,"
said Osiris. Atum brought the god air. "I hunger," said Osiris. Atum
shared his beer and bread. The food was tasteless, the beer dry as sand.
Then it was quiet in the land of the hidden god. No shadow of a sound
moved through limitless desert. Black night was the stillness of the god's
heart, the absence of its beat, beat, beat. No footsteps, no sighs, no joy, no
peace in the silence. All was isolation, desolation, hard rock in the land of
Atum, where Osiris would remain forever.

"Shall I see your face?" asked Osiris.

"No," said Atum. "Mine is the face of emptiness. You will not suffer
its sorrow."

"I long for light," cried Osiris. "Even eternal night in Egypt has its thousand stars. Every other god grips the staff of life in his hand. Every other god sails in the Boat of the Millions of Years. At dawn, at noon, at dusk with the sun, they come and go, drift amid lotus, slice through light's dancing waters."

"That is the talent of the living," said Atum. "Your place now belongs to your son. Horus will become the warrior of light, a god begat by a god . . ."

Osiris wept, saying, "Then I am renewed and life returns. Light shines in Egypt. I did not know I had a son."

The Imprisoned Isis

Seven drops of rain fell from a cloud. The Sky Mother of Osiris was weeping, and the Earth Father of Osiris drank up the dew. Return. Return. Return. The power of genesis swelled the belly of the goddess. Like a moon, like rising water, Isis grew round. Each time she approached the temple of Osiris, the child within the womb kicked. Two goddesses, Isis and Nephthys, stayed with the village women. They gave barley beer and bread to the *ka* of Osiris. They carried water; they planted seed. They slept not as goddesses, but as tired women curled up on the ground, side by side, their feet dusty, exhausted. They bathed and praised the Sun each morning; they read the movement of the stars each night. And always they kept their faces covered.

Yet they were slow and too visible. While offering bread to the *ka* of Osiris one morning, the two were found by Seth's men and bound like slaves. The wounds of the ropes that cut their flesh, though, were not as deep as the wound of the loss of their beloved.

In the caverns below Osiris lifted his head. "I want to see my son," he demanded. "If I cannot see your face, Atum, obscured as it is in its terrible veil of mists, then I must see the face of my son. One god must gaze on the face of another."

"True," said Atum. "You see me not, but my face gazes on you. Life is the shape in the mirror. I am sunlight, a desert, a man, a woman, serpent, lion, lotus. I am form in waiting. I am nothing. Do I not resemble the terror and joy of your own heart? I am all of it, the thousand names within the one, the one within the none. So shall you see your son and your son shall see you."

"How long will I live?" asked Osiris.

"Millions of years, an era of millions . . ."

"And in the end?"

"It shall be as it was in the beginning. Empty past. Empty future. The pause, the waiting. I'll destroy what I have created, swallow it whole as the serpent swallows its tail. The Earth, Egypt, its flowers, cattle and wheat, men and women, beasts and stones, the Sun, the Moon, the stars: all will be again as it was—primeval ocean, the waters of Abyss. Nothing. Not fate. Not fact. Not memory. I am that I am. I am and am not. I will be what remains. Just Atum and his possibilities, his eternal son Osiris. I come back to myself, one being, the same snake who knew no man and saw no god."

Seth brought the goddess, bound and fettered, before him. He asked her to kneel. The goddess kneeled. "Sad widow, my sister, Isis, poor woman who once was my brother's wife," Seth said mockingly, "do you miss your kingdom? Shall I make you queen again?"

"I am queen, my own mistress, and my kingdom is love," Isis answered quietly.

"Wedded to death," retorted Seth.

"Wed to eternal life."

"Osiris is dead."

"He is not. I have raised him up. With words of power I set waves of sunlight in motion. He is beyond the limits of time, the limits of this place. He is light eternal; you are but his shadow. You are mighty, Seth, a man to be obeyed, feared as a cobra is feared. I am your twin, and a serpent, too. But whereas you creep on the ground and strike terror into the hearts of children, Osiris rides the winged serpent of the sky. I have raised him up. Osiris lives in each particle of light, in each stone, in your wheat, in your bread. Sir, he lives even in you. Life unending, he returns, he lives again."

"She is a witch," Seth's companions whispered to him. "Lock her up where she'll do no harm. You rule Egypt now. Lock her up. What good is she?"

"She can spin," said Seth, tugging his beard. "Isis, sweet sister, you who so love sunlight, shall live in darkness. Take her to the caverns, seal her inside a tomb," he ordered his guards. "Give she who so loves the dead a corpse for a husband. Shut her up with a loom, make her spin endlessly. Make her work night and day. Give her cause for sorrow."

Seth sneered at the goddess. Isis returned him a smile.

"For the knowledge of death while I yet live," she said, "I thank you. For the dark quiet of my mother's womb I am grateful. For time alone to commune with the spirits of the unmanifest, I praise thee. For the loom and thread, I am grateful. For myself, I weave new life."

Osiris gazed in the empty mirror that was the face of Atum. He beheld Isis chained alive inside the tomb. He beheld the satisfaction of Seth. He saw himself a corpse, his flesh eaten by beetles. He trembled in fear, everywhere engulfed by shadow. He suffered. He watched.

In the face of terror he grew strong. He underwent his transformation. There was work yet for the Lord of Death to do. A god cannot remain idle. It is against the nature of gods. Osiris set his hands to the task of building a city, a place of welcome, home eternal for the dead. To this task he gave his own dark body and about it grew a field of reeds. He gathered his sorrow and made a river flow in the world beneath. His troubled thoughts twisted into dark labyrinthine chambers. His desire for truth and life eternal became the scales of justice, the maintenance of order amid chaos. Yet his mind was always on Egypt, his people, his wife, their sufferings.

He asked Atum, "What will become of Seth?"

"He shall ride with the gods in the Boat of the Millions of Years," Atum said.

Saddened by his brother's good fortune, Osiris wept for his own loss, for the loss of the comfort of his wife's breasts, for the sight of the tender buds of spring. His lips twisted in anger, rage—and his heart knew jealousy, terrible hideous jealousy, the fear and loathing in the dark heart of Seth. Then he saw himself in his brother and embraced the shadow. He suffered his last death. He left off dreaming of things that might have been.

"I am," he said, "and I am not. All this and more lies in the body of Atum." Then into the dark heart of Osiris came an illumination. The lightning bolt of understanding filled his soul with light.

While Osiris lived and suffered in his grave land, Isis remained in the prison of Seth, a sunless room beneath a mountain filled with the voices of the dead. She gathered their words, their memories, and spun them into song, lullabies for an unborn king. Day and night she worked the spindle, recalled the turnings of a life.

Because Seth wanted fine linens fit for a king, he sent his courtiers to Isis.

"Teach them something useful," he instructed her. "Teach them the lessons of bondage. Show them the truth of the role of weavers."

Isis taught them the art of transforming flax into thread, of thread into linen, of dead matter into new life. She combed the flax, she saved the seed. She taught them the cycles of transformation, separation, unification, desire. She named her flying shuttle the Barge of Ra. She taught them the stringing of the loom, the plucking of individual strings, the insertion of fine golden threads. She taught them the precognition of the shuttle's path, the making of patterns. She gave them her love, the song of the wheel, the prayers of spinners, the binding of the cloth of life.

Each day the courtiers came to admire her handiwork and the fullness of her belly. "Teach us the magic of weaving fine children," they said.

"Pray as you weave," said Isis. "With prayers clot the blood and knit the bones into form. Bind red and blue threads, black and white. I weave what I envision: a ladder to Heaven, threads of sunlight through gold wings. I make a web of flesh and ensnare in it a soul shining and silver as a fish. I weave a story old as memory, long as the life of a god. Sing to the child: may he live long, flourish, and grow in health. Bind his fate with love and blood and desire. With every thread speak his holy name. That is the cloth of life."

The Moon flew through the sky. It waxed and waned, and the belly of Isis grew round. Each morning she wove; each evening she spun. At night she dreamed the patterns of stars, the battles fought, the gifts of mothers, the losses. And in the morning she rose to weave and spin again.

The Birth of Horus

Then Thoth, the Moon god who also knew about time, began to fret over Isis ensnared. He sent his sisters, Seshat and Ma'at, disguised as weavers, to the spinning mill. "Isis," said Ma'at, "the world outside is still filled with sunlight. There is life yet, as your womb attests."

"There is life for she who heeds advice," said Seshat. "Thoth has sent us. Leave this place. Hide your son. Seth has no good intentions for him."

The womb of Isis jumped at the name, and the goddess ceased her weaving.

"Save yourself and your child," said Ma'at.

"Hide him," said Seshat, "and he will grow strong, his arms filled with twofold strength. On golden wings he will soar to touch the highest visions of the gods. He will sit on your lap, and he will sit on the throne of his father. He will avenge Osiris. He will possess the Two Lands."

"Name him Horus, the twice-born," said Ma'at.

That evening seven stars descended from the sky, and in the shape of scorpions they crawled beneath the prison door. With their pincers they sliced the ropes that bound Isis. She came forth from the spinning mill accompanied by the scorpions. Those who tried to stop her, the creatures stung to death. The henchmen of Seth writhed in pain, burned with poisonous fire.

In the cool of morning and under the cloak of evening, hiding herself by midday, Isis walked from sandy plateau to delta. At last her waters broke forth; the river flowed, moving toward eternal sea. The Sun had not yet shown its face and a mist still hung above the river, when Isis collapsed amid a clump of papyrus and let out a groan, like the bellow of a cow. "I birth myself now. I am made mother," she cried.

A fire, a quivering, moved along her spine. Gripped in its motion, she could do nothing but dance, belly big in the growing dawn. Air hissed through her teeth like the stirring of snakes.

Nephthys, who knew her sister, who knew how life quickens in the belly, felt the womb of Isis stir and hurried to attend to her. All the divine creatures who attended the birth of the world attended the birth of the child of Isis. The ram god Khnum snorted out his breath of life and pawed at the muddy riverbank. The serpents Wadjet and Renenutet slithered out of the marsh grass, changing themselves into goddesses. The frog goddess Heket leaped from the muck of the river bottom onto the wet bank. Selket, the scorpion, her own pale, translucent children still clinging to her back, lifted her tail and scrabbled onto the nearest rock.

Isis danced. She spun in great circles. Bellowed. Rocked. Hissed. Sighed. She cried, "*Iiiieeeew!*" It was a hawk screeching, the soul of Horus circling above her, spinning in the air above, darting in beneath the limitless souls of Heaven. He flew east and returned with the disk of the Sun in his beak. "Make way," cried Isis. "The child tears through with the claws of a falcon."

"Come, Horus," cried the goddesses.

"Appear," said Khnum.

Squatting there, her feet upon two mud bricks, Isis delivered the child into her own hands, caught him red and raw as he pushed from the dark world into light.

"My son," she cried. "I created your name. In the dark world before time, I formed the egg. You emerge from it shining, wet, and beautiful. Splendid seed," she cried. "Child of my flesh, strength of my bones."

The newborn's limbs were overlaid with gold, and the blue cord of life wound about his head like the uraeus serpent on the crown of Egypt. His male member stood erect and firm. "Warrior king," said Heket and cut the cord of his navel, binding to him his fate. Just as the Sun disk burst above the horizon, the child opened his eyes. They were blue as the belly of the Sky. "Child of Dawn," cried Wadjet. The boy's eyes flashed red as desert sands, red as the blood of life. "Child of the Two Horizons," cried Selket. His eyes grew dark, black as obsidian flecked with gold. "Dispeller of Darkness," cried Renenutet.

Isis blew her divine breath upon his face, and Horus inhaled his mother's essence, a perfume sweet as incense and melilot flowers. She bathed him in cool waters, then laid him to rest in a nest of papyrus. From her own dress she made his loincloth, tying his girdle and sealing it with a magical knot. At her breast the infant suckled. The milk of Heaven flowed to Earth the way the graceful light of stars streams down onto the heads of dreamers. Isis murmured the songs of changing, words of power, a mother's protections. In this moment of transformation lay the seeds of the past and the coming to flower of the future.

"Horus twice-born," said Isis. "He makes answer for his father."

The Sun was made glorious, dawn resplendent; the stars ceased wheeling on the birthday of the falcon. By that sign, Seth knew. In his distant city his heart filled with rage. "Find the child," he said. "Slay the child. As Isis clothed her boy in light, so clothe yourselves in darkness. Go forth as serpents, scorpions, crocodiles, creatures of the dark and deep." Chaos slithered on the ground; possibility lay hidden among the rushes. Months passed, a year, two. The goddess kept watch.

Horus the Twice-Born

A round the time of his second birthday, Horus lay amid papyrus stalks watching the sky, the darting swallows, a calligraphy of birds. The wind and the child were at rest. At dusk when the edges of opposites touched, everything appeared unreal—light merged with shadows, serpents came and went.

Two asps, green as living reeds, slithered into the nest where the boy lay absorbed in the dance of birds and the quivering curtain of tall, green papyrus. Slow as growing vines they climbed onto the child's bare white foot. As he sucked his thumb, an asp reared, striking his foot. Horus stamped and killed the serpent, stamped and killed the other before it could strike. Then he lay down amid the lotus, wounded.

Isis washed his feet, calling forth the poison with the kiss of her mouth, then tied about the wound magic knots so that no serpent might rise up again. Horus whimpered in pain the first day, was lame for several days thereafter, then walked again.

Yet Isis worried, afraid to leave the boy alone. By day she traveled to nearby villages to trade her magic for food. The women met her at the well with cries of joy. She taught them to weave, to plant, to read stars, to birth children full of beauty. They gave her raisin cakes, pomegranates, dates, pumpkin. They gave her herbs and she showed them the ones that relieved fevers.

Disguised as cobras Renenutet and Wadjet watched over Horus in her absence. Every goddess on Earth and in Heaven took her turn at keeping watch. Horus grew up in the company of seven cobras, seven cows, seven scorpions. He delighted them with his stories of the world of Heaven. They educated him in the ways of Earth.

Two more years passed. Seth was not content and again sent forth his spies. On a morning filled with dust and flies a red-haired stranger entered the village. Amazed, the children surrounded him, for they had never seen such a man. They touched his sun-reddened skin, they tugged the red hairs of his beard. The women at the ovens baking bread scolded the children good-heartedly.

"So many children here!" exclaimed the stranger. "And all of them well fed, well loved." The women smiled and offered the man bread. "Of all these," he asked, "which child is best loved? Which mother loves her baby best?"

Suspicious, the women made no answer, but the children playing outside the temple heard the stranger's questions and teased each other. "My mother loves me," cried one child. "Mine loves me best," said another. "But it is Horus whom all mothers love."

"Where is Horus?" the stranger asked.

"We've never seen him," they answered. "His mother hides him in the papyrus swamps."

The stranger returned to Seth to say he had found the child.

And then, once again, one morning when Isis was absent and while Nephthys as nursemaid looked away, a scorpion crawled into the child's bed and stung him. In the village Isis felt her own throat constrict and her heart begin to pound. Overhead a hawk shrieked once, then dropped like a stone from the sky. The pot Isis was making crashed to the ground. Her heart filled with terror. She screamed and tried to run, but her legs crumpled beneath her and she fell like a woman stricken. "My son!" she wailed. "My son!" Then she rose and ran toward the papyrus swamps.

The goddesses clustered around the child's lifeless body. White foam bubbled from his lips, his spittle clumped in the dust. Helpless, heart still, eyes clouded, the child lay rigid as stone. In the wound of his leg Isis saw the poison and gathered the boy into her arms. Weeping, she pressed her lips to his, trying to blow into him the breath of life. She embraced him, pressing a milky breast to his mouth. But he moved not his lips; he took no food. Her heart cleaved like an ancient stone. She shrieked like a hawk. She howled like a jackal. She thrashed like a fish over a hot fire. She flung herself about the circle of goddesses. Heart and mind flew from her body. She screamed, "Horus is stung! O gods, the golden child, heir of Egypt, has fallen!"

Hearing her cries, farmers threw down their hoes and ran from their fields. Fishermen stopped their boats and drew nigh. Women dashed from their houses with herbs and shredded linen sheets. But what good were these if Isis, who taught them the healings, could not save her own child. The gods and goddesses glanced from one to the other, helpless.

"My child! My child! Some god or goddess speak! Do something. He dies! The fiery poison rages on."

"Call on your mother!" cried the children.

"I cannot. My mother is Heaven itself. Her appearance here would crush the world."

"Call on your father!" cried the men.

"My father lies inert in the ground, helpless as Osiris."

"Call on your kinsmen!" cried the women.

"Who remains? My husband lies in his coffin. My brother Seth is my constant enemy. Horus dies as surely as sunlight dies at close of day."

Then all the people were silent in the midst of her misery. Stiff with pain, swollen by poison, the child shuddered and stopped breathing. At the edge of the fields, where the desert began, the goddess Selket heard the wail of grief and hurried to her sisters.

"Why do you weep, Nephthys?"

"A scorpion has stung Horus," Nephthys answered.

"I know a scorpion's sting as surely as I know my name," said Selket. "Isis must pray to Thoth. The child lives while the Sun stays in the sky."

"Thoth," cried Isis, raising her arms. "Stop time. Stay the Sun. Stop the Boat of the Millions of Years!"

"Stop the boat," cried Thoth. The god descended and knelt before Isis and her child. The boy did not move. Breath stopped. Heart stopped. Sun stopped. Still as death lay Horus.

"I called too late," said Isis. Nephthys could only weep.

"No fear, Isis," said Thoth. "No tears, Nephthys. I come equipped with words of power. Ra lives; the poison dies."

Thoth whispered the words to Isis, and Isis whispered the words into the child's ear—hot language, white words, breathings, the *heka*, how the universe talks to itself. After a moment breath returned; the child's eyes fluttered, then opened; his twisted limbs relaxed.

"I am thirsty," said Horus.

He drank from his mother's breast. Thoth returned to Heaven. The boat of the Sun sailed on.

When news of the miracle reached Seth, he cursed both mother and child. The resurrected child had caused much talk; the goddess had been revealed. Knowing she could not stay in the delta because Seth would be seeking a mother and child, Isis left the young boy Horus in the care of his nursemaids in Buto.

She dressed him in his loincloth and handed the little bundle to the goddess Renenutet, saying, "You who tear your gowns with your hands and beat your breasts for the slain Osiris, watch over his little child. Ra in the sky will answer for him. His father, Osiris, will watch over him. A mother's love will protect him. From time to time I will return."

With a heavy heart, she covered her head in a veil of blue and hurried away. Seven scorpions followed. Now and again they stopped to gaze back at the tearful Horus. The boy put a trembling finger to his mouth as he watched his mother leave. "Turn your faces to the ground," commanded Isis, because her own heart was breaking. She feared if she looked back, she might never walk with her eyes straight ahead again.

The world was in chaos; her people suffered. She was a goddess and there was yet work to be done. The temples of Osiris needed offerings; the *ka* of the god needed to hear its name so that the white flowers might drift upon the waters again with the perfume of the goddess, so that green shoots might rise up through the dry, mud-cracked Earth.

Although she had raised her child these five years, and although the boy still wore the sidelock of youth, the heart of Isis longed always and eternally for her husband, Osiris. She spoke words of power and assumed the forms she pleased. On Earth she was the shape of things as they are, as Osiris in Amentet was the shape of things to come.

She knew the byways into the realm of dream, the land of the dead, the hidden Amentet. There she joined Osiris for a time, breathing with him, sleeping, dreaming the bright fire in the dark, dreaming the green rupture of seed, stealing the names of demons who guarded the gates. And when she returned to the villages by day, she met her priests and priestesses beside the sacred water and taught them the prayers the dead needed the living to recite.

"There is life," she said. "I have seen it. The dead go to another place. My husband, Osiris, lives and your ancestors are with him. Say their names. Bring them beer and raisin cake. Love life, love the dead and each other. As long as we live, the dead may live."

While Isis worked her magic, teaching the people the ways of Duat[1] and the blessings of Earth, Osiris opened the channels from this world to the next so that the river of life might flow freely. He established the Hall of Justice, erected the scales of justice, and set truth in the place of chaos. He heard the petitions of those in Amentet and shared the meals of his temples. He taught the souls that live forever to build their houses and fill the rooms with music.

And in each temple on Earth the goddess Isis lay down to dream with Osiris, and their dreams infused each other with magic. The belly of the goddess again grew round as the crescent Moon grows day by day toward full.

Horus spearing Seth in his form of a hippopotamus. In his left hand he holds two ropes already lodged in the hippopotamus. Isis kneels in the bow and holds two similar ropes.

3

The Battle between
Light and Shadow

When Isis returns for Horus, the boy has grown into a man. Her adventures have led her far from the realm of the boy's understanding. Through her suffering, she has become a wise woman, a shamaness. It is time for her to teach her son about his soul's true destiny. As a woman, she is unfamiliar with the ways of the warrior, so she teaches the boy how to contact his father in dream. It is through the psychic and intuitive realm that Horus receives the blessing of his father and his spiritual guidance.

Now the focus of the story moves from the matriarchal point of view to the patriarchal. This is no longer the story of Isis and Osiris; it is now the story of Horus and Seth. The two must wage the eternal battle of opposition, of good and evil, of light and dark, of life and death. This is not just a human battle, but a contest that involves all the powers of the universe, all the gods and goddesses in Heaven, as well as those on Earth. It is a tale of the emotions—of sensuality, jealousy, rage, trickery, bitterness, and deep compassion. The realms of the male and female have never seemed so far apart.

When the battle troubles the heart of Isis and she tries to offer compassion for Seth, Horus, in his haste and anger, cuts off his mother's head. Thoth restores it with his magic. Even Horus himself is wounded in the battle, and it is only after he has been blinded by rage that he comes to understand the healing power of love. In Heaven Isis wins her own battle with Seth by showing him the result of his greed and jealousy. In the end, order is restored. Osiris has established order in the neterworld, where death cycles again into life. Seth is given the realm of the sky along with the Sun god Ra, and Horus is given the throne of the king to rule the realm of Earth. Isis, who has traversed and understood the great mysteries on Earth, in Heaven, and in the Great Below, becomes Queen of the Universe.

So the tale concludes . . .

Isis Returns for Horus

Isis was sad for the loss of her husband, the loss of her kingdom, and her absence from her son. She gathered her scorpions and said, "I am alone and in sorrow greater than anyone's in all the villages of Egypt. My child is far from me. I am widowed. I am alone, alone, like a man grown old. Alone like a man who has ceased to search after and look upon women in their houses. O scorpions, turn your faces again to the ground. Find me a straight path into the swamps. Lead me to the hidden place on the island that I might see my son, who has grown up in my absence—no longer a child, but almost a young man."

Much of the scenery had changed while she was away, but at last Isis found her way to the thatch-roofed houses of the snake women, her sister goddesses Renenutet, Wadjet, and Uto. The serpent goddesses who had helped her birth the boy had raised him in her absence. When she knocked at the door, a young man answered. He was strong of limb, powerful of back, and straight in his gaze.

"I am Isis, your mother," she said. She threw her arms about him, touched his gleaming face, and gazed into his golden eyes. Yet he pulled back and stared at her, at her full breasts and the lump of flesh knotted in her belly.

"Where have you been?" he demanded. "And who is it you love more than me or my father?"

He clenched his fists, and she saw in him already the posture of the warrior. "You serve your father well," the goddess answered. "He was mighty on Earth, and is mighty in the land of the dead. Look deep into your heart, Horus. Perceive the source of your strength and do not use it against those who love you."

That night Isis told her sisters the news of her pregnancy, that she had conceived a second son, Harpokrates, by Osiris while in a dream. The goddesses rejoiced and knew now that the way between the two worlds lay open. The guardian scorpions again transformed themselves into stars, and the cobras slithered back into the primordial waters.

While she slept that night, Horus stood outside his mother's room, listening to her breathing. The soft rhythm of the air escaping her nose perfumed the room with the odor of lotus. Horus listened as the breaths turned slowly into sighs, then shuddering breaths of pleasure, then the vowels of a woman loving. He burst into her room to observe what manner of man or beast slept upon his mother's breast. No man of flesh lay there. Isis slept immobile on her bed. But in the candlelight, the shadows on the wall revealed a man and a woman in the ecstatic pleasure of embrace, arms and legs twined together like two serpents, sexual parts dancing, testicles swinging, buttocks pounding like a bull and a cow in a field.

Horus cried out, afraid. The dream shattered. Isis awoke. The shadows vanished.

"With whom do you lie?" he asked.

"I commune with Osiris, your father."

"Then tell my father for me that I am his son, his servant. I wish to communicate with him, too."

Horus Communes with Osiris

Now Isis could see that the time had come for her to teach her son the ways of the warrior, the means of the hero, lover, and magician. It was time to take him to the temples of his father, but Seth, knowing the boy was of age, would be looking for them. So they traveled transformed as a pair of hawks circling the skies of Egypt. They sailed from one Nile city to the next. In each nome the goddess Isis paused to show her son Horus the temples that had been built for his father. And in each temple she taught Horus the words of power, the breathings, the sacred names of gods, and the map of the caverns in and out of Amentet. Disguised as a cow with her young bull, Isis and Horus arrived at last in Abydos at the shrine of Osiris.

"Your father lies here in these western hills. You must go there alone," she told him. "You must lie down in the sand. The serpents that come to lie with you will not harm you. The sand that covers your belly will not smother you. The darkness that fills your mind will not consume you. The voices you hear are only the chants of the souls of the dead. Do not be afraid, Horus. Osiris longs to penetrate your heart."

Then Horus took his reed mat into the desert and lay down beneath the thousand shining souls of the night sky. He closed his eyes and began his breathings. Deeper and deeper he sank into the dream of death. His eyes opened and closed until his form lay still on the sand.

The souls of the dead began to sing: "*Osiris went away. He fell asleep. He died. Behold, he returns—a son with his father. Osiris comes back. He awakens. He lives. He encircles everything in his arms.*"

In his dream Horus knew his father's death, lying in the floating coffin of Byblos. He knew his mother's magical conception of himself, and he felt the rending of his father's body. In his dream Horus saw his father's phallus swallowed by a fish. He heard the cries of Osiris, saying, "Come to me. Come to me. Come to me." He tasted sand, he felt the pressure of Earth upon his head, he entered into darkness deeper than night.

Yet while he slept, the soul of Horus spread its wings and rushed to the aid of his father. He lifted him up. He opened his mouth. He gave him beer and cake and words of power. And his father whispered, "Raise my soul, Horus. Spread the word of my authority. Defend the gates of

Amentet on my behalf, that he who harmed me twice may not draw near a third time, nor see me in this house of darkness, still of heart and helpless."

Then the fists of Horus closed in anger that the communion he desired with his father seemed to him now somehow diverted, and he said to Osiris, "Look to yourself, to your own condition. Set your own soul in motion. Are you not a god? Move as the others move, as the stars wheel through the night sky. I am a young man and life yet lies ahead. Must I live always with my mother? Must I entertain, amuse, and divert your brother, he who sent you here into this helplessness? Mine is the way of the roads on Earth, of the limitless light of sky."

"Mine is the way of the barley," said Osiris. "Whether I live or die, I am Osiris. I enter and reappear through you. I decay in you. I grow in you. I fall down in you. I rise up. I have entered the order of things. I emerge in the cycles, the double house of truth. I have reached my limits."

Then the souls of the dead began to sing: *"Osiris went away. He fell asleep. He died. Behold, he returns—a son with his father. Osiris comes back. He awakens. He lives. He encircles everything in his arms."*

Horus felt ashamed, knowing now that his way and his father's were different, and he lowered his head in the presence of Osiris. "What would you have me do?" he asked.

"Return tomorrow," said Osiris, "and I will teach you the use of the bow and arrows, the spear, knife, and mace."

So did Horus spend a part of his life in the desert, apart from his mother in the embrace of his father. He journeyed by day into the upper worlds as a hawk above the plain. By night, he descended in dream to do the work of his father. Osiris gave him the seeds of possibility, the scales of balance, the knowing of the two ways.

At last, when Horus was made into the image of a warrior, Osiris asked, "What is the best thing any man might do?"

"To revere the gods," said Horus. "To restore the balance of order, to love life, to face death, and to avenge the injuries sustained by one's mother and father."

"And what animal serves such a warrior?"

Horus answered, "A horse."

"Not a lion? A lion is strong, brave in battle, fierce, loyal."

"But a horse is fleet," said Horus, "and more useful in cutting off fleeing enemies."

The answer pleased Osiris, for he knew that his son thought now like a warrior. Then he withdrew from his communion with Horus in dream. Although Horus lay dreaming three nights more, Osiris did not appear. At last, Horus felt that his father believed him to be ready. Gathering his mat and weapons, he left the desert.

At his back he heard the angelic voices of the dead souls singing: *"Osiris went away. He fell asleep. He died. Behold, he returns—a son with his father. Osiris comes back. He awakens. He lives. He encircles everything in his arms."*

The War in Heaven

When Horus left the mountains, he appeared on the streets of Hierakonpolis in shining glory, with girded loins, the muscles of his arms straining against the gold bands of the warrior, the disk of the Sun bright on his head. He came forth with no need to hide himself, and the people of every city—of Dendera, Abydos, Coptos, Edfu—fell down on their knees, knowing that a king and a god had revealed himself to them. Horus reminded them of the ways of his father.

Horus established the festival of the gods so that the land again would be filled with greening, with dancing, and with sowing, reaping, and feasting. He reminded the sons and daughters of Egypt to remember the souls of the dead. He spoke his father's name. He told the old stories of glory. He established the scales of justice, and he set the land in order.

Wherever he walked, children followed, serpents parted, the cattle of the field bellowed, the scorpions lay still, and birds of prey dipped and swooped overhead. Those outlaws of Seth, who came into the cities to raid the townspeople during the festival, spied the god Horus and witnessed the goodness he had brought. Tired of life in the desert, they joined with Horus, pledging their swords to his side. He, in turn, taught them the use of his weapons of iron, the loyalty of the lion, the fleetness of the horse.

Now the goddess Hathor, the golden one, came down to the river one morning and spied Horus. The sight of him caused her to dance, to sing, to shiver in excitement, and whomever she held in her gaze or whoever gazed upon her form fell immediately in love. She stood ever near the god Horus, who grew enchanted by her. But in his confusion, he knew not what to do, having never known the company of women except his nursemaids and his mother, Isis. And Hathor was not alone in her affection for the handsome god.

When the concubine of Seth, the goddess Tauret, heard of the young, virile golden hawk in Thebes, she hurried to him to make of him a husband. For Seth, it was bad enough that the name Osiris was being spoken again, bad enough that his men had deserted his camp, bad enough that the boy had grown up to become a man. But when he heard that his concubine had deserted him, it was too much. As his wife had left him for Osiris, so had his concubine left him for Osiris's son. Too much. Too much. Too much. He sent an enormous serpent slithering after her, ready to devour her. She ran in fear. But the companions of Horus trapped the snake and chopped it to pieces with their axes. The serpent's blood seeped into the Earth, mixed with the clods of the field, and Osiris in Amentet knew that the great battle had begun.

Enraged, Seth himself put on the war crown, took up the knife, and hunted for Horus as if he were hunting a boar. Rather than fight, however, Horus took wing in the form of a hawk and flew straight to Heaven, where the council of the great gods sat in the branches of the tree at the center of the world. Shu, the god of air, lifted Horus up, and Thoth was there to greet him. "The time has come," said Thoth. "May justice prevail over strength."

Horus stood before the council, glancing over the faces of the gods and goddesses there as if he had seen them before in a dream, in another life perhaps. He did not bow his head. He was neither brash nor weak. "My father is dead," he said. "I am his son, and he has taught me the ways. It is his wish that I preside over the Black Land, but Seth has stolen my father's fertile land. I come on behalf of my mother and father. I have come to receive Osiris's crown."

"Give the office of rulership to Horus," Thoth said, and the lesser gods brought forth the white crown.

"Stop!" Atum cried out. "This is not justice. How can you decide among yourselves when you've not heard Seth speak?"

Then Seth entered the great council hall to address the gods. He looked upon his nephew Horus, the golden child, with the bitterest hatred. "I watched over the land of my brother after his untimely death," he said bitterly, "before ever this pup of a boy was conceived. (And, I ask, by whom?) Now he tries to take from me what already lies in my hands. If you want fair, I am fair. I am willing to fight him for the crown. I have been a warrior all my life. I'll show him the ways of the club and knife. I'll hack to pieces the little boy's pretensions. Give me but a day and let the stronger god prevail."

The gods murmured among themselves, taking sides and arguing until the heavenly council had entered into chaos. Thoth rose and shouted above the others, "Why give the throne of his father to Seth while Osiris' son stands before you? Born of Osiris, conceived on Earth, the son is the true heir."

Then Ra trembled in rage at the words of Thoth. He was already angry with him for cheating him out of his five days during their game eons ago. It was his fault that these children of Nut were bickering. "The heir born on Earth!" he shouted. "Then give the throne of Osiris to Seth, the son of Nut. The throne of a god was meant for a son of the sky goddess."

Now the two brothers, Thoth and Ra, began to argue bitterly. In the high heavens the Sun and Moon stood against each other. For an entire day the skies of Egypt darkened, and the Earth quivered. The goddess of Heaven was incensed with her children. What right had they to destroy the balance of things, when all the universe, the Earth, and stars were wheeled about by her command? What right had the thousand souls within her to bicker, to destroy her peaceful dreams?

"No one can decide," said the gods. "Now what shall we do?"

Knowing that his mother, Nut, commanded the patterns of Heaven, knowing that she who had shone forth in primeval time was mother of them all, held the past and the future—knowing all this, Thoth agreed to write her a letter and lay out the predicament.

In a responding letter the goddess Nut replied, "Give the Black Land of Osiris to his son, Horus. Double the size of the Red Land of Seth. If my son is unhappy about his concubine and his wife running off, well, perhaps that is his problem. Nevertheless, give him two more: Anath and Astarte. But, please, don't bother me with such things again. And don't undo the balance again, or I'll get angry and hurl myself to the ground, smashing Heaven against Earth."

"The goddess is right!" exclaimed Thoth.

But Ra was still angry with Thoth and Horus, and even more angry now with his mother. "You'd give the best land in Egypt to this smart-mouthed stripling?" he cried. "Why, look at him. He's barely left his mama's teat. He couldn't bear up under the strain."

"And you're an old eunuch who can't keep his own house in order," hissed one of the serpent gods.

At this Ra turned his back on the council and left, retreating behind a veil of clouds, leaving the upper and lower worlds in darkness. But Hathor, goddess of love, had been listening all this time, and she entered her father's chambers. "Don't be angry," she said. "Let me dance for you." She swung her long hair, she shook the sistrum, she whirled cloud to cloud on dancing feet, drawing nearer each time, removing, one by one, each of her seven veils.

At last she stood before the Sun god naked, and she bent over, showing him her private parts. "Do you think the hawk boy would know what to do if I showed him this?"

Ra laughed. "Funny girl," he said. "Show him any of your secrets. If he's really a god, he'll know what to do."

Then Hathor and Ra returned to the council to hear what both plaintiffs had to say. Seth bent his knee before Ra. "I am older and wiser than the boy," he said humbly. "For you, Ra, I can slay the serpent of darkness."

Ra said, "The son of Nut is right."

Horus raised his spear, exclaiming, "I'm being cheated of my father's throne because I've never fought a serpent? Why give the office to my mother's brother when I am the son of a king?"

Thoth placed his hand upon Horus' shoulder. "The decision of the sky goddess," he reminded Ra, "the decision of the mother of Seth and Osiris was to give the throne to Horus."

"And what of Ra's decision?" spat Seth. "What of the decree of the most high god? He chose me. Doesn't that count? Throw Horus into the Nile and let me fight him there fair and square."

"This I can do," said Ra. And the vault of Heaven split asunder, sending Horus and Seth splashing into the Nile.

The Battle of Horus and Seth

And they wrestled. For eighty years they wrestled, clashing their knives, swinging their clubs, and shooting their arrows. The two gods emerged from the Nile as men, their hair dripping with water and standing on the backs of crocodiles. They flung their spears at each other, took glancing blows, and returned assault for assault. A year passed. They changed themselves into bears, yowling, howling, biting, pawing each other's heads, stamping their feet and thundering above the ground. Five years passed. Seth transformed himself into a snake, Horus into a mongoose. They hissed and spat and danced through the sands, tearing at each other's flesh.

Ten years passed. They transformed themselves into ferocious beasts, the likes of which were known only in the underworld. Seth, with the head of an ass, kicked and bucked and brayed through the desert. Horus, with the head of a lion, roared and leaped onto the back of his opponent, teeth bared. Twenty years passed. They were two gods raging throughout the Red and Black Lands of Egypt, fighting with scorpions in their hands. Forty years passed. They were the gods of night and day, the Sun and Moon, the eastern and western horizons, the heat and rain, the sandstorm and the light. Seventy-five years passed.

If either one or the other began to win, if Horus brought Seth under the knife, or if Seth set his mace against the head of Horus, Thoth held up his hand and stopped the battle. On and on the war waged. The bodies of the brave men who fought with Horus and Seth littered the fields, their empty eyes reflecting the gray skies, their mouths open and filling with sand. Their souls crowded the halls of Osiris's underworld. The women wept loudly and beat their breasts. The children held their breath in fear.

"This fighting must stop," cried the gods in Heaven. "The world and its people are all in chaos."

Yet the two gods fought on, blow for blow, transforming themselves into a pair of hippopotamuses who, biting each other's throats, plunged deep into the river Nile, neither one of them to emerge for more than three months. There in the mud they clawed and bit and held one another down, trying to drown each other. The water churned with their fighting, the river grew wild with splashing. Isis sat on the edge of the bank,

ling the contest, fearing the worst. "Stop them, Thoth," she begged.
Thoth did not stop them.

; took up her yarn and wove a sturdy rope. She broke a branch from
amore and formed for her spear a copper point. What mother would
ght for her son, for her husband, for those she loved? Then she tied
ie around the spear and plunged it deep into the frothing waters
e the two forms wrestled. The weapon bit deep into the body of one
opotamus. A voice cried out.

ome to me! Mother Isis! I am Horus! Tell your weapon to release me!"
hen she realized what she had done, her heart was filled with re-
e. From her breasts flowed the milk of love. "Back, spear!" cried Isis.
\y from my son!"

ith tears she plunged the spear again into the waters. The copper point
esh. Red blood pooled to the surface like a hideous, gaping red mouth.
cried out, "Sister Isis, what have you done? It is I, your brother Seth,
knew you in the womb. Tell your weapon to release me!"

ain, her heart was filled with ambiguous grief and love. "Back,
!" cried Isis. "Away from my brother!"

:aring his mother on the bank, Horus grew furious. Why was she
sing Seth when at last he'd been bound and beaten? Why did
release him, who murdered her husband and usurped her son's
ie? What right had the woman to change her mind? And his fury
immense, raging through him.

: charged from the waters like a wild panther and ran after Isis, who
ike a frightened gazelle. She heard his footsteps pounding behind
nd at last he caught her, raised his knife, and with one quick slash
ed her beautiful head from her neck.

ie gods in Heaven gasped. "Who is that pitiful headless woman?"
ied.

is," answered Seth. "Horus attacked his mother."

unish him, then," cried the god.

alizing what he had done, that his anger had betrayed him, and that
ad mortally wounded Isis, Horus threw down his bloodstained
on and ran into the mountains, intending never to return, for who
l he face after such a horrible crime?

:anwhile, Thoth had witnessed the unfortunate tragedy at the
s edge and ran to the headless goddess. Quickly, by means of his
s of power, he set upon her shoulders the head of a cow. When the
ess saw herself reflected in the pool of water, she said, "I am remade
: image of my mother."

th followed Horus through the snaking pathways of the desert
ıtains and found him at last in the moonlight asleep in an oasis un-
date tree. He seized him. Horus awoke too late. Seth tumbled him
e ground and plucked his two eyes from their sockets, then cast
far away on the side of a mountain. There the eyeballs came to rest

and from them sprang up two blue lotus flowers that sent forth a light seen throughout the Earth. Leaving the blind hawk god to founder alone in the heat of the desert sand, Seth returned to Ra, saying, "I was unable to find him."

Yet Hathor, following the light of the blue lotus, found him on the mountainside, lying facedown and weeping. She began to sing, which comforted the injured Horus. Then a gazelle, which had been following her melody, came to her. Hathor milked the gazelle and poured the liquid into the hawk god's empty eye sockets, first the right eye, then the left. "Open your eyes," she commanded.

He opened his eyes to look full in the face of the goddess of love. His heart opened. Horus was healed by Hathor. Now Hathor escorted him to Heaven and into the council chambers. Seth was already there, drinking wine and whispering his lies in Ra's ear.

"Seth tore out my eyes," said Horus. "Hathor healed them."

"That isn't true," said Seth. "I was nowhere near him."

Ra turned his back on Seth and Horus and said, "I am sick of this, the two of you fighting all the time. You are worse than the humans the gods created. The whole affair disgusts me. You've turned my hair white. You've made an old man of me." He rose slowly, his golden face now red with anger, now purple with rage, and he went away to his chambers for the night.

"The fighting must stop," cried the gods. "Do as Ra commands. Go home, eat your honey cakes together, drink your barley beer, make yourselves a festival, but leave the gods of Heaven in peace!"

Then Seth smiled, stretched his hand toward Horus, and drew him away from Hathor. "Ra is right. Come, nephew. At my house we will feast." Horus went along with Seth as the gods had commanded.

The house of his uncle was large and illumined with candles. Horus had heard of such houses from the stories of his mother, how the palace of Osiris had been filled with music, wine, and good food. He believed that since he had come at last to inherit the throne of his father, he would eat the food of gods and sing the songs of kings. The two gods sat side by side upon their mats, sniffing perfumes of lotus and sandalwood while Seth's seven concubines danced. The women were full-breasted and beautiful; their arms and legs moved like light upon water. Horus thought of his mother's shadow dancing, of the dances of Hathor. For the first time he longed for the company of women in the manner that a god and a king might possess.

For Horus, Seth brought out the ripest fruits, the finest colored vegetables, and the choicest cuts of meat. But he himself ate nothing except lettuce. They drank much beer, growing sleepy, trading kind words about how their two lands might live. At last the beds were prepared. Seth said, "If you and I are to coexist in harmony, then we must embody the Earth of our two lands and lie down next to each other like the black loam and red sand." Too tired to disagree, Horus lay down next to Seth, his back facing east, while Seth turned his back to the west. For a moment they resembled the two lions of Aker, the vision of yesterday and tomorrow. But in the night Horus awoke to find Seth trying to seduce him. Humiliated, he leaped from the bed and ran home to find his mother.

The Recrowning of Isis

Horus was much surprised to find Isis awake, waiting, seated at the edge of the river and wearing the head of a cow. "Forgive me," he said. "I will make you again the beautiful Queen of Heaven and Earth." He brought forth her head, set it on her shoulders, and gave her a shining diadem like the crown of horns. Then Horus laid his weary head in her lap and wept for himself. "I am a fool," he said. "I believed Seth and he tried to seduce me."

"It is time you understood the worlds of your uncle and your father," Isis said. Taking Horus by the hand, she led him by moonlight to a farmer's field. "Look there," she said, pointing across the plain. "Tell me what you see."

"I see pigs groveling and grunting with their noses in the dirt," said Horus. "I see green shoots of corn pushing up through the rich soil."

"That is all you need to know," Isis said. "Remember this, Horus. From pigs you get pigs; from corn you get corn. Through Osiris you reap your harvest, but through Seth, you reap only dirt, more pigs, and sorrow. I've a plan for your uncle Seth," she said.

The next morning Seth again called together the greater and lesser gods, demanding that they meet in council to hear his latest petition and decide on the ownership of Osiris's throne. "Eighty years now," said the gods. "All this fighting, all this confusion and chaos. Let's end it once and for all. Speak, Seth. You called us."

Then Seth paced magnificently before the gods, measuring his words, sure of his triumph. "This boy who stands before you is not a warrior. I am the legitimate heir, son of Nut and Geb. I bothered no one. Instead, it was Horus who first attacked me."

"You killed my father. You imprisoned my mother . . ."

"You have no proof of the falsehoods you raise against me!"

Isis shouted above the din of their voices, "My mother, Nut, the great goddess, has already addressed this council. Her decision was to give the throne to Horus."

Seth banged his staff upon the vault of Heaven. The thunder rolled and lightning flashed. "Shut up! Shut up, you old witch," he shouted. "You with your magic and ridiculous headdress of horns."

"You corrupter of children . . ."

"Children! Children? I thought he was a man . . ."

"Be quiet, you two," said the gods. "What is right is right. Justice will be done."

"This is between Horus and me," said Seth. "I won't have any more to do with this council as long as Isis is here."

"Fair enough," said Ra. "Take this council to the Island of Reeds in the Midst of the Stream. Tell the ferryman not to let any woman come across who looks like Isis."

Then the gods descended to their boats, carrying the noontime offerings—the loaves of bread, the wine, the grapes. They sailed to the Hall of Justice on the Island of Reeds in the Midst of the Stream. Hungry now, they sat down to eat.

Isis tiptoed to the shore after them. Dressed as an old beggar woman, head veiled in rags, her beautiful form draped in black, stooped and bent above her walking stick, she smiled at the ferryman with snaggled teeth. On her shoulder sat a vulture, on her finger shone a gold ring. "That boy who tends the cattle on the Island of Reeds in the Midst of the Stream," said Isis. "I was told he is hungry and needs this bowl of flour and these raisin cakes. You must ferry me over. Poor little boy. Five days without food."

The ferryman shook his head. "I was told no woman may cross."

"No woman who looks like Isis, they said. Look at me. Do you think I look like Isis?" Then she began to cough in his face and hurled drops of spit from her mouth.

"Not in the least," he said.

"So now, take some of these cakes and ferry me across."

"I cannot."

"All right, all right," said the goddess. "Take this gold ring, but hurry. The boy is hungry."

Then the ferryman took her to the Island of Reeds in the Midst of the Stream. Once on the other side, Isis walked quickly in the shadow of the trees, changing herself yet again into a beautiful woman with shapely, firm breasts, dazzling eyes, and gold bands on her wrists and feet. The god Seth, who was eating bread with Ra, saw the young woman from afar. Seth rose quickly and walked between the sycamores where no god could see him or her. "Beautiful woman," he whispered. "Would you commune with a god?"

Isis lowered her eyes and sighed. "I thank you," she said, "for I am in need of talking. My heart is sad. You see, I am the wife of a herdsman. My husband and I had a child; then he died, leaving the boy to tend his father's cattle. But a stranger came, saying, 'Boy, leave your father's cattle and your mother, or I'll throw you out.' If you are a god, honor the right and defend my son. Whatever you want I shall grant it to you."

Seth was quite sure of himself and answered her. "What! O noble woman, I cannot believe it. A stranger comes to steal your husband's cattle while the son is yet living there! This is horrible. It cannot be." He moved closer to the beautiful woman. "I weep for you, my dear."

Then Isis transformed into a swallow, shrieking through the air, crying, "Weep for yourself! Your own words condemn you."

Seth was angry. He howled. He raged. He wept. He shook his fist at the bird perched in the acacia tree and shouted to the company of gods, "Damn that evil woman. She has tricked me again. She changed herself into a young woman. She said," and he repeated her words, mockingly, " 'A stranger steals my dead husband's cattle while his son yet lives.' "

"What did you say?" asked Ra.

"Well," said Seth, "I felt sorry for her. I said something like, 'Poor woman, I cannot believe it. This is horrible. It cannot be.' "

"Then our work is done here," answered Ra. "You've answered your own question. Give Horus the white crown of his father, Osiris."

Seth drew out his lance and held it to Ra's throat. "Give me one more battle to fight," he said ominously. "Allow me the honor of winning back my throne. If you do not, I will kill all of you, every god and goddess, one every day."

"No more fighting," said Ra. "I can't stand the fighting. I'm sick to death of all of you. Thoth, whom have we not petitioned?"

"Osiris," answered Thoth. "It is his throne. They are his son and his brother. Let Osiris decide."

"Then send a letter to Osiris," Ra commanded. "Tell him that Seth has the power of the upper world aligned with him. Tell him for me that Ma'at was in Heaven when the world was made. Had he not existed, if he had not been born, yet would the barley and the corn still grow in my light."

Seth Becomes the Barge of the Sun

Thoth wrote his letter in gold, and the god Osiris responded. "Ma'at, the goddess of truth, resides now in Amentet with me. If Ra doubts this, let him attempt to sail his barge through the dark passageways of my world without the assistance of Ma'at. Tell him for me that these chambers are filled with savage creatures who fear no god or goddess. I have chained them now, but I can release them. Tell Ra for me that I hold the scales of Ma'at, and the hearts of all who do wrong will be devoured. The souls of evil will exist no more. Tell Ra for me that my father has said I will prevail to the end of time, I will prevail long after the age of men and gods. Tell him for me that this is my final judgment."

Then Ra began to tremble, fearing he had sided with the wrong party after all. Seth, recalling the ages present and past, said at last, "Give Horus the white crown." Now Isis rejoiced that her son was made king. On Earth below, sunlight now flooded the fields of Egypt. The land rejoiced and brought forth the flood and the harvest.

"What becomes of Seth?" asked Thoth.

"Give him to me," answered Ra. "He is strong. He is mighty. He is feared alike by men and gods. He is like a son to me. Therefore, let him live with me. Let him be my thunder and my rain. Let him transform himself into the hull of my boat to slice through the darkened waters. Let him stand in the prow with his spear and slay the serpent of darkness. Let him become the warrior, the provider of limits."

And Thoth replied: "It is good that there is order, stability, truth, and foundation. It is good also for things to change, to transform, to become. Movement and foundation are the essence of the creation of gods. Therefore, is the invisible made visible. Let Seth become the iron of Earth, his bones the bones of Earth, as the bones of Horus are the lodestone. Let the warriors learn what to attract and what to repel."

"And twice a year," said Ra, "let the two estranged brothers come together as once they lay side by side in the womb. Let the bones of Seth plough up the Earth of Osiris. Let the bones of Seth reap the harvest of Osiris."

"Let the two changing gods establish an order," replied Thoth.

Now did Ra see with his own eyes how indeed Ma'at lived with Osiris, for Osiris had lived his life in both the light and the dark. And he saw how Thoth expressed the universe through the words of Ma'at. He sighed, saying, "I am old. I will leave this world to the young at heart. A god must be capable of changing his mind. He must see the two sides, weigh the good with the bad."

Then he left the upper world in the hands of Thoth, the lower world in the hands of Osiris, and Earth in the hands of Horus. And Isis, who had perceived it all from the beginning, who communed with the gods above and below, was named Queen of Heaven, the Underworld, and Earth.

In the end was the beginning. There was Life. Possibility. Desire. Passion. Diversification. Communion. Return. There was ever and always the constant business of Heaven and Earth—the multitudinous ways of Becoming. And in the cosmic dust of Heaven slept the ourobouric serpent, Atum, biting its tail.

PART TWO

Egypt: Land of the Ancient Soul

Step Pyramid at Saqqara, circa 2600 B.C.

4

*Mythic and Historic Time/Space:
Background for the Stories
of Isis and Osiris*

> To me every hour of the light and dark is a miracle,
> Every cubic inch of space is a miracle,
> Every square yard of the surface of the earth is spread
>   with the same,
> Every foot of the interior swarms with the same.
>
> To me the sea is a continual miracle,
> The fishes that swim—the rocks—the motion of the
>   waves—the ships with men in them,
> What stranger miracles are there?
>
> from "Miracles," *Leaves of Grass*
> by Walt Whitman

In the predawn call of the muezzin, in the late afternoon playing of a flute in the marketplace, I have heard the melody that ripples across the friezes in the tombs of ancient musicians. On the curved lips of merchants in the night bazaar, I've noted the same beatific smiles as those that appear on the granite faces of the kings in Karnak.

The same dawn that bespoke the moment of creation to the ancient priestess washes across the faces of countless Egyptians—the light-skinned young businessmen in Cairo crossing the street, the dark Nubian children of Aswan weaving garlands, the sun-bronzed bedouin camel drivers walking through the smoke of campfires below the dusty yellow plateau of Giza, and the almond-eyed gatekeepers smoking cigarettes outside the temple of Edfu.

At the heart of the Great Pyramid, I've spent the night staring into the darkness, hearing the echo of ancient cantors, and feeling the timeless pulse of the universe. On the edges of the desert, at the foot of the pyramids, I have looked up and seen the vibrant stars that are the gods in hiding, the souls waiting to be born. As the wind blows across the desert sands, I can imagine the shushing sounds of the bare feet of dancing tribal women as they make supplications to their goddess.

Egypt is not only a culture that existed in a certain time and place, with a certain history, geography, and economy, Egypt is also a state of being that exists eternally in archetypal realms. The historical Egypt was but a backdrop for the essential Egypt, the Egypt of the eternal return. In this view, Egypt did not have, but rather was, a quality of intelligence.

In ancient Egypt, at least for a period of time, substance and essence bloomed simultaneously. The pattern of primary essence that resonates through archetypal Egypt—through the Egypt of our psyches—represents the creative potency of universal form and power. It is that which unfolded into what we know as the historical, exoteric Egypt.

It is my belief that this template of essential and archetypal reality, along with the concept of the gods and goddesses, created the charge and possibility for the pattern that became ancient Egypt.

"The First Time,"
or How the Gods Created the Universe

The story of Isis and Osiris is a story about time. It begins before the birth of the universe. It begins inside the dark and empty belly of the serpent who is the Great Abyss where nothing yet exists—not men, not Earth, not the gods, not even time or space. It is almost too impossible to think about this circular, ourobouric asp with neither head nor tail, beginning nor ending, since we cannot fathom the concept of what never existed. Life, the dream, the illusion of Being, happens in the midst of the great serpent's belly. Before that, there is only desire, the will to exist, the great hidden progenitor of the universe whom the ancient Egyptians called Atum. From him the world sprang in its great cosmic combustion of energy, expanding whirring gases and contracting matter into stars. And to him all will return at the end of time like a black hole in the universe, sucking in matter that disappears.

But between the beginning and the end, there is time and space. There are men and women, gods and nature. All these spring from the first creation. First came Light, whom the ancient Egyptians named Ra. In the light of consciousness of time/space there came into being Nature, or the "neters," as we call the gods of ancient Egypt. Time and space, as we know it, came into existence when the gods were born, gathered together from the cosmic dust of Heaven (from Nut, the goddess) and the matter of Earth (Geb, the god).

The myth of Isis and Osiris is about primordial time, The First Time, as the ancients called it. Isis, the goddess of Heaven and Earth, measures archetypal time, what we might call the "durative realm," the everlasting. Her dying and renewing husband Osiris is the measure of cyclical time, the eternal return, as well as the seasons and the recurrent patterns of life.

When Seth places Osiris in the wooden coffin, he traps the god in time. He fragments the god's time into years and months by hacking the lunar body of Osiris into pieces. He further attempts to confine and control Isis (durative time) by trapping her inside his spinning mill. Yet she transcends this realm by tapping psychically into the eternal and durative realm of Osiris. She enters the land of the dead in trance and dream and brings back her vision of time eternal through the conception of the divine child, Horus.

Ever after the death of Osiris, the pregnant Isis now lives in three times: what happened previously, what is happening now, and what will happen in the future. This knowledge of both the temporal and the eternal realms allows her to transcend the limitations of time and create a renewed vision of Egypt. When we say that the goddess has become Queen of Heaven and Earth by the story's end, we also mean that she operates in full glory in both the durative and the temporal realms.

Horus, son of Isis and Osiris and heir to both durative and cyclical time, is the hero of this myth. Horus performs the action of the hero by walking in both worlds—one foot in eternal time, the other in cyclical time. It is Horus who becomes the pattern of a man that the ancients emulated. If we view the myth this way, we begin to understand how the Egyptians divided their story of becoming into three realms: the time of gods, the time of heroes, and the time of men.

Exploring the Durative Realm

It would be tempting to think of these realms as historical eras—first came gods, then heroes, then men. But in fact, the ancient Egyptians perceived these separate realities as occurring simultaneously. Every sunrise revealed the story of creation. Each dawn and dusk reenacted the battle of Horus and Seth. Every day a man lived and breathed, his life and his death recurred from waking to sleeping.

As Sir Alan Gardiner noted in his *Egyptian Grammar*, the ancient Egyptians had only two verb tenses. These revealed either the singleness of an event or its repetition—they recognized only the "present" or the "eternal present." Although the "present" could have happened today or yesterday, the significant distinction in the two verb tenses was revealed in a difference in whether perceived events occurred in man's time or in the gods' time.[1]

This dual notion of time permeated all of ancient Egyptian life. The mud brick and thatch houses of the people were temporary affairs, never meant to last, for the Nile floods came annually and washed everything away. But the houses of the gods, the temples, were built of stone. They were to last for eternity, the lifetime of a neter.

The ancient Egyptians believed that a divine spark resided in every human being. Although the mortal shell of flesh and bone disappeared at death, the spiritual self remained. The Egyptians lived full lives, planted corn, birthed children, and enjoyed music, but they focused on what was eternal. They existed not within the temporal time of men, but within the eternal present time of gods. As the poet Octavio Paz has said:

> ... there was a time when time was not succession and transition, but rather the perpetual source of a fixed present in which all times, past and future, were contained. When man was exiled from that eternity in which all times were one, he entered chronometric time and became a prisoner of the clock and the calendar. As soon as time was divided up into yesterday, today, and tomorrow, into hours, minutes, seconds, man ceased to be one with time, ceased to coincide with the flow of reality.[2]

The Durative Realm and Ritualistic Time

As a student at Barnard College and Columbia University, I was much moved by the lectures of Professor Theodor Gaster, the great scholar of Near Eastern and Hebraic studies. He drew a remarkable distinction between the "durative" and the "punctual" realms, especially as they were used in the ritual dramas of the ancient Near East.

The durative realm was the realm of gods, of archetypes, of essential qualities, of Christ crucified and resurrected, of Buddha always under that bodhi tree finding enlightenment, or of the constant re-creation of the world. In the punctual realm of here and now we are able to draw down the durative, archetypal event through our reenactments at Christmas and Easter and on Buddha's birthday.

In this way these great happenings, eternally recurring in the durative world beyond time and space, continue to give their enduring potency to the temporally limited world of the here and now. Thus, in his important work *Thespis*, Gaster shows that, for example, the Egyptian New Year festivals involved the punctual enactment by the pharaoh, or priest-king, of the drama of creation, and he explains how, for the Egyptian, the dying year was renewed through these incursions from the durative world of the eternal springtime of creation itself.[3]

In his brilliant presentation and commentaries of the extant scenarios of these sacred festivals, Gaster reveals the immense psychological power of these dramas to renew the heart of self and society. One can imagine what would happen in America if each year around July 4, in addition to hot dogs and firecrackers, we suddenly dropped our boundaries of space and time and received Thomas Jefferson into our midst, declaring our independence over again with the same fervor as in 1776.

On a much larger scale, the ancient Egyptians were constantly invoking sacred time. As one sees from ritual funerary papyri, as well as in the wonderfully colorful friezes of sacred festivals, Egyptians used the three critical turning points of the year (the flooding of the land, the retreat of the Nile, and the time of drought) as opportunities to bring the eternal, changing patterns of durative, archetypal Egypt into punctual, everyday Egypt. Their agricultural, festival, and personal lives centered around no less than three calendars.[4]

The lunar calendar kept cyclical time. As the oldest measure of time, it was the instrument of the moon goddess and the record of her patterns. When passive hunting and gathering gave way to agricultural concerns, the solar calendar evolved, including the five epagomenal days honoring the five great gods of Egypt. Solar calendars kept more accurate agricultural time. The Sothic calendar marked the helical rising of the Dog Star, Sirius (or Sothis), which every June 21 heralded the arrival of the Nile inundation.[5] In addition, there were gods and goddesses of the epoch, of the season, of the month, of the day, and of the appointed hour.

After the birth of Isis and Osiris, historic time in Egypt was also a part of the gods' time. From 3000 B.C. onward, every June 21 the goddess Isis shone her brilliant face upon the thirsty land of Egypt, blessing it in her form as the rising star Sothis. Every June 21 the god Osiris rose up from his underworld depths, appearing as the swollen river Nile, and flooded the land with his life-giving waters. Every June 21, then, Isis and Osiris blessed the people of Egypt and gifted them with their life-sustaining powers. The star rose, the river overflowed its banks, and the fields were made fertile. In the punctual realm it was the New Year festival; in the durative realm it was the dawn of eternal creation and regeneration.

Egyptian civilization lasted thousands of years. One wonders if the present ephemeral lives of countries would endure longer if they, too, received the great greening thrusts of energy and renewal that came from regularly tapping into the durative realm, for it is there in the deep patterns of perfect harmony and knowing that the dynamic purpose of the relationship between the land, humanity, and the gods eternally resides.

Prehistory: The Time of Gods

It was said that before the reign of Narmer, the first pharaoh of Egypt, the gods (Osiris, Isis, Seth, Nephthys, and Horus) reigned. How long they reigned we do not know, for that is the gods' time. For all intents and purposes, the gods still reign. Time, or at least the gods' time, began when Osiris and Isis, who were children of the sky goddess Nut and star-dwellers clothed in bodies of light, descended to the earth. These divine neters immersed themselves in matter by taking human form, and they taught a message of love and nurturance that became the archetypal pattern for later kings and queens.

The importance of these mythic origins is that the Egyptians believed absolutely in their own antiquity and divinity. They accomplished all they did because they believed they were descended from gods. All art and culture, all science and agriculture were possible because the laws governing them were handed down by the gods communicating through the higher minds that inhabit those of ordinary men and women.

Believing themselves to be born into this world from divine dimensions, the ancient Egyptians unequivocally accepted an eternal spirit. They dedicated their lives to religious devotion to the ancestors and gods, planning continually for the moment of their return to their spiritual source. They lived like gods, thought like gods, built a high culture worthy of the gods' wisdom, and erected cities, temples, and monuments on a divine scale. Even their collective memories were the memories of gods.

When Herodotus, the ancient Greek historian and traveler, first landed on the shores of Egypt, he shook the dust from his tunic and the sand from his feet and stood in awe of what he perceived to be the oldest civilization in the world. The Egyptians, he wrote, "have existed ever since men appeared upon the earth."[6] After he had proved himself a worthy man and a seeker of truth, the priests of Egypt gave him their histories, stories, and mysteries that heretofore had been passed orally from generation to generation.

Their land, the priests said, was first ruled by ten gods who reigned for some fifteen thousand years. These gods, called the *paut*, were born from the chaos of whirling star dust, and among the last of them were Isis and Osiris. In turn, these primordial beings engendered other gods, the last of whom was Horus, son of Isis and Osiris, and on whom the later pharaohs patterned their own heroic lives.[7] In Horus, Herodotus saw his own Greek god, Herakles, a son of Zeus, who when only an infant strangled the snakes of darkness.

After Horus there came nine dynasties of "venerables," god-men equivalent to the Titans. Called the Shemsu-Hor, these human companions of Horus reigned 13,420 years, beginning about 18,000 B.C.[8] Their reign ended around 3000 B.C. with the legendary king Menes, the first recorded human ruler. Perhaps he was Narmer; perhaps he was not. This "perhaps," then, is where our revisionist knowledge of ancient Egyptian history begins.

Curious about their own origins, the Egyptians kept extensive lists of their kings. In the third century B.C. a priest-scribe named Manetho documented a history of ancient Egypt accurate enough that modern Egyptologists still base their knowledge of the Old, Middle, and New Kingdoms on his designations. Manetho stated that there were 15,150 divine dynasties, 9,777 years of kings before Menes, then 3,000 years of known pharaohs in thirty dynasties. His computations place the date of the divine origin of Egypt as far back as 28,000 B.C., a date that coincides with the historical influx of nomadic tribes into Egypt.[9]

The Multicultural Origins of Egypt

Around 30,000 B.C. the Sahara was a vast savanna and forest, teeming with exotic plants and animals. At various times waters from the melting polar ice caps covered most of Europe and submerged the Sahara plain. A land bridge connected Europe and North Africa. Blond and red-haired Ice Age hunters followed the animals migrating along the isthmus between Tunisia and southern Italy.

Around 10,000 B.C. the land bridge vanished, trapping these nomads in Libya. A brief two thousand years later, the grassy savanna shriveled and turned to desert. Once the trees that held moisture were gone, the land turned to sand. No rains fell. In search of food, the nomads moved east, making their way into the green, fertile Nile Delta of Egypt, where the floods assured them abundant food.[10]

This same catastrophic drought forced African tribes in the Sudan, Nubia, and Central Africa to launch their boats downriver along the Nile, seeking sustenance. They carried their boats on their backs, traversing the dangerous cataracts from Khartoum to Aswan on foot, until they passed the island of Elephantine where, again, they set sail until they reached Upper Egypt, settling in the area around Thebes.[11] In addition, Semitic tribes arrived in Egypt from two directions. Those who crossed the Sinai Peninsula into the northern Nile Delta merged with the European-Libyans. Those traversing the southern Arabian peninsula into Ethiopia mingled with African cultures.

Between the ninth and sixth millennia B.C. the inhabitants of the entire area were afoot, hauling with them not only their children but their cultures, their dreams for the future, their gods, their myths, and their truths. A great many people in search of a better life migrated simultaneously to the southern highlands and the northern Nile Delta. The religious myths intermingled, as did the races, resulting in a people who looked at various times during the millennia more or less African, Asian, Mediterranean, and European—all of whom were worshipers of the natural cycles of the earth and the Great Goddess.

Isis: Queen of Heaven and Earth

At first, women followed the tribes, but as the herds shrank and hunters ranged farther afield, they stayed behind, camping where foods could be foraged. As they waited, women discovered a few things—crop cultivation, weaving, pottery, art, and sacred storytelling. Thus began the transition between hunting tribes and agricultural peoples. Isis, the myth tells us, taught women to weave, to grow crops, and to breed animals. She taught them to tell the stories, to draw the pictures, and to remember the dead. Above all, she taught them to praise the divine and follow the natural, rhythmic cycles of time.

Around 7000 B.C. Neolithic women became the world's first farmers. The simple headband often seen adorning the forehead of Isis represents not royalty, but the linen rag tied about the foreheads of field women to keep their hair and sweat from falling into their eyes.[12] Alongside agriculture grew the cult of the cow goddess, who embodied motherhood. Like human females, cows bore their young in nine months, nurtured them with their milk, and even ploughed the fields that grew the grain. Their crescent horns symbolized the waxing and waning moon that coincided with the monthly renewal of the womb.

The cow goddess first appeared in Egypt around 5000 B.C., a precursor to Isis. If one travels through the wind-sculpted dunes into the sandstone hills beyond Faiyum, the large Saharan oasis near ancient Memphis, one finds Egypt's oldest known deity. The goddess of fertility reigns no longer in a land of abundant field and savanna but in what is now endless desert sand, heat, and sky. Carved into the sandstone cliff, she wears long plaits of hair and a linen gown. Her naked followers have brought their cattle for her to bless.

Isis was queen of both the heavens and the earth. An embodiment of the rich soil, she made agriculture possible. Women prayed to the dark, fecund Earth to grant renewed life from her own body. They geared their labors in the field to the rising of the star Sirius, which they named Sothis, that annually heralded the coming flood. The appearance of Sothis was perceived as a message from Isis herself, a promise of the planet's renewal. Where the vast desert night sky is littered with stars, Isis appears as the cow of the Heavens. The Milky Way is the product of her breasts.

The myth of Isis is as old as human memory. The Faiyum cult of the cow goddess clearly predates the bull cult of Egypt's Old Kingdom by two thousand years. In Upper Egypt stories of the sky goddess center around the divine son, who is a hawk god. But in neither Upper nor Lower Egypt do the tales of the husband appear until the mention of Osiris around 3000 B.C. Whereas the function of the hawk god—the later Horus—is mainly as a warrior, the chief function of Osiris was to die and be reborn as the grain.

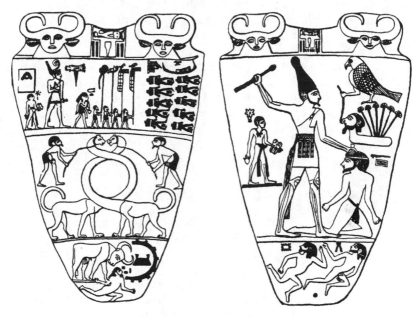

Front and back of the Palette of Narmer, circa 3100 B.C.

Agrarian and Nomad: The Roots of Conflict between Osiris and Seth

A s the desert encroached, former hunters came to see that cooperative agriculture provided a more stable life. But little arable land was available. Those tribes who settled and claimed the fertile delta were constantly attacked by these nomadic tribes who had no land or resources of their own. Thus the stage was set for the war between farmers and hunters—the setting for the mythic battle between Osiris, the "civilized" man, and Seth, the barbarian. The remembered stories of the warring and marauding gods represent two thousand years of tribal skirmishes between Libyans and Asiatic intruders, between African southerners and Nile Delta northerners, between farmers and nomads.

Until 3000 B.C. Egypt operated as two distinctly different countries. The northern people in Lower Egypt, called the Black Land, were primarily farmers since the Nile deposited tremendous amounts of black fertile soil into the delta area, resulting in a large amount of arable land. The southern people lived in Upper Egypt, the Red Land, a comparatively narrow strip of fertile land bordered on either side by high, dry desert plateaus composed of reddish sandstone. They supplemented their passive agricultural practices by hunting wild game and making forays into the delta. Each civilization developed according to its needs. The northern culture advanced as farmers and builders, while the southern culture advanced as warriors.[13]

The myth relates that the gods gave Osiris, the firstborn son, all the fertile black land, while to Seth was given all the red, dry desert. Seth, then, was the god of hunters, whereas Osiris was the god of farmers. Seth envied the fertile land of his brother and determined to kill him so that he might rule all of Egypt.

Northern Egypt: Land of Isis and Osiris

Little remains of the early northern settlers. What the river left uncovered by alluvial deposits, modern inhabitants stripped for *sebbakh*, the fertile soil found in mounds of rubble marking the site of ancient mud-brick houses. Today, the stones of the earliest temples have been dismantled and hauled away to support the massive building projects in Cairo, Heliopolis, and other nearby cities. The seven gentle arms of the Nile that once formed the delta, creating a flowering lotus-shaped pattern, are now clogged. Only two rivulets remain, the Rosetta to the west and the Damietta to the east.

Nevertheless, now—as it was then—the Nile Delta and the Faiyum oasis are where the majority of Egypt's food is grown. Modern roadsides are cluttered with the stands of vendors selling ripe melons, onions, cucumbers, tomatoes, dates, grapes, and grains. Bright yellow cane cages hold geese and ducks for sale. Sleepy cattle, sheep, and goats lie in the shade of palm tree–lined roads, while camels clomp through the dusty streets, chewing their cud, hauling hay, sugarcane, flax, wheat, and corn.

Even modern farmers live in mud-brick houses covered with thatched roofs, sometimes sharing their evening shade with donkeys and other beasts of burden. In many ways, especially in the rural areas of the delta and the Faiyum oasis, life has not changed substantially for thousands of years. Emmer is no longer cut with wooden sickles set with flint teeth, but the donkey and the wooden plow are still the barefoot farmer's mainstays.

Around 5000 B.C. the earliest settlers came from Mesopotamia, following the coastline of the Mediterranean along the Sinai Peninsula. They settled in the delta—along the riverbanks and in the surrounding foothills—bringing with them their most valued possessions, their gods, their rituals, their ingenuity, probably their cattle, and, more importantly, wild emmer, previously unknown on the African continent.[14] They erected temporary thatch houses of reeds and palms that were easily rebuilt following the annual floods, but these farmers settled in for the duration.[15] After centuries of cultivation, they reaped domesticated crops of barley and wheat from which they baked high loaves of fine bread and brewed barley beer, the two most important ritual offerings of the cult of Osiris.

Other settlers migrated from Libya to the Faiyum oasis in northern Egypt. They camped in marshes and on the riverbanks in low, clustered, oval huts of dried mud and thatch reminiscent of the houses of Faiyum residents today. Their burials were marked by the beliefs of pastoral people. Spelt, a type of wheat, was scattered over the corpse, for perhaps it had occurred to these newcomers that the grasses grew greener in the Fields of the Dead. Thereafter, the ritual linked the dead with Osiris, the black-faced god clothed in green who, like the black delta soil sprouting vegetation, signified life resurrected.

The mythic Isis and Osiris arise in Egypt as early as the fifth millennium B.C.[16] They resemble the Sumerian and Babylonian gods Inanna/Ishtar and Dumuzi. Like Isis, Inanna, goddess of heaven and earth, lost her husband to the dark forces of the land of the dead. Originally a shepherd king, Dumuzi became, like Osiris, a farmer intimately connected with the grain, the natural cycles of time and seasonal regeneration.

Southern Egypt: Land of Anubis and Seth

Beyond the Nile Delta, most of Upper Egypt is a wasteland. The eastern desert is bordered by high cliffs, dry wadis, and sparse vegetation. To the west lie the endless yellow sands and high hills of the Sahara. Agriculture is limited to a strip of land on either side of the Nile. From the air the river and its surrounding fields resemble a long, thin green snake, striped with blue and slithering along the hot sand.

Into this harsh land of southern Egypt, around the first Nile cataract at Aswan, came tribes of predynastic African people who carved out a life for themselves. Like the Nilotic tribes of the Sudan even into the late twentieth century, these nomads camped along the riverbanks, scattered millet seeds in the mud, then left to hunt and gather in the desert, returning to the millet at harvesttime.[17] Between the sowing and the reaping, they traveled from one end of the Nile to the other, finally contacting the Faiyum and delta peoples.

The myth of Isis and Osiris tells us that the god and goddess "civilized the barbarians"; that is, they taught the people agriculture and social organization. Contact with the delta tribes had an enormous impact on these early nomads. From the northerners, the southerners learned an agrarian lifestyle that they combined with their own traditional hunting skills. As a result, they emerged as a more fully rounded culture, sparking a new cultural climate. Grain was cultivated year to year. Goats, sheep, cattle, pigs, and geese were domesticated. In time, the nomads cast off the animal skins that marked them as hunters and began wearing coarse woven clothes.

When they buried their dead in the desert facing the setting sun, the inhabitants of this area began a tradition in the western hills of Abydos and Thebes that continued for four thousand years. The black lacquer and gilded statue of Anubis—the jackal that the archaeologist Howard Carter found guarding Tutankhamun's tomb in 1922—followed a tradition of burial nearly three thousand years old. As early as 4500 B.C., Upper Egyptian chieftains, called *khenti*, were buried side by side with their sleek saluki hunting dogs.[18] Even that symbolic gesture was the remnant of a nomadic past, perhaps a link to Seth the hunter. The dog buried at his master's side became the pattern for Anubis, who played the role of guide for the dead into the underworld.

Seth: The God of Craftsmen

A large number of modern Upper Egyptians are dark-skinned, tall, and Nubian in appearance. Many are farmers, but a majority work as skilled craftsmen, like their ancestors—potters, stone masons, jewelers, and artisans of all kinds who eke out a living by quarrying the hard bedrock, sculpting the mud, weaving the cloth, and selling their wares. The land does not give forth its riches as easily as it does in the Nile region. What living is to be made here is gained by clawing at the hard heart of the rock—the sculpting of statues, the baking of faience, the digging of alabaster, and, from ancient times down to modern, the plundering of tombs.

From Aswan to Luxor, the Nile River is crisscrossed by a constant flotilla of luxury boats, small skiffs, ferries, and sleek white-sailed feluccas. Its markets throng with vendors of African spices, metal works, replicas of ancient statues, and colorful, vibrant textiles. Its streets are congested with camels and garden-variety hucksters whispering, "Mummy beads, miss, ancient Egyptian mummy beads." If you are lucky enough or look especially gullible, a *galibeya*-clad man will pull you to the side, look furtively up and down the street, then take from some hidden pocket a noxious, desiccated foot smelling of turpentine, saying, "Found in the tomb, by my grandfather. For you, my sister, only a thousand dollars." And when you try to hurry away, he will run after you, calling, "How much you want to pay?"

Tourism supports the modern Egyptian economy the way trade supported the ancient culture. Both the ancient and modern lifestyles have relied on a quest for the beautiful, the exotic, the hard to obtain, and, recently, the false.

As far back as the fifth millennium B.C., trade and travel were an essential part of Egyptian culture. From the Sinai and Nubia the Egyptians imported malachite for eye paint and cedar, juniper, and resin from the forests of Syria. They traded in turquoise and carnelian. Necklaces of perforated seashells from the Mediterranean, Red Sea, and Indian Ocean decorate the Neolithic dead, and amazonite stones, carried in from the central eastern Sahara, found their way into prehistoric graves.[19]

The myth suggests that, in addition to hunting boars with his Ethiopian entourage, Seth was the god of metals. He ensnared Osiris in a jeweled coffin encrusted with gold, malachite, carnelian, and other precious stones. These gems were mined in the mountains of the eastern desert, an arid hilly land dotted with small oases. As these athletic and resourceful former hunters learned to mine copper in the eastern desert, tool and jewelry making appeared, including beautiful faience beads covered with a green alkaline copper glaze.

Carnelian and malachite could have been ripped from the mountain core only by instruments hardened through the process of the forge. In addition to jewelry making, metals were used in both agriculture and warfare. The blade that plowed the field and reaped the grain also severed the heads of enemies. The rise of metallurgy, a craft unknown in the Nile Delta, gave the Upper Egyptians an advantage over the delta dwellers and allowed them to invade and conquer the delta lands around 3000 B.C.

Osiris may have tried to civilize Seth and his barbarians, but Seth built the beautiful jeweled coffin that ensnared Osiris. He developed the knife that hacked his brother to pieces as surely as metal scythes cut wheat. The bones of the war god were bones of iron. Seth himself was called "the bones of the earth." The task of the culture was to learn to transmute the incredible power of the knife into a more beneficent use.

Horus: The Time of Heroes and Kings

Around 3500 B.C. the winds of change blew through Egypt. The hunting dog no longer appears in its master's grave. Round African huts give way to rectangular mud-brick houses. Permanent towns arise near Naqada and Hierakonpolis. A new people have arrived. From the east they traveled down the tip of the Sinai Peninsula, crossed the Gulf of Suez, and followed the coastline of the Red Sea. Then, turning east, they meandered through the many dry, twisting wadis that led to Middle Egypt and the Nile.

With them they bore the creative spark and technical know-how needed to greatly advance primitive civilization. Writing developed, along with new art forms. Brick structures replaced simple dwellings.[20] Chiefs and kings of this "dynastic race" lay stretched out in walled-in tombs and coffins reminiscent of later pharaonic burials, and in direct contrast to the common fetal-position burials of the previous chiefs. An apparently different racial strain, their bodies were larger and their skulls wider, traits similar to those found during the dynastic period.[21]

For the two thousand years before these people appeared in Upper Egypt, a nameless, birdlike sky goddess reigned. She bore all the characteristics of the goddess Hathor, who was similar to her sister, Isis, in the delta. The goddess of fertility, life, and death, she guarded the cycles of time, brought the crops to fruition, bore the children, and received the dead into her arms. The newcomers named this Great Goddess Hathor, meaning "house of Horus." She birthed the new heroic god, Heru, who became the "savior king."[22] As the new main god of the region, Horus joined the myth as the son of Isis/Hathor who fought Seth, the god of the barbarians. The new rulers were equated with the mythic "companions of Horus"—the kings who ruled after the first appearance of Horus.

History: The Time of Men

We leave prehistoric Egypt shrouded in the mists of time. The historic age is opening before us. The gods no longer rule. Egypt is ruled by men descended of gods.

In 3000 B.C. a southern chieftain named Narmer journeyed to the Nile Delta. He marched under the symbol of the falcon, Horus, and the cow goddess, Hathor. He found there, camped by the riverbanks, tribes of bearded "foreigners," probably Semites. He slew their chief, Washi, and married the dead man's queen, giving Narmer the status of being the uniter of the Two Lands, the first king of both Upper and Lower Egypt. His conquest was chiseled into stone, the first known historic record of ancient Egypt. It is called the Palette of Narmer.

The widow he married was Neit-hotep, a high priestess of the ancient delta goddess. Narmer's marriage to the embodiment of the Great Goddess cemented his right to rule. To make peace, he accepted the gods and goddesses of the north, incorporating their theology into his own. When Isis merged with Hathor as the mother of Horus, the Great Goddess encompassed all the attributes of the creative matrix—mother, wife, lover, sorceress, warrior, protectress, and comforter of the dead. The pharaoh attained divine status as the incarnation of the goddess's consort, Horus. Now the queen's role, like the goddess's role, was to birth heroic children and to nurture. The role of the pharaoh, who embodied Horus, was to rule his nation and protect it.

After the time of Narmer some three thousand years passed. In that time well over two hundred known pharaohs reigned, some for as long as sixty-seven years, some for as little as a month. (More information on Egyptian history can be found in Appendix D.) The rulers followed the pattern of civilization set by the divine pair, Isis and Osiris. They worshiped the gods, honored the dead, cultivated the fields, and continued their endeavors in art, craft, and industry. They patterned their lives according to the rise and fall of the Nile and of the stars. The duties of the pharaoh followed the pattern set by the god Horus and first enacted by King Narmer. To these ancient patterns we attribute the glory of the pyramids, the magnificence of the burials, and the overwhelming social organization of ancient Egypt.

Isis and Osiris in the Punctual Realm

The ancient Egyptians believed that their gods came to Egypt from a mythic land called Punt. Punt has never been located.[23] We do not know the origins of the ancient Egyptians. We believe they were a mingling of bodies, minds, and psyches from the three major continents. And we can't be entirely sure that the mythic rulers, Osiris and Isis, weren't real people. A number of ancient sources insist that they were a real man and woman, the Adam and Eve of Egypt. They became deified through their developed spiritual powers, attaining god- and goddess-hood through their divinely inspired intelligence and wisdom.

In Abydos, the same site where Isis was said to have found the severed head of Osiris, the same site where the temple to Osiris was erected early in Egyptian history, there existed a tomb of an ancient king who was simply called Khenti. It was this tomb that was discovered by the ancient Egyptians of the Nineteenth Dynasty—already archaeologists of their own lost history. They believed this to be the original tomb of Osiris.[24]

The ancients made no distinction between myth and history. These people endeavored to conduct their lives according to the great unfolding story of their gods, mythic heroes, and archetypes. It is a common human impulse to take actual historical people, like Christ or Buddha, and turn them into an archetype. As the mythologist Mircea Eliade observes, even Goethe was conscious of trying to live a life of mythic proportions, to create an example by all that he did. The poet Paul Valéry said that Goethe "represents for us, gentlemen of the human race, one of our best attempts to render ourselves like gods."[25]

Durative Egypt

Durative Egypt is outside local space and time: it exists in time/space and is available now, an ever-present and ever-recurring possibility of transformative consciousness. Perhaps this explains the deeper levels of fascination that many have felt for Egypt for thousands of years, a fascination that transcends its obvious mysteries and aesthetic glories. In Egypt we have a still-living metaphor for the deepest creative impulse in ourselves. If we could gain from within ourselves but a fraction of what caused historical Egypt to flourish, then our lives would be extraordinary cocreative partnerships with evolution.

Egypt cannot be explained as the product of an earlier high civilization. Nor was it a leftover colony of extraterrestrial visitation (as some of my more interesting friends profess). It is, I believe, an example of the magnificent achievement that can be attained when a culture taps into its durative base. The Egyptologist R. A. Schwaller de Lubicz (of whom we will learn more in the next chapter) suggested this when he stated that, in order to understand the heightened state of mind that was durative ancient Egypt, we have to enter into its mind, and psyche, and spirit.

Schwaller de Lubicz took the Egyptologists who preceded him to task for succumbing to the seductive lie inherent in theories of evolution— that species were always moving upward toward a state of perfection and that new development in a culture meant "improved" intellectual and spiritual development. This is not necessarily the case. Hitler, for example, was arguably not more highly civilized or evolved than the ancient Egyptian sage Ptahhotep simply because Hitler was born nearly four thousand years later. It is dangerously presumptuous and egocentric to base one's knowledge of a past civilization on a comparison to our own. Evolution, Schwaller de Lubicz said, was merely a study of the stages of transmutation:

> Past civilization is held to be inferior to ours since it has preceded us! In fact, neither time nor space separates [changes in consciousness] profoundly. In order to obtain true [separation], there must be a difference in mentality. The state of mind separates or unites; we must search the state of mind for the mainspring of all behavior.[26]

Many Egyptologists have hoped to enter into the ancient mind in part by learning the language and its symbols. But that is not enough. Indeed, it may not even be critical to understanding that state of mind. What is essential is awakening to a living rapport and identity with durative Egypt so that it takes up residence within us. This means more than immersing ourselves in the myth, and the inscriptions, and gazing upon a few artifacts. It means entering an Egyptian state of mind, allowing for the simultaneous existence and experience of all things in motion, and recognizing their synchronistic functions for a brief but eternally absolute moment.

One reaches these states through love, attunement, and fully conscious incarnation. This doesn't mean that we have to drop our present psyche and history, but rather that we expand our awareness by attuning first to the durative aspects of ourselves, then to the realm of the durative that is eternal Egypt. This necessitates journeying from our daily time/space consciousness through the gateway of the eternal mind of the neters. Yogis know that each breath, each heartbeat, is surrounded by emptiness, that all is transitory. They live each moment in its time—a breath, a second, a heartbeat, a life—thus moving through the doorways of space and time. This knowledge, this expanded existence, is available to us as well, as "Process 1: A Visit to the Durative" will demonstrate.

☥
PROCESS I:
A Visit to the Durative

TIME: 60 minutes.
MATERIALS NEEDED: Notebook and pen or pencil.
MUSIC: Quiet, reflective music from Area 1 throughout the journey, concluding with vital, celebrational music from Area 3.
SPECIAL NOTES: In reading the processes, the guide should pause whenever an ellipsis (. . .) appears. Instructions to the guide, which should not be read aloud, have been set off in parentheses.

INSTRUCTIONS FOR THE SOLO JOURNEYER: You can reflect on durative events in your own life by following the instructions below. Before you begin the process, however, you may want to look through a photo album that chronicles the places, people, and events of your life. Remember that time is flexible and that what you remember will be whatever you need to recall in accordance with your soul's journey. Don't worry if you discover later on that you have overlooked some major event. What comes up for you now, at this time and place, is what's important. If you wish, you can imagine a partner—a friend, a departed relative, a guidance figure, a neter—to whom you are describing these events. It may work best if the partner is someone to whom you are not close, as we often tell our life stories to strangers in an attempt to tell ourselves about ourselves. Then record the guided meditation and follow the instructions.

SCRIPT FOR THE GUIDE: You are now going to pay a visit to your own durative realm. You are about to enter a time out of time. The categories of your local time will be strained by the tensions of eternity. Eternity and what lies there will flood the gates of the times of your personal story.

Open your notebook and write at the top of a new page the words *My*

Life in the Durative Realm. Now find a partner, if possible someone whose life story is relatively unknown to you. With your partner, begin to remember joyful celebrations in your lives, turning points, critical times, and name them aloud to each other. Naming these events will often serve to jog your memory for related occurrences. Recall events that you would like to believe are stored in durative time/space. Name the events that you would like to believe are stored in the mind of God—perhaps a certain birthday, a first love, an engagement or wedding, a baby's arrival, a family holiday, a triumph in your school or professional life, or an especially blissful day.

As you remember these times and places, events, moods, and people, jot them down in your notebook. Don't write any details, just a few words that will help you remember. List as many of them as you can in the allotted time. Should you fail to find any happy events that you want to visit in durative time, use your creative imagination to invent several. (Allow ten minutes.)

Now let us begin to engage and experience the concept of durative time/space, which lies beyond what we normally think of as either time or space.

Study your list of events. Allow your eyes and brain and memory and heart to feel energized, filled with a kind of heavenly light. Let your eyes of Light shine upon the events of your life, as if Ra, the sun, streamed his being through them. Let your brain and memory fill with the Light of these events, as if Osiris himself remembered the pieces of you. Let your heart fill with Light, love, and compassion, knowing that, as you look, remember, and feel, the divine Light of Isis looks, remembers, and feels through you.

Begin to endow the events of your life with the feelings that these godded beings might bring to them. See them with the eyes of Ra. Revisit them with the memory of Osiris. Feel them with the heart of Isis. Now let your hands of Light reach out and arrange or rearrange these events playfully, out of any logic or time sequence, so that, for example, your daughter at her graduation is present at your fifth birthday, your favorite pet from early childhood is a celebrant at the office party marking your promotion. Mix and match and know that all these events are occurring in durative time, eternally. (Allow two minutes.)

Hold out your hands and begin to mold the material of time/space. Become an Isis assembling your own Osiris. Pull time and space apart and see the events of your life wildly separate and disconnected from one another. Then bring them together so that in your private durative realm these separate festivities are happening simultaneously and the celebration never ends. (Allow one or two minutes.)

Now share with your partner this mammoth celebration. All of the joyous events of your life are occurring at this moment, in the continual now. Describe each scene with rich vividness: the sounds, sights, tastes, and feelings; the other people who are there with you. See them. Touch them. Tell your partner about them. And tell it dramatically, with all the detail you can remember or imagine.

Decide which of you will speak first. Each person will have five minutes to describe this eternal celebration happening in the durative realm. If you find yourself without sufficient words, let your hands begin again to mold and stretch and play with the stuff of time and space. You'll find that more memories will pour out. If you who are listening feel moved to act out a moment of joy, or dance and sing in response to the celebration of your partner's life, do so. Then quickly return to your deep listening. (Allow five minutes for the first speaker.)

Let the first person come to a natural conclusion. Then let the partner begin to speak of the events of his or her life being celebrated in the durative realm.

(After everyone's five minutes are up, say:)

Come now to a natural conclusion of this exploration into personal durative time/space.

Let us drop into the durative realm of our planet. Let us choose an event that made a difference—a mythic event or one of historic significance—and let us go to that place in time and space where it is always happening. We will place ourselves there as witnesses to that event.

For example, you might choose to be present in the durative realm at the birth of Jesus, or at the signing of the Declaration of Independence of the United States, or with Buddha at the time of his enlightenment under the bodhi tree, or at the first performance of *Hamlet* or *The Magic Flute,* or watching that woman of the Paleolithic Age painting bison on the walls of her cave at Lascaux.

Feel the great godded connections between your brain and heart and hand, then begin to write on a new page a list or cluster of those events you wish to visit. Do this privately without talking with your partner. (Allow several minutes.)

Now put the notebook aside and make yourself comfortable while maintaining a connection with your partner. You may sit back to back, lie down with your heads together, or just sit facing each other while lightly holding hands. Make yourself absolutely comfortable, knowing that your partner can be comfortable only if you are comfortable. Begin to follow your breathing as you inhale and exhale . . . Feel the presence of the neter Shu, the god of air, as you breathe in and out . . . Easily, fully, breathing in and out . . .

Let the god Ra come and neter your eyes once again, so that they become bright orbs illuminating your insight. Let them close gently. Continue to breathe easily, in and out, the breath of Shu, the eyes of Ra . . .

You find yourself on an ancient barge being borne down a great river past green fields. You feel the soft slosh of the water as your barge moves through it. Above your head a bright sail catches the gentle winds that guide you. The sky is blue and utterly cloudless.

You become aware that the sky and the fields around you are the setting for eternity, that you are floating gently within the durative realm, and that you may choose the scenes in this realm for which you want to serve as High Witness. These scenes will simply appear in the sky or along the banks of the river as you float past. Should you want to move closer to the banks, know that the barge will move you wherever you want to go and welcome you back when you are ready to move on. (Allow three minutes.)

Return to the barge, knowing that you are an ever-present participant in the events you have chosen to witness within the durative realm. Once again, make yourself comfortable, breathing with the breath of Shu . . . See with the inner eyes of Ra . . . Open with the great heart of Isis, and imagine with the brain of Ptah . . .

All time is present in the sky above you and the fields around you. All time is present, including the future. Create now an experience in the durative realm that you can believe in. Draw it down to quicken your life and the life of the whole planet. Create a template of a new high civilization, a new kind of Egypt of the soul, a pattern of possibility and probability. It need not be huge; it may in fact seem very small. But it yearns to exist. It deserves to be brought into being in the punctual realm of present time and present space.

Find such a pattern of a wonderful new possibility for your life in the archetypal durative realm and experience it fully with all your heightened senses. Create it or let it reveal itself. (Allow two minutes.)

Now allow a golden fishing net to float out from all the places and spaces of your body of Light under the guidance of Isis in her role as weaver of the patterns of time and space. Enfold the vision, or pattern, or whiff of possibility, and gently pull it in from the durative realm toward you in your barge.

Let the net and the pattern of possibility melt into your body. Feel it melting into you. Feel it moving within you in so vital a manner that you begin to stretch and move and sit up and yawn and stretch again and open your eyes and find yourself back in the realm of present punctual time. When you are ready, write in your notebook what you saw or felt or experienced, and how you can engage these events of durative time to manifest and activate them in this present reality, in the here and now. (Allow several minutes for writing.)

Now share your experience with your partner as fully, dramatically, and vividly as possible. (Allow at least five minutes for each partner to share. If appropriate, encourage some pairs to share their experiences with the whole group. If there are those who say they felt nothing, ask them to write and discuss an experience of the durative they would have enjoyed having. Creative imagination can often provide as meaningful and useful an experience as can the actual visionary one.)

It is time now to celebrate together the durative realm and the opportunities it offers us to live in a richer set of realities.

(Music for vigorous communal dancing is appropriate here.)

⚛

JOURNAL PROCESS

Set your clock to get up at dawn. Write about the sunrise as if it were the moment of creation. Write about yourself at the moment of conception. Write about everything you thought the day you were born. Imagine that today is the day you are being born.

Respond to each of the following questions. Write quickly, in a stream of consciousness:

> What do I want from the universe?
> What does the universe want from me?
> What do we, the universe and I, want together?

Write a letter to a higher principle or presence in the durative realm. Begin the letter "Dear Friend." Ask your Friend in the durative realm to tell you something of the divine design of your life that is stored there as a potential to be realized. Then answer the letter as the Friend writing to you and addressing you as "Dear Friend." Just let the answer flow from the durative realm, and be open to anything that may come.

Hieroglyphic Text of Popi I.

5

The Quickening of Reality:
Hieroglyphic Thinking

Complete mystery prevails as to the real meaning of the representations
[inscribed on walls and papyri], the pantheon and the myths. . . . We
stand before a strongbox containing the greatest wealth concerning the
history of humanity; we have insisted on using the rationalist key,
rather than that which the makers of this jewelcase used—the symbol
and the symbolic.

from *Symbol and the Symbolic*
by R. A. Schwaller de Lubicz

Around 2640 B.C., when historical Egypt was less than 400 years old, a
common man, a scribe and a radical thinker, embodied the high wisdom
of the ancient gods. His name was Imhotep, and he moved through the
ranks of Egyptian officials, elevating the dreams of Egypt in the process.
A high priest of Ptah, the god of craftsmen, Imhotep was the first to
build in stone. On the golden sands of the Saqqara plateau he erected a
temple for the pharaoh Djoser—a kind of stairway to the sun. So perfect
was the Step Pyramid and its surrounding complex that it became the
model for other pyramids, yet no other single building project in Egypt,
including those of the New Kingdom, equaled its glory. Its dimensions
were ascribed to the holy numbers of the neters, and even Egyptian sages
born 250 years later looked back on the glory of Imhotep's work, bemoaning the fact that such wisdom had already been forgotten.[1]

Yet the composition of the Saqqara pyramid and complex was more
than a mathematical game. It was a deliberate attempt to set into practical form the harmonic resonances of the cosmic order of creation. The
triangle itself resonated symbolically as a tangible image of the three-in-
one aspect of the sun god: he was Ptah in the morning, Ra at noon, and
Atum in the evening.

Imhotep had the gift of genius, and he fired the creative ambitions of
not only his generation but of generations to come. Through his mind
and hands all the spiritual philosophy of Egypt was molded into practical

realities, taking form in art, architecture, and religious instruction. He was a high priest, vizier, scribe, and architect, as well as a gifted poet and a healer, whom the Greeks equated with the god Asclepios. In his own right, Imhotep was deified by the ancient scribes of the New Kingdom, who honored him by pouring a libation from their ink pots before beginning to write.

Then came the time of the great forgetting, when intruders from the east overran the streets, when monuments fell and temples filled with sand. The ancient language was neglected and traditions were abandoned. All this was in reaction to a new religion that followed one man, the Christ, whom certain of the mystery texts of Nag Hammadi say spent his youth among Egyptian priests.

In A.D. 1799, when Egypt's marvels lay shattered in the dust and buried in the mud, when the language of the gods was lost and the glory of the ancient kingdom no more than a vague dream, a nine-year-old French boy looked upon a copy of the newly discovered Rosetta Stone and determined that his life's work would be the deciphering of the hieroglyphs. At age thirty-one, having mastered twenty-four related languages of the ancient world, Jean-François Champollion—in a moment of radical inner knowing combined with years of study—finally understood the hieroglyphs. He rushed into his brother's study and shouted, "I have done it!" then fainted on the floor.[2]

Because Champollion combined his intuition with the scientific process, and because he believed in his own soul's duty in this life and acted upon it, the world was flooded anew with ancient light. Unfortunately, he died soon after his discovery. The translators who followed him only glimpsed the power of the ancient mysteries. They were powerfully drawn to the language but could not penetrate it, for they failed to think like the ancient Egyptians—with their hearts as well as their minds. Their translations lay dry as desert sand, for while they had the mental intelligence, they lacked the heart wisdom of the ancients.

The Unique Discoveries of Schwaller de Lubicz

Into our own era was born the remarkable Alsatian philosopher and Egyptologist R. A. Schwaller de Lubicz.[3] He took the dried and mummified historical understanding of Egypt and enlivened its spirit. His extensive studies of Egyptian monuments, and his research into the psychology of ancient Egyptian symbolic thinking, challenged the tradition that declared ancient Egypt a country filled with primitive, priest-ridden, death-obsessed mummifiers with a penchant for art. Schwaller de Lubicz helped to reveal ancient Egypt as one of the most highly advanced civilizations, one whose art, architecture, symbolism, medicine, mathematics, astronomy, and psychology were profoundly interrelated and whose culture was based on a precise tradition of the mysteries of creation.

Born in 1891 into a family of pharmacists, Schwaller de Lubicz early in his life showed a penchant for philosophical and mystical subjects. Even in his youth he combined an intuitive and inner understanding with scientific perceptions, often questioning himself and others about the "true" nature of substance. One look at a tranquilizer or a laxative in his family's drugstore, for example, and he would begin contemplating the philosophical nature of serenity or purgation.

Practical pharmacology did not satisfy Schwaller de Lubicz. He moved to Paris and at the age of twenty began to study the ancient art of alchemy—that blending of scientific and mystical philosophy that had originated in Egypt, the Land of Khemt. His explorations led him to spiritual studies with such groups as the Theosophical Society, an esoteric group who called themselves The Brothers of Heliopolis, and several other alchemical lodges. He eventually received the title AOR, Light of the Higher Mind.

For a while he worked on the problem of the effect of sound vibrations on matter with a mysterious alchemist dubbed Fulcanelli. (Schwaller de Lubicz had sworn never to reveal the man's true name.) At the same time he pursued a study of the symbolism of Gothic cathedrals, in the process re-creating glass with hues of red and blue equal to the great windows of Chartres—knowledge that had been lost for six centuries. Under Henri Matisse he took up painting. Later, his insights influenced such artists and poets as Jean Arp and Fernand Léger.

Philosophy, theology, science, art—Schwaller de Lubicz's interests crossed all disciplines. He studied with the masters, becoming a master himself. All welcomed his company because he reflected the philosophy of nature implicit in their own work and its relation to symbolic and artistic endeavors. Now Schwaller de Lubicz began to develop and share his own theories of symbolism. All his work in technical sciences, artistic pursuits, and philosophical inquiry into spirit and form were preparing Schwaller de Lubicz for the task of a lifetime, but he was not yet aware of his destiny.

In 1937 he went to Egypt simply to visit. The power of its symbols moved him greatly—the temples like music in stone; the hieroglyphs like philosophy made visible; the sky, the river, the sands, the fields as vibrant and vital as if upon the first day of creation. As he stepped through the first gate of the Temple of Luxor and beheld its columns, its light, its images, its shape, he was seized by radical intuition. He believed this vast, asymmetric ruin to be a deliberate exercise in proportion and meaning—an anthropology, a science, and a psychology in stone. He immediately moved his family into a small hotel near the site. There they stayed and worked for the next fifteen years, his wife and her daughter assisting him with the painstaking measurements of this great Eighteenth Dynasty monument.

Symbolism and Hieroglyphs

Long before the theory of relativity was conceived, the sages of Egypt knew that material reality consisted of movement, measure, and proportion. For example, in their creation myth of Atum, the great unified god divided himself into two parts; his two children, Shu and Tefnut (space and cosmic fire), begat two children, Nut and Geb, or Heaven and Earth. Like the fissure of an egg cell in the womb, one divided into two, and two divided into four, and four into eight, and so on. Schwaller de Lubicz insisted that the ancient Egyptian philosophy of life was embedded in the way the Egyptians viewed mathematics. "It makes a fundamental difference in the entire scientific structure," he said, "whether you conceive of two as one plus one or as the dividing of one into two."[4]

Atum, the great nothing from which everything sprang, was no more than cosmic dust living in the eternal moment before the Big Bang. Likewise, Atum knew that one day he would swallow everything and return it to the nothingness from which it came. Today, this reminds us of the astrophysical phenomenon of the black hole.

In Egypt this dualistic vision of the universe—where Nothing precedes the Everything that one day returns to Nothing—did not produce uncertainty and doubt in the natural values of life, for the Egyptians also perceived a mystical creative reality underlying the material world. They believed that the neters themselves embodied the sciences and the arts, and that the great Neter of neters held the cosmic pattern.

We tap into this layered sense of deep knowing symbolically each night when we dream. Images rise up, one after the other, linking themselves through the emotional and spiritual tones implicit in each image. The symbolic dream is not consciously woven; it simply appears, without effort, forming a constellation of meaning.

Poets use this clustering process when they write, catching a glimpse of the images and tones, then honing the work until it resounds in a fine cluster of gold. Read a line of poetry and watch the lightning-quick explosions of associations your mind makes. For example, this from Kenneth Patchen:

> Be music, night
> That her sleep may go
> Where angels have their pale, tall choirs.[5]

If we are thinking hieroglyphically, one falls into both image and sound. One feels the music of the first two words. "Be music!" the line commands, and one becomes music. Then "night," but the music of night is also silence. It becomes the music of the cosmos, the darkened skies humming and aglow with fire. The images of stars spring to mind, their twinkling like musical notes, clear and in concert. We are being that music of the universe.

"That her sleep may go . . ." Now we feel in that musical body, the body of sleep that moves, floats, an image of the astral self, the dream self that rises up into the music of night. We drift up like white evening clouds against the moon, toward that place "where angels have their pale, tall choirs." There the angels are in their shining, gossamer astral bodies—enormous pillars of light, singing, like the stars. Perhaps they have become the stars themselves. Such poetry is filled with wonder!

The amazing thing about learning to think hieroglyphically is that, once you accomplish it, you begin to live this way entirely. That is, a tree is no longer simply a tree; it is a treatise on growth and form, a discourse on change and endurance. Every moment of life attains that dreamlike resonance. It is no surprise, then, that those sacred scribes, the high priests of Egypt who read and thought and wrote in symbolic images, were also adept at dream interpretation.

My friend Ellen Burstyn once related a dream to me in which she said a word appeared, and as it came floating toward her she could see behind it all words, colors, shadows, a towline of related resonances trailing out toward infinity. Now, that's hieroglyphic dreaming!

Hieroglyphic Thinking before the Birth of Writing

To convey the nested, multidimensional reality that operates simultaneously on mythic, archetypal, scientific, and practical levels, an abstract language will not suffice; therefore, the symbol becomes essential. Well before literacy, an inscribed or painted image could evoke all the interwoven layers of meaning and association needed to understand a symbolic image.

Around 4000 B.C., before the advent of hieroglyphic writing, hieroglyphic thinking was already in evidence. An unknown artist of the Upper Egyptian Amratian tribe chiseled an image of the celestial cow goddess onto a slate palette. Like some M. C. Escher painting, this simple artistic representation of the divine feminine has the amazing ability to transmute itself into a dual image. The palette depicts a woman lifting up her arms, and in her hands she holds two stars. Where the head should be there appears a star, and stars appear on her breasts.

This indeed is already two-directional thinking, combining the image of woman and sky; but when viewed for an extended period of time the image flips into yet another dimension. Suddenly, the woman's uplifted arms transform themselves into cow horns, the bottom of her dress becomes the cow's muzzle, and the stars of her breasts become the ears of the cow. Star-woman and star-cow have become one and the same. Perhaps this ancient neter was Hathor, the sky goddess who was the patroness of astrology and who took the form of a cow.

Within this image, too, lie all the connotations behind the actual picture. The sky-woman/cow is linked with the galactic clouds that form what we know as the Milky Way. As the Egyptians knew it, it was the milk of Mother Sky; thus her association with the cow. In such a loaded super-saturated consciousness, steeped as it was in the religious and spiritual life, it is no wonder the ancient Egyptians perceived their hieroglyphs as "sacred writing," given to man by the hands of the god Thoth himself.

With such rich symbolic art to draw upon, when the ancient Egyptians did begin to write, they did not use abstract letters and words as we do, but instead evoked an entire revelation of ancient mystery through concrete symbols made dramatically visible: a sun, a tree, a tied papyrus scroll. Their language made no distinction between "writing" and "painting"—both transformed eternal, netered realities into symbols. The power of image was thus wedded to the power of sound and a resonance of onomatopoeic words—words that sounded like what they represented—appeared. For example, the phonetic glyphs of the word for "bee" (🐝 🐝 🐝) spelled the sound of the bee (*zit-zit*), and the image of the bee itself appeared at the end of the word as representative of the land of milk and honey.

Symbolic and hieroglyphic thinking gives us a sense of the ancient Egyptian mind, one that is drastically different from our own.[6] At worst, we use symbols to obscure our elitist knowings from the masses. At best, we offer them as subconscious representations of archetypal content. In ancient Egypt, however, the function of symbol was very different. For the Egyptian scribes, symbols bridged the sacred and secular realms, the inner and outer realities. Symbols merged the myths of gods and the reality of the lives of men. In pharaonic Egypt the symbol was a deliberately chosen pictorial device used to offer inner understanding as well as to convey information. The visible image has the tremendous power of being able to bypass the left brain and go straight to the viscera. Like poetry, it speaks to an intelligence of the heart. Symbolism in ancient Egypt evoked an idea in its entirety, establishing a network of meaning.

Symbol as Natural, Organic Thought

The symbol was concrete in its representation of qualities, functions, and principles. A great deal of an ancient Egyptian's life was spent observing the natural world, noting the life cycles of animals, their gestations, mating customs, and other vital characteristics. The animals were not symbolic abstractions but living embodiments of spiritual principles. The bird in flight represented the flight of the spiritual essence from its earthly body. The vulture, who brought bits of carrion to feed her young, represented the process of the death-life cycle. The Egyptian phoenix, or *bennu*, was represented by the image of a stork, a migratory bird that always returned to its own nest. Thus the *bennu*/stork symbolized the reincarnating soul, for a soul may wander where it wishes but must return to the nest, which is the physical body.

The serpent symbol, bearing both a forked tongue and a double penis, clearly spoke of duality. As a symbol of duality, the serpent also represents intelligence, which discriminates and breaks the whole into its constituent parts. Since intelligence without assimilation and nourishment is dangerous, the royal diadem worn by the pharaoh showed both the cobra and the vulture Mut (mother), the symbol of gestation and reconciliation. The diadem of cobra and vulture thus illustrated the union of intelligence with mothering, of gestation with discrimination. The pharaoh, therefore, in wearing the royal crown, symbolized the wholeness of the perfected human. This does not negate the fact that the royal crown simultaneously symbolized the unification of Upper and Lower Egypt by merging the images of the vulture of the desert plateau (Upper Egypt) with the cobra of the Nile Delta (Lower Egypt).

A further ancient symbol of spiritualized humanity is not, as our culture might have it, an angel hovering in the sky, but rather a winged serpent. This typically Egyptian metaphor represents the union of heaven and earth, of spirit and matter; it represents what can happen when duality transcends itself.

This multilayered symbolism is not a primitive lexicon of animal-headed gods. Egyptian symbolism is to our metaphor what Bach is to folk melody: cosmically meaningful principles taken from relatively simple forms. Symbolism in ancient Egypt was a sacred science designed to cultivate perception of all the phenomena of nature within the written image, while also revealing the forces and laws that govern the energetic and spiritual aspects of the universe. Every image carried an immediate understanding of the "real" world and of the cosmos.

This rich multiplicity of meaning is largely absent from the language systems of the modern world. This is also what makes simple word-for-word translations of the hieroglyphs unacceptable to us, for they are far from the poetic wisdom texts they were meant to be. An abstract language cannot reach beyond itself. But symbolic language is designed to make echoing and reechoing connections in our hearts and minds. In such a language a serpent is more than a serpent, a bird is more than a bird—and a winged serpent tells us yet another thing.

Symbol and symbolic language attempt to move us beyond the ordinary consciousness of daily speech. As J. J. Bachofen said in *Myth, Religion and Mother Right:*

> The symbol awakens intimations; speech can only explain. The symbol plucks all the strings of the human spirit at once; speech is compelled to take up a single thought at a time. The symbol strikes its roots in the most secret depths of the soul; language skims over the surface of the understanding.[7]

Recently, though, scientists have been writing luminously, in a manner that would seem familiar to a citizen of ancient Egypt, about the relation of the part to the whole, of the microcosm to the macrocosm. Loren Eisley and Lewis Thomas describe with wonderful clarity the "immense journey" of natural phenomena and the workings of the cosmos itself implicit in the "lives of the cell."[8] Their sensibility is deeply needed at this time, when our culturally induced inability to perceive these relationships is creating dire consequences in many spheres.

One wonders what would happen in education, for example, if from the start children who now suffer through math and science were shown the excitement of the sheer wondrous mystery of nature instead of being forced to learn sequential principles unrelated to the glory of the universe. I always advise math and science teachers who come to my training seminars to teach mathematics by starting with the wonder of the nature of infinity.

Abstract vs. Symbolic Thinking

The ancient Egyptians did not use language as we do—with sounds or symbols linked in fixed associations, which in turn evoke sequential patterns in the brain. Instead, it was the Greeks who gave us our use of language. From the Phoenician alphabet the Greeks created a language of abstract forms, in which words stood for concepts. Such a language gives us a certain science, a certain distancing of self from nature, a certain dialectical interplay between self and nature, and a belief that we can control nature as if it were separate from us.

Schwaller de Lubicz reminds us that there are two distinct traditions of knowledge. On the one hand, there is Aristotelian logic, which is deductive and scientific and which focuses on form rather than on content. On the other hand, there is Pythagorean philosophy, which synthesizes perceptions of form into an overriding unity of content. Pythagoras derived his philosophy of the spiritual meanings of numbers while studying with the priests of Egypt. Schwaller de Lubicz points out that, throughout the history of Western thinking, there is this split between the Pythagorean and the Aristotelian, only the split goes back further, to Khemt versus Babylon. Contemporary society is the inheritor of Babel. But right along with it runs the line that starts with the Pharaohs, and [their] mentality is opposite.[9]

Rather than move into a rapidly written cursive and abstract language, as the Sumerians and Babylonians did through the use of cuneiform script, the ancient Egyptians retained two systems of writing. The daily cursive scripts were used chiefly by scribes in business and administration. These scripts were first in hieratic, a cursive form of hieroglyphs that developed as early as 2700 B.C., and then in demotic, similar to the modern stenographer's shorthand, which developed later. The hieroglyph, however, remained the primary vehicle of transmission of the wisdom texts through the priesthood. This symbolic language remained intact from the beginning of Egyptian civilization to its end. For the ancient Egyptians, a writing system handed to them by the gods themselves was too sacred to truncate into abstraction.

Hieroglyphic Sound

Ancient Egyptians exhibited a very sophisticated form of hieroglyphic thinking and writing. For them, words created a vibratory field that evoked and generated an identity with whoever or whatever was being spoken to or spoken about. We know that in the ancient Egyptian temple the human voice was used to summon archetypal realities. It was the instrument par excellence of the priest and the enchanter, and there was both great art and great science in the careful and specific use of tones, each of which had a particular force. Of special sanctity were the breathy vowel sounds, the combinations of which were the sacred names of the gods escaping the lips.

Because of the potency of these sounds that were said to have been uttered at the creation of the world, the ancient Egyptian hieroglyphs, as in ancient Hebrew, indicated only consonants and not vowels. To understand the important connection that sound played in pronouncing the sacred names of God worldwide, one need only compare the name of the Hebrew god Yahweh (or Iaooua) with the ancient Egyptian name of the goddess Auset, whom we call Isis (Iaaw).[10]

In his study of sound, entitled *Eurythmy as Visible Speech*, the Austrian mystic Rudolf Steiner proposed that consonants intimated the sound of external event, while the vowel imitated the sound of the inner experience of event. In other words, consonants exist in the temporal realm, while vowels exist in the durative realm. He also noted that the sound of the letter *h* exhibited decidedly both consonantal and vowel sounds, or inner and outer realities.[11]

A similar teaching is found in the Vedic traditions of India that speak of the "inspirational breath." It is no surprise to discover that the Egyptian god who created the world by means of speaking the inner and outer realities is named Ptah (explosive *p*, with an aspirated *h* sound). The sounds of words, therefore, were as important as their meanings, as was also the case with ancient Hebrew, Sanskrit, high Javanese, and old Chinese; indeed, sound and meaning were inextricably linked.

Recent years have seen some corroboration of this vibratory power, especially in the work of Dr. Hans Jenny, a Swiss physicist specializing in the study of wave forms, a field he has named cymatics. Dr. Jenny has demonstrated the effect of different sounds on physical matter, from violin playing to electronically amplified tones that produce changing rhythmic patterns in sand according to harmonic proportions. Jenny experimented with many different materials and sounds, and was actually able to show patterns of evolutionary design emerging from an ascending scale.

In Jenny's movie *Cymatics*, one sees and hears a violin being played, or whatever is making the sound, then watches in astonishment as tiny particles move around and form ever more complex organizations in direct response to the sound waves. In the same film Dr. Jenny demonstrates the remarkable effect of the human voice on pattern. With the tonoscope, an instrument he invented, one can watch sound being converted into image. In one particular scene, the classical Sanskrit sound of *om* is produced over iron filings, which begin to move and waver until they form the Sanskrit glyph for *om*. This is not as strange as it may seem, for certain sacred glyphs in Sanskrit, Hebrew, and high Javanese are said to be rendered from the sounds forming themselves on substance. In certain spiritual practices one contemplates the glyph while making the sound.

This connection between sound and meaning, form and content, is not practiced in most people's daily speech. It retains its resonance, however, for poets who view the craft of language as the ancients did—as a sacred task. The poet Octavio Paz reiterates this in *The Bow and the Lyre* when he says, "The poem is a shell that echoes the music of the world, and meters and rhymes are merely correspondences, echoes, of the universal harmony."[12]

This tradition of sound and form reached its highest sophistication in ancient Egyptian for, as Egyptologist John Anthony West has observed,

Egyptian was a language in which images contained profound clues to the cosmic meaning of each letter, and this meaning was undoubtedly amplified by the sound of the letter itself. Words were compounded of these letters in a manner incorporating and amplifying the meaning of the individual letters, so that the meaning of a word emerged from the interplay of letters, just like the meaning of a chord or a musical phrase results from the combination of notes.[13]

Hieroglyphic Sounding, Writing, Thinking

The argument that troubled and baffled translators for two thousand years as to whether the hieroglyphs were phonetic or symbolic—that is, whether they were sounds or pictures—wouldn't have caused an ancient Egyptian any consternation at all. Of course they were both images and sounds. For the ancient Egyptian, life was seldom viewed as this *or* that, but often this *and* that. With nearly six hundred glyphs to choose from in their alphabet, as opposed to our meager twenty-six, they could pick which glyphs provided both the image and the sound necessary to a word's meaning.

Let us look, for example, at the Egyptian word *heka*, which means "words of power," what we might think of as incantation or the magic of the chant. It begins with that same aspirated *h* sound found in the name of the god Ptah, a sound poised between the inner and outer world, between durative and temporal time. The long *ahh* sound at its conclusion brings us to the sound of wonder itself, "Ahh!" It is the same word the ancient Egyptians exclaimed when gazing upon the brilliant light of stars that were themselves the bodies of gods. *Heka* is the magic of creation.

The glyph for *heka* (𓏤 𓂝 𓏛) appears to us as the signs for a twist of fiber, two arms uplifted, and a rolled papyrus tied with a string. The twisted fiber recalls the dance of the intellect, the act of thought intertwining. We recall the serpent image as the snaking action of the brain pattern. Then we see the glyph for spirit, the *ka*, with arms open in supplication and reception of divine blessing. *Ka* provides the essence of inspiration. The rolled and tied papyrus represents the sacred word ready to be disclosed. The dance of the intellect and the spiritual state of mind result in the words of power. We see, then, how the word operates in a multidimensional realm, incorporating sound and image, and providing a metaphysical treatise on the act of creation itself.

The ancient Egyptian language was constructed very differently from ours. It contained an enormous number of word plays, puns, anagrams. The names for things often contained clues to their meaning and interrelatedness. The biblical story of the pharaoh's daughter naming the infant she found Moses, "because she drew him from the Nile," has further meaning when we understand that *mose* in ancient Egyptian meant "child," but the similar-sounding word *moshe* meant "crocodile." The children of ancient Egypt were often dedicated to a particular neter and named as the "child of" that deity. For example, Thutmose, the name of several famous Nineteenth Dynasty pharaohs, meant "child of Thoth." Ramose, or Rameses, as we call him, meant "child of Ra." The child drawn from the water is simply *mose*, or "child," but the word is similar in sound to the ancient word *moshe*. In a way, he becomes the "child of the crocodile." The princess's pun takes on near prophetic resonance when we view Moses as both the end of an era (the crocodile) and the beginning of a new one (the child).

The ancient texts are full of double meanings and hidden clues. The name of the lion, for example, was *ra-ra*, an onomatopoeic word in imitation of the sound of a lion's roar. Is it any wonder, then, that we often find the sun god Ra appearing as a lion, or that the lion that runs beside the chariot of the pharaoh Rameses II is a direct sign that Rameses (Ramose) is the son of the sun god Ra and the lion-headed goddess Sekhmet?

The anagram was a favorite Egyptian expression of the dual nature of the world. For example, *ais* (☞ 𓀀 𓃾 ☜) is the word for the physical mass of brain tissue. *Sia* (☜ 𓃾 𓀀 ☞), which is *ais* spelled backward, is the word for consciousness. The difference is that *ais* is merely intellectual ability, which in itself is of less value than *sia*, the wisdom that applies the talents of the mind. In these examples we see that the language embodies both the connection and the distinction and graphically suggests the cosmic principle of inversion—the calling forth of matter out of spirit and spirit out of matter.

Other examples noted by John Anthony West are:[14]

akh = spirit	*kha* = corpse
akhakh = to grow green	*khakha* = to storm
ben = negation or "it is not," "there is not"	*neb* = gold, lord, master, owner, all, every

Hieroglyph as Total Meaning

The pictorial aspect of the hieroglyph contains total meaning. The hieroglyph of the giraffe, for example, means "to foretell," because the long neck of the giraffe allowed it to see farther into the distance. The picture of a wall falling down carries the message of something being overthrown, and the hieroglyph for a jackal means "to digest."

In modern Western languages writing is used in an abstract, linear fashion. If we read the word "jackal," for instance, the mind conveys memorized sound and visual associations. Hieroglyphic writing and thinking works in a circular fashion. The hieroglyphic image—jackal—is there before our eyes and can expand, evoking within the prepared viewer a whole complex of qualities and associations from abstract, intuitive notions or states of being to relationships and understandings that cannot be defined but must be experienced on many levels.

A jackal, for example, buries its kill until the natural elements have digested it. It knows the right moment to dig up the carrion and finish the eating and digestive process itself. The jackal-headed god Anubis was not only the neter for the human digestive system, but also the one who knew just the right moment to lead the newly dead person before Osiris and the forty-two Assessors, who test the spirit for worthiness to enter the Immortal Realms. Jackal thus represented readiness, timing, preparation, digestion, and immortality: these are some of the images and knowings that would be evoked in the mind of an ancient Egyptian when seeing the hieroglyph for the jackal.

One of the most important of all hieroglyphs is the scarab. The word in Egyptian is *kheper* (🪲), and it represents the scarab, or dung beetle. It also contains the idea of the stages of growth that the insect undergoes—egg, larva, nymph—so that the word represented the idea of metamorphosis and transformation, that is, the idea of becoming in all of its possible verbal forms. The word is the entity embodied in the new sun as it rises in the morning.

The dung beetle has the astonishing habit of laying its eggs in cow dung, then rolling the dung along until it forms a hardened ball. This unusual egg case is buried, then unearthed later, whereupon the ball cracks open in the hot sun and the winged children fly forth. The transformation of life from something as vulgar as a ball of dung speaks worlds about our own notions of what is sacred and profane. But to the universal mind of God all matter is holy.

The reader might enjoy reciting from an ancient Egyptian creation document to get some sense of a theology of creation based on highly expressive sounds and resonant fields of meaning:

> *Kheper-i kheperu kheper-kuie em kheperu*
> *en kheperi kheper em sep tepi.*

This translates as the Creator God saying:

> When I became, the becoming became. I have become in becoming the form of Kheperi, who came into being on the First Time.

For us, this is very abstract theology, but for the ancient Egyptians it was a series of very powerful images, a resounding of images of the understanding of the heart that unfolds in the listener. For the Egyptians, the seat of intelligence was thought to be in the heart.

Sonically, the repetition of the variations on the sound *kheperi* for being and becoming acts as a kind of drumbeat that lulls the conscious mind, allowing the individual to fall into a near-trance state where the message can enter through *sia* (the wisdom) rather than through *ais* (the brain alone). Recall the kind of trancelike sounds of Edgar Allan Poe's work, where, for example, in the poem "Annabel

Lee" we are immersed in the repetitive rushing in of the tide through such sentences as

> I was a child and she was a child in my kingdom
>   by the sea
> And we loved with a love that was more than love
> I and my Annabel Lee.[15]

To return to our ancient Egyptian incantation of becoming, the image of the dung beetle appearing again and again in this line works symbolically to give us the ability to see in all of nature, throughout each day and at all times, the transformative power of life. The scarab elevates the base material of life (the dung ball) and through her diligent efforts transforms it into the spiritual essence of the sun. Thus the symbolic image enters into the reader's and listener's consciousness like a musical tone, which then resonates with the inner meaning, calling forth a creative partnership with many more levels of thought than alphabetic writing allows.

Ancient Hebrew is grounded in the same thought processes. According to the kabbalah (the Hebrew mystical tradition of the revelation of words), the opening passages of Genesis have a similar quality of compact richness and depth of meaning. The first word of the opening passage can be broken down into a sentence, which itself is an extraordinary document of many teachings, that standard translations do not render. Thus what most translations show as "In the beginning, God created . . . ," in kabbalah could be rendered as "Patterns of creation by the Elohim." By adding the deeper meanings of each letter of the word *Elohim* (aleph—lammed—hay—yod—mem), the text would read: "Patterns of creation by the Immeasurable Potencies or Potentiators channeling life into the containment of the biosphere!"

Or, as I have said in one of my more whimsical lectures, this opening line of Genesis appears to be a graduate course listing in the Godschool catalog *Creation 101: How to Create a Planet and Its Life Forms.* Again, using the kabbalistic key, the next two chapters of Genesis can be seen as an extraordinary presentation of the nature and practice of the creative process.

Hieroglyphic Thought as Incarnation

As mentioned earlier, alphabetic writing provides a distancing from creation so that one can control and order things. Hieroglyphic writing and thinking, on the other hand, cause one to incarnate, to actually become deeply the things about which one is speaking and thinking. Alphabetic writing distances; hieroglyphic writing incarnates.

With so many more associations circulating in each image, the symbol gives to the prepared consciousness a flexibility and brilliance that we may not normally display. But as we read hieroglyphically, we feel each line quickening and stimulating our dendritic associations and brain growth.

The Egyptian consciousness may have floated within this style of knowledge in much the way that some marine biologists believe that dolphins do. Cetaceans communicate by emitting hieroglyphs in sound—patterns of sonar whistles and beeps that re-create the characteristics of the thing being described. With a smooth and streamlined body in an open sea, and having no hand for grasping things, the genius of the dolphin is naturally not going to be put to mastering and manipulating its environment. Rather, it seems to evoke games and high play, with very complex social interactions in a sea of music that some think affects the actual shape of the surrounding ocean topography.

After many experiences swimming with dolphins, I believe there is no question that human moods and attitudes are positively affected by being "pulsed" and "sonared" by dolphin companions. It feels as if one is being "pulsed" into one's optimum state of mind. In addition to the high game, what philosophies and metaphysical speculations the hieroglyphic sonar mind of the dolphin might imagine, only the neters know.

Schwaller de Lubicz wrote about hieroglyphic thought in a way that could also pertain to dolphins:

> The aim is no longer to translate things into sensory terms, but to put ourselves into the state "magically" identical with the symbol-object, so as to become heavy with the quality of weight, to become red with the quality of redness, to burn with the quality of fire.[16]

If you do that when you read—become red with the quality of redness, burn with the quality of fire—your memory will vastly improve. Short-term electrical memory will shift very quickly into long-term chemical, highly associative memory.

Our normal mode of writing is analytic. We reduce the abstraction of letters to a defined image, which then builds on associations of disconnected facts. But the ancient Egyptian form was analogical. It both expanded the image into far-reaching associations and then inwardly unified the associations—as seen, for example, in the jackal image. Analytic thinking is reductive; it asks how things differ. Analogical thinking is inclusive; it asks how one thing links with another.

Perhaps the greatest talent of Schwaller de Lubicz was his ability to think both analytically and analogically, that is, scientifically and intuitively. But it was his analogical thinking that prepared him for his journey to and ultimate work in Egypt. In some way, when he gazed upon the windows and architecture of the cathedral of Chartres, he was preparing himself to study the hieroglyphs. The alchemical formulas he found in that Gothic church taught him what the architects of the cathedral knew and what the scribes of ancient Egypt's hieroglyphs knew, which is simply this: "God exists in the details."[17]

Toward a New Translation of Hieroglyphs

We must also remember that not all hieroglyphs were clear depictions of a particular species of animal, or even of the way the natural world appeared. The puns of Egypt were not limited to sounds and words; they also included images. Thus one finds on the wall of the Temple of Luxor the image of a sacred cow sprouting a human head. The cow's horns have transformed themselves into human arms uplifted in the *ka* position of prayer. Cattle were long considered sacred animals wherein the spirit of a god or a goddess might reside. At the same time, the holy cow was offered as a sacrifice to the divine being. The intertwined human/animal image on the wall of the Temple of Luxor seems to suggest that we, too, are receptacles for the spirit of the divine. Like the sacrificed cow, we die but are returned in spirit to the welcoming, open arms of the great neters beyond.

Often a single image was made up of a collection of parts drawn from various species—the head of a lioness with the body of a woman, for example, referring to tenderness and healing with the capacity for ferocity. This is the image of Sekhmet, the goddess of creative healing, magic, and justified rage. In this way the hieroglyphic symbol could depict with remarkable fluidity many subtle combinations and interchanges occurring between nature and reality.

One can appreciate the enormous difficulties analytic, alphabetic minds have in translating analogical, hieroglyphic texts. Word-for-word translations of a symbolic language are impossible. That is why many modern texts of sacred Egyptian literature sound like so much gobbledygook. For example:

ī - ná	*āa*	*er*	*maa*	*neteru*	*āāaiu*	*ānχ - á*	*em*
I have come	advancing	to	see	the gods	great,	and I live	upon

ḥetepet	*ámu*	*kau - sen*	*un - ná*	*er*	*t'eru*	*ba*	*neb*
the offerings	which eat	their doubles.	I have been	to	the borders of	the Ram,	lord of

Teṭteṭ	*tā - f*	*per - á*	*em*	*bennu*	*er*	*t'eṭet - á*
Tattu.	He granted	that I might come forth	as	a *bennu* bird,	that	I might speak·

un - ná	*em*	*átru*	*uṭen - á*	*em*	*neter sentrá*
I have been	in	the water of the river.	I have made offerings	with	incense.

He cannot be sculpted in stone; in the images on which men place crowns and uraei he is not made manifest; service cannot be rendered nor offerings made ·to him; not can he be drawn in his form of mystery; not is known the place where he is; not is he found in the painted shrine.[18]

These lines taken from the Book of the Dead (Papyrus of Ani) were translated by E. A. Wallis Budge, the former curator of antiquities of the British Museum. Budge was a fine compiler of data—through his scrupulous efforts we have an abundance of factual material on ancient Egypt. But he was not able to think hieroglyphically. His translations cannot convey the power of the true meaning of the sentences in the ancient language. We must look again at the images and sounds.

Un-na, which Budge translates as simply "I," refers to "the good being," related to the name of Osiris in his underworld manifestation—Unnefer. The *un-na* refers not to temporal being but to eternal being, to unity and oneness. It is possible that the name Unnefer, meaning "the beauty of the united oneness," also relates to the word "universe" (Latin, *unifers*): "the many parts combined into the whole." Consider that Osiris is dismembered into parts and is then reunited to himself in the underworld, where he creates a new world order, a universe. Consider, too, that Osiris unifies the sacred and the secular—the resonance between universe and Unnefer may not be accidental.

Returning to our retranslation of the text, the good and eternal being has journeyed to the edges of the road where matter and spirit are found together. In this place on the path of initiation and enlightenment the good being experiences his *ba* (ram), or soul nature. This ram glyph would remind an ancient Egyptian of the god Amun, the neter of hidden potentialities who also appears in a ram form. The soul that the good being experiences, then, is all of his possible selves, his own hidden manifestations.

Now he comes forth from the house. While the word *per-ah* means "to come forth," *per-ah* is also a homophone meaning "the pharaoh." At last having seen his eternal nature, he is liberated from the body; in other words, he becomes a shining being, free in flight, as boundless as a bird that flies through the sky, resurrected as the *bennu*, the phoenix, the reborn sun. He has entered his own god nature. Literally, the text does not say "I must speak," but rather "I speak." It may imply that the good being now has the words of power, the *heka*. This means that he can travel to inner and outer realms, that he now lives in both the durative and the temporal, that he is an eternally resurrecting being, like the phoenix. His words of power are the magic of his transformation, the text itself, the journey of which he speaks.

Next, the good being has immersed himself in the purified waters, a symbol of having "come clean" before his god. Like Osiris cast into the Nile, the good being has gone all the way from death in nothingness into the primordial chaos of new creation. In other words, the speaker of this text has died, gone to the other world, met his soul, seen himself reborn, and is coming back to tell us what it was like. This meditation differs wildly from the one Budge offered.

Given what we now know about the text and what we know about the combination of imagery, sound, symbol, and meaning, a new translation using hieroglyphic thinking would not resemble Budge's. It would, like the ancient text, work through images, poetry, sound, and mythic allusion to describe a man's thoughts as he travels through the land of the dead. It would evoke an emotional understanding even deeper and more powerful than the intellectual and discursive one presented in the previous analysis. Consider this variant translation by Normandi Ellis from *Awakening Osiris*:

I stand before the mirror looking back in time. I was born a man. Before that I was a god. I was with you when time began. I have not denied you. To do so would be to deny myself. Because I delight in fresh bread, the smell of clover, and the thighs of women, I live; therefore, you live with me. We are the same—more than brothers. We are one heart, one fire—a shining hawk suspended between heaven and earth, its wings aflame.

I was a man of Egypt, born of woman on a sheet of linen in a green valley rent by a river between two worlds of sand. I was earth in the hands of the potter who gathered me, who molded me in fire and air, who made me a child and gave me to my mother, a poor woman and a goddess. She suckled me, gave me the power of words. . . .

I was a man of Egypt going to the river often to behold the gods who dwell in the rushes, who dwell in frogs and in the heron. In my hands I held the divinity of colored stones, and in time I learned to handle the delicate hearts of men. . . . I burned incense in the temples, but offered only myself for nothing else was mine to give.[19]

Modern translators are doing their work with great literalness, but the result is that a high culture of multidimensional meanings is made to sound like necrophilic nursery rhymes. As one insightful commentator, Bika Reed, has shown, many translations could be compared to what would be understood of Shakespeare if, after many thousands of years, a linguistic archaeologist uncovered a torn fragment of *Hamlet*:[20]

KING: Now, Hamlet, where is Polonius?
HAMLET: At supper.
KING: At supper? Where?
HAMLET: Not where he eats, but where he is eaten; a certain convocation of politic worms are e'en at him. Your worm is your only emperor for diet; we fat all creatures else to fat us, and we fat ourselves for maggots; your fat king and your lean beggar is but variable service; two dishes, but one table; that's the end.

The archaeologist, Reed says, using a magnifying glass to read the moldy leaf, would carefully examine the text and compose an article on it for the scientific Ancient British Excavation Society. Entitled "The Gastronomic Habits of the Ancient British," the paper would give evidence for the following conclusions:

> The ancient British considered maggots as their main food. It must have been a long-extinct variety (*Maggot comestibus*) unknown today. The flesh of the maggots was highly esteemed, for even the king ate it, as indicated in line five. The text, though obscure and corroded, leaves no doubt that social distinctions were clearly demarcated by size: to be fat was clearly both an honor and a social advantage, while to be lean was the stigma of beggary and low birth. Eating maggots was so important that all state functions were concluded by this gastronomic event.

Modern Hieroglyphic Thinking

One of the things that Schwaller de Lubicz demonstrated so brilliantly is the profound difference between our material thought and what we might call our soul thought or hieroglyphic thought. In hieroglyphic thought many disciplines and knowings converge in a synergistic way. The expression of this synthesis of art, science, religion, and architecture is reduced to its crystalline form in the hieroglyph, and as such the hieroglyph imposes pattern upon pattern upon pattern of thought and meaning upon meaning upon meaning, with all forms and persona inherent in it. It is a seed crystal that, if dropped into the supersaturated solution of time and space, will require volumes to express its meaning. But if it is dropped into the human brain, the hieroglyph creates a tremendous resonance of activity, associations, brain growth, and dendritic and chemical growth, thus providing the connections that allow us to receive the unfolding of essence.

"Form," as the poet Robert Creeley has said, "is no more than an extension of content."[21] Thus the form is determined by what is placed in it. Form and shape are charged with the capacity to receive the unfolding patterns of creation itself. Our lives flow from our patterns of thought, and our spiritual longings affect our thought forms. By consciously shaping our lives through spiritual attunement, by viewing the multidimensional viewing of depth realities, by thinking hieroglyphically, analogically, and symbolically in charged multipatterns with webs of meaning, we can begin to create changes in our own forms—in our bodies and our minds. Thus we approach the *enantiadromia*, "the big turnaround" that leads to a higher and deeper culture for us all.

With the enormous growth in complex coherent realms of knowledge, I suspect that we are again on the verge of hieroglyphic thinking.

A modern example is the writing technique of James Joyce. In *Ulysses* a Jewish Dubliner, while purportedly thinking of his son, simultaneously experiences a compass of visions containing zoology, Babylonian astrology, Gnosticism, and cosmology—a natural process of the hieroglyphic mind:

> On the highway of the clouds they come, muttering thunder of rebellion, the ghost of beasts. . . . Elk and yak, the bulls of Bashan and of Babylon, mammoth and mastodon, they come trooping to the sunken sea, *Lacus Mortis*. Ominous, revengeful zodiacal host! They moan passing upon the clouds, horned and capricorned, the trumpeted with the tusked, the lionmaned, the giant antlered, snouter and crawler, rodent, ruminant and pachyderm, all their moving multitude, murderers of the sun.
>
> Onward to the dead sea they tramp to drink, unslaked and with horrible gulpings, the salt somnolent inexhaustible flood. And the equine portent grows again, magnified in the deserted heavens, nay to heaven's own magnitude till it looms, vast, over the house of Virgo . . . the everlasting bride, harbinger of the daystar, the bride, ever virgin. . . . It floats, it flows about her starborn flesh and loose it streams emerald, sapphire, mauve and heliotrope, sustained on currents of cold interstellar wind, winding, coiling, simply swirling, writhing in the skies, a mysterious writing till after a myriad metamorphoses of symbol, it blazes, Alpha, a ruby and triangled sign upon the forehead of Taurus.[22]

The Egyptians lived closer to the depths of their intradimensional minds than we do. Indeed, by our standards their consciousness was diaphanous to its various levels. Joyce's work has proven prophetic of how the stress of living in a time and space of overload is forcing us to return to an ancient knowing in order to recover the lost art of analogical thinking. By learning to perceive hieroglyphically, we can tap the many levels of consciousness; we can accommodate ourselves to the many transformations of a lifetime. We can discover the many meanings, the sacred ambivalences. We can live simultaneously in the temporal and durative realms as we move forward into the past and pastward into the future to recover the who and what of the many strands and layers of our identity.

⚶

PROCESS 2:
Hieroglyphic Thinking

We are about to embark on a process of learning to think and write hieroglyphically. We might call this an exercise in sacred writing, for the kind of information contained in this writing is not linear and sequential; rather, it offers itself to the whole of the mind, and on many levels of knowing and understanding. This it does with a simultaneity of symbol, sound, pun, dream, myth, rhythm, philosophy, emotion, and worldview that is virtually impossible for alphabetic writing to achieve. Thus it allows for an opening of mind and feeling to levels of understanding often closed to the "normal" point of view.

Madeleine L'Engle, in her book *The Irrational Season*, posed a marvelous question that illumines the nature of the hieroglyphic mind. She wondered what the kingdom of heaven would be like. Pondering this question, she finally concluded that the kingdom of heaven would be like finding yourself on the most beautiful planet in the universe but able to perceive it with only one sense. Utilizing this one sense, say, the sense of smell, you know that this particular planet is special, and certainly aromatic, but you're literally deaf and blind to its glories, as well as being unable to touch or taste it.

Then, suddenly, not five but a million senses open up within you, and you realize that you are on this planet—the earth—and that you are now seeing it in its full glory as the kingdom of heaven. The analogy is apt, for with the tragic closure of so many of our available doors of perception through cultural conditioning and our abstraction and distancing from the reality around and within us, most of us are living behind shutters, not in the kingdom. Let us try to open a few of those shutters and see what we begin to see.

In this exercise you'll start simply and work with an ordinary image. You will then draw and learn how to see the image from many different perspectives and senses. The image will seem to look back at you, now regarding you from many different perspectives. You and the image will come to reflect each other from many different perspectives, roles, and contexts.

Next you will find and draw some of the associations the image suggests. These images and associations will begin to cluster in such a way that they quicken a whole new way of thinking and writing in you. Putting them together in a sentence, you will write hieroglyphics and hieroglyphic sentences. These may well provide you with fresh ideas as well as innovative thought patterns. Recalling that inversion of sounds and letters is critical to understanding the intricacies of the Egyptian language system, you will invert the process. The image itself will then reflect upon you in the same way that you have reflected upon it. Between the two of you, you may soon begin to see the birth of new thought.

After you have done the exercise once, I recommend that you practice it regularly. As a result, many new ways of thinking and looking at the world may begin to occur to you because of the hieroglyphic channels you are laying down in your mind. This is because hieroglyphic thought can contain many different frames of mind and styles of seeing that are normally inhibited by the conditioning we receive from culture, family, friends, schooling, and most of the circumstances in modern life. As you begin to see through and past your conditioning, multiple associations will arise and you'll start to tap into a lode of natural creativity.

What actually happens, of course, is the expansion of your whole concept of the uses of thought. You become thought; thought becomes you. Making multiple associations in different contexts results in new ways of thinking.

TIME: 60 minutes.
MATERIALS NEEDED: Unlined paper and drawing materials.
MUSIC: If desired, music from Area 1.

INSTRUCTIONS FOR THE SOLO JOURNEYER: This process lends itself to the solo journeyer. Just record the instructions and follow them. Remember to leave long pauses where appropriate. When you get to the sharing part, you may want to imagine how various people you know would respond to your hieroglyphics. You may want to show your work to several people who are close to you. You also may want to lead them through this exercise and compare results.

SCRIPT FOR THE GUIDE: I would like you to take a piece of paper and focus your attention on it. Just begin to breathe with the blankness of the paper. Just breathe easily, in and out, focusing on the blankness until a concrete image occurs to you—the image of an actual thing that exists in physical space. It could be a bird, a star, a tree, a wheel—whatever comes to you. It may seem to appear from within the paper or it may float into your mind. Whenever or however it appears, draw that image in the middle of your paper.

Very quickly draw the image so that you can view it clearly. You have about one minute to draw it, no more than that. Think of it as drawing a hieroglyph. (Allow one minute.)

After you have drawn the image, enclose it in a box or a circle, as for example in the following illustration, where my image is a bird. (The guide demonstrates something like this:)

Now, just reflect on your image, with no particular thoughts or feelings. (Allow one minute.)

Continuing to reflect on the image, see how the borders between you and the image are beginning to dissolve. Let yourself gradually become the image. Imagine yourself able to do what the image does. Thus if you have drawn a bird, sense yourself flying like a bird. If your image is a tree, feel your branches waving in the breeze. Do what the image does. Stay focused; be the image; do what the image does.

Come back to yourself and look at the image again from many points of view:

See the image from the point of view of yourself as a child, a child looking at that image . . .

Now consider it from the point of view of a dog or cat looking at that image in its concrete manifestation. For example, if the image is a bird, how does the dog or cat look at that bird?

Now look at the image as an extremely angry person would.

Now look at the image as someone who is deeply in love would look at it.

Now look at the image as a wise older person would look at the image.

Now consider it from the perspective of another version of that same image—say, another bird.

Now examine it from the perspective of the god or the neter of the image.

Now see the image under different climatic conditions:

In the midst of a storm . . .

On a hot summer day . . .

On a crisp spring morning with everything greening around it . . .

During a snowfall . . .

Draw lines coming out from the box or circle around your image that indicate other thoughts, images, or ideas that the central image suggests to you. For example, the image of a bird might call forth images or associations of worm—freedom—nest—love—soul. You may want to draw these related images or write words that seem associated with the image. Just do that for the next several minutes, noting clusters of thoughts, images, ideas, or associations suggested by the image. (Allow five minutes.) The following illustration indicates one way that this might look. (The guide draws something like the following:)

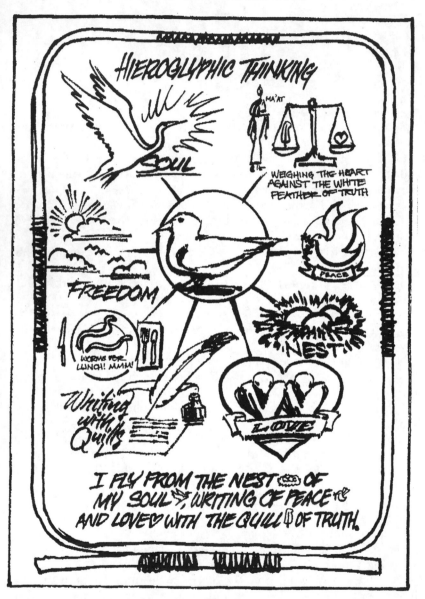

Write a sentence or several sentences using those image and thought clusters. You can express it in words, pictures, or both, the way the ancient Egyptians did, sometimes spelling things out, sometimes using pictures. You can have alphabetical sentences or all pictures, or even a combination of the two.

Your "sentence" may look like English, but it may also have parts that are not English, but hieroglyph. The symbols will be included in the sentence. But do it in a way that is meaningful, that gives a story or communicates some ideas or information or way of seeing. Let your mind have a party with these images. Be as inventive and outrageous as you like in the combinations you bring together. For example, the cluster of images around the bird could be brought together to read:

> I fly from the nest of my soul writing of peace and love with the quill of truth.

All right, begin to put it all together. (Allow five minutes.) Go back and look at the original image. Breathe into it. Breathe with that image until you find your consciousness passing into the image. If the image is a bird, become that bird on the page. Now identified with that image, say, a bird, look up at your human face. Let the bird, who is now you, look back from the page and look upon you. Egyptian thought always contains its inversion. You are the image—bird, tree, star, or whatever—reflecting on your human face and human beingness, finding it strange or wondrous or scary or whatever. Not only are you becoming the image, you are that image looking back at you. (Allow one minute.)

Now let the image regard you from many points of view:

Let the image regard you as a child version of itself. If the image is a bird, it is a baby bird in a nest looking at you . . .

Let the image be an angry version of itself looking at you . . .

Let the image be a compound version of itself looking at you . . . If it is a bird, for example, it might also have a dog's head . . .

Let the image be the lover version of itself reflecting back on you . . .

Let the image be a wise old being version of itself reflecting back on you . . .

Let the image be the neter of itself regarding you . . .

Let the image regard you under different climatic conditions, so that if it is a bird, it is the bird looking at you:

In winter snows and storms . . .

In crisp, windy autumn . . .

Under hot summer skies . . .

In budding, greening springtime . . .

Take a fresh piece of paper. Let the image make a box and draw its version of you. The image is drawing its version of you in a box in the middle of the page. It isn't you drawing you; it's the image drawing you. How would a bird draw you? (The guide draws an example, like the following:)

(Allow one to two minutes.)

After you have done that, let the image allow itself various thought boxes to cluster around you with various drawings or words for ideas or associations that the image has about you. The image is thinking about you in images. If it is a bird, what are the bird's associations regarding you? Draw these as clusters of words or images, as in the following manner. (The guide demonstrates with something like the following:)

Now you do it. (Allow three to five minutes.)

As you did before with your human self regarding the image and forming a sentence or sentences out of the multiple associations, do the same with the image. The image self will bring its cluster of associations together in sentences that can be put together in pictures or in words or in a combination of both. So now, the image is writing its own brand of hieroglyphics. Following our example, then, the image might decide to write something like the following:

With holding wings and speaking beak I hatch ideas from my flying imagination.

Let the image self write the sentences. (Allow five minutes.)

Once you have done this, compare the two hieroglyphic thoughts that you have just written, one being you reflecting on the image and the other being the image reflecting on you. You thought hieroglyphically about the image, and the image self thought hieroglyphically about you. This excursion into the analogical processes of hieroglyphic thought, and the kinds of meanings that are revealed, is perhaps different from your usual kinds of writing or thinking about things. (Allow two minutes.)

If you choose to do so, join in groups of three: to appreciate fully the vast range of form hieroglyphic thinking allows, it is helpful to get the input of others. Share with one another the. variety of images and sentences that you have produced. If you prefer to remain absorbed in your own process instead, feel free to do so. We will have five minutes to reflect by ourselves or with each other. (Allow five to ten minutes.)

♠

JOURNAL PROCESS

Use the hieroglyphic clustering technique around an idea drawn symbolically. Follow the process given above to create hieroglyphic sentences. Do the same with an event drawn from your life, then an event from history, then around a person living or dead. Always remember to treat the subject of the process symbolically. You might try to use this hieroglyphic technique around the following: God. Earth. Me. Then, regardless of what series of images you have used, take the sentences you have come up with and put them all together into a more complex or elaborate paragraph of ideas and feelings.

Today you are not writing in your journal. Words will not come. Instead, pick up a pack of magic markers and draw, doodle, sketch out emotions, abstractions, images. Take a walk and pretend that each thing you see on your way is a word and begin to think about it as a cluster of thoughts, emotions, images, phrases. Find one particular tree or leaf and have a hieroglyphic conversation with it.

The Metternich Stela (Obverse).

6

Neters: Agents of Creation

The human heart can go the lengths of God.
from A *Sleep of Prisoners*
by Christopher Fry

We think about Egypt. We are drawn into Egypt. Egypt is farmed in our souls. During all my years of working with the imagery of the inner life, the emblems and attributes of Egypt recur again and again. In dreams and reveries, the symbols of Egypt rise to the inner vision: we see scarabs and ankhs, winged disks of the Sun. We long for our pilgrimage to the foot of the Sphinx, as if it could speak our deepest knowing. We imagine ourselves inside the Great Pyramid, dying each night and rebirthing ourselves with the sun. We recognize and relish the images of pharaonic masks and animal-headed gods that reside in every major museum throughout the world.

We close our eyes on a summer day and perceive the eye of Ra always looking, watching, loving. We imagine vividly that eternally green oasis of the Nile valley, split by the life-giving blue river. Egypt seizes the Western psyche, and we feel a collective shock of recognition. She seems to promise, "Travel where you may, do whatever you must; you will never forget me."

Imagine a myth so vast, so deep, so rich and multilayered that it would take a lifetime to discover the length and breadth of it. The record of the world's spiritual yearning is carved into the body in the way the Nile carves itself into the rock bed of Egypt. Within our bodies the sacred rivers run in gently moving streams, then surge forth in powerful torrents. Within our eyes dwell the light of the sun and the moon; behind the eyes, the greater, hidden illuminations. Within the chakras, those magic circles of power held in the body—the crown of the head, the forehead, the throat, the heart, the solar plexus, the pelvis, the base of the spine—unfold all the teachings of the sacred temples.

Indeed, when we stand at the base of the Great Pyramid, the immense size and age of the structure overwhelm us as we gaze backward through nearly five thousand years of history to the last of the Seven Wonders of the World. Throughout history the eternal and persistent images of Egypt's ancient gods and sacred sites have touched humankind to the core, moving them to speak in tones of reverence. On the Giza plateau Napoleon, humbled by the immensity of all he saw, addressed his entourage of soldiers, scholars, and artists, saying, "From the summit of yonder pyramids, forty centuries look down upon you."[1] Likewise, Jean-François Champollion, the translator of the hieroglyphs, expressed the depth of the ancient mind when he said, "The Egyptians of old thought like men a hundred feet tall. By comparison, we in Europe are but Lilliputians."[2]

Part of ancient Egypt's power to enthrall lies in a great paradoxical mystery. How did it happen that, somewhere between 3100 and 2600 B.C., an aboriginal people on the banks of a swampy delta recovered the land and invented an agronomy that has lasted for five thousand years? What leaps of imagination caused them to discover many of the fine points of astronomy, architecture, medicine, mathematics, and literature? What infusion of wisdom, intuition, or intelligence conceived the enormity of pyramids, their eternal presence, and also created the delicate balance of *ma'at*, a system of governance and law based on principles of cosmic truth? What priests or kings divined in their hearts a consummate theology and symbology, an enormously artful and enduring culture, and a written language based on hieroglyphs? How could it be that in so short a time the Egyptian people's bodies, minds, and souls entered into a congruence that quickened a surge of creativity that has not been seen since?

The Neter as the God in Nature

Of the forces contributing to the intense and complex growth of ancient Egyptian civilization, one of the most vital was the notion of the living gods, or the concept of neters. Egyptian gods and goddesses are the divine impulses that reveal themselves in the natural world and in the body. The neters of Egypt are the rock bed of our first spiritual longing. If we trace the Egyptian word *neter* through the Coptic and Greek, we arrive at the root form of our word "nature." Male or female, the neters revealed their divinity through nature, and divine nature was present in all things—animals, plants, moving water, the heavens, the earth.

The universe was alive from end to end. Rocks were stable; the heat was debilitating; the desert was deadly; trees were rare, vital, and wondrously refreshing; cows were nurturing; snakes were dangerous but powerful. Divine power confronted men and women wherever they turned. Many, many neters inhabited the animal, vegetable, and mineral world of Egypt.

The neters are drawn from the creative images of the land itself. Imagine the enormous length and power of the Nile arising in the southern mountains. Its source may have been unknown to the ancients, but it was abundant, overflowing with water; and it dug itself into divergent channels that spread out, becoming individual streams that formed the green growth of the delta and sustained life. The overflow returned to the Great Green, the Mediterranean, the cosmic primordial waters. Those diversified channels stem from the one true Nile, the great flood of abundant divine energy. Imagine those channels being the many neters, but with one divine power flowing through them all. That image of the simultaneous unity and diversification of nature lies at the core of Egyptian religion.

One of the most popular Egyptian deities was the goddess Isis, whose cult arose early during prehistoric culture. By A.D. 300, her temples appeared not only in Egypt, but also in Greece and throughout the Roman Empire, even in the British Isles. All the powers of the gods and goddesses before her were manifested in her form. In Apuleius's *The Golden Ass* she appears to her servant Lucius and reveals to him what it means to be a goddess (or a god):

> I am Nature, the universal mother, mistress of all the elements, primordial child of time, sovereign of all things spiritual, queen of the dead, queen also of the immortals, the single manifestation of all gods and goddesses that are. My nod governs the shining heights of heaven, the wholesome sea breezes, the lamentable silences of the world below. Though I am worshiped in many aspects, known by countless names, and propitiated with all manner of different rites, yet the whole round earth venerates me.[3]

Neter as Archetype

The neters operate on a psychological level, as well as on a spiritual level; that is, they are not only the creators of patterns but the holders of patterns, the embodiment of an ancient consciousness. In his memoirs Carl Jung recalled his journey from Khartoum down the Nile and his encounter with the dog-faced baboons of Abu Simbel. It was there, in Rameses' temple, that the solar myth of Horus returned to him in full force. "It is a myth," Jung wrote, "which must have been told after human culture—that is, consciousness—had for the first time released men from the darkness of prehistoric times. Thus the journey from the heart of Africa to Egypt became, for me, a kind of drama of the birth of light. That drama was intimately connected with me, with my psychology."[4]

Known from the earliest times, then, the neters resembled what we could call gods, but they are diversified gods, each with a specific function. They served as dynamic archetypes and motivating principles to which the Egyptians consciously attuned themselves. Neters presented themselves symbolically in animal and human forms, as well as with a combination of animal and human features. Their diverse outward appearances were not arbitrary fantasies, but symbols based on careful consideration, deep meditation, and meticulous observation of the nature of reality.

Although we cannot know the neters in a deep way until we have meditated on them to the point at which they hold a charged space within us, we can nevertheless accustom ourselves to thinking of them in relation to our emotional and intellectual responses to their symbols. For example, when we observe the snake, what do we associate with snakeness? Perhaps its ability to shed its skin, its ability to coil back on itself, its rearing strike and poisonous bite, its consumption of its prey whole, its intimate knowing of the earth through its belly. Then we might begin to understand the powers of the gods and goddesses who appear to us as snakes. The goddess Renenutet partakes of the snake's ability to shed its skin, to be reborn, and so she manifests as a snake goddess of birth. The goddess Wadjet manifests as the rearing, striking cobra, and thus becomes the goddess who protected the king. The god Apophis partakes of the snake's voracious appetite, and he appears as the god of darkness, intent on devouring the sun.

The Appearance of Neters

When appearing entirely as animals—like Sobek, the crocodile god of the Nile, or Kheperi, the sacred beetle of transformation—the neters illustrate the principles of organic life on Earth. These animal neters might embody birth, fecundity, decay, and regeneration. When shown in human form with an animal head—like Thoth, the god of wisdom, depicted with the head of an ibis, or Sekhmet, the goddess of magic, depicted with the head of a lion—they symbolize a function of activity within the human sphere.

These anthropomorphic neters might embody wisdom, instinct, or strength. Whenever they are shown entirely in human form they represent the transcendent gods who command creation itself, such as Amun, as the hidden, unmanifest god; Atum, as the great nothing from which everything sprang; or Ptah, as the author of the world through the Word. Human/divine forces also appear in the shape of such neters as Isis, the ultimate female or creative matrix, and Osiris, the ultimate male or vivifying principle.

Ancient symbology also reveals the precise role of the neters. By their dress we understand their roles in mythic life, whether they appear in the animal skins of the high priest or priestess, in the war kilt of the pharaoh, in the close body wrapping of the mummy, or in the breast-revealing dresses of the divine mother. By their crowns we recognize their spiritual manifestations, whether they wear the hieroglyphic signs of their names, the symbolic images of their associated animals, the festival crowns and war crowns of Upper and Lower Egypt, or the feathers emblematic of the sky deities.

The symbolic equipment they hold in their hands gives us the image of their earthly power. The flail appears as the symbol of authority; the crook, as the symbol of the shepherd caretaker; the crossed arrows, as the emblem of the warrior; the *waz* scepter, with its forked base and jackal-headed knob, as the sign of dominion. The ankh is seen as an image of the knot of life; it symbolizes the life-giving force of creative power. The multibeaded *menat* necklace, with its phallic counterpoise that hangs down the back, symbolizes fertility and happiness. Through color, position, size, and gesture, other symbols associated with each neter provide information that is at once physical, psychological, and spiritual. These symbols are never static but always in action, illuminating a living process.

The divine attributes of neters are present and active in human life: the human being always contains the potential to be raised to the gods. Thus neters serve as evolutionary principles of reality, engendering a higher development by functioning on a psycho-spiritual level in much the same way as DNA functions on an organic level. At any moment the possibility exists for us to make the next leap to a higher level of spiritual understanding and creative fulfillment. In essence, we are made of cosmic dust, of wavering particles of light, of the great, expansive, creative "Ahhh!" We are the latest product of the metabolism of the galaxy. We are the substance of gods. We are made from the body of gods, all the bits of humanity moving like atoms in the body of the divine. As the ancients said, "The divine mother of the universe [Nut] has many souls."

Neter as Science

For the ancient Egyptians, life was a dynamic interaction between essence and existence, between theocentric reality (divine-centered) and anthropocentric reality (human-centered). Man was a model of the universe, and the universe was a model of god. When he understood himself fully, he could also understand the universe: its laws of astronomy, astrology, proportion, mathematics, geography, measure, medicine, anatomy, rhythm, magic, art. All were linked in one dynamic scheme. One part could not be understood if separated from any other part.

Anthropocentric thinking and theocentric thinking were not opposed to each other at all, but formed an essential bridge as a way of understanding the relationship of the self to the divine. As the German poet Rainer Maria Rilke said, "Take your practiced powers and stretch them out until they span the chasm between two contradictions. . . . For the god wants to know himself in you."⁵ This acceptance and application of the dual principles operating in the cosmos create the tension and energy necessary to project us toward great leaps of culture and development. The merger of human and "netered" knowing, a psychology unique to the Egyptians, helped to create in a brief period, and literally from the mud, a complex and brilliant civilization.

We come to understand the dynamic vibration and effect of the creative principle in all things by discovering the interrelationships of the neters. Certain avant-garde students of ancient Egypt (such as R. A. and Isha Schwaller de Lubicz, John Anthony West, and Lucie Lamy) have suggested that we may find close parallels between the dynamic interaction of neters in ancient Egyptian symbology and the similar interaction of matter and energy described in modern physics.

When we discuss the theory of spiraling black holes, or what preceded the Big Bang, for example, we can also understand the creation of the time-space continuum in relation to the Egyptian notion of divine creation. In the beginning, lying with primordial chaos (Atum) are the principles of darkness, inertia, the void, and hidden energy (the ogdoad). All of these are the precursors to the spontaneous explosion of light (the birth of Ra). In the end of days, so say the Egyptians, all of these return again to Atum, to chaos, to the swirling void, the inert, and the dark, as the circling serpent, Atum, swallows its tail.

Furthermore, these interpreters of Egyptian symbolism have claimed that certain aspects of modern physics are already implicit in ancient Egyptian understanding.⁶ West, for example, in *The Serpent in the Sky*, suggests that both modern physics and Egyptian mathematics reveal the unfolding spiral action of the Golden Section as the creative primordial principle. What the physicists discovered by observing the patterns of moving subatomic particles, the Egyptians discovered through the manipulation of numbers. (For a fuller discussion of sacred geometry, see Chapter 7, "Magic of Magic, Spirit of Spirit, Part 1.")

Neters in the Physical Body

Not only do the neters operate in the intellectual realm of mathematics and physics, but they manifest themselves as well in the level of the body; that is, the bodily functions are the functions of universal spiritual principles. The Egyptians consecrated different parts of the body to different neters according to the gods' symbolic actions.

In *The Opening of the Way* Isha Schwaller de Lubicz—wife of R. A.

Schwaller de Lubicz and a mystic in her own right—discusses the heads of the four sons of Horus (a man, a hawk, a jackal, and a baboon), which appear on the canopic jars that held the organs of the mummy.[7] For example, we might imagine that the jackal-headed god presides over the stomach's processes because the stomach breaks down or decomposes food in order to transform it into nourishment. The linking symbol is that jackals were well-known visitors of the necropolises, where bodies decomposed in the process of transforming their gross matter into spirit matter.

There were neters for every part of the body. There was a neter of the heart, usually Ma'at, the goddess of balance, justice, and truth; a neter of the hands, the ram god Khnum, who fashioned the body and soul out of clay on his potter's wheel; a neter of the tongue and lips, the god Ptah, who spoke the world into being. By bringing together a balance between divine principles in oneself, by aligning the godded heart and hands and speech, one brought health to the body and enlightenment to the spirit. This participation in highly sophisticated archetypal thinking was implemented in the practice of health, architecture, medicine, and other pragmatics of daily life. I believe it served as a key to the unleashing of the phenomenal creative energies of predynastic and Old Kingdom Egypt.

Beyond the Pagan Gods

We have a difficult time today understanding this ancient concept of gods and neters because we are still under the influence of the early Egyptologists, good Judeo-Christian souls who saw in the neters not gods, but the heads of demons and a pagan religion. They interpreted the awe and mystery of the ancient Egyptian cosmos as "quaint," "unsophisticated," and "primitive." Late-nineteenth and early-twentieth-century Egyptian scholars, such as F. M. Cornford and E. A. Wallis Budge, regarded the work of these ancients as an expression of largely irrational and mythopoeic thought that could not have been produced by "logical" people, but rather by the near-ancestors of African primates. (One can almost hear a tea-table conversation at Lady Stumbleton-Smythe's, circa 1904: "They were largely necrophiliacs, those Egyptians, don't you know. But they seem to have chanced upon a fairly interesting architecture.")

These early anthropologists, largely educated at Cambridge, were the products of their time, scholars with a linear Aristotelian point of view. They insisted on understanding Egypt by dissecting its minutiae, by "deducing" it through intellectual exercises, "scientific" research, and scholarship rather than by experiencing the enthralling nature of it. The Platonic approach, with its emphasis on transcendent feeling and the spiritual ideal, might have permitted them a greater understanding of the highly sophisticated, polyphrenic,[8] and multileveled thought inherent in the complex, mythical conceptions of the ancient Egyptians. In his book *The Time Falling Bodies Take to Light*, the cultural historian William Irwin Thompson describes such thinking:

> One single myth can be a narrative about the formation of the solar system, the seasonal movement of planets and stars, the formation of civilization in the shift from Neolithic matriarchy to the patriarchal state, the development of consciousness in the emergence from the Great Mother to the fully individuated being, and, finally, the transformation of the central nervous system in the yogic achievement of illumination. A mythic narrative works through a system of correspondences, so a god is at once a principle of order, a number, a geometrical figure, a dancing measure, a mantram [sacred phrase], a special planet, and a heavenly body.[9]

Most sophisticated students of mythology would agree that this is true of any mythic tradition. However, within their concept of neters the Egyptians wove a very conscious sacred science from physical, psychological, mythic, and spiritual threads. On the physical level, the god or goddess embodied a planet, a plant, or, as we have seen, an organ of the body. The ancient Egyptian met the grain god Osiris, for example, in any wheat field.

On the psychological level, the archetypal neter served as a great animating force whose actions mimicked one's own, giving one's life purpose, meaning, and even the momentum behind taking action and making choices. Whenever he fought an oppressor, the ancient Egyptian reenacted the battle of Horus and Seth.

On a mythic level the god represented an entire story that illuminated the stages, sufferings, and ultimate ennoblement of existence. By recalling the sorrows of Isis, the birth of her child, her wanderings, and her ultimate triumphs, the ancient Egyptian entered into a deeper pattern encoded in both psyche and spirit that allowed for the unfolding of her imagination and a deeper connection to her own life.

Finally, on the integral or religious level, the neter was a great mediator between the earth realm and the transcendent realm, helping to seed or crystallize within the individual higher patterns of existence in the way that spiritual yearning allows one to transcend the temporal and contact the divine in one's own nature. These patterns manifest in time and space in the devotee through the neter's communion and love. This integral spiritual level embraces and infuses with its qualities the other levels.

Traces of this way of experiencing a netered world remain in the contemporary Egyptian's psyche. While leading a tour through Egypt not long ago, I performed an engagement ceremony for two of our Egyptian guides at sunset atop the Temple of Hathor, a monument to the Egyptian goddess of love. During the ceremony the planet Venus rose, and the young couple exclaimed, "Look! Hathor is rising and blessing our engagement!"

Toward Understanding the Neters

The neters had their origins in the prehistoric mists of the tribal cultures of each nome. The gods of the pharaohs were the divine beings and archetypes of the community in which each pharaoh had been born. We find in the early dynasties of the Old Kingdom that the great sun god was the falcon-headed warrior, Horus the Elder, but by the Fifth Dynasty of the Old Kingdom Ra had emerged as the supreme solar power. During the New Kingdom, when the capital city was moved from Memphis in Lower Egypt to Thebes in Upper Egypt, the great supreme god was Amun, or Amun-Re. And then, of course, the pharaoh Akhenaten upset everything by declaring that the real, true god was his solar disc, Aten.

Certain pharaohs held an affinity for particular neters, perhaps the neters of their forefathers. Seti I was well known as a dutiful son to the Great Mother, and, unlike his predecessors, he honored a great number of goddesses. Queen Hatshepsut was fond of the goddess Hathor, and in her own mortuary temple she built Hathor a beautiful chapel, now open to infinite blue sky, dramatic shadows and light, and a panorama of the high plateaus of western Thebes.

On the other hand, the tomb builders of ancient Egypt might have paid more due to the snake goddess Meretseger than a pharaoh did, as the tomb builder was more likely to encounter her incarnation in the hot desert. There were also occupational gods: Thoth, as the record keeper of the gods, was paid great honor by scribes, just as judges paid honor to Ma'at, the goddess of truth. Ptah, the builder of the universe, was the patron neter of architects, just as Khnum, the sculptor of souls and humans, was for the potter.

Even the ancient Egyptians did not know the names of every god and goddess. One story recounts that during a particular pharaoh's reign, the land was plagued by drought. The king called his chief counsel to his side and bade him consult the oracles and divine the reason. The dutiful scribe obeyed and returned to tell his king that in the underground caverns of the island of Elephantine lived the river god Hapi. Hapi was unhappy because he had been forgotten and discounted. Once hymns and prayers were composed for the god and temples erected in his honor, the normal inundation of the Nile returned.

One can see, then, that a linear understanding of Egyptian neters is not entirely possible. There exists no single authority or hierarchy of neters. The neters are the universe itself, a reflection of the rhythm of both durative and punctual time, as well as symbols that snap and glitter and crackle like sparks of fire sending light in a thousand directions. Like the universe, the neters are too complex to be understood with a single system of thought. They are a bundle of contradictions composing a harmonious, balanced whole. As the Egyptologist Barbara Mertz said,

"There are a dozen different ways of explaining anything that really matters; and *all of them are right.*"[10]

The natives, scholars, and guides of Egypt have lived so long with the gods and goddesses whispering in their ears that their appearance in these forms, whether as plants or planets, seems an almost instinctual recognition. Most Westerners, however, are not familiar with looking for the symbols and manifestations of gods in everyday life. Therefore, before continuing to Process 3, it may be helpful to read through Appendix A to familiarize yourself with some of the major neters of ancient Egypt.

In the appendix you will find descriptions of the gods' and goddesses' animal, vegetable, and mineral appearances, their functions, their emblems, and their particular domain within the physical and mental realms. You will also find, whenever possible, images of these divine beings. Look upon these images with your newly opened eyes of Light. Study them with your hieroglyphic mind. Try to imagine what dialogues you might have with these neters in the durative realm. Hymns were written to the neters for their feast days. You'll find some of these hymns to the neters in their descriptions.

Remember that the gods and goddesses were the neters of the natural world in a particular place. Two or more neters may serve similar functions in various parts of Egypt. For example, the protective mother goddess of the Lower Egyptian delta is the cobra goddess Wadjet, because such powerful creatures were commonly found curled up beside their eggs amid the tall papyrus grasses. Yet the same protective mother goddess is seen in the Upper Egyptian desert plateau as the vulture goddess Nekhebet (or Mut), because in the desert vultures and their eggs were seen more often than cobras. As you look upon these neters, try to imagine them in their proper surroundings, in their regions, in their times.

It is not necessary to be able to distinguish all the neters, just the ones that speak to you particularly. The important thing to remember is that all neters are aspects of the Great Divine Light. They are the brilliant multiformed petals of a single lotus. One may name and admire the individual petals, or simply relax and enjoy the perfume of the entire lotus.

When you feel comfortable with these gods and goddesses, proceed to Process 3.

♣

PROCESS 3:
Infusing the Body with Neters

Because we are a part of nature, the neters live in us and are always there at our depths to be called upon to infuse our bodies, our minds, and our spirits with new and renewing vitality. In this exercise we are calling upon the divine beings and archetypes who were birthed from the light of stars millions of years ago. We are calling upon primordial events in the durative realm to enter us and infuse us with the wisdom and understanding of a netered mind.

We make of our selves, as the ancients said, one heart, one mind, one body. R. A. Schwaller de Lubicz suggested that the temples of ancient Egypt were built according to the proportion of the divinely infused man and woman. The body itself is an adytum, a temple filled with neters. Ancient Egyptian priests and priestesses never entered the temple unless they had first washed and fasted. You also might be more comfortable during the netering process if you avoid rich meals. Also, bathing before and after the exercise with Epsom salts or Dead Sea salts and baking soda will clarify the body and spirit.

By now you should feel at ease in the neters' presence. In this exercise you will receive the images of the gods. You will find them compassionate, protective, loving, emboldening, perhaps even shy at times—as diverse and pleasant a company as your circle of friends.

Within you, the neters work as healers upon the psyche and the soma. Some people experience the neters more bodily than others, particularly in the areas that need the neters' attention. Memories and emotions are stored in every cell of the body—memories especially in the bones, emotions in the soft tissue. On occasion, people find that their joints are stiff or slightly swollen due to the unaccustomed charge of high energy pouring through these parts of the body. This is perfectly normal and should cause no alarm. Again, the Epsom salts bath or a good aromatic balm or body oil will take care of these problems.

Repeating this exercise often can result in a quickening and an enlivening of vitality. The neters will always be on call to heal any minor upset—a strained muscle, clogged sinus, overstimulated brain, and so on. Also in this way, various gods and goddesses will take turns being the predominant archetype, and your vision of your self, your body, and your mind will expand to fill wider and wider dimensions.

TIME: 90 minutes.

MATERIALS NEEDED: The participants should have familiarized themselves with the descriptions of the ancient Egyptian gods in Appendix A.

MUSIC: Music from Area 2, for example, Deuter's *Ecstasy*.

INSTRUCTIONS FOR THE SOLO JOURNEYER: You can conduct this process simply by reading the script into a tape recorder, allowing for the many needed pauses. By doing this, you will, of course, have the advantage of having gone through this process once already, so you will be more familiar with the bodily territories of the neters.

SCRIPT FOR THE GUIDE: We will lead you now in an exercise of letting your body and mind become netered. You will receive images of the great principal neters of pharaonic Egypt. I ask you to sense them and feel them physically, psychologically, mythically, and spiritually, so that you may awaken to the subtlety and complexity of the images.

Before we begin I want you to lie down, close your eyes, and breathe deeply . . . Breathing deeply and regularly, scan your body, starting at the toes and letting the toes relax. Continue to breathe slowly and deeply. Now let your feet relax . . . and now let all tension drain out of your legs . . . relax your hips, continuing to breathe slowly and deeply . . . Now let your entire torso relax . . .

Your shoulders now, losing all tenseness, become utterly and completely relaxed . . . your arms become so relaxed that they could reach through the floor. Stretch your hands and fingers for a moment and then relax them . . . let go.

Move to your neck . . . lose all tension there; now your face . . . so relaxed, so very relaxed, your mouth letting go, then your cheeks. Your eyes relax . . . relax. Your forehead lets go of all strain, all tension. The top of your scalp now and the back of your head become so very relaxed as you continue to breathe deeply. Breathe deeply and let all remaining tension be exhaled on the outgoing breath. Breathe and relax now. Relax and breathe.

(This is the relaxation exercise that we will do to prepare and be receptive to a number of the processes in this journey.)

So now . . . feel deeply relaxed. Continuing to lie on your back with your eyes closed, think of your whole body as Egypt, your whole body as the realm of pure potential: your blood as the Nile; your body as the green land; your mind and spirit as the place of the gods . . . And having that thought, release it and let it just continue in the background of your mind.

Think of the joints connecting the bones in your body. Begin with the joints in your toes and your ankles. Think of those joints of which you are conscious, the ones you feel. Now think of the major joints of which you may not be aware, such as the ones connecting the vertebrae of your spine . . .

As you think of the joints throughout your body, suggest to yourself that the relevant muscle fibers are relaxing, becoming longer and looser, so that the joints can release and you can prepare yourself to be flooded with new life, as the Nile floods its banks and brings the green world back again . . . In your thoughts consider your entire body, suggesting from the toes up to the top of your head that the muscles are relaxing, becoming longer, becoming looser . . .

I will now invite you to welcome into your body the great Egyptian neters. We begin with your eyes. Think of your eyes as the eyes of Ra, the sun god . . . Sense your eyes being filled with his luminous warmth . . . Pay attention to your breathing. In Egypt the breath is associated with Shu, the god of the invigorating spirit. Breathe deeply the breath of Shu . . . Sense the eyes of Ra netering your own eyes . . . Now breathe with the breath of Shu . . . the eyes of Ra, the breath of Shu . . .

Become aware of Shu and Ra together, and notice how this presence affects your eyes. Notice how your eyes, the eyes of the neter Ra, open and close with your breathing . . . And notice that when you exhale with the breath of Shu, your eyelids get heavier and your eyes close even more. Let your eyes close tighter with each exhalation, each breath of Shu, but do not tighten any of the muscles of your face. Just experience your eyes closing a bit, more and more. This breathing of the breath of Shu and the sensation around the eyes will continue to affect you as you travel deeper through the Egypt of the self . . .

Altering your consciousness, deepen your state of being so that you become available to the goddedness, to the netering in yourself. Focus again on your breathing, the breath of Shu. As you exhale, go deeper and deeper into the realm of the gods, the realm of the neters. Feel your eyelids closing a little more each time . . .

As you continue to do this, be aware of the top of your head. Feel your skull where it encloses the brain space. The ancients would say that this area belongs to the neter Ptah, the great god of creativity, who is often shown with a wonderful bald head, symbolizing perhaps his enormous intelligence. One of the ancient names for Egypt was Hiku-ptah, Realm of the Soul of Ptah, realm of the soul with tremendous intelligence. Feel the neter of Ptah in the skull and brain space . . . Explore the netering of Ptah. Be aware of the top and back of your skull . . . Then explore the sockets around your eyes, the god Ra. Be aware of your jaw and jawbone, your teeth, your mouth . . . the creative orifice of Ptah.

Now focus on the spine. The neter of the spine is Osiris. Begin to move your spine gently. Concentrate on the movement, the movement of Osiris, all the way down your body . . . Be aware of the shoulder girdle and the shoulder joints . . . the ribs . . . their connective tissues . . .

Focus on your upper and lower arms and hands. Your hands are the hands of Khnum, the ram god, the potter god, the god of high craft . . .

the hands of Khnum, who, it was said, fashioned human beings on the pottery wheel . . .

Become increasingly aware of your skeleton . . . the pelvis . . . the hip joints . . . the upper legs . . . the lower legs . . . the feet. Become more and more aware of your skeleton . . . It was thought that the skeleton was the province of Seth, the god associated with rocks, dry places, and the bones of the earth. The bones of Seth.

Now become aware of your muscles and the organs of your body. Feel your body as a body with no facade, no skin on the outside. See yourself as an anatomy chart with just the inside showing at present. Feel something of what you are like without your facade. What would it be like to walk along, all your organs exposed, without that surface that presents your image to the world? . . .

Let us go into those organs. Let us begin with the heart, the heart belonging to the neter Isis, goddess of heartfulness and compassion, as well as of wisdom . . . Feel Isis netering your heart . . . The heart is also the goddess Ma'at, the winged Isis, goddess of rhythm and balance . . . Feel the beating of your heart. This is the place where the life memories and emotions are stored . . . Feel Isis as Ma'at netering your heart.

Move into the solar plexus, the place of power, the place of the goddess Sekhmet, the goddess of power, the lion-headed goddess . . . Go into the digestive tract, the place of the jackal-headed neter Anubis, the god of digestion . . . Return again to the lungs and breathe deeply. Breathe in the place of Shu, the neter of the creative vitalizing breath . . .

Add the reproductive organs. For women, the neter of the womb is the big-bellied hippopotamus goddess Tauret. For men, the neter is the phallic god Min . . . Feel the reproductive organs, the site of deep regeneration being netered by the god Min and the goddess Tauret . . .

Now move deeply, deeply into the internal organs—the places where the four sons of Horus reside. Become aware of the stomach. See the stomach, the place where nourishment begins, the food breaking down into particles of sugar, fat, albumens . . . Feel the nourishment . . . The god of the stomach, the first son of Horus, the jackal-headed son, Duametef . . . Now see the liver . . . Feel the blood cells forming . . . The god of the liver, the second son of Horus, the human-headed son, Imset . . . Moving on deeply through the body's processes, see the intestines . . . Feel the chyle that separates what is useful from what is not . . . The god of the intestines, the third son of Horus, the falcon-headed son, Qebehsenuf . . . Moving on, visit the kidneys and the spleen . . . Pass up into the chest, the lungs, the place of Håpy, the fourth, baboon-headed son of Horus. Observe the lungs, the air coming into and then out of your lungs as you breathe . . . the place of Shu, the neter of the creative, vitalizing breath . . . The vital organs, the four sons of Horus . . .

See the circulatory system, the blood flowing, and the lymph, and know this as one of the neters of the Nile, Hapi, often seen carrying water jars. Sense the great flowing tides of your body . . . Sense the abundance flowing through your body . . .

Now sense the electrical activity, the great wisdom that creates the connections between your brain and other parts of the body through the nervous system. The god of the nervous system and of the great connections is Thoth, the god of wisdom, the god who sees all the patterns and connections, the ibis-headed god. Feel Thoth, the great, magical Wise One who knows the high magic of connections. Feel that neter in your body . . .

Realize that you can pass into your body at any point, at any point you like, with your mind. Begin to explore inside, exploring wherever you like. Observe the activity in different parts of your body and have the sense of each part of the body being under the rule of a high principle, a god, a neter, or, if you like, a principle of intelligence . . .

Try to explore inside one of your hands, sacred to Khnum, the god of creative craft . . . Travel up your arm, sacred to Selket, the goddess of caring, often seen as a lovely little golden statue, her arms outstretched in a gesture of protection, the goddess of nurturing . . .

Continue exploring. Pass up through your throat into your head. Observe your brain, the place of Ptah. Move around, in, and through your brain. Feel the electrical activity of the various parts of your brain communicating with each other, and every cell and neuron. Feel the conversations of Ptah and Thoth.

Now come out to the tip of your nose as we begin to explore at more and more microscopic levels. Exit your nose. Find yourself standing on the end of your nose, looking at a cell. What a huge nose! And so intriguing to see the cells of your own skin laid out like huge pieces of a mosaic floor. Ghost whispers of steam are pocketing out of holes in the mosaic. Either you are getting smaller or the mosaic cells are getting bigger. In fact, they are rapidly expanding in all directions. Choose to stand now in the middle of one cell . . .

As you continue to shrink, the steam rising out of the floor of the cell is more noticeable. Other things become apparent as well. What are those tall reeds growing up so quickly before your eyes? Now they seem to have become a dense grove of palm trees. It's hair. You didn't know that you were growing so many trees of hair on your nose, but you are. The breaks in the mosaic pavement now seem more like cracks in the land after an earthquake. In fact, a large cavern opens up before you and you enter it, continuing to get smaller and smaller and smaller. The great cavern is one of your pores. The walls of the cavern seem to have been constructed by some master architect, or perhaps a jeweler, certainly a neter, so powerful and beautiful are they. And these walls are flexing and stretching and rippling like a snake. Perhaps here is one of the many domains of the snake goddess, the neter Wadjet.

As you continue to get smaller, you become aware of large intricate networks of multicolored tubing, holy channels of veins, nerves, dendrites, oil ducts, and muscle fibers governed by the neter Neith. Neith, the goddess of the network and patterns, is there, orchestrating these many channels, carrying their juices through a single pore.

You go in deeper and deeper, and you get smaller and smaller. The tunnel has swelled to the proportion of a great pyramid or temple, the Temple in Man.

You stand poised on the edge of a single cell, your feet balanced on an enormous ridge, trying not to be blown away by the hot, strong, gaseous winds. Who is lord of the winds? Is it the neter of deserts, Seth? For it's becoming warmer and warmer. Great balls of luminosity roll and bump through the air of Seth. They smell of minerals and chemicals, these globes of hot water vapor. You feel the steam escaping through the pore now with almost hurricane force . . . You grow smaller and smaller. Now you watch sea monsters and dragons rushing by. O snake neter, O Wadjet, be with me now! These are microbes, but they look like whales invented by a mad scientist.

And you get smaller and smaller and smaller. You see that you are standing on a crazy-quilt webbing of elastic balls, enormous globules, some red, some white, some transparent. You watch as they slip in and out of the webbing in the company of exotic, frenetic, shape-shifting globules. You are looking at the bloodstream with its red and white corpuscles and its shape-shifting phagocytes. You are watching air, oxygen, coursing between the cells in this giant, swirling exchange.

But is there not another reality present in the midst of this one? You call upon the neter Ra and look again at this scene with the eyes of a god, and suddenly you are amazed at the numinous glory that is present before you. You are present at the electromagnetic level of your own cellular life. You are watching phosphorescent fields of electric blue and magenta, sparkling streamers weaving their pulsing, shimmering way through cells and fibers, blood platelets and microbes. Each is fed, sustained, and illumined by the force fields circulating throughout this microworld.

This, too, is the province of the goddess Neith, the weaver, she who sustains the net and the subtle networks of life. And so with the help of Neith, the neter of the pattern that connects, you are looking now upon the physical, energetic basis of that pattern, the energizing life force that gives the impetus as well as the pattern to all forms, however infinite or infinitesimal.

You shrink now at an even faster pace. Great ballooning cells and gleaming, rippling trunks like the outreach of a thousand elephants swoop by you. You fall through the ceiling of a domed temple whose inner recesses contain treasures so strange that there is no naming them— jellyfish jewels perhaps, or transcendent sausages. Mad, ecstatic dances are performed here by ones who seem inhabitants of another planet, extraterrestrials given to dervish spinning.

Becoming smaller and smaller still, you find yourself climbing down spiral vortices, for you are in the nucleus of your own cell. Little shimmering balls dot the surface of these vortices—chromosomes, DNA, RNA, all interweaving in a fantastic dance of connections. This is the realm of the neter Atum, the god of atoms, the god of the beginning of creation.

There is a presence here, wise and deep, solemn in its ancient knowings. You find yourself able to talk to this presence, which is the nucleus of the cell. It tells you:

"I am a very old cell. I am the progenitor of many who surround me. My life has been one of service to the Creator in whom we live and move and have our being. I hope that I have imparted this devotion and these ideals to my children and their children after them. My long life has given me the time to reflect on the Great Life, the Life of the One of whose body we are a part. So great is this One that its being is beyond our conception or even imagination. Our Creator depends on our service and harmony for its own well-being and development. If we meditate and tender our devotions to this great neter and obey its injunctions, we will in time become initiated so that we will eventually share in the wonders of the Divine Being's mind."

You wonder who this neter is. Who is this god? Who is this great divinity? This, of course, is a forbidden question for the cell. But you know who it is. This being, this divinity, this high and holy neter, is yourself. And your little, wise, ancient cell nucleus is longing for conscious union and copartnership with you, Great Neter, for that will bring on the communion of the saints.

And so you decide to go deeper. You become smaller and smaller and smaller as the cell swells in greatness. Soon you pass within a molecule itself. It seems to be a highly charged, pulsating space. Every now and then there is a sweeping pull, as if from some invisible magnet. As you continue to shrink, the walls of the molecule recede into electric blue dreams.

You are shrinking and entering now into one of your own atoms. You are becoming a million times smaller. Finally, you become aware of something caught in the strong, intermittent magnetic current. There is something gleaming ahead of you.

You come up to it. It is a fiery ball, which looks very much like a sun poised in the middle of space. It is the nucleus of the atom. You think of it as the neter Horus, an energetic, perennially youthful neter of governance. You notice way off in the distance a large, revolving electrical spark flashing rapidly by. Then there's a smaller one, and another one, and another. Electrons . . . protons . . . neutrons . . . zipping particles of energy, Horus energy.

You become smaller and smaller. The electrons look like planets, and the sun is resplendent in its shining beauty. Horus is beautiful! Planetoids and comets, shooting stars and cosmic dust, are also apparent. Are these the subatomic particles you've heard so much about? Are these the quarks and the tachyons and the goodness-knows-whats? And who, pray, is their neter?

You see that there is an electric web from the nucleus of the atom to all of the protons, electrons, neutrons. This web is a living being. You see finely divided webs of shimmering light and delicate rainbow-colored strands reaching out from the heart of the sun and linking to the little planet of electrons. You know that you are in the center of all reality. Is this perhaps the province of Aten, the neter of illumination, whom the pharaoh Akhenaten believed was the unifying neter for all the neters, the neter who held the secret of life?

Suddenly, your mind expands. Your mind expands and expands in a quantum of cosmic dimensions. You are in a galaxy of galaxies, a galaxy containing a trillion galaxies. You look out at these shimmering smudges and you realize they are not stars. They're galaxies! Each galaxy contains a hundred billion, two hundred billion stars with an infinite number of planets. You are looking out at a galaxy of galaxies. And your mind is that galaxy of galaxies . . . You are in the core nature of the god Amun . . . Amun, god of vibrational forces, of forms spiraling, bending, singing, shaping, and reshaping. The black holes, the Big Bangs. Then, *SHOOM!*

You're back in your own atom. You inhale the breath of Shu, and your mind expands to the galaxy of galaxies. You exhale the breath of Shu, and you're back in the nucleus of your own atom. You inhale the breath of Shu, and you're in the galaxy of galaxies. You exhale the breath of Shu, and you're back in the atom. Inhale the galaxy of galaxies with its webbing of interconnection and light. Exhale the being of the atom. Back and forth. Back and forth. Both of them know each other very well, and they sing to each other. They sing the song of creation . . .

Your body of imagination is now drawn within your real body, strengthening it with the knowledge, the gnosis of connection between atom and galaxy. You know that you are netered. You are netered with trillions of gods who are singing to trillions of gods.

Somewhere in your mind/brain/body you are always in a constant creation, moving from atom to galactic being, from galactic being to atom, from atom to galactic being. You breathe deeply of the essence of the fields within fields surrounding each atom, filled with the knowledge of billions of years, filled with the charge of the radical microsecond.

And you know, finally, that you are godded, you are netered. You are at home in the universe, for you are at home in the pluraverse. You are ubiquitous through the stars and the atoms. You are singing with all that is. And all that is sings in you, "Welcome home, welcome home, welcome home, welcome home."

Your mind fills this galactic being, which is yourself, and your mind is also godded and netered. It has deep, deep, deep levels of mind: the inscape of mind from the microcosm of mind in that tiny cell, to the macrocosm of mind in the galaxy of galaxies. The Great Oneness, the Great Goddedness in the mind of the cell and the mind of the galaxies sing to each other.

You now have one minute of clock time, equal subjectively to a very long time, to go back and forth and explore the deep, netered, godded realities of mind and body, or perhaps the single reality of body/mind. Explore and ask yourself, What is mind? Is it real, or an illusion? Is the body real, or an illusion? Might they both be real? Or both illusion? Or both real *and* illusion? Are they more real than real? Fill and feel the gods of your body and your mind, the great creative principles, beginning now . . .

And your spirit expands. You've gone into your mind. You've gone into your body. Now your spiritual being expands and expands. You will know yourself in the fullness of your spiritual dimension as well . . .

Travel deeply. Travel far. For having gone into the galaxies of yourself, you see the energy interchange between the great fields of life and the great fullnesses of spirit. You see ideas and gods and patterns playing on the great charges of light and connection that is your body/mind. Be in the realm of spiritual reality . . .

Observe dimensions that are beyond any particular existence. Cosmic dimensions. Transpersonal dimensions. Whatever you call them. And find the atmosphere increasingly holding a sense of great power . . .

Enter a place, a temple of holiness, that is your own body/mind/spirit. It is a place of very great power, but a power that is tranquil and serene. A very powerful force, powerful without any hint of menace, a creative power of love. Remain in that space, the space of the spiritual dimension, of the great spiritual power of love. Let the power of that spirit permeate you. Let it fill your spirit, your mind, your body, your whole self . . .

Allow yourself to be netered. And allow the neters, the different gods, the different parts of yourself, to be netered by the One, the ultimate spiritual source of reality, the final neter of which these other neters are but a part.

Receive . . . Receive . . . Receive . . . Receive . . . Receive . . . Receive . . . Receive . . . Receive . . . Receive . . . Receive . . . Receive . . . Receive . . . Receive . . . Receive . . . Receive . . .

Then, with that powerful, benevolent life force, the force of deep spirit, in you, its serenity filling you so that you are like a glowing body of light, make your way back through the cosmic transpersonal realm of the deep oneness, the one neter, into your own spiritual world, the world of many neters. Through your mind and through your body, feel the goddedness in your body. Feel the neters of your body.

The neters of the left foot . . . and right leg . . . and generative organs

... and intestines ... the liver ... and spleen ... and heart ... and lungs
... and throat ... and tongue ... and nose ... and eyes ... and ears ...
and brain ... and all the joints ... and the left arm ... and the left hand
... and the right arm ... and the right hand ... the nervous system ...
the enzymatic streams ... the lymph streams ... the throbbings ... the
poundings ... the molecules ... the DNA ... the atoms ...

Fill with neters. Fill with gods. Fill with high patterns. Feel and be
filled with those gods.

If there is any part of you that needs netering, any part that needs a
healing or "wholing," then in a minute or so of clock time open yourself
to receive those patterns of rejuvenation, of relieving, of healing from
the mighty pattern or neter of the organ.

If there are problems in the heart, or liver, or lungs, or throat, or whatever, then, as in ancient Egypt, feel the gods of those places coming together, reaching over to each other and performing the dance of the
neters, the dance of reconnection, that your systems of body or mind
may be rewoven and reconnected. Let the obstructions be eliminated.
Let the parts be healed.

Do so now ... The god of healing at the physical and intellectual levels is the god Thoth. The healing goddess at the magical and astral levels
is Sekhmet. The healing god and goddess at the spiritual levels are Horus
and Isis. Feel the gods and goddesses coming together ... Heal now ...

If you have had experiences and painful memories around sexuality,
then let the neters of that function come and give you healing. These
neters are Isis and Osiris, and also Isis in her guise as Hathor and Osiris
in his guise as Min. Let the neters of these functions, whether of sexuality or of generation, come and restore these areas to health of function as
well as health of memories so that the memories are healed. And let that
happen now ...

Know that you have performed a meditation that is a modern form of
an ancient Egyptian meditation of bringing the neters into the body.
You have passed through different levels of your own being to further
unify yourself, moving to integration of more and more profound levels
of yourself. Some of the obstructions have been eliminated as you have
moved toward deeper becoming, fulfillment, a larger humanity, a greater
realization of your own potential. So in a few short years did ancient
Egypt move to the deeper levels, to the larger humanity, to the larger
creativity by understanding the process you have just experienced.

I will now recite the names of the ancient Egyptian gods, and as I do
so, you will emerge from the state that you are in, stretching and bringing back with you experiences, images, ideas, understandings that you
may want to write down. Perhaps parts of your body were filled with gods
in such a way that you may want to draw them or reflect on them or
record them. Whatever you want to bring back, bring.

I will name the gods of ancient Egypt, the neters that stand for the great principles or qualities of being and creativity. And you will stretch and enjoy and feel your body netered.

I call now upon the images of the gods, the neters:

Isis . . . Osiris . . . Seth . . . Nephthys . . . Thoth . . . Anubis . . . Horus . . . Ra . . . Khnum . . . Neith . . . Wadjet . . . Nekhebet . . . Selket . . . Shu . . . Amun . . . Ptah . . . Sekhmet . . . Mut . . . Ma'at . . . Hathor . . . Aten . . . Wepwawet . . . Amun-Re . . . Atum . . . Harpokrates . . . Hapi . . . Anuket . . . Satis . . . Bes . . .

And rise, rise now to consciousness. Stretch and feel these gods flow through you. Receive their forms, the creative forms of life. Rise up to consciousness.

Neith . . . Selket . . . Bast . . . Min . . . Tauret . . . Hathor . . . Ma'at . . . Sekhmet . . . Isis . . . Osiris . . . Horus . . . Thoth . . .

Let life fill you. Let life fill you. Let life fill you. Allow yourself to be netered. Netered. Netered. Netered. Netered. Netered. Netered. Netered. Netered. Netered. Netered. SO BE IT.

⚜

JOURNAL PROCESS

In your journal, trace the outline of one of your hands. Know that this is the hand of the god Khnum. Inside the outline of your hand, write a list of all the things your hands and heart have created.

Draw an image of your body on a large piece of paper, or have someone trace around you. List all the major scars. Then, one by one, from each of your fingers and toes, from the top of your head to the soles of your feet, from the front and back and sides, write what each part of your body knows, loves, and remembers.

The cow-headed Isis pouring out a libation in honor of the soul of Osiris, which rises in the form of a man-headed hawk from the plants growing in a sacred lake. From a bas-relief at Philae.

7

Magic of Magic, Spirit of Spirit, Part 1

THE KNOT OF ISIS

At the ends of the universe is a blood red cord that ties life to death, man to woman, will to destiny. Let the knot of that red sash, which cradles the hips of the goddess, bind in me the ends of life and dream. I'm an old man with more than my share of hopes and misgivings. Let my thoughts lie together in peace. At my death let the bubbles of blood on my lips taste as sweet as berries. Give me not words of consolation. Give me magic, the fire of one beyond the borders of enchantment. Give me the spell of living well.

Do I lie on the floor of my house or within the temple? Is the hand that soothes me that of wife or priestess? I rise and walk. The sky arcs ever around; the world spreads itself beneath my feet. We are bound mind to Mind, heart to Heart—no difference rises between the shadow of my footsteps and the will of god. I walk in harmony, heaven in one hand, earth in the other. I am the knot where two worlds meet. Red magic courses through me like the blood of Isis, magic of magic, spirit of spirit. I am proof of the power of gods. I am water and dust walking.

from *Awakening Osiris*
by Normandi Ellis

The Teachings of the Temples

Egypt for millennia was synonymous with magic. One of the earliest names for Egypt, al-Khemt, meant "the black land," or "the place of alchemical transformations." The many thousands of spells and amulets that have been found, the arcane magical practices surrounding the process of mummification and burial, the ritualization of magic in virtually every aspect of Egyptian life show that what we might consider magic was the normal psychological stance of daily life in ancient Egypt.

My friend has a bumper sticker that reads MAGIC HAPPENS. And it does. I have taken well over five hundred people to Egypt with me on various visits, and you would be astonished by the things I've seen:

I saw the power of a woman's desire for a simple statue of the lion goddess Sekhmet spontaneously shatter the glass in a merchant's store. I saw a young woman begin to pray in a language she never knew, a dead language known only to the amazed priest at the Coptic church who heard it. I saw fifteen women begin their periods on the same day—including a sixty-five-year-old woman who hadn't had a period in a decade—because of a prayer for cleansing spoken in the Temple of Isis. I heard spontaneous songs of praise rise from the lips of visitors.

I've seen deaths and marriages, even healings, from afar. A visitor entered each ancient temple speaking the name of a friend's sister who was in the United States gravely ill with cancer; when the visitor returned from her trip, her friend called to say, "The most amazing thing happened! Mary's cancer has apparently gone into remission!"

Those who meditated through the night and lay down in the sarcophagus inside the King's Chamber in the Great Pyramid of Cheops reported feeling the pulses of electrical energy surging through them head to toe; and although they did not know it at the time, when they walked out into the dawn on the Giza plateau the next morning, it would appear that for some of them their lives had changed. Legal battles were won; failed relationships fell away; healings between estranged family members occurred; serendipitous jobs appeared. Was this just the normal course of things, or something more?

It is not uncommon for people who travel to Egypt to come away with a sense that they have changed, their hearts opened, their spirits rejuvenated, their possibilities extended. How can we explain such miracles, except that the sacred temples—even the earth beneath one's feet—still reverberate with ancient power, charged by five thousand centuries of conscious invocation, prayer, incantation, and meditation. We are not talking about average Sunday churchgoers; we are talking about a people for whom every animal, plant, and stone embodied the divine, a people for whom daily life vibrated spiritual meaning, for whom the mere act of waking from sleep was a resurrection from death, akin to Ra being reborn each morning.

When we view the world as sacred—when every beast, grain of sand, molecule of air, tree, seed, and river is viewed as being empowered with neters—then the world views us as sacred, too.

It is true that the Colossus of Memnon no longer sings, that the Nile no longer overflows its banks, that the paint is now flaking from the tomb ceilings, that ancient glyphs crumble every day to sand, and that these losses are deeply felt. And still the power thrums beneath the sand and under the blue sky, the light of heaven pierces the hearts of those who come to revere this place. While traveling through the Egyptian countryside, I once met an old peasant farmer. The fellahin said to me, "The gods want you here. They need someone to speak their names."

"When we of the twentieth century find ourselves moved (often to tears), awed, staggered by Egypt's amazing works," says John Anthony

West, "it is because, without our consent, and without knowing why or how, we have been put momentarily in touch with the gods by people who knew precisely what they were doing and why they were doing it."[1]

The Magic of the Temple

Generally, a temple was erected at the center of a village, with the dwellings of the townspeople built around it. Spirit was the keystone of life. The temples were laid down during the dawn of Egyptian history, according to plans designed by the mysterious and godlike companions of Horus. Each new temple was erected on the site of an earlier one, with careful observance to details ranging from architectural structure to astrological significance, from symbolic meaning to functional aspects. Each temple's construction began with an invocation to the gods and goddesses. The invocation called forth the powers of universal harmony, mathematics, myth, and symbolism, powers that were then incorporated into the temple design so that the temple on earth would reflect the same design principles used by the divine architects of the universe.

The stones of the Great Pyramid were cut to such precision that, to produce such fine work these days, we would need to employ lasers. If we are to believe the historians who tell us that primitive ancient Egyptians used only copper and bronze tools and had no knowledge of the wheel, how can we explain that they moved over six million tons of stone to build a single structure containing more masonry than all the churches and cathedrals built in England since the time of Christ? The alignment of the pyramid's base to true north is so precise that even the most perfect astronomical building today—the Paris Observatory—is still six minutes off true north, while the Great Pyramid is off by only one-twelfth of a degree.[2] Obviously, these "primitives" knew exactly what they were doing.

Why shouldn't the Great Pyramid be perfect? It was thought to be divinely inspired. It represented the primordial *benben* stone, the first hill of the earth to rise above the primordial waters at the dawn of creation; it represented order emerging from chaos. The temples of Egypt were built by people conscious that every action and detail was a deliberate expression of the god who dwelt within each temple. The ancient Egyptians well knew that their earthly lives were temporal but the souls of gods were eternal, so while they built their own homes of mud brick, they built the temples of stone. The "houses of the gods" were meant to last an eternity.

R. A. Schwaller de Lubicz spent years studying the structure of the Temple of Luxor, its mathematical genius, its symbolic resonances, its hermetic meanings. He believed that its every detail was intended to imitate the act of universal creation to evoke an intuitive understanding of the creative power of the neters in everyone who saw it. The temple, he said, is alive.[3]

Schwaller de Lubicz noted that temples in Egypt were often rebuilt on the site of older temples, and that these new structures were enlivened by the conscious placement of what he called the "seed stone"—a stone that was once part of the former building and was now incorporated into the new temple. In the Temple of Luxor, for example, we find the full image of the god Min perfectly chiseled into smooth, similarly hewn stones, with the exception of the erect phallus of the god. This one stone is definitely worn, somewhat ravaged, and pock-marked by the blowing sands of time; its age predates the raising of the temple as we know it. It is the seed stone of the Temple of Luxor, perhaps taken from the previous temple on this same site, and its deliberate placement emphasizes its most efficacious meaning in so far as "revitalizing" and "impregnating" the new temple with its renewed, creative power.

What is amazing is that, just as the sages of Egypt consciously invoked the cosmic creative principles in their construction of the temples, so they also consciously disassembled the temples when the time was right. Although this practice of rejuvenating the temples is often attributed to simple pharaonic egomania, Schwaller de Lubicz believed that the temples were not razed, but dismantled "carefully and deliberately when their predetermined symbolic significance had passed. The new temple was then constructed and consecrated to whichever neter the changing cycles of time pushed forward into prominence. . . . The sages of Egypt were deliberately and knowledgeably organizing the ambiance or atmosphere of an entire civilization in harmony with cosmic requirements."[4]

The function of a temple—whether that temple is an actual architectural structure or a group of initiates who form a template, an intellectual structure—is to maintain and perpetuate a vast body of knowledge. The establishment and maintenance of any temple requires extraordinary skill by knowledgeable and dedicated individuals who believe that adherence to divine creative principles is the sacred task of all, who view themselves as artists and craftsmen imitating the creative acts of the divine.

Judging by the recent findings of the well-furbished tombs of the builders of the pyramids, these people were not slaves; they were, so it appears, middle class. Says John Anthony West, "It's quite clear when you look at what they [built] that slaves don't produce that kind of work . . . slaves don't produce masterpieces of art."[5] Nor would slaves have the training and initiation to understand the higher spiritual principles inherent in the movement and alignment of stones, in the precision needed to carve a glyph, in the preparation of ritual foods. Sacred works must be consecrated by sacred hands.

Ancient Adepts in the Wisdom of Egypt

The ancient Egyptians were not reticent about their belief in spiritual practices, but they did protect their inner wisdom. Although sacred texts were written, the vowels were not pronounced, thus keeping the proper sacred names intact. What wisdom was handed down, was passed on orally under the tutelage of the high priests of the temple.

Because the teachings were multitudinous and included nearly every aspect of life, many years of study and hard work were involved. Initiations into the higher levels of mysteries had to be earned. The Greeks who studied with the priests—Pythagoras, Herodotus, Plutarch—were quick to say that although the priests revealed their secrets to them, they could not repeat what those secrets were. Even so, one of the problems with Greek interpretations of myth and mystery is that they attempted to explain too much. The truth, so the Egyptian scribes have told us, is always more than one thing; that it, the core truth, resonates with multiple meanings, emotions, resonant states of mind.

We know of two Jews, Joseph and Moses, who were initiated into the greater mysteries of ancient Egypt. Joseph, according to the biblical story, was given the ring of the pharaoh, dressed in fine linen, and rode in the pharaoh's chariot. He married the daughter of a high priest of Heliopolis and was undoubtedly initiated into the worship of Ra. An adept at the art of divination—perhaps even a priest of Egyptian religion himself—he was named Psonthomphanechos, meaning "Revealer of Secrets."

Of Moses, we know that he was raised in the court as a child of the pharaoh's daughter. There he learned all of Egypt's wisdom and was mighty in words and deeds. Certainly Moses was a high initiate as well; like Joseph before him, he married a high priest's daughter and became a priest himself. The Egyptian scribe Manetho, compiling a history of Egypt in 30 B.C., mentioned that Moses was a priest initiated into the mysteries of Osiris. The commandments, the principles of law, the sacred rites that Moses later brought to the Jewish nation, are in many ways markedly similar to the practices of the initiated high priests of Egypt.[6]

The Tale of Eucrates, Coveter of Magic

Apparently, the sacred names of the gods were closely guarded (not to be spoken in vain) because they were potent enough to be misused. One delightful ancient story tells of a Greek named Eucrates who met one of the sacred magician scribes of Memphis. This man was very learned and had spent twenty-three years in the underground sanctuaries of the temple, where Isis herself, his personal neter, had taught him magic.

While riding with this magician in a boat one day, Eucrates saw him perform such curious feats as riding crocodiles and commanding lost objects to rise up from the water. Much impressed, Eucrates told the magician that he wished to study with him, so the magician invited him to visit. Eucrates wanted to bring a retinue of servants with him, but the magician told him to dismiss them for he would not be needing their assistance. When they arrived at the magician's house, Eucrates could see that the magician had no servants at all, but clearly he needed none. When there was a chore to be done, he would put clothing on a door bolt, pestle, or broom. Then he would utter some magic words, and the object would come alive and do his bidding. When the service was done, the magician would say some other words, and the servant would turn back into an inanimate object. Eucrates, naturally, was eager to learn this trick, but the magician was extremely secretive.

One day Eucrates eavesdropped as the magician said a three-syllable word over a pestle. Eucrates learned the word, and when the magus went out, the eager student of magic said the word and instructed the pestle to fetch some water. The pestle fetched the water, and kept fetching water, on and on, because Eucrates had not learned how to command it to stop.

In desperation, Eucrates hacked the pestle in two, but that just compounded the disaster, for now there were two pestles hauling water. The house was almost floating away, and so was Eucrates, when the magician returned and gave the order to stop. (Now you know the origin of Mickey Mouse's adventure as the sorcerer's apprentice in *Fantasia*. Either Walt Disney read ancient Egyptian hieroglyphs or he tapped into them in a durative realm vision.)

White and Black Magic

Many Egyptian legends speak of the locally famed sorcerer-priest who severs the head of a goose, then reunites it by magical words, or who calls forth from the depths of the river the harem girl's missing jewelry. Even in some popular women's magazines, we see ancient Egyptian love spells repeated around Valentine's Day. They combine the ancient prayers to Isis, the mixing of aromatic herbs and spices, and the anointing of the sleeping body of the beloved. Suffice it to say that if you can get that close to your intended, a love spell is hardly necessary.

This is not to say that such magic-making does not work—often it does; this is simply to make a distinction between spiritual practice and showmanship. Those who take the transformative arts of the ancient Egyptians seriously are careful to distinguish between magic and sorcery. Paraphrasing Schwaller de Lubicz, West says:

> Magic is a summoning-up and utilization of *natural cosmic energy* by harmonic means. Sorcery concerns itself with influencing the psychological ambiance, thus with an energy *emanating from* the complex of human life. Both are valid, both "work." There is both "white" and "black" magic and "white" and "black" sorcery; and there are higher and lower forms of both magic and sorcery.[7]

In other words, there is magic and there is Magic. There are lower mysteries and Higher Mysteries. As lower magic is the manipulation of forms, so Higher Magic is the urge toward consciousness, which is an understanding of the universe itself. Egyptian priests and priestesses were adept at both.

Temples of the Priest-Magicians

The temples of the priest-magicians were called *per ankh*, the House of Life, and the priest-magicians were the *sesh per ankh*, or scribes in the House of Life. These temples were often several buildings, some open to the public, others secluded for the training in the high arts of human evolution and spiritual transformation. To the public house people came for psychotherapy and often, in the temples devoted to Sekhmet, for healing of the body as well. Here they came to incubate dreams, or for dream interpretation, to be put into an altered state to explore the depths of some problem or concern. Here, too, they learned powerful psychological chants to turn away disaster or malevolent influences.

As keepers of the records in the temple library, the priest-magicians had access to the highest written wisdom in the land, such wisdom as was kept under lock and key. They were not copyists of texts but interpreters of the sacred hieroglyphs. They determined which glyphs were inscribed on the walls of the new temples, as well as which rites were read in which services.

At the great magical House of Life at the Temple of Horus at Edfu, one of the walls is engraved with a list of sacred books kept there. Their titles give us some idea of the powers possessed by the ancient priest-magicians: The Book of Appeasing Sekhmet; The Book of Magical Protection of the King in His Palace; Spells for Warding Off the Evil Eye; The Book of Repelling Crocodiles; The Book of Knowledge of the Secrets of the Laboratory; The Book of Knowing the Secret Forms of the God.

The Functions of the Temple Priests

Those who formed the priesthood of the temple were as diverse in their understandings of the mysteries as they were in their temple functions, but even the lesser priests had to have been initiated into at least the lower mysteries. The most common member of the priesthood was the *wab* priest, meaning "a pure one." The hieroglyph depicts a person over whom water is poured, indicating that, on a literal level, the priest or priestess had bathed in the sacred lake, was spiritually clean, and had been initiated (or baptized, perhaps, in Christian terms) into the sacred mystery of merger with the cosmic waters of creation.

Like other priests, the temple priests served only three months out of the year, or one month every season. When not attached to a temple, they lived with their families in the community and continued their daily businesses, whether as merchants, scribes, farmers, or artists. Yet while they were attached to a temple, they lived cloistered inside where incense burned, praises were sung, and the sacred rites continued in shifts throughout the day and night. Isolated from their families, they abstained from sexual intercourse, wore pure white linen robes, ate no fish, and took very little meat. "Pure ones" bathed four times a day, twice in the morning and twice in the evening. Like most Egyptian men, they were circumcised, and while they served a temple, their heads and bodies were shaven.

Many priestesses who served the temple were singers, dancers, and musicians living at home with their families and performing their religious duties only on special occasions. The *khenerit*, however, were cloistered priestesses who lived within the temple itself. As keepers of the innermost sanctuaries, they were adepts in the same high wisdom that the priests knew. The higher priestesses were called "the wife of the god."

The astrological forecasts of the *ounuit*, or "priests of the hours," kept track of divine, netered time, rather than of human hours. Their predictions were not personal, but focused on keeping track of the three festival calendars—the lunar, the solar, and the Sothic, the Sothic being the true agricultural calendar based on the accurate rising of the Dog Star, the herald of the annual flood. These priests determined the minute and hour when the doors between the worlds would slide open and a given neter would appear.

Some *ounuit* priestesses acted as midwives, assisting in the birth of children. Through divine channels to Isis and the Seven Hathors, the goddesses of fate, they were able to read the future of the child in the cracked birthing bricks upon which the laboring mother had squatted. A few honored priests and priestesses were the "stolists," as the Greeks called them; that is, they clothed the god, bathed the cult statue, presented it food several times a day, opened the inner sanctuary at dawn, and closed it at night.

The high priest, or *sem* priest, was called "the first prophet of the god." Only the *sem* priest or priestess wore the traditional panther skin; otherwise, it was forbidden to wear the skin of any animal. Perhaps this was because the wearing of animal skins recalled more barbarous times, but more likely it was because one needed to have attained higher levels of initiation to control the intensive solar energies with which the lion or panther skins were associated.

Pharaoh as High Priest and Sacrament

As the god's son incarnate, the pharaoh was the highest priest of all. Bearing both the crook and the flail, he was equally shepherd and warrior, lamb and lion, propitiating the gods and rejuvenating the entire country. In the early dynasties he literally sacrificed himself for the salvation of his people, thereby assuring them of abundant life and fertile fields.

Records from as far back as 2800 B.C. depict the pharaoh's *heb sed* festival, a theatrical, public drama of sacrifice and renewal taking place in the pharaoh's thirtieth year of reign. The Christian tenets of faith in Jesus as the Son of God sacrificed in his thirty-third year for the salvation of his people are not so dissimilar. The complete meaning of the *heb sed* festival is still mysterious, but the weeklong passion play took place at the beginning of the Egyptian spring season. The passion play involved ceremonial rites and preparations, including bringing festival meat and drink to the temple, processions of the pharaoh through throngs of his people, a solemn moment of divine illumination of the pharaoh's divine task before the god Anubis (Opener of the Way), and physical trials of endurance. Although we cannot be sure, the very early festivals may have involved ritual sacrifices, perhaps of an honored stand-in for the pharaoh. Later, the sacrifices were symbolic, substituting a sacred animal for the human being. After the blood ritual came the sacred eating of the sacrificed god, the celebrations of spiritual renewal and the return to life, and the bestowal of blessings.

During this ceremony the pharaoh "dies" and is no longer seen on earth. When he reappears in glorious raiment, he bears "The Will" or "The Secret of the Two Partners," a sacred papyrus scroll that contained the testament of his father in the neterworld, Osiris.[8] As we will see later, the rituals and drama of the *heb sed* festival form the basis of the Osirian mysteries in which Egyptian initiates into the temple wisdom participated.

Pharaoh as Magician and Miracle Worker

Many pharaohs were adepts in the making of magic and the working of miracles. The last native Egyptian ruler, Nectanebo II, was greatly skilled in magic. By making a wax statue of the Macedonian queen Olympias, he caused her to dream that the god Amun had made love with her and that she had conceived a divine child. He then sent King Philip a dream in which a golden hawk told him that Olympias would birth a god. This legend establishes the divine origins of Alexander the Great who, when later presented to the oracle of Amun in the Libyan desert, was declared the son of the god (that is, pharaoh) before witnesses.

Nectanebo not only sent dreams, he read stars, interpreted omens, and fought battles by means of magical figures. After fashioning ships and soldiers of wax, then speaking magical incantations over the battle scene, he would cause the winds to overturn his enemies' ships; this would invariably happen in the next day's actual battle. One day, though, the Egyptian ruler made his images and recited his incantations, yet he saw the winds of the neters turn against him, sinking his own ships. Distraught, Nectanebo shaved his head and beard, put on the clothes of a commoner, and fled to Ethiopia, leaving Egypt helpless before the Persian invaders.

In the Arab tradition, the historian Mas Udi tells us that an unnamed woman pharaoh, a sorceress, protected Egypt by magical spells for the thirty years following the time of Exodus; that walls that she built around the borders of Egypt held magical statues of crocodiles, lions, and other fierce creatures that she could summon to life. She collected many magical papyri, learned the properties of plants, animals, and minerals, and controlled the powers of nature. By burying magical wax men in the ground, she caused the enemies of Egypt to be swallowed by the earth.

The pharaonic sorceress must have been none other than Hatshepsut, the only woman pharaoh to rule Egypt for thirty years. (In scope and brilliance she reminds us of the great medieval abbess Hildegard of Bingen, also one of the most learned and powerful people of her time.)

We know that after the pharaoh Ahmose expelled the Hyksos (Semitic foreigners) from Egypt in 1553 B.C., Hatshepsut came to rule and established Egyptian outposts deep within Asia, as far as Syria. She also declared that the gods hated those who "had ruled without Ra [and] had acted without divine command." Because the gods so despised them, the "earth carried off their footprints."[9] This story suggests that the biblical pharaoh of Exodus was not Rameses II, as is commonly believed, but rather the pharaoh Ahmose.

Of Healing and Medicine

Perhaps Hatshepsut was a healer as well as a sorceress. On the upper terrace of her temple in Deir el-Bahri sits a small healing chapel dedicated to Imhotep and Amenhotep, both fabled scribes, physicians, priest-magicians, and wise men. Here the infirm came to be cured, and graffiti on the chapel walls bear the names of those who received cures and healing dreams.

The ancient Egyptians practiced different types of medicine, much of which has been attributed to the knowledge of the priest-physician Imhotep. He wrote the famous treatise now known as the Edwin Smith Papyrus, which accurately details surgical techniques performed as early as 2575 B.C. He is also the same man who envisioned and designed the Step Pyramid for pharaoh Djoser. The Greeks identified Imhotep with their healing god Asclepios.

For ancient physicians, the magician's box was as ubiquitous as the modern doctor's black bag. Made of wood and covered in white plaster, each box bore an image of the practitioner's patron healing neter on its lid—perhaps Anubis, Horus, Isis, or Sekhmet. The box held specific medical papyri and magic wands with animal heads. With these gilt wood or ivory wands, the magician drew circles around certain sick people and their houses, something like an ancient quarantine. As early as the Old Kingdom, the physicians knew that diseases were carried by flies, and that germs were airborne; thus the ancient medical texts put enormous importance on rites of purification and cleanliness.

The boxes also contained healing talismans, perhaps the tree of Osiris called the *djed* pillar, used for the fast mending of broken bones, or a red carnelian womb of Isis, an amulet for fertility. One of the most popular healing talismans was the Wadjet eye, or the whole eye of Horus. This amulet recalled the blinding of Horus by Seth during battle and the healing of that blinded eye by Thoth. The eye of Horus, perhaps because it was torn to pieces in legend, was also an ancient Egyptian unit of measure for fractions, all its fractional parts totaling one, the image of wholeness. Therefore, the restored eye of Horus was a healing talisman that brought one wholeness or health.

It is interesting to note that when the pupil of the eye in the hieroglyph is combined with the tears that flow beneath it, the ancient image of "Rx," or the modern symbol of the physician's prescription, is produced.

Ancient Spells and the Roots of Modern Medicine

Many early Egyptologists scoffed at papyri that advised women to pour urine on wheat and barley to be certain of fertility. They assumed that it was an ancient spell to assure fertility, a prime example of superstitious, primitive thinking and nothing else. In truth, the ancient texts were giving a precise medical method for early determination of pregnancy. Not only that, but the text also indicated how to predict the sex of the unborn child. The researcher Colin Ronan reported that under scientific investigation, the "spell" actually did predict pregnancy:

> The method used was to take a woman's urine and soak bags containing wheat and barley with it. They found that if the subject was pregnant, the urine would accelerate the growth of the wheat if the child was to be a boy, or the barley if it was to be a girl. Yet such a test is only a comparatively recent innovation with us; not until 1926 was a urine pregnancy test discovered, and it was another seven years before the acceleration of [growth of] wheat and barley was confirmed by laboratory tests.[10]

Ronan also noted that a four-thousand-year-old tomb painting in Beni Hassan shows contraceptives being made from acacia spikes, honey, and dates. Four millennia later, scientists came to realize that acacia spikes contain lactic acid, a known spermicide, finally rediscovering what the ancient Egyptians already knew. It makes one wonder about the ancient spell "How to Turn an Old Man into a Youth." What exactly was the *hemayet* plant that could remove wrinkles and age spots when ground into a pulp?

Indeed, one wonders how the ancient Egyptians could have known so much. Perhaps all their knowledge of science, anatomy, botany, nutrition, mathematics, astronomy, and so on can be attributed to simple observation, trial and error, and accurate record keeping. Or, perhaps it was just as the ancient Egyptians said—the gods themselves taught the sciences to them. Perhaps they simply looked to the neter in order to understand nature. Greek philosophers, among them Heron of Alexandria, who lived during the second century A.D. and studied with the Egyptian priests, suggested that the soul possessed an innate universal knowledge that exterior objects awakened through the senses.

This idea is similar to the notion of Jung's collective unconscious, which is reached by the senses and speaks through the emotions. For example, the strong sense impressions of memory and childhood can be explained biologically by the way the brain stores information, yet they remain a mystery of utmost importance. When we begin to see memory and learning passed on genetically, it is even more amazing.[11] We keep coming back to the old metaphysical notion that somehow thoughts are things and perhaps, conversely, things are thoughts. This could mean that our intuitive impressions of things out there are actually symbolic, perhaps even holographic, rather than logical readings. As the magicians say, "It's all a trick with light and mirrors."

Of Dreams and Oracles

Egyptian medicine was holistic. The healers treated body, mind, and spirit, working on a multitude of levels. They knew that there were deep connections between physical ailments and psychological and spiritual malaise. The easiest way to tap this transpersonal level was through patients' dreams, where images linked events occurring in both earthly and spiritual realms.

Sleeping in a temple to incubate a healing dream was a common practice among Greek pilgrims, especially at the healing centers devoted to the god Asclepios. The healing Temple of Hathor in Dendera included a long corridor filled with numerous statues that bore healing incantations and inscriptions. Water poured over these images drained through stone channels into sunken tubs, where the sick bathed in the healing waters.

Dream-seekers at Dendera passed the night sealed in almost total darkness inside a small crypt, searching for the healing image that arose from the psychic depths. Priestesses brought each dreamer a special lamp containing a kind of aromatic oil designed to place the patient in a state of hypnosis, which allowed the dreamer to hold a conversation with the healing neter. The techniques are not dissimilar from modern techniques of combined aromatherapy and the use of isolation tanks. Studies by Karlis Osis and J. Fahler have determined that prehypnotized subjects dream more deeply and more precognitively than those who are not hypnotized.[12]

Shamanic Dreaming

It has been suggested that dreamers tap into the deeper psyche, where the primordial patterns of past, present, and future are held. There, we have access not only to the archetypal past but also to the future. Says historian of religions Mircea Eliade:

> It is in dreams that the pure sacred life is entered and direct relations with the gods, spirits, and ancestral souls are re-established. It is always in dreams that historical time is abolished and the mythical time regained— which allows the future shaman to witness the beginnings of the world and hence to become contemporary not only with the cosmogony but also with the primordial mythical revelations.[13]

It is no surprise that Egypt's priests and priestesses were adept at dream interpretation. Those learned scribes who deeply understood hieroglyphic symbols made little distinction between whether those images appeared on the wall of a temple, in a scroll of papyrus, or in a dream. Because the priest-magicians could read the archetypal patterns of the past, by the same token, they could decipher a dream image and its pattern for the future.

Even the pharaohs had their dreams interpreted. Divine will often manifested through psychic connections with the neters during sleep. The famous stela that lies between the paws of the Sphinx details the dream of a young prince, Thutmose IV. While he was hunting one afternoon, he fell asleep in the shade of the Sphinx, which lay half hidden in the sands. The Sphinx told him that if he cleared away the sand that encumbered it, the prince would become pharaoh. Thutmose IV cleared the sand, and the Sphinx kept its promise. Later, when the pharaoh's country was under siege and it appeared that he would lose an important battle against the Nubians, he received another dream telling him which neter would bring victory if he made the proper offerings. He prayed, made his offerings, and was victorious.

In shamanic traditions the shaman-to-be often receives the call to destiny during a dream. Some dreams are personal and herald the entrance into a deeper and renewed life of the spirit. Others, like the dream of Thutmose IV, bear cultural and historical importance. The dream exists beyond local time and space, and while the ego is stilled in sleep, the dream provides the clearest channel of divine direction, piercing the veil of the everyday and bringing deep knowledge into consciousness.

In his memoirs Carl Jung recalls dreaming about an old house with a vast library of arcane, leather-bound books containing curious symbols he did not recognize. He knew that the library was some aspect of his personality of which he was not yet conscious. And, indeed, when he first encountered alchemy two years after the dream, he felt it to be "nonsense." However, fifteen years after his initial dream, he himself had assembled an alchemical library very much like the one he had seen in his dream.[14] An early dream of mine also related to a mysterious house filled with rare books and manuscripts and many ancient statues. I now live in such a house surrounded by those things.

Contacting Neters through Dream

Because Egypt is one of the oldest civilizations, and perhaps because its highly spiritual culture was charged daily by chanting priests and peasants for four thousand years, Egypt itself has entered into the collective unconscious. It provides a limitless fount of images that flow from the unconscious and are available to today's dreamers just as much as to ancient ones.

In his study of human consciousness, the psychologist Erich Neumann spoke of the eons of ancestral experience stored in the instinctual nature of the body, which forms a "living knowledge." It is only in the past few thousand years that the human mind has attempted to make conscious the wisdom of this kind of cellular knowledge. Yet, as Neumann implied, this is the true primordial wisdom—the mind of the genes, the full knowing of the DNA, the collective unconscious of the ouroboros. "The Great Mother," he wrote, "has a wisdom infinitely superior to the ego, because the instincts and archetypes that speak through the collective unconscious represent the 'wisdom of the species' and its will."[15]

Queen of Heaven and Earth, mistress of the upper and lower worlds, the goddess Isis often appears in dreams to bear messages, challenges, and warnings, or to offer succor to the troubled. She and the god Bes often bring hidden information into consciousness from the durative realm. Many a bedroom in ancient Egypt held a niche containing the statue of either Bes or Isis, who drove away nightmares and brought prophetic sleep. Those who could not afford to incubate their dreams at the temple often sought the advice of Isis the sorceress while asleep.

A number of spells for inducing dreams can be found, including drawing an image of the dwarflike god Bes on the dream-seeker's left hand. The ink was made of blood, frankincense, myrrh, cinnabar, and rainwater. Then the dreamer wrapped his hand in a long strip of black cloth consecrated to Isis. A petition to Bes or Isis needed to be written out before sunset. That night the dreamer lay down to sleep without speaking a word, wrapping the cloth about his hand, and winding a length of it about his throat. If the dreamer didn't strangle himself in his sleep, a dream might come. It could be interpreted by consulting the Dream Book, a kind of ancient Egyptian do-it-yourself dream-interpretation guide.[16]

A Modern Encounter with Remnants of Ancient Magic

If the scribe who chiseled the temple hieroglyphs knew the precise manifestation of the neter being invoked, then certainly the craftsmen of the temple statues and cult objects knew the power inherent in their symbols. If magicians could heal illnesses through healing waters poured over empowered statues, they could also create disease. Just as the priests of Egypt deliberately erased the power of certain temple hieroglyphs, so they also protected the statues of the gods from misuse.

I know this only too well through firsthand experience. Several years after my husband, Robert Masters, and I were married, we found in an antiquities shop a beautiful bronze statue of the goddess Sekhmet, dating from before the first millennium B.C. We had been saving for over two years to make a down payment on a house and the statue cost everything we had in the bank. Naturally, we bought the statue. Soon after, ancient Egyptian artifacts began to arrive. They would come as gifts or we would find them in the antiquities shops we haunted, often costing very little. (As a child in New York City I would visit the Madison Avenue shop of an old gentleman who in Vienna had been Sigmund Freud's antiquities dealer. Seeing my face pressed against the pane of his shop day after day, he finally invited me in, and for the next few years gave me an invaluable training in how to recognize authentic items. This permitted us to buy many things that were authentic but which at that time the dealers had no great interest in.)

Soon we had a fine complement of the gods of Egypt, followed soon after by the gods of Greece and Rome, of Tibet and Micronesia, and of China. And they are still coming. Yes, I will aver to the jaundiced reader, perhaps it was merely a matter of coincidence, a fortuitous freak of circumstance, but perhaps it was not.

Anyway, one day I decided to give the Sekhmet statue a good cleaning. I was wearing shorts at the time and had just been scratched on the back of my leg by Psyche, our Siamese cat. I lifted the statue from its base and began to carefully wipe the dust of centuries out of its hollow interior. At one point, I recall swatting the dust cloth on my leg. A few days later, on the site of the cat scratch a black necrotic crater formed, then another, and still another. Whatever it was, it wasn't modern. Before long, I looked like the biblical Job on the back of my leg.

I went to see an elderly physician friend of ours, Dr. William Wolf. He seemed very puzzled and took a biological assay of the crater. After the test came back, he called me into his office, saying, "Do you know what you've got? You've got anthrax! How could you possibly catch anthrax in the modern world? I thought I saw the last case, and that was in 1917. No, don't tell me. Have you been around anything ancient?"

"Oh, yes," I replied. "All the time. I have a mummy case in the dining room, Isis and Osiris in the living room, Thoth in the study . . ."

"But have you been touching any of these things, cleaning them perhaps?"

"Well, there is a three-thousand-year-old statue of Sekhmet that I was sort of cleaning."

"Let me see it immediately. In the meantime, let's get you started on a course of cortisone."

Due examination of the statue indeed showed that there were anthrax spores within it, and we had to go through quite an elaborate procedure to get rid of them. Anthrax was one of the diseases of the ancient Egyptians; it recurs throughout the Old Testament whenever one god or another is smiting somebody. Spores do not die. In fact, they can live on for millions of years. What evidently happened is that when I swatted the anthrax-ridden dust cloth on my newly scratched leg, the spores woke up from their long sleep and happily went to work again. Ergo, the black necrotic craters.

But why anthrax, you may wonder, in this particular statue? We know that often, when a statue was to be buried after it had been in use for some time, or was placed in a tomb to guard the dead, it would be rubbed down with the bandages or cloths from a person dying of a deadly disease. This was probably part of the source of the legend about the curse of the pharaohs, a curse to protect the statues of the gods from grave robbers and modern archaeologists.

The Living Neters in Stone

For the ancient Egyptians, the choice of building materials was deliberate, which is why the pyramids were originally encased in highly polished white limestone that glittered at dawn, and why the rose quartzite obelisk of Hatshepsut at Karnak rings like a bell when struck, and why the larger statues of the fiery goddess Sekhmet were carved of black granite, a volcanic stone, and why the wooden sarcophagi of the pharaohs resembled the tree of Byblos in which Osiris was encased. All the paintings on the tomb walls, the furniture, the amulets, even the mummy itself were created with high spiritual intentions and focus, imbued with the power of constant religious devotion, prayer, and attention.

Rather than viewing the abundant funereal provisions of the dead as evidence of rampant materialism, we ought to see each object as the ancients did. Each was imbued with magic, ritually empowered by priests with the specific intent of invoking perfected life and harmony in paradise.

The statues in the temples themselves were the earthly residences for the neters. Because a divine soul could inhabit any form it wished, the statues were bathed, clothed, and fed as if they were living neters. It was not the statue of Amun-Re itself that was revered, but the cosmic principle of divine light and becoming that resided within the form. The ancient Egyptians had no doubt that the images of the neters were alive, for, as you recall, all beasts, animals, and stones held the spark of the divine. Thus the living statue of the god also contained that god's visionary powers and the ability to know what existed in the durative realm. If a high priest or initiate had the same visionary experience of the durative powers, then it was possible to perceive the oracles of the gods. The divine light in the statue communed with the divine light in the human form. One could speak with gods *khu* to *khu*—mind to Mind.

On festival days the god's statue was carried on the shoulders of priests outside the temple gates and through the streets crowded with worshipers. At designated rest stops along the way the priests paused, and those who needed the intervention of the neters came to the image of the god to ask for favors or decisions. When the parading cult statue of the god Amun stopped before the young boy Thutmose III and appeared to single him out for notice, the priests were assured that he had been chosen by the god as the future pharaoh. Similarly, Queen Hatshepsut undertook her noble journey to the land of Punt when the god Amun asked her to search out the highways to the myrrh terraces. One of the colossi of Memnon delivered seven oracular verses at dawn to the Greek Eucrates, who was studying with the Egyptian priests.

Astrology and the Cycles of Time

Still other prophecies regarding the fate of the country were made by the *ounuit* priests based on astrological data. Because for thousands and thousands of years the priests had kept accurate records of the solar and lunar calendars, as well as the risings of the Dog Star, Sirius, they noted the inevitable procession of the equinoxes in which approximately every 2,160 years the date of the spring equinox moved from one zodiacal constellation to another. That is, the spring equinox (March 21) in the year 4240 B.C. occurred when the constellation Taurus was highest in the sky. Then, around 2080 B.C., the spring equinox coincided with the sign of Aries, the ram. The Piscean age occurred around A.D 80 when the equinox coincided with the rising of the constellation of the fish, which is where it still rises. But as we approach the Aquarian age, the spring equinox is moving inevitably toward the constellation of the water bearer.[17]

The priests determined that the opening of each of these ages heralded a new era of human development and planetary energy related to that constellation's particular zodiacal sign. In order to cojoin their old world order with the new cosmic order, the priests erected new temples for the emergent neters of the times. Thus we find that during 4240 B.C., the age of Taurus, Egypt, as well as other global civilizations, was thoroughly immersed in the cult of the bull and cow. It is during that period of time that the predynastic images of the cow goddess Hathor appear and her cult temple was first erected in Dendera. John Anthony West notes that also at that time

the symbolism of Mentu, the bull, becomes the most salient feature of Egyptian art; architecture becomes monolithic, is carried out on a scale never equaled throughout recorded history and performed with a finesse never surpassed. Old Kingdom Egypt radiates a kind of gigantic calm assurance. What little is known of other civilizations of the Taurean age suggests they shared these qualities. It is just possible that the veneration of the cow in India dates from this period. The parallel civilization of Crete was also consecrated to the bull. And while the case cannot be couched in terms acceptable to the skeptic, the astrological nature of the sign of Taurus (feminine, fixed, earth, and ruled by Venus) corresponds neatly with Old Kingdom Egypt.[18]

Before this period of time, beginning around 7400 B.C., Egypt was under the influence of the astrological sign of Gemini, the twins. An interesting note is that it was during this period of Neolithic history that Egypt was a land of dualities. Upper and Lower Egypt exhibited distinctly separate cultures. The Tasian and Badarian cultures succeeded one another in the desert plateaus of the south, while at approximately the same time the Merimda and Faiyum A cultures followed each other in the northern delta.[19] The southern cultures, you will recall, are associated with the warrior god Seth, patron of the hunters and gatherers, and the northern cultures with the agricultural god Osiris. In addition, the two lands were ruled by twin goddesses (Mut and Wadjet, the vulture and the snake) who were worshiped in their districts within twin cities.

An even earlier era, in which Neolithic peoples began settling into the Nile river valley and delta, was ruled by Cancer, the water sign that symbolizes the "first" or ancestral home. The Greek historian Plutarch reported that the reason the Egyptians revered the lion and ornamented their temple doors with lions' mouths that sprayed fountains of water was that the Nile had spread its new waters over the seeded lands of Egypt during the time that the spring equinox was in Leo, that is, around 10,000 B.C., when the constellation of the Lion (Leo) was moving inevitably toward the constellation of the Crab (Cancer). Plutarch said that the Nile arose from the mountains of central Africa, an event that would have followed the retreat of glacial snowcaps in Europe, the wasting of the Sahara savanna into sand, and the settling of previously nomadic peoples close to the Nile, their source of sustenance.

By 1990 B.C., when the procession of the equinoxes had moved into Aries, we note that Egyptian religion simultaneously experienced a dramatic change from the worship of the bull and cow to the worship of the ram god Amun. At this time, construction of the glorious Temple of Karnak and its avenue of ram-headed sphinxes was begun. The dawn of the Piscean age in the first century A.D. was marked by the rise of the Christian religion, symbolized by the fish.

Thus, as we approach the year 2000, we find ourselves nearing the age of Aquarius. Will our new spiritual foundations for the next two thousand years spring from the image of that water bearer? Certainly the image of fresh water is apropos in these times when our planet suffers from pollution of its seas, rivers, and lakes. When sea life is dying, when droves of whales and dolphins beach themselves, we find ourselves in desperate need of that water-bearing Aquarian. Perhaps the new Aquarius is manifest as twentieth-century ecologists who have come again to understand the deep connection between nature and neter.

Anubis, under the direction of Thoth, reconstituting the body of Osiris with the help of the frog goddess Heket. Nephthys sits at the head of the bier and Isis at the foot.

8

*Magic of Magic, Spirit of Spirit,
Part 2*

When the ripe fruit falls
its sweetness distills and trickles away into the veins of the
earth.

When fulfilled people die
the essential oil of their experience enters
the veins of living space, and adds a glisten
to the atom, to the body of immortal chaos.

from "When the Ripe Fruit Falls"
by D. H. Lawrence

Initiation into the Way

In this time of whole system transition we have extraordinary opportunities for both global and personal transformation. If we look to ancient Egypt, we may find that the tools we need to recover and transform our world are not unlike those of the ancient practitioner of natural philosophy and sacred psychology—the Egyptian sorcerer:

· A knowing of the cycles of time with a deep understanding of the durative and temporal realms. One knows when to enter into *kairos*, the "loaded time," when the doors between the worlds open.
· A deep belief in and an understanding of the powers of the neters. One works in alignment with the elements of the natural world that each power represents. In other words, one taps into both the scientific and intuitive relationships between cause and effect.
· An understanding that Spirit manifesting as light is the charge of the universe. Because one realizes that energy does not dissipate, but rather circulates, one observes and uses the transformation of matter to release energy into a new form.

These were the basic tenets of faith behind the act of magic-making. This is also the meaning behind the hermetic wisdom of generations, professed by the magical adept, "As above, so below; as below, so above," or when the Christian adept professes, "I and the Father are one."

Working from this belief system, sorcerers or priest-magicians could affect matter by aligning themselves with divine will and drawing down the power through incantation and ritual. Their most effective tools were the *heka*, the words of power, the deep images, and the spiritually supercharged phrases that "cast a spell." By *heka* the ancient Egyptians meant that words spoken in proper sequence, with proper intonation, and with the power of intent could produce magical effects. In modern terms, *heka* may be seen as "incantatory prose," as language elevated to poetic art, with all its attention to music, myth, and symbol. Or it may reside in mantras recited in meditation, or in spiritual affirmations. Words of power are those uttered with clarity and vision and precision of execution.

One of the primary ways to participate in the divine energy of the universe is to speak it into being. We must come to know that what we think, and feel, and say affects the world around us. Prayers are magic-making, but even thought is magic-making. As we move through this chapter, we will begin to take the first steps to learning to apply the principles of magic to growing in our own lives and in the world.

How the Gods Speak the World into Being

Just as the ancient Egyptians believed the world sprang from the lips of the neter Ptah who uttered the first word, so the Christian New Testament reads, "In the beginning was the Word and the Word was with God and the Word was God" (John 1:1). The Old Testament tells us, "And God said, Let there be Light, and there was Light" (Genesis 1:1). In the Hindu tradition the world springs from the skulls forming the necklace of the goddess Kali, and each of these skulls is a letter of the Sanskrit alphabet.

Naming, or creative utterance, sparks Light—that is, consciousness; we see things as they are. Simultaneously, naming evokes comparison, an awareness of dissimilarity; we see things as they are not. Selection and perception begin at the moment of consciousness, perhaps before consciousness is aware of itself, and it is precisely this dual knowledge of being and nonbeing states that forms the core of Egyptian spirituality. To the ancient mind, nothing existed before the Word. Nothing lived until it was named, and once named, it could be known. What could not be named remained nameless and did not exist, because it could not be known.[1] Knowing and unknowing underlie the Egyptian notion of *heka*.

In the Heliopolitan tradition we read that at the moment of creation Ra is accompanied by Thoth, the god of wisdom, and Ma'at, the goddess of truth. The two neters represent mindfulness and heartfulness in the moment of the fully conscious creative act. What we can conceive (as Ptah conceived the world) in our heart (Ma'at) and mind (Thoth) already exists. What we believe, we become.

Consciousness is creative, and naming acknowledges existence; therefore, thoughts are things. This places the responsibility upon us as individuals who daily must remain conscious of our thoughts. This, in turn, reinforces our positive habitual thoughts and helps us guard against negative patterns of thinking.

The gods Sia, Hu, and Hike also daily accompany Ra in the solar barque. Thus we are to simultaneously understand that creation is based in divine intelligence or perception (Sia), in ritual or divine authority (Hu), and in the affirmation or the magic of the utterance itself (Hike).

As the cosmic patterns are duplicated in the architecture of the earth, so the history of a lifetime is embedded in every human being's name. The angel tells Mary and Joseph to name the holy child Jesus, or Yeshua, for the name held special powers. The Book of Enoch said that it was the secret name given by God to the Son of Man, meaning "Yahweh saves."

The Ren *or Sacred Name*

So were the ancient Egyptians given a sacred name, the *ren*, which resonated with the powers associated with each individual. Amenhotep meant the "peace of Amun"; Meriaten meant "beloved of the sun god." It was said that each person's *ren* was the spiritual link with the divine patron neter, and that "the name was his for a lifetime in one of the knotted loops on the infinite thread of Eternity."[2] Therefore, when someone died, his name lived on as long as the person was remembered; as long as one's name was spoken by family and friends, one lived. The Book of the Dead contains a marvelous spell to assure one's remembrance in eternity:

> Give me my name. Say it over red jasper dipped in an unguent of flowers. . . . I am more than flesh and bone. I am more than the deeds I have done. I am more than all I remember. Give me my name. Say it over red jasper laid in the heart of sycamore. Give me my name that gods may call me to soar like the hawk and crane.[3]

More important, to speak the name of a god was to feel enfolded in the divine presence. Sacred names fed the gods' souls as well as human souls. By chanting a neter's name, one is blessed with divine power, one sees the divine manifestations of the neter on earth, the grace, the blessing, the peace.

At death, one meets one's Creator face-to-face. Yet this meeting holds no terror; it is like coming upon an old friend along the way. One text in the Book of the Dead shows an immortal soul in the underworld calling out heartily to the gods: "I know you. I know your names."

To speak the *heka* of self-becoming—as the Great God created and recognized himself—was to bear the same spark of divine creative power. We find this tradition in the Sanskrit where the devotee chants the creative *om* of Kali, or repeats the mantra *om mani padme hum* ("All hail the Jewel within the Lotus"), which means that one has perceived and honors the divine child within the universal matrix.

Connecting with such potent logos, with such primal utterance, one contacts the god-in-hiding within oneself. To speak the neter's name invokes a divine transference of that spiritual essence into the body. If the neters may manifest themselves in nature, then certainly they may reside in us and in each other. Therefore, it is not so astonishing to find one ancient text declaring: "God is my name. I do not forget it, this name of mine."

The texts of the sacred union with god and the calling down of the divine are more ancient than the pyramids themselves, predating even the first pharaoh of Egypt, King Menes. The first extant holy words of power were called the Pyramid Texts because they appear, inscribed in beautifully rendered hieroglyphs, in the tombs of the late Old Kingdom pharaohs (circa 2494–2181 B.C.). To this day, the images seem as fresh as the day they were carved. They speak of the union of the human spirit with the spirit of the neters. For example, this brief but beautiful poem to the goddess Nut found in the pyramid of Pepi I shows us how the pharaoh revered the great sky goddess as the source of spiritual light:

> O Great One who became sky, you are strong; you are mighty. You fill every place with your beauty. The whole earth is beneath you, you possess it! As you enfold earth and all things in your arms, so have you taken this Pepi to you, an indestructible star within you![4]

In yet another text, Pepi asserts his divinity by emphasizing that his soul is part of the immortal soul of the god, that this cosmic inheritance existed before the birth of the world, and that his true life began at the beginning of time:

> Pepi was born in Nun, before there was sky, before there was earth, before there were mountains, before there was strife, before even the struggle of Seth and Horus came about through the Horus Eye.[5]

These ancient hymns are not grandiose self-elevation, but reminders of the merger of the lower self with the Higher Self, of illumination of one's Osirian nature. Arthur Versluis, a longtime student of Eastern and Near Eastern religions and the author of *The Egyptian Mysteries*, states that he believes that although most of the Egyptian texts are written in the first person, "their focus is one of widening, or perhaps better, heightening the amplitude of consciousness, in one sense expanding the I, and in another virtually eliminating it."[6]

Words of Power for the Dead

The oldest chapter in what later came to be called the Book of the Dead is the one known as The Coming Forth by Day in the Underworld. The Egyptians themselves considered this text very ancient, very mysterious, and very difficult to understand. It was said to have been found by the pharaoh Cheops in the city of Hermopolis, to have been written in letters of lapis lazuli on a block of ironstone, and to have appeared lying beneath the feet of a god.[7] In addition to its hymns, words of power, and prayers, as well as its initial map of the underworld, this work represents the primary text of ancient Egyptian religion, the understanding of the unification of the souls of Ra and Osiris.

Those texts inscribed on the pyramid walls were later expanded to include other texts, specifically religious "spells" or rituals that were inscribed on the sarcophagus itself. These "Coffin Texts," as they were called, relied more heavily on the use of magical words of power than did the older ecstatic hymns of the Pyramid Texts. The German Egyptologist Erik Hornung has called this era of magic (the First Intermediate Period) "the nuclear energy of early civilizations," implying both *heka*'s creative and destructive energies.[8] He goes on to explain:

> The powers of the chaos before creation are never conquered entirely, but provoke a continual struggle which is fought by the gods in the sky and in the underworld, and on earth primarily by the king. In strict terms the most powerful weapon, the creative energy of "magic," should be available only to the gods; a magician on earth must therefore take on the role of a deity in order to exploit this dangerous and potent force.[9]

Hornung further recounts the misuses of magic, specifically the love spells, a subversion of the little will, rather than the alignment of the human will with the will of the neters. The use of the selfish, human will is termed "evil." As to the neters, there is no evil. There is chaos, yes; there is confusion and confrontation and limitation. Seth may act as a sort of trickster who disturbs the world order, but Seth is an essential element of limited disorder that is essential to change and to living order. Duality is part of the ancient Egyptian concept of the double, *ma'at*, or truth. The goddesses Isis and Nephthys were said to represent the twin *ma'aty*, that is, the active and the receptive, the glorious, and the veiled knowing.

True magic was possible only with an understanding of Thoth (wisdom) and Ma'at (truth). The greatest offering a pharaoh or priest could make was to offer *ma'at* to the neter, to say, in effect, "I have experienced your truth; I have applied your truth to my experience, and I offer back to you *ma'at*." Neters require nothing more. They do not need bread or wine. They need only the *ma'at* of the heart of a godded love. "The gods do not need any material gifts," says Hornung. "But they do need human response to their existence; they want to be experienced in the hearts of men, for only then does their work of creation acquire its lasting significance."[10]

The Importance of the Heart

One of the most mystical and essential texts of the ancient Egyptians is the text called the Chapter of Not Losing His Heart in the Underworld. The heart was the storehouse of the human soul—all its memories, deeds, words, emotions, and longings. It is the heart, the *ab*, consciousness itself, that is weighed in the Scales of Ma'at before Lord Osiris in the neterworld. The heart speaks its truth (not the brain, which can become entangled in thought). If that truth is found good, if the heart is found to be as light as the feather crowning the hair of the goddess Ma'at, then one lives eternally with Osiris in abundance and continual renewal. But if the heart speaks against a man, for hearts cannot lie, the *ab* is thrown to the monster Ammit, the "Great Devourer of Hearts," whose name is Death.

The deceased is made to cry out, "My heart. My mother. My heart. My mother. My heart of my coming into being. My heart of my transformations . . ." The *ab* was the "blood-soul," the connection to the womb of the Great Mother, the creative matrix. Connected as the heart was with the goddess Isis and Isis with the words of power, the heart was thus the source of all desire, and desire, the love nature, the passion for existence, was the catapult for one's transformations. The heart, with its continual beat-pause-beat-pause, is the symbol of the universal dance between death and life. The hieroglyph for "to dance" is the image of the heart.

The *ab* connected one with one's potentialities as well as with one's past deeds. During the trial in the underworld the heart stands in judgment of the soul. It speaks of all it has seen. It bears within it the transcendence of the small, temporal now and a movement toward the pulse of eternal time.

The *ma'at* of the heart connects a man with his Osirian nature, with his continual regreening. It is that small, light part of the self—light as a germ of a seed—that is the source of one's renewal. The Vedic notion of Atman as the primordial state of unity with the godded Self is similar. Arthur Versluis, quoting the Chandogya Upanishad, says:

The Atma, which dwells in the heart, is smaller than a grain of rice, smaller . . . than the germ which is in a grain of millet . . . this Atma, which dwells in the heart, is also greater than the earth, than the atmosphere, than the sky, greater than all the worlds together.[11]

Initiation into the Osirian and Eleusinian Mysteries

The seeded nature is the key element in both the Osirian and the Eleusinian mysteries, in which the main characters—Osiris in the Egyptian mystery, the goddess Demeter in the Greek mystery—were divinities of agriculture, particularly of the grain. We know that the story of Isis and Osiris is a tale of anguish, grief, loss, redemption, wisdom gained, and final ecstatic reunion. So, too, is the Eleusinian mystery drama of Demeter and Persephone, wherein the mother goddess loses her child Persephone to Hades, the god of death and the underworld. Persephone becomes queen of the underworld while her mother, suffering the same immense grief as did Isis in the Egyptian tale, searches everywhere for her lost daughter. Even the depictions of Demeter and Isis at the sacred well are similar, as are the mystery and magic of both goddesses attempting to make a child immortal by placing it in a fire. Demeter's grief causes the crops of Greece to wither as surely as the death and dismemberment of Osiris creates the dry, devastated Egyptian land before the return of the floodwaters.

We know, too, that both rites involved transpersonal experiences of spiritual teachings about loss, sorrow, and rebirth. An initiate into either the Egyptian Osirian mystery or the Greek Eleusinian mystery received special knowledge and training into the deeper meaning of the story as part of the initiation. Initiates experienced a physical and symbolic descent into the darkened underworld where the initiatory experience occurred. In essence, during the night of initiation the individual died to the old self as surely as the seed dies in the earth; then the transformative experience of that death germinated within the soul, and the person arose reborn. A fragment of a work by the Greek poet Pindar says of the initiates upon their return: "Happy are they who, having beheld these things, descend beneath the Earth. They know life's end but also a new beginning from the gods."

The revelation of the final secret, the presentation of the sheaf of wheat at Eleusis, was a symbolic image imbued with spiritual meaning and charged with the emotional catharsis experienced during the previous death-life experience. The ceremony placed its emphasis on the epiphany of the individual wherein the ineffable "mysteries" (rebirths) of the god Osiris and the goddess Persephone resided. The myth was no longer a legend happening out there, but a living story that resonated each day now within the human psyche. The paradox was that immortality, that is, life eternal, could be experienced only by experiencing death.

The Greek historian Herodotus recorded that the rites of Demeter were carried to the temple at Eleusis by fifty daughters of Egypt whose husbands had been murdered.[12] He further stated that "the names of nearly all the gods came to Greece from Egypt . . . for the names of all the gods have been known in Egypt from the beginning of time."

In Egypt the Osirian mysteries were already being practiced when the First Dynasty began around 3000 B.C. Comparatively speaking, the Eleusinian mysteries were a reflection as well as a revision of the ancient Egyptian rites, following closely both the pattern and the experience of the more ancient mystery. Not until 1700 B.C. did the ancestors of the Greeks settle into the hilly slopes of Eleusis, and although rites of some kind were performed at that time, no temple arose until 1500 B.C. Egyptian faience plaques discovered under the corners of temples at Mycenae date from 1400 B.C., giving further evidence of the Egyptian influence and the carrying of the Osirian mysteries to Greece.

The Greek mysteries continued the rites of the similar Egyptian mysteries, and the Christian mysteries reflect both. The Egyptian mysteries were based soundly on symbol and ritual. No writings were necessary, as the hieroglyphs and images contained the keys. The transmission of the secrets was oral, and the initiatory experience was one of pure outpouring of Spirit. Of the Greek mysteries we know slightly more; of the Christian mysteries, most exist in writing. But the problem may be one the ancients anticipated. When a mystery is written down, rather than learned, it tends to be "forgotten" by the poorly schooled initiate who believes he can always grab a book and "look it up later." In the ancient tradition, there was no forgetting. Either one learned the lessons or one lost paradise.

The sad reality is that the reenactment of the mysteries themselves eventually vanished in proportion to the amount of information that was written about them. The fact is that a mystery must be experienced, it cannot be understood intellectually—a fact that sheds light on the Greek reluctance and inability to discuss what occurred during these ancient rites.

Mystery and Sacred Drama

As both the Greeks and Egyptians were well aware, the dream was an unconscious enactment of the great mythos, but drama itself was a conscious connection with the ancient spiritual powers. This is one reason why in Greece the temples of healing, dedicated to Isis or Asclepios, were built next to the amphitheaters. Within the power of heightened language, as presented during theater, lay the power of catharsis, the naming and exorcism of spiritual, psychological, and physical disease. Following a dramatic retelling of the Lamentations of Isis and Nephthys, for example, one might go to the healing temple in order to be relieved of one's own ills and suffering.[13]

Group participation in these mysteries heightened the initiate's awareness that his own life was not unlike the lives of others, that all men and women are sojourners on similar quests, and that the death of the god was for the enlightenment of the whole. Most important, the initiate saw that the death of the individual self joined him to the universal mind of the Higher Self. Although some rites were kept strictly for the pharaoh and the high priests of Egypt, nearly everyone in the culture could participate in the Osirian and Eleusinian mysteries.

Certainly not everyone understood the larger importance of the ritual, but the attention drawn to the rite by means of a mass festival unified the nation in its longing for the same spiritual ends represented by Osiris. As the people of Egypt lamented and wept with Isis for the lost Osiris, as they wailed and mourned and threw dust upon their heads, their ritual grief mirrored the grief of all humankind in its loss of the sacred wisdom, without which they were condemned to live in fragmentation and ignorance.

Mass worship satisfied the spiritual longings of the group and focused an entire culture's attentions on the inner sanctuary—the adytum or shrine of gold inherent within the "seed" of humankind. Such losses as the death of a child, the death of a spouse, or the death of a parent would tend to draw individuals closer to the transformative experience, as would the challenge of facing imminent death in battle or childbirth. The Osirian mystery was one that lay close to the bone for everyone. Certainly, if one did not experience knowledge of it in this lifetime, one was sure to experience it at the moment of death. In a time when few people lived much beyond sixty, there was little opportunity for leisurely self-understanding.

Mircea Eliade reminds us that the death ritual moves us from the profane, nonsanctified state of the human condition to rebirth into a sanctified state. "The mystery of initiation," he says, "discloses to the neophyte, little by little, the true dimensions of existence; by introducing him to the sacred, the mystery obliges him to assume the responsibilities of a man."[14]

Temples of Initiation Rites

In Egypt both men and women were ordained as priests and priestesses, although the majority of the clergy were men. All the townspeople—

men, women, and children—celebrated the rites of Osiris. However, only priests and priestesses were involved in the ceremonies that occurred within the sanctuary. On the other hand, very few people were excluded from the ceremonies in ancient Egypt. Noblemen and noblewomen in the ancient cities acted as clergy, attendants, musicians, dancers, singers, fan bearers, and participants of one sort or the other.

The rites of Osiris and of Eleusis continued unabated year after year. While many people flocked to the temples to become initiated for the first time, many of the initiates also returned annually to celebrate the festival of renewal. The sacred act of the Osirian rites is the remembering of Osiris. To forget one's name, to forget one's sanctity, to forget one's relationship to the divine was to die while still living. It was the worst of all possible sins. Therefore, the rites were celebrated yearly. Each spring, Osiris was mourned; each spring, his body and spirit were reunited; each spring, he was remembered and reborn.

Just as the Eleusinian mysteries involved a weeklong initiation and a sacred walk from the Parthenon in Athens to the temple at Eleusis, so might the initiations into various Egyptian cults have involved travel from one temple to another. Once a year the goddess Hathor of Dendera sailed, amid clouds of incense and throngs of singers, dancers, and priestesses, to the Temple of Horus at Edfu. So might the temples of Osiris, Isis, Horus, Ra, and the other gods scattered throughout Egypt have formed a holy pilgrimage that every initiate took at least once in a lifetime.

The ritual offerings chiseled in elaborate detail and magnificent inscriptions on the wall of the Temple of Osiris at Abydos are not mere portraits of Seti I's egomania. They are acknowledgments that the divine appeared robed in flesh, and their gestures and propitiations are less politically motivated superstitious rituals than they are reenactments of the sacred rites of initiation. The Egyptian scholar and symbolist John Anthony West points out that when one sequentially follows these exquisite relief carvings in Abydos, one invokes "a knowledge of, reverence for, and power over the cosmic principle of renewal, personified as Osiris."[15]

Some believe that the oldest prehistoric initiation site may be the Sphinx itself. By means of geological dating of water and flood markings on the Sphinx, West has argued that it is much older than the First Dynasty of the Old Kingdom, as is commonly believed.[16] West and a team of scientists led by a geologist from Boston University are now searching, by means of projected sound waves, for possible initiation chambers within the Sphinx itself. During initial research they found some suspicious-looking cavities in front of the Sphinx and on either side. Although these hollows may indicate a natural deformity of the bedrock, the way they are situated makes them appear to be deliberately man-made features. West details the investigation, saying:

We were looking to see if there were any possible chambers or cavities under the Sphinx which might corroborate, say, Edgar Cayce's readings, which suggested that there was a so-called "hall of records" under the Sphinx in which the whole history of mankind could be read out.[17]

The Lesser and Greater Mysteries

The priest-magician, the magus, the sorcerer or mighty adept, received training through various levels of initiation into the Lesser and Greater Mysteries. The sorcerers and sorceresses who worked miracles and had the capacity to live in several worlds at once had all undergone some form of death to the old self and rebirth to the Higher Self, and these were the mysteries of Osiris and Ra. The Lesser Mysteries taught the initiate stability, creativity, and strength in order to become a fit vehicle for the Great Work. The Greater Mysteries made rebirth of the new self possible by releasing attachment to the here and now. As the ancient magus proclaimed:

> I've walked the long road and kept to my journey . . . I have lost and found myself in every rock, field and tree. I know what I am and what I imagine. I know shadow and light, and I have never been satisfied with shelter and bread when the great was left unattained. This I have done to enter death and turn from nothing toward life. I shall pass into heaven, even I shall pass like eternity, quietly in the fire and flesh.[18]

The true magus sees all life as a series of initiations. Birth, learning to walk and talk, working at a craft, marrying, having one's firstborn—all these are leave-takings of old habits of being, and openings up to enhanced communication with larger patterns of existence and the use of responsible power. The magus reminds us that other initiations are intentionally undertaken at the price of great effort and risk, but these initiations herald spiritual and personal unfoldment beyond that which one normally expects in a lifetime—the path of choosing copartnership with the neters.

The magus must enter a ring of fire and be forged to an extraordinarily fine temper. The psychophysical and psychospiritual powers that are developed join to the tempering, and these powers render the initiate able to play reality, to be immensely more responsive to what is there than most people ever dream of.

Carlos Castañeda says that shamans or magi have an aura of uniqueness, as well as an air of mystery and "lightness." Where the magi came from, where they are going, no one can tell. They may even present themselves as being completely without ties on either the psychic or the physical plane. They may baffle their followers by showing up in unexpected places and saying outlandish things. Unpredictable, sometimes cranky, and frequently fascinating to be around, shamans seem not quite human in the usual sense, yet they are not gods. There is an aura of inbetweenness about them.

This notion of in-betweenness is actually a manifestation of *ma'at*, or cosmic balance. The magi seem to be at rest at a central spot in the universe where the forces of darkness and violence, light and creativity, balance each other. Having learned to orchestrate these forces, they choose not to look on them or label them as good or evil. Seen in the appropriate way, all oppositions seem allies. This unique vantage point gives shamans unusual power.

In ancient Egypt the magus always experiences the cosmos as interconnected. Mind and Nature, here and there, near and far, the very small and the very large, microcosm and macrocosm—all are parts of a larger unity, and inextricable ties bind these seeming opposites into an organic unity.[19] Thus the magus knows that anything set into motion—a work, an idea, a thought, a ritual—sends resonant waves throughout the whole system, changing everything. Most of us are continuously being buffeted by these lines of forces, but the magus remains true, in a state of high witness to these vibrations and energy transactions. As one student of this phenomenon put it, the magus "is able to play upon the universe as though it were a flute."

As we have seen, ancient Egyptians were entirely aware of the laws of correspondence, under which a small operation done precisely right can have far-reaching effects by stimulating the same vibration, in higher octaves. Above all, the ancient Egyptians had the wisdom of seeing things as they are in all their interrelationships. In such a culture one learns that everything is alive, and that the invisible consciousness from the mind of stars to the sprites of springs can become allies. Everything is netered. What one sees as "normal reality" is but the tip of the iceberg. Since the universe is made of mind, and since manifest responses or entities are projections of the universe in one's own mind, magic becomes a way of projecting mind into time. Or, as one modern adept has put it, "Magic teaches you how to write your own universe."

The key emotion of the magus is the sense of wonder. How natural to stay in the sense of wonder if you are always seeing eternity in a grain of sand! When you are at home with angels and neters, your friends are literally everywhere. Your sense of the weave and correspondence of all things keeps all things full of meaning, full of presence, full of power, full of response.

When you look at the historical figure of Jesus from this perspective, he fulfills the portrait of the ancient Egyptian magus, a portrait that one could rightly argue provided a source for his own miraculous works. After all, he grew up just a few miles north of the place where the model of the magus was given. We see this Egyptian patterning particularly in his enigmatic comings and goings; his awesome initiations in the wilderness and on the cross; his calm aura of more than normal power and of having friendships beyond this local reality; his walking his own path, sometimes even leaving his disciples behind. Above all, Jesus exhibited the quality of lightness that brought those near him into a high energy field and an extended reality in which they, too, were filled with wonder for what might and must be.

Life as Constant and Ceaseless Becoming

The Egyptian idea of eternal life had to do with the notion of constant and ceaseless becoming, of decayed matter releasing its energy, becoming what the poet Dylan Thomas might call "the force that through the green fuse drives the flower." At higher levels the energies generated in the mental and astral states, when aligned with Spirit, were able to affect physical matter. The Book of the Dead provides the words of power that enable one to perform "all the transmutations which the heart bears within it." These transformations were attunements with the potentialities of the heart. The ability to transform by desire and by alignment of the will with the divine was the revelation of the higher-level initiates.

In the works of the Greek satirist Lucius Apuleius, the writer speaks of watching a woman transform herself into a raven by means of magic. Throughout the world, magi in every culture are said to enter visionary states through chant, drugs, dance, or other ritual, and in these states they contact their totem animals who bring in the power from other realms. So, too, were the "spells" of the Book of the Dead addressing those who transform and project themselves into the lotus, the *bennu* bird, the hawk, the god Ptah, and the hidden "god who giveth light in the darkness." All these were images of rebirth, of channeling death in one form into living, creative power in another.

To achieve the highly creative, transformative state of the adept took many years. Before the initiate entered into the Greater Mysteries of the solar, transformative god, he was first allowed into the Lesser Mysteries of Osiris. These Lesser Mysteries were preparatory levels, learning to see that the earthly cycles were mirrors of the cosmic pattern, learning to see the neter manifest in nature. The secret of all art, love, and life, says Versluis, is that "it is only through union with anything that it can be truly possessed."[20] The Lesser Mysteries developed the initiate's powers of concentration and strengthened his ability to receive instruction through powerful psychic channels.

In her work *The Opening of the Way*, Isha Schwaller de Lubicz gives us a luminous explanation of the true meanings of the wisdom texts written by high priest-magicians for the benefit of scribes and would-be initiates. At first blush, these "Instructions" (as they are called), written by Kagmeni and Ptahhotep, appear to be nothing more than fatherly maxims. But on deeper inspection, their practical occultism stressed the seven spiritual accomplishments of the initiate, which Schwaller de Lubicz lists as the sense of spiritual presence, concentration, serenity, appropriate gesture (or the following of *ma'at*), silence, thankfulness, and generosity. The texts also warned against seven obstacles to spiritual fulfillment. These were:

1. *Personal concern, or anxiety for self-preservation and attachment to the personality.* "Everything comes to him who has the courage to lose himself in order to find the Universe."

2. *Wrong notion of providence.* That is, a belief in a god who corrects one's flaws, changes history, and prevents inevitable consequences from happening. In the ancient Egyptian concept of neter the sacred act, or divine providence, is viewed as a combination of destiny and free will. This philosophy is more in line with the Chinese notion of the *tao*, which sees things, not in terms of good and evil, but in terms of yin and yang. The ancient Egyptian would believe in the saying "The Lord helps those who help themselves."

3. *False pity.* Schwaller de Lubicz sees suffering as "the school of consciousness," and true wisdom cannot be gained without it. One consents to experience the trials of human suffering in order to better transmute them with the manifestation of love. At best, pity is based on fear. It is a personal reaction to the suffering of others as it appears to affect oneself. At worst, pity is merely condescension.

4. *Quest for sanctity.* One conducts one's life not according to the straight and narrow, but according to the wide and deep. As Schwaller de Lubicz says, quoting the Bible, " 'He who hath not put his talent to use shall be deprived of all that he hath.' The wise man tends the divine fire in himself until it overcomes all lesser fires."[21]

5. *Sentimentality.* That is, judgment of the world through personal feelings and intellectual notions. The ancient Egyptian believed that only the spiritual and the physical were real realms. Mental and emotional planes were temporal and could be true only if aligned to physical and spiritual planes.

6. *Satisfaction.* Longing is an eternal spiritual state, and those who are satisfied on physical, emotional, or intellectual planes are closing their eyes to all that is yet possible. "He who is satisfied with the mediocre will never attain the great."

7. *Routine.* Blindly maintaining the status quo for fear of recrimination was to lose one's own true nature. At times bucking the system was a sacred task, especially when it meant aligning action on earth more closely with spiritual truth.[22]

All these were the concerns of the individual who wished to undergo initiation into the Lesser and Greater Mysteries. When the initiate claimed to be "a pure one," it meant that through daily spiritual practice he had aligned himself with Ma'at. The Book of the Dead contains an unusual prayer called the "Negative Confession," a speech delivered by the pure heart at the moment of trial. Read by the living, it is a treatise on thinking *ma'at*, on living the ethical life.

Similar to the Ten Commandments, the prayer lists forty-two confessions, among them the statement "I have not repulsed the divine." By this one means that one no longer views the divine as separate from the self. We accept responsibility for our words, thoughts, and deeds. We love others as ourselves. We love the heavens and the earth and all things therein, for they are the bodies of the neters. We realize our own interconnected nature with the manifest world in the same way that Christ said, "That which ye do to the least of these, ye do to me." As R. A. Schwaller de Lubicz pointed out in *The Temple in Man*,

> The universe is nothing but consciousness, and in all its appearances reveals nothing but an evolution of consciousness, from its origin to its end . . . it is the goal of every "initiatory" religion to teach the way to this ultimate union.[23]

Facing One's Own Death

An initiate might achieve this state of wisdom through years of chastening life experience, or could undergo a rite in which the doors of perception were flung open, as happens sometimes in the drug experience of the shaman or in an induced hypnotic trance. In his book *The Goddess Sekhmet*, Robert Masters says:

> [During these trances, initiates] experienced themselves as dying and going into the underworld where much of what then befell them was believed by the Egyptians to be the same as what actually happened to the newly dead.[24]

To die and be reborn was to remove the fear of death that prevented the individual from attaining the higher powers in the Greater Mysteries. Although mass rituals of certain Osirian mysteries were public events, the higher grades of initiation took place in secret, for it was only in the solitude of the self alone in the dark that the initiate could face his own origin and return.

The initiation rites, writes Masters, were sometimes so terrifying that they drove the initiate mad. Certainly the rite of being buried alive screened out the timid and fainthearted. In the trial in the Qerti, or cavern, the initiate experienced the terrors of hell in the labyrinth. It was only by facing up to fear, to the most gruesome visage that could be imagined, that the initiate could achieve mastery over the emotions and temper the body with the spiritual fire of the warrior.

> This terror is exactly homologous with the confusion and suffering of all beings, lost as they are in the samsaric labyrinth of birth and death. . . . The initiate "takes on" the suffering of all beings, and for them, with them, attains liberation, only to enter again into life, save with widened awareness, heightened compassion, greater wisdom and serenity. In this, the initiate suffering for and with all beings, we can see how Christianity is essentially the Mysteries laid bare. The Trial is followed not by "pride of attainment" but by compassion.[25]

The individual would know the initiation had taken root within the self when he saw that the ordinary life had become extraordinary. It would simply be impossible for an initiate into the Mysteries to live his life in the same way as he had always lived, for the door between the worlds had blown apart. Having died to it, having contacted his origin—the primordial realm of Nun in which all time and form exist—the initiate's consciousness had been changed, and so, too, his life ever afterward. It was not a matter of assuming a new identity, but rather of receiving a revelation of true identity, an identity of the individual's origin in the transcendent divine.

Entering into the Fire

Much less is known about initiation into the solar energies, the fire energy of Horus or Ra. The Greater Mysteries of Ra were reserved for the high priests and pharaohs. These taught the art of heroism, of burning with the fire in the belly; of entering fire and becoming fire; of raising the kundalini energy, which in the Indian spiritual tradition is the serpent energy coiled at the base of the spine and asleep within the natural man. This kundalini energy is the very life force of the universe. It is the fire of life, the magic, the means of manifestation. The sun, as personified by Horus or Ra, was the most perfect symbol of Light, the radiant energy—both visible and invisible—that is the energy of all things at their source.

"From fire, out of fire, and into fire," as the ancient texts say, this fire at the end of time will consume all: "This is the realm of Truth that encircles Ra." One may either pass into the flames, what the ancient Egyptians called the Island of Flame, at the end of time, or pass through it voluntarily in this lifetime and be changed by it. The challenge was to overcome the destructive solar energies in this lifetime. Says the Litany of Ra: "Whosoever has knowledge upon earth has knowledge after death." That is, one learns not to fear the fire, but to enter blissfully into it, into the unmanifest in a final merger with the divine.

Once awakened, the kundalini serpent rose and filled the divine human with its energy. The uraeus on the pharaoh's forehead was the image of his mastery in the use of divine fire, the spitting cobra that was the eye of Ra. Whereas the mysteries of Osiris were meant to reveal the unity of all forms through natural transference of energies, the mysteries of Ra taught the conscious art of manipulation of forms. Such high magic was said to allow the pharaoh to manifest the unmanifest, to command winds, water, and earth. At its lower level, it was throwing a staff to the ground and watching it change into a serpent; at higher levels, it was the alignment of will with the Divine Will and the manifestation of desire.

"The nature of existence as desire is existence in fire," Versluis reminds us. "It is the constant pain of burning."[26] Out of control, this fire consumes one, manifests as lust, greed, envy, jealousy, and anger, but these are the plagues of the little will out of alignment with the Divine Will. The greater fire is the yearning in every human being—the yearning for union with the beloved, the yearning for union with the divine. In fact, it is this yearning that pulls us through every great heroic act of our lifetime. When handled correctly, fire is the most useful natural element. When handled roughly and with primitive force, that fire, like the lion symbolic of Ra and Sekhmet, will turn on us and devour us.

Heb Sed: *The Pharaoh's Transformative Journey*

Perhaps this was the meaning of the curious *heb sed* festival, which the pharaoh underwent during the celebration in his thirtieth year. The *heb sed* festival resembles the classic adventure of the hero known in all sacred literature of the world. In fact, the word "hero" is thought to be linked with the Egyptian word *heru*, that is, the golden hawk god Horus manifesting as the sun in heaven and the spiritual warrior on earth.

Knowing the cycle of time was upon him and he must change himself, become spiritually recharged, or die, the pharaoh set out by means of the *heb sed* ritual to procure a token of his qualification for continued possession of the throne. This is what Joseph Campbell meant when he said the hero heeds the call to adventure.

Led by his guide Anubis, the opener of the way into the lower worlds, the pharaoh received the magical aid of the gods in his quest. It was only by means of magical protection that he could enter into the land of the dead or move through the labyrinth. In the underworld, the Amentet, or "hidden place," the pharaoh stood at the center of death and nonexistence. There he "touched the four sides of the land," as the ancient texts say; that is, although he had died, he experienced himself simultaneously as everywhere at once. He saw that he was and he was not—a difficult and nearly impossible task, but one in which the micro-macrocosmic world can truly be seen. This was the cosmic revelation.

In his death the pharaoh became Osirified, but he was aided by Isis and merged with the magical goddess of the land. Here, too, he was given the wisdom of his father, Osiris, receiving atonement, or "at-one-ment." "I and the Father are One," the mystic proclaimed. Symbolically, the pharaoh attained the divine blessing of his father; he had been given the charge for the sacred task, for returning to life and performing the Great Work. Osiris bequeathed his divine son a scroll, which was the Testament or Will of the Father. Now the pharaoh appeared again before his people in new attire, the apotheosis, resurrected, returned, and ready to take up his throne again.[27] He had not died in Amentet. He had not vanished into the nothingness. He had touched it and been reborn.

Attaining Illumination

In *The Golden Ass*, Lucius Apuleius spoke of such illumination as the mysteries of Isis, saying that "in the middle of the night I saw the Sun shine with a brilliant light. I approached the gods from below and from on high." He meant that in nothingness, in the bliss of nirvana, he had attained the *khu*, the divine intelligence of the gods—in other words, illumination. One of the most ancient texts in the Book of the Dead, called Not Dying in Amentet, speaks of death as the transcendent experience of the hidden world of Osiris. The text reads:

> The house of Ptah opens. The mouth of Ptah opens. Light *(khu)* falls within darkness. The true eye of Horus healed me. Anubis nursed me and opened the way. I have hidden myself with you, O never setting stars, I am a messenger of Ra. My mind opens. Isis in my heart utters the words of wisdom. In truth, I am Ra himself. . . . I see now the hidden things. I shine forth like a god. I shall not die a second time.[28]

Now that the initiate had seen the hidden things and the wisdom of Isis had spoken within his heart, he could never forget his own divine nature. He had become immortal. He had been illuminated.

On the lintel above the entrance of nearly every tomb in the Valley of the Kings one finds an image of the golden ball of the sun between the goddesses Isis and Nephthys. These two goddesses are the *ma'aty,* or double truth, worshiping the emblem within the solar energy. Within that sun disk there is another illustration, an image of the beetle Kheperi, the symbol of transformation, and a ram-headed mummy representing the union of Osiris and Ra. This message reads: "This is Ra when he has come to rest in Osiris, and this is Osiris when he has come to rest in Ra."[29] When Osiris is within Ra, an initiate has merged with the divine and been transformed by it. No longer can we believe that our transient mortal existence is the only realm of life.

The Secret of the Two Partners

The Will, or Testament, that the pharaoh received from his father was called "The Secret of the Two Partners." It was the blessed wisdom of sacred ambiguity, the wisdom of duality. The Will contained not so much the virtue of merging Osiris with Horus, but of merging Seth with Horus. It was the hidden understanding of these two gods who, as Joseph Campbell said, "though they appear to be implacable enemies are of one mind." With this came the understanding of the duality of not only male and female, but of being and nonbeing, of good and evil. Said Campbell:

> [In] the inevitable dialectic of temporality, where all things appear in pairs, Horus and Seth are forever in conflict; whereas in the sphere of eternity, beyond the veil of time and space, where there is no duality, they are at one; death and life are one; all is peace.[30]

To be both Ra and Osiris, Horus and Seth, is to be both inert and alive. It is to become the universe (Unnefer) itself, where the pair of opposites are united in cosmic harmony.

The Great Work

With such an expanded awareness of the interconnectedness of ourselves with the One, of the above and below, of the here and there, of the then and now—with such an awareness of our potentialities as well as actualities—we as initiates are ready to take up our work again on earth. We are ready to manifest our true selves because we have tapped into the primordial fount of true being. In alchemical terms, the philosopher's stone has been attained, for alchemy is the science by which one is restored to the primordial self. Now we are ready to begin the conclusion of the Great Work.

In their chosen perfected crafts, adepts reveal the divine. The scribe composes luminous hymns to the neters, the dancer lets the gods dance her, the judge speaks *ma'at* and embodies the wisdom of a Solomon. In essence, daily life is imbued with spiritual meaning. In such states we tap into our greatest life powers, each of us performing our sacred task and elevating the world around us: "Every figure is become a holy figure; every field ploughed recapitulates the primal breaking of the Earth; every work of art [every craft] recapitulates creation itself, the ordering of the cosmos."[31] In essence, this is the meaning of all sorcerers and alchemists when they refer to the Great Work.

Modern Miracles

What, then, do the ancient Egyptians have to teach us moderns? Perhaps simply this: With God all things are possible. When the ancients speak of performing "all the transmutations which the heart bears within it," they refer to the yearning and potentiality that lies within each heart for higher states of awareness, for understanding the divine in one's own being. They refer to eternal life, eternal space, eternal time. The Litany of Ra proclaims, "I know yesterday, and I know tomorrow."

Understanding the proclamation of Ra in his form as the beetle Kheperi is to gain the key to understanding the deeper ancient Egyptian wisdom. The sun god shouts his magic from the highest heights, saying, "When I became, the becoming became. I have become in becoming the form Kheperi who came into being on the first time." In essence, throughout all the becomings nothing is lost. Forms do not die; they transform. Energy does not dissipate, it is released and transferred. Potentiality is everywhere, inherent in all things. If the ancient Egyptians were anything, they were human possibles. If they have anything to teach us, it is this: that the one and the many are here in the eternal us in the eternal now.

The question inevitably arises: Did the ancient Egyptians believe in reincarnation? I believe they did, and they called it *kheperi*, or becoming. In *Egyptian Mysteries*, Lucie Lamy explores the possibilities of reincarnation by examining the ancient texts and temples. She says that two ways are offered to our soul after death: either a final liberation or a return into incarnation and the experience of becoming conscious.

A striking example of this symbology are the dual air shafts found in the King's Chamber in the Great Pyramid of Cheops. Anyone who has ever lain inside the great stone sarcophagus in the King's Chamber can attest to the fact that while there one feels the pulse of the stars surging through one in a kind of electrical current. At first it appears that the direction of the energy is moving from negative to positive pole, then it switches from positive to negative pole.

Lamy points out that one air shaft aligns itself perfectly with the three stars in Orion's Belt to the south, which is the land of Seth; the other air shaft aligns with Draconis, the pole star to the north, which is the land of Osiris. These air shafts, she maintains, are actually guideways for the soul. They offer a choice at death between final liberation and eternal life in the north, or, to the south, reincarnation in a mortal body (the limits of Seth) and new life experience.[32]

Because initiates have in some sense died to their modernity and been re-born to their eternity, they are empowered to make conscious choices in the life they must live in this lifetime, in this place and time. John Anthony West believes it was this spiritual insight that allowed the ancient Egyptians to perform the magical and spiritually meaningful things that they did.

> In a true civilization, human beings generally understand that we are on this earth for a purpose, that our lives have a certain meaning. In Egypt if we wanted to apply a single definition to the Egyptian esoteric doctrine, it would be *the transformation of the soul*: the possibility that we have to transform ourselves from the material beings that we are by birth to the spiritual beings that we are by birthright. And all of the Egyptian doctrine, all of their temples, all of their tombs, everything that they ever did, was directed toward that tremendous aim.[33]

At this moment, at this time, we are the seed stones for the new Temple of the Spirit. We are the initiates. And our magic can be the utilization of more of our capacities than are usually perceived by our everyday or linear mind. The miracles of old are merely the conscious activation of more patterns of reality than are usually seen through the linear, analytic lens. It may be time to look again at the nature of miracles. If nothing else, they are telling proof that the laws of form in the world of space and time are only a special case of the eternal world. If we are mindful of the truth within, if we love, then we change ourselves and transform the world around us. If we die into that divine love, we are welcomed into that unity of eternal love, eternal life, eternal flame. Then, like a magus of old, we are able to proclaim:

> This I have done to enter death and turn from nothing toward life. I shall pass into heaven, even I shall pass like eternity, quietly in the fire and flesh.[34]

PROCESS 4:
The Magic of Mindfulness and the Receiving of the Words of Power

In the sacred psychologies belonging to both magical and spiritual disciplines, great importance is attached to practices furthering mindfulness and an intensely aware state of consciousness. Such work is considered important for all people, whatever their beliefs or objectives, but it is essential for the spiritual or magical practitioner. For it is only through mindfulness that one is able to wake up to all the realities both within oneself and without. Life is no longer a dream but a vast creative enterprise in which one can focus one's enhanced energies and attention to partner creation itself.

Our immediate purpose in doing Part 1 of the following process is to break through the robotlike functioning and automatic behavior that afflict too many of us too much of the time. As we move into mindfulness, we will attempt to become aware of the different streams of consciousness that compose us—physical and emotional sensations, ideas, inner and outer perceptions—so that finally we move into an integrated awareness. In this integrated state we can then begin Part 2 and encounter the divine inner companion (in this case, Isis) and receive from her the words of power in the form of our *ren*—the sacred name of our integrated self.

Part 1 of the following exercise is one that Robert Masters and I developed to introduce students to techniques and practices they can employ for their own development in attaining mindfulness and can be done by itself and apart from the more esoteric process in Part 2. In any system of development, whether physical, spiritual, or magical, one should generally begin with the physical body because it is tangible, tends to be obedient, and is easier to sense. You can tell in a general way at least what it is doing. Trying to follow only your mental processes can lead to confusion as the "monkey mind" goes swinging through the jungle of thought and feeling.

The combination of exercises in Part 1 includes many traditionally used by Buddhists and Sufis to achieve states of mindfulness. Some of them derive from the work of G. I. Gurdjieff, the Russian mystic and teacher of esoteric philosophies and disciplines. These practices help to facilitate what is sometimes called self-remembering. The self-remembering exercises are thought to derive from ancient Egyptian training practices for magicians and spiritual adepts. Similar to these are the methods of self-observation developed by F. M. Alexander, the modern psychophysiologist and a pioneer in body movement and awareness. We will work both with elements of Alexander's famous inhibiting technique and with the Gurdjieff stop exercise, which is similar to a Sufi practice.

Part 1 will require about ninety minutes. In the context of a spiritual or magical discipline, or The Work, as Gurdjieff referred to it, such exercises are practiced during every minute of a student's "waking" day. That practice is continued for however long may be required—until a student has broken free of his or her half-asleep state of normal "waking" consciousness and true wakefulness has become the norm.

TIME: 90 minutes for Part 1, 15 minutes for Part 2.
MATERIALS NEEDED: A carpeted room.
MUSIC: Include meditative background music from Area 1 for Part 1. At the beginning of Part 2, stirring music from Area 3 would be appropriate. During the meditation with Isis in Part 2 there could be the sound of a heartbeat as well as meditative music from Area 1.

INSTRUCTIONS FOR THE SOLO JOURNEYER: The solo journeyer will have no problem doing this process. Just record the instructions, including appropriate pauses and music.

♣

PART I: MINDFULNESS

SCRIPT FOR THE GUIDE: To begin with, lie on your back for a moment in any way that is comfortable for you . . . Now sit up . . . The first thing we'll try should be very easy. It's a children's game in many parts of the world. Tap the top of your head with one hand while you make circles on your stomach with the other. Make circles now on your stomach for the next few moments . . . All right, now stop. Put your hands down on the floor or on your legs, wherever you like, and simultaneously rap four times with the right hand while you rap three times with the left. Simultaneously. If it takes ten seconds or four seconds or three seconds or whatever, the four raps and the three raps should be done together within the same unit of time. Keep breathing and keep rapping simultaneously—four times with the right hand, three times with the left . . .

All right, lie down on your back a minute and rest. Now conceive of your body from head to toe as being divided into ten equal spaces. Just count from one to ten, beginning at your toes, so that at the count of ten you arrive at the top of your head. Is that clear? But the spaces should be equal. Then count back down from ten to one from your head to your feet.

Stop. And remember that you were sitting down a moment ago and then you went from a sitting to a lying position. See if you can remember how you did it. What was the sequence of your movements? Did you put one hand behind you first? If so, which hand? Did your shoulders touch the floor simultaneously? In what sequence did your head contact the floor in relation to the other movements that you made?

Now think about sitting up. If you're going to sit up, how are you going to go about it? What will move first? Will you tighten your buttocks? Will you contract your abdomen? Will you do the worst possible thing and stiffen the muscles of the neck and try to get up head first? Will you find a way to use your legs to do it? Try to *think* about how you're going to get up. Plan it as completely as possible.

See if you can now stand up exactly the way that you planned to do it. How many different activities were you aware of when you did that? Do you know what you did with your toes? Do you know what your eyes were doing? How was your breathing involved in it? On which foot did you put the most pressure? Which hand did you use? Did your head go to the left or to the right? Did you throw back your head? Did you move it forward? What did your fingers do? Was your action at all consistent with what you supposed you were going to do?

Now that you're standing up, walk around and try to sense as completely as possible what you do as you walk. Several times at some point I'm going to tell you to stop. Then you should freeze, no matter what position you may be in, unless you might lose your balance. Then arrange yourself so that you don't fall. Now, walk around a little more, quickly, paying close attention to what you do . . . Stop.

Scan your body. See if you're doing what you thought you were doing. The next time you walk, try to be aware of your feelings and your thoughts. See if, when I call "Stop," you can stop these thoughts and feelings as well.

All right, continue to walk around. Remember that you are simultaneously trying to be aware of all parts of your body as they move, of the position of your body in space, of your physical sensations, of the emotional content of your experience, and of your thoughts and ideas.

To what extent can you think about other matters while still attending to the sensations and the movements and the feelings? Try thinking about the second law of thermodynamics or the mind of the dolphin, or something like that, that will titillate your mind and exercise it while you do these other things. Are you still aware of what each part of your body is doing? How are your legs moving, your arms swinging? What is the position of your shoulders, the feel of your feet as they move along the floor? Stay aware of the emotions that run through you and, of course, the ideas you're thinking about. All of this should be done simultaneously . . .

Stop. Take this interval to sense the position of your body in space. You've stopped almost everything except your heart and your breathing. Everything feels almost frozen—all your movement, feelings, ideas. See if your situation is what you were aware of the moment you heard me say "Stop."

Now walk around again, this time repeating to yourself your full name, "I am _____. I am _____." Keep repeating your name, being aware of all the things that you were aware of before—the parts and feel of your body as you walk, the play of your emotions, your ideas . . .

Continue doing all of this and repeating your name. At the same time in your mind count from one to ten . . .

Stop. All right, now just comfortably walk around. Pay attention to nothing except the part of you that's saying, "I am (your name)" while counting from one to ten at the same time. See if you can do it in such a way that you are not counting in the spaces between the words. You are simultaneously speaking and counting—there are two voices speaking at one and at the same time.

Normally within you there are many voices speaking at the same time, so this is not such a novel experience. The novelty is becoming conscious of it in this way, and without conflict. Generally, if you are conscious of the two voices, they are arguing. One is saying, "Eat," and the other says, "Don't eat." Or smoke, and don't smoke. Or drink, and don't drink. Something like that.

See if you can detect any movement of those thoughts, if they seem to you to move at all in your own internal space. Some people feel it moving in their chest, others in their head. Some feel the counting in one place and the speaking of one's name in another . . .

Stop. Now lie down and rest a little. Any one of these practices done as meditation or exercise will begin to alter the functioning of the nervous system. It goes against everything that is normal and thus prepares the way for us to break down habits and habitual modes of functioning. Some of these exercises also activate higher brain centers because the lower centers have never in the course of the evolutionary development of human beings behaved in quite this way. They are all keys to freedom.

One of the most intriguing keys, if we speak in terms of a single technique and not of the effects of prolonged, disciplined work, is the Alexander inhibiting technique. F. M. Alexander's discovery was that, from the moment that one decides to do any action, there is an interval between the impulse or idea and the act itself, during which one can say no, and that this is, you might say, freedom itself.

If you watch people, you will see that as soon as the impulse arises, the act is usually performed. It is done unconsciously and almost always with excessive force. It is done clumsily, it is done by someone who is more asleep than awake.

However, if you decide you're going to do something and then you don't do it, you're saying no to the initial impulse. At that point, you can decide whether you really want to do that action. You can then consciously go ahead and do that thing. Or you can do something else. By repeating this process of stopping yourself at the point of impulse over and over, you gradually find that you do the action with greater and greater awareness or consciousness—and greater awareness of choice. You'll also find that the quality of the act improves. You'll do it with a freedom and a wakefulness that is quite uncharacteristic of the rest of your behavior. It will be so clear to you when it happens that there will be no doubt at all in your mind that almost everything you have done in the past has been done in a kind of trance or sleep state.

When teachers such as G. I. Gurdjieff, for example, speak of people being asleep, they're talking about walking around in our lives in a hypnotic state. It is a state in which we are responsive to suggestions from the environment and to suggestions from our own conditioning—everything seems to be acting on us. We can change this, though, with thoughts. As soon as a decision to act arises, say no. At this point, it's your choice to go ahead and do it, or not to do it, or to do something else. Whatever you choose, choose it consciously.

To really make this technique successful you have to work very hard at it. You have to practice it for hours at a time. You have to apply it to thousands of actions until it becomes your response to every impulse and thought. Why should you want to take all that trouble? Because then you will experience being awake and being free, which means that you're not responding to any coercion from within or from without. For the first time in your life you may have the sense that you're really doing something yourself. You may feel that it is a conscious, integrated person who is doing these things, a person who can choose to do them or not. And the person who is doing them knows exactly what he or she is doing. We have reason to believe that the spiritual and magical adepts of ancient Egypt prepared themselves with just these kinds of practices for becoming conscious.

Just to get a taste of it now, stand up. Whatever comes to your mind to do, inhibit that impulse. Say no to it for a moment, whether it is an idea, a movement, or whatever. Then if you go ahead and do it, you should do it very consciously. If you decide to do something else, inhibit that for a moment and then either do it or do not do it. But with each thing that you start to do, do not do anything as you ordinarily do. Stop, then go ahead or do not go ahead, consciously.

You can walk around, or stand, or whatever, but practice that for a few minutes. See if you can at least understand what it is to take advantage of that interval between the impulse and the act that offers you the potential for freedom . . .

Now lie down and rest a little, closing your eyes. Lie on your back with your palms down, arms at your sides, and scan your body. Go over your body image, your body as you sense it, beginning at the lower part. Feel where your body is clear, where you can sense it clearly, where you cannot sense it so clearly, and where you cannot sense it at all. See if there are parts that are simply missing so far as your ability to sense them is concerned.

How many of your toes can you really sense? Can you sense anything inside your head where your brain is located? Most people sense their heads as empty. What feature of your face do you sense most clearly? Is it your mouth? Your eyes? If not, then what? Can you sense your fingers individually? These are also comparatively clear in the body images of most people. See if you can sense your ears. Try to sense as much of your body as you can . . .

Attend to your mental processes for a while, to see what comes into your mind. Deliberately think about something . . . Now see if you can stop thinking—if you can think about nothing. For how long? Each time you start to think about something, stop. See if you can stop the mental processes with an instruction to stop—the same as you can stop your physical body, as in the stop exercise . . .

Ask yourself, do I give the command to stop? Or do I disobey the order and refuse to stop? Which feels more like the conscious self that you think of as being yourself? Is it the observer or the process? Try making a number of movements and focus on the sensations. By concentrating on what you sense, can you eliminate the need to think, to verbalize anything, or to image anything? See if the sensations will satisfy your need for experience so that you do not have to have ideas at the same time . . . Then, if by sensing, you have managed to purge your mind temporarily of ideas and verbalizations, stop and see how long the mind will remain free . . . Now just rest for several minutes.

Lie quietly on your back with your arms at your sides. Remember that what we are doing in this exercise can be done for any length of time and that it can be done, and should be done, during all kinds of experiences—at work or wherever you may be. It should be practiced for longer and longer periods of time to further your capacity for mindfulness.

Become aware now of your breathing. See if you can tell, for example, whether you are breathing more through one nostril than the other. To check it out, put one finger alongside the first nostril to close it off and then inhale. Repeat with the other one, and see if your breathing is equal through the two. If it isn't, see if it is as you sensed it to be.

Having established that, try to follow the breath as far into your body as you can. See if you can follow it to the lungs, and feel the lungs inflating and deflating. Try to really follow the passage of the air in and out. If you have trouble at first, follow your breath a little farther each time, or be aware of the place where you lose track of it, both going in and coming out. Then try to extend that awareness.

Pay attention to the sound of my voice. See whether, when I speak, you seem to hear me with your ears. Is it a real sensation that comes in through the ears? Or are you hearing me with the top of your head or through your solar plexus? Can you really say, based on sensing, that my voice or any other sound that you are aware of is coming through your ears? If not, try to define for yourself your auditory sensing. If you do sense that it is coming through your ears, then try to follow it inward and see how far you can sense the sound.

Now listen to the sounds in the environment around you. Try to make those observations about hearing. You assume that you hear with your ears. But do you hear with your ears the same way that you smell with your nose and taste with your mouth and touch with your hands and see with your eyes?

And what about seeing with your eyes? Look around you, or look above you, lying down, and be aware of those visual sensations. What is it that you see, and how do you see at the sensory level? Do you feel anything going back through the eye to the brain? Obviously something has to get beyond the surface of the eye. And what gets beyond the surface is, as you know, not what you see. What you see is what the brain organizes from the raw stuff of visual perception that never gets into your consciousness. What you think you see is the symbolic coding that the brain does on the external world. But try to sense your seeing and be aware of it in a way that you have never been aware before . . . Then close your eyes again and try to be aware of other cavities of your body—the inside of your mouth, for instance, is the easiest one perhaps to be aware of. See if you can sense clearly your tongue and the space inside your mouth. What is your awareness of your teeth? Try sensing other body cavities . . .

Turn your attention deeper and see if you can sense your heartbeat. Look for the flowing of your blood . . . Let your consciousness move slowly down your body and into your right leg. Follow it from the pelvis on down to the knee, down to the ankle, and around the foot to the toes, then come back again . . . See if it seems to you that you have an awareness at all of the activity in the nervous system, if you have any other sorts of sensations of energy flowing in your body, other internal processes or activities . . .

Focus on whatever internal awareness you have, maintaining it while you also scan your external body. Bring as much of your body image into awareness as you can without losing your internal awareness . . .

Shift your awareness from your physical self to the physical world around you. Sense it with your eyes closed. Clearly separate your self from the not-self around you, whether it is sound or tactile impression, the air around you, whatever it is. Focus your awareness on what you are conscious of that is not your self . . .

Return your awareness to yourself. Slowly get up and move around, retaining that self-awareness—you'll find it easier to do when you move. Getting up and moving around, see how much you can be aware of now. See how it feels to put one foot on the floor, then the other, then sensing on up to the ankle movements, the legs, the knees, the hip joints. Sense the surface of the body . . .

Continue to move. Make your awareness of what you're doing just as intense as you possibly can. No movement escapes you, no sensation. Your body image is as fully within your awareness as possible. At the same time, affirm your personal identity by recalling your name, keeping your name in your awareness. Try to listen to what I'm saying without being distracted from either that total sensory awareness or the awareness of your own identity through your name.

It is our name, according to some teachings, that gives us the illusion of being one person. Having one name tends to inhibit the awareness of the different kinds of consciousness and personalities within us. If we were to do it differently—if, for example, we assigned one name to the intellectual center, one to the emotional center, and one to the sensing and moving center—then our whole lives would be very different. We would perceive everything differently and think differently. We would organize ourselves differently and probably perceive a quite different world. In a few moments that is what we will attempt to do . . .

All right. Now, in addition to recalling your identity and being as aware as possible of what you do, try counting from one to twenty, then from twenty to one. Simultaneously, try saying your name without inserting your name in the pauses between the numbers. Keep the two tracks going, one counting, one saying your name over and over. You may find it easier to do this exercise by counting quickly. Keep going without straining or trying too hard. If you think about it at all, then you know that it's almost possible for you to think of two things at once. Doing this exercise in a controlled way, that is, verbally thinking of two things at once while also sensing, is even more difficult, however.

Your awareness should keep you from holding your breath or tensing your muscles, making this into a strenuous effort. As much as possible, what you do should be on the mental side. Now stop counting.

When I next tell you to stop, you will stop exactly where you are in terms of your ideas, your feelings, and your movements, continuing only to breathe. You will then conduct a very thorough self-study to determine whether you indeed were doing what you thought you were doing. Try not to let anything escape your awareness, so that when the stop command comes, you won't discover that you were barely aware and didn't really know what you were doing. Also, make sure that you really stopped and did not continue with a few unconscious movements afterward.

Stop. If you begin to think—stop . . . It's not thinking you're doing here, but sensing. You're noting whether everything was as you sensed it to be. It's nonverbal. Note whether it was your feelings that you were conscious of.

All right, now move again. Silently holding on to the awareness you had when reciting your name, discover a descriptive name for your physical being. Allow the name to arrive from your deep psyche. It will just rise up and may surprise you. The name should be one that gives you a sense of your body and its energies and functions, like Sensuous, Sprightly, Powerport, Leaper, Dancer, or even affectionate names like Buddy, Cara Mia, Sport.

Just let the name for your body or physical being rise up and try to get inside all of its meanings and nuances. Speak it aloud as you move around the room. Become aware of how your awareness and perspective on things are changing as a result of identifying with this name. At the same time, try to remain aware of your given name . . .

Stop. Try to hold all your feelings about your name for your physical body while holding on to your given name . . .

Begin to move again, allowing yourself to be aware of both your given name and the name for your physical self. But this time, find a name for your emotional self. Let the name for your emotional being rise up out of your own depths. Some have found names coming up like Dreamer, Violet, Strongheart, Loving Man, Kindness, Vulnerable, or even Venus, Marilyn, Rainbow.

Just let the name rise up. Try to get inside all of its meanings and nuances, speaking it aloud as you move around the room. Be aware, too, of how your perspective is changing as you identify with this name. At the same time, try to remain aware of your given name and the name for your physical being . . .

Stop. Try to hold on to your conscious awareness of all the feelings about your name for your emotional self. At the same time, continue to be aware of your given name and the name for your physical being . . .

Now, begin to move again. Allow yourself to be aware of your given name, the name for your physical self, and the name for your emotional self. But this time, add the name of your intellectual or thinking self, letting it rise up out of your depths. Names that others have come up with have included Smarty, Thinker, Big Brain, Knower, Whiz Kid, High Mind, Sage, Philosopher, even Socrates, Hypatia, Merlin.

Just let the name rise up and try to get inside all of its meanings and nuances, speaking it aloud as you move around the room. Be aware, too, of how your perspective is changing again as you identify with this name. At the same time, try to remain aware of your given name, as well as the names of your physical and emotional selves and the content they hold for you . . .

Stop. Try to hold on to your conscious awareness of all the feelings about your name for your intellectual self. At the same time, continue to be aware of your given name, and the names for your physical and emotional selves and their content . . .

Now, begin to move again. Allow yourself to be aware of your given name, as well as the names and content you're aware of for your physical, emotional, and intellectual selves. But now add the name for your spiritual self. Let this name for your spiritual self rise up out of your depths. Names that others have come up with have included Adventurer, Angel, Spirit Body, Shaman, High Priestess, Athena, Apollo, Soul Partner.

Just let the name rise up and try to get inside all of its meanings and nuances, speaking it aloud as you move around the room. Be aware, too, of how your perspective is changing as you identify with this name. At the same time, try to remain aware of your given name, as well as the names for your physical, emotional, and intellectual selves and the content they hold for you . . .

Stop. Try to hold on to your conscious awareness of all the feelings about your name for your spiritual self. At the same time, continue to be aware of your given name, and the names for your physical, emotional, and intellectual selves and their content. Be aware of how many identities you hold and the different perspectives you gain from each of them . . .

Now try to take your attention away from yourself completely—be as fully aware as possible of the not-self. Sounds, sights, objects—no affirmation of your own identity. Release, for the time being, all of your names, all of your identities. Put them away. Try to expand the awareness as much as possible so that you are taking in as many objects visually, as many sounds, as many tactile sensations, awarenesses, as possible. See if, instead of being aware of ten or twenty sensations, you can be aware of forty or fifty or a hundred or whatever is your capacity . . .

Stop. Be aware just of what you were doing when the stop command was given. Think only of that.

Now lie down a moment. Once again, take stock of yourself and see what you are able to bring into awareness. In the most detailed way go over your body and your body image, your sensations and feelings, any movement that you can detect, internal or external, in your breathing, everything. See if you can extend this awareness considerably beyond the inventory you took the first time . . .

Add the awareness of all the different names you've given yourself, your given name as well as the names and content you hold for your physical body, your emotional self, your intellectual self, and your spiritual self. Hold all of this in your awareness now. Hold it all within you.

You can do it, for it is all part of you . . . The greater the range of your awareness and the greater its contents, the better it corresponds to the actuality of the situation, and the closer to freedom you get.

Make this a very, very detailed exercise in awareness and self-remembering so that you're able to keep adding on more and more to what you're aware of, without losing anything. You'll find that if you focus, you can keep adding on for a very long time. This in itself will reveal to you how partial the awareness was before.

Then let the self-awareness go and, with your eyes closed, do the same thing with the environment. As you allow your awareness to expand, you'll discover how much more aware you are of what's going on all around you than you ordinarily think you are. How much can you sense of what's really out there that is not-self?

Get up and move around now. Continue to do the same thing to gain an absolutely maximum awareness of the contents of your senses, of what is not you. What is approaching you through your senses? Become a recipient of all that passes through you from the environment, not remembering yourself now, but rather acting as a recorder, a device that receives information.

Continue moving around, acting as an un-self-conscious being that records everything around it. You're not itemizing one thing at a time;

you're recording on multitracks, expanding your awareness of the content of what you've recorded. Observe things without naming them.

Stop. Return again to the self-remembering. Focus your awareness back on yourself. Be aware of every movement, every thought, every feeling, every sensation that you have. Remember all of your different names for yourself—given, physical, emotional, intellectual, spiritual, as well as your various other identities. Your awareness now is entirely of yourself, as completely as you can make it. You're aware of your breathing, your toes, your fingers, your armpits, under your chin, and in your mouth. And you're also aware of all your names and identities.

Stop. Now, take this a step further, do both. Expand your awareness to encompass both self and environment. Self-remember, affirm your full identity, but at the same time, be aware of everything around you without saying that this is self or this is not-self. Just expand your awareness, trying not to differentiate between what is you and what is not you, being equally aware of your body, your sensations, your thoughts, your names, your environment. You're eliminating what, in large measure, is an arbitrary distinction anyway. Try to give equal awareness to self and world without saying this is one or the other.

You're probably experiencing a much larger awareness than you had when you were aware of only one or the other. Now you must be aware of the whole. As you combine this expanded awareness of your thoughts, senses, and feelings, along with how you are moving through an ever-enlarging awareness of your environment, you will find yourself seeing, observing, and feeling yourself in ways not previously experienced before. You will gain a view of yourself that is simultaneously objective and subjective. You will gain an awareness of yourself in the environment as simultaneously objective and subjective. This expanded awareness can be carried with you throughout your daily life. It is available to you to tap into at any moment. It is not the most expanded consciousness or the most profound understanding possible, but it is the most complete awareness you can experience in your everyday functioning.

How much can you hold in your consciousness when you are aware of everything about yourself and everything about your world without establishing any boundary between the two? Regarded this way, a chair is as much the content of your consciousness and your identity, your self, as the movement of your knee, or your breathing. Everything has equal status. Are you aware of fifty contents of your consciousness? Or a hundred? Or two hundred?

Stand quietly now. See if you are aware of more when you're not moving, or less. There should be a very large number of items in your consciousness as you do this . . .

Stop. When you can really stop in such circumstances but continue to hold the contents of your consciousness, then you will be on your way to enlightenment.

(If the guide or group or solo voyager decides to do only Part 1 of this process at this time, say the following:)

Now, moving again, continuing to walk, notice how you feel. How do you relate to your environment? Do you feel at one with it? Do you sense it with more than just your eyes and ears? Do you notice changes in your perception? As you walk, are you conscious of being simultaneously aware of what is above you, below you, and on either side of you? Does this help you realize that ordinarily we use a kind of tunnel vision? Notice that, as you move now, your perception expands in all directions. Notice how you're seeing. Try to remember how you ordinarily perceive things.

If you continue to practice this exercise, you'll find that you feel much more at one with yourself and the environment. You'll have a much more expanded awareness of the world. You'll feel it through all your senses. And through your emotions, you'll have the feeling of not being separated from the world—that it is not quite so "other" as it seems to most people.

♀

PART 2: RECEIVING THE WORDS OF POWER

(Rousing music from Area 3 should be played at this point.)

Continue to walk around, moving with that greatly heightened awareness. You feel as if you're seeing it all for the first time, that you're fully experiencing that much of yourself for the first time. You're moving like a primitive or a new arrival on the earth, eagerly and pleasurably enjoying this wealth of sensation and awareness. Take in everything existence has to offer at this moment in the way of self-knowledge, your body, and your world. Move around in it with maximum awareness.

Move around, not as somebody in a trance or somebody who is too relaxed, but as somebody who is feeling totally alive and eager to experience all these sensations as keenly and as sharply as possible. Tell yourself to wake up! Wake up! Wake up! And experience it again and again on the multiple levels of your consciousness—not as a sensory bombardment, but as a much greater enrichment . . .

(Music ends.)

Now, stop. We are now in that state of enhanced aliveness and awakeness in which we can enter into states of consciousness associated with magical ways of knowing. Within such knowing one can create or cocreate one's reality and learn how to live within it. For this step into creation, one generally needs a partner, an ally from the archetypal world, a guide and protector. In the context of the work we are doing here, it is only proper that it be Isis.

(Meditative music should begin here.)

I want you to imagine that standing before you is Queen Isis. She is dressed in a long linen shift knotted around the waist with a red sash. She wears golden sandals. Her hair is long and black and gathered perhaps in many braids. On her head is a crown that is in the form of a solar disk, with the horn of a cow on either side. A wonderful perfume seems to emanate from her, perhaps like all your favorite odors combined.

And yet, as you become aware of her, Isis may change for you in form and face and dress, for she is a goddess for all seasons, for all people. Thus her eyes may appear almond shaped, and in color very dark, or green or sky blue. She may be very light or dark in complexion or the many shades between. She may appear petite or remarkably tall, supple, and sinuous, or generously endowed. She holds a flower in one hand, perhaps a lotus. With her other hand she reaches out to you and you extend yours to receive hers.

Perhaps you feel now or can imagine that you feel a subtle current, a cloud brush of texture, or even the feel of a true hand in yours. Allow yourself to feel her hand in yours as tangible, real, and her presence as fully alive to you as possible. She is Queen Isis, your guide and friend, Friend to the Universe, Great Mother, Teacher, and Guide to the mysteries. Know that she knows you in ways that you do not yet know yourself. For she is ageless wisdom, immortal mind. She is all time, all space, all life eternal—the punctual and the durative. She exists in action and in stillness. And she exists in you and you in her.

Feeling her presence grow more and more real to you, seeing, sensing, or imagining her before you, her hand in yours, let her lead you forward now, your eyes still closed or half opened. Let her lead you forward into her embrace. She embraces you like a mother, and you feel that you have come home at last in her arms. You feel loved and cherished by her, nourished and nurtured, able to take on new life and a deeper identity. There are no words as yet, only love . . .

But now you seem to hear or sense her speaking to you. She asks you, "Would you like to know the words of power that are your *ren*, your secret name, the name for your highest self?" You answer, "Yes."

(The sound of a heartbeat could be played here.)

She draws you nearer. You hear and sense the sound of a heart. It is the thrum of the universe, the beating of her heart. The sound and sense and feel of the heartbeat grow and grow until they seem to take up all time and all space. It is all that is . . . And now it seems as if you have entered her heart, just as she entered the heart of Ra to learn his secret name. That is what gave her the power to resurrect Osiris and to restore Horus when he lay ill and dying in the papyrus swamps. Isis entered the heart of Ra and learned his *ren*, his secret name.

And now you have entered into the heart of Isis. Listen now and feel with the fullness of mindfulness that is yours; listen, and be mindful of

Isis as she names you as she named her child Horus, as any mother names her child. Here in the heart of Isis will arise a new name for yourself. It might be some sacred Indian name like Peace Maker or White Raven Woman. It might be a Sufi name like Bijili, the Lightning of God, or some ancient Egyptian name like Beautiful Image of Kheperi.

Listen for the sound of your *ren*, your higher name, as it comes to you from the heart of Isis. It will be your new charge. It will be your *heka*, your word of power. And with your new name you will have the ability to transform yourself throughout the rest of the processes you will experience while entering into the passion play of Isis and Osiris. You will be invested with the power of magic, of mystery, of embodied spirit and spirited body. Your mind and heart and hands and all your now-integrated selves are sourced in the heart of all Becoming. Let your name arise now . . . And when it does, know it to be a holy and hidden name, your *ren* name, known only to yourself and used by you to call yourself into richer and truer being . . .

Thanking Isis for the great gift she has given you, feel yourself withdrawing from her, her presence becoming fainter for now, but knowing that she is always available to you when you need her. She will be your ally and protector throughout all the processes yet to come in this great adventure we are taking into her myth and reality. She will be a Virgil to your Dante, your Great Friend and Guide to the deeper mysteries and magic of Becoming.

TAKING THIS PROCESS HOME: Take this new pattern of awareness back with you into your daily life. Know that you can reenter it at a moment's notice, for example, when you're walking outdoors for an hour or two at a time. By systematically increasing the contents of your consciousness, you will find that you can expand your awareness to a degree that will eventually astonish you and that will make you feel much, much more connected and alive. Try doing this process all day, and you will see that you've broken out of a limited habitual context into a world much more like the freshly perceived world of childhood.

The so-called cerebral reducing valve of the brain that, as we age, screens out more and more of our perceptions to try to make life simpler for us—and that thus limits our consciousness and awareness—will cease to perform that reductive function. You can easily demonstrate this. Ask someone to walk through a room and tell him to list every last thing that he's aware of. Then put him in a meditative state and ask the same question. The person will double or triple the list of what he perceived. He had recorded it all before, but he hadn't brought it into his conscious awareness. While this may be of some benefit if you don't know how to cope with the totality, think how rich it must be to have the kind of awareness that more "primitive" people have. They don't need to screen their awareness, for they simply integrate all that information and deal with it as a part of the glory of life.

✣

JOURNAL PROCESS

For the next ten minutes write down all the words of power you can think of.

Rename many of the common things in your life or home with titles of power. Your cat, for example, might be renamed Queen Purrilla, Stainer of Valuable Rugs, while your dog could be called Barker of Great Noises. Your stove might be Cauldron of Fire. You get the idea.

PART THREE

The Passion Play of Isis and Osiris: A Journey of Transformation

*Osiris wearing the white crown and menat and holding the scepter, crook, and
flail. Before him are the four sons of Horus, and behind him is his wife Isis.*

9

Entering the World
of the Myth

The Egyptians are the first who have told this story . . . that the soul of man is immortal and that, when the body dies, the soul creeps into some other living thing then coming to birth; and when it has gone through all things, of land and sea and the air, it creeps again into a human body at its birth. The cycle for the soul is, they say, three thousand years.

from *The Histories*
by Herodotus

A myth is that which is always unfolding in time—unfolding and unfolding like the thousand petals of the lotus that opens at the dawn of creation. The roots of the lotus reach deep into the waters of the unconscious and arise from the obscurity of our depths. The substance of living is released as the petals open one by one. As each stage of being unfurls, the layers of our life's mythic meaning are revealed to us, released into the divine Light. That perfume called our essence, sweet and hard-won, returns to its source. Such is the gift of life lived mythically.

Myth abides from beginning to end. Coded into our being, the very sea of the unconscious, it thrums in the background of the mind like an Egypt, a remembrance of a time when men lived lives as large as a god's. We may spend our lives journeying toward that sacred, mythic place only to find it retreating in the distance, but it may appear without warning before our eyes at precisely the right moment, as if the veils between worlds had parted.

Neither fiction nor fact, myth is coded essence. It is about growing your soul. Its purpose is to bridge the local time/space continuum with what abides, what is transcendent and eternal. Myth shapes our being by merging the personal with the communal. It provides individual meaning while simultaneously uniting us with the collective, universal mind, and ultimately with all humankind and nature.

As a part of the creative process, myths tell us how to wake up to ourselves, how to transform. Through myth we contemplate our origins and become initiated into the creative process of growing and rebirthing our own lives. Even in the smallest of things there resides the realm of god. Myth throws us back upon our primary resource, the human spirit, manifest in its desire and longing for the beloved, in the quest for wisdom or the pearl of great price.

Touching the Ancient Soul

Three thousand years have passed since the glory of Egypt's New Kingdom; three thousand years since Rameses the Great won the Battle of Qadesh, since he begat his ninety-eight children who begat their children. Six thousand years have passed since the mythic coming of Isis and Osiris, when the companions of Horus laid down their laws for the ancient civilization. And, if we are to believe Herodotus, we may have been there, we may have been not only the people of Egypt, but the Nile lotus, the ibis, the sky, the sand, the river, the mud itself.

Through the four previous processes, we have entered into the durative Egypt, into the sacred time and place. Perhaps our souls remember once having scuffed papyrus sandals along the hard-packed earth of the ancient city of Pe or Bubastis. Perhaps we can almost remember what it was like to be a young Egyptian child, the heavy sidelock of hair swinging upon our shoulder—that braid that symbolized our youth and our innocence. Perhaps then we stopped to squint in the glaring sunlight and gaze upon the beautiful newly inscribed hieroglyphs at the Temple of Luxor. How we longed to study in the school, to enter the temple, to understand these beautiful, graceful words in images!

We may be feeling a surge of longing by now, what Normandi Ellis, our teller of the myth, has described to me as "nostalgia or homesickness for a place I've never been." Or we may be feeling, quite to the contrary, as though we are strangers in a strange land. Either way, we have been charged by the storehouse of countless collective memories, and perhaps a few of our own images garnered from lives past but still resonant in the energy fields of planetary memory. It is the power of the neters flowing through us, the power of the ancient light that once stirred and skipped along the sands and the river, now coursing through us—for energy never disappears, it simply recombines into new forms. We are as old as the stars, the latest product of the metabolism of the galaxy. Our atoms, the light energy running through our cells, is primordial. Parts of us are ancient Egypt.

By now we have been filled to the brim with neters and know that natures—the world's and our own—are but the signposts of gods in hiding. Our bones are the bones of Egypt; our blood courses through our veins

Osiris on his throne. From the Papyrus of Nesi-ta-neb-ashru.

like the rich stream of the Nile. We have been prepared now to enter into the myth ourselves, where past and future are a knot of time and space intertwined.

What Isis and Osiris Can Teach Us

We will now experience the myth of Isis and Osiris in a very personal, very existential way. Through this tremendous story we begin to explore what marriage to the soul can really mean. But before we do, let us recall that as early as 1948, Joseph Campbell noted that within "progressive societies" every vestige of the ancient heritage of ritual, morality, and art was in full decay.[1] Today, the outward decay is decades worse, yet curiously there is new hope, for the decay commands us to become aware and conscious of our actions and to seek new sources and resources for our lives. People can no longer bear the spiritual aridity and meaninglessness that come from living too long on the surface, even a successful surface.

The trouble is that the lines of communication between the conscious and unconscious zones of the human psyche have been badly eroded by our concentration on external and superficial realities and by our denial of the deeper, inward worlds. Through all of this, the soul has suffered most. It has either been abandoned as nonexistent or felt to be so ephemeral as to be unworthy of notice. At worst, it has been filled like a garbage dump with the flotsam of all manner of projections that find no other home.

However, it is also possible to perceive the current breakdown of the membranes between cultures and ecologies, both inner and outer, as a sign that the depths are rising, that the soul is returning to court and be courted by consciousness to renew their ancient partnership. This is happening in ways that will allow us to build new bridges, new marriages between soul and consciousness, between inner and outer worlds; perhaps even to make them stronger than they were when first forged in the childhood of humanity. For now that we have raised the stakes to almost unbearable heights, we know what we have to lose.

Although today the bridges between realities offered by the great religions may be in disrepair, these faiths are also seeding and crossfertilizing each other in a new sacred conjunction of the souls of each of the faiths. As the gods and guides of East, West, North, and South become available to us all—and to each other—this creates many fascinating new connections to the realms of Spirit. Athena and Spider Woman meet and compare notes. Isis and Sophia, the feminine principle of wisdom, trace their common lineage. Apollo and Krishna play duets together on the lyre and the flute. Oya, the wild goddess of Africa, exchanges plants with the Greek Demeter and tales of triumph with Durga of India.

The growing threat of ecological disaster has, miraculously, brought about a renewed appreciation of nature, of plants and animals, and of the spellbinding mystery of the movements of the sun, moon, and stars. Just as it did in ancient times, this fierce appreciation informs our knowings and provides the scaffolding for new bridges of communication and communion with nature. Out of this has come a fervent revival of interest in archetypal realities, without which there can be no real comprehension of the nature and practice of myth, for archetypes are residents in the world of myth and great story. They may even be the creators of that world. Learning to become a "cocreator" with one or many archetypes means learning to build bridges to the source levels, the soul levels, of our lives.

Searching out and testing these patterns of partnership from the places where we find them embedded and embodied in the great stories of humankind—waiting to usher evolutionary change into our lives—is the heart of the work of sacred psychology. And while it is work, because we use myth and story to anchor us and to provide the guidelines, it also becomes "play for mortal stakes," as Robert Frost reminds us, "for heaven and for future's sakes."[2]

Living the Mythic Life

Because of the acceleration of human experience in our time, each of us, in his or her own way, is becoming a mythic being. We have undergone as many unusual experiences and suffered as many woundings as any mythic character. As in the traditional model of stages along the hero's journey of transformation, we have heard and answered many calls, discovered remarkable allies, crossed and recrossed many thresholds of experience, found ourselves swallowed and regestated in the belly of the whale, entered upon a road of trials and high adventures, died many times to outworn and restrictive aspects of ourselves, and been chronically resurrected. We have fought monsters of our own and others' making, tried to right wrongs or enhance the condition of life wherever we have found it, and have even discovered a path to the beloved and marriage to the spiritual partner within. Our lives could hardly be called humdrum, but any time they seemed dull, we went out and did something about it. Or, perhaps, some archetypal force entered in and livened things up for us.

In my travels I have discovered this phenomenon occurring worldwide. We are all engaged in a mythic experiencing of the life of the soul and, by extension, of the Soul of the World. Indeed, marriage to the soul may be the preeminent occurrence in the life of the psyche today. But what is unique about our time is that our lives are not amplified by reflection in the cultural mythic hero or heroine. Our lives are as mythic as theirs. We are direct participants in the story of the Soul of the World. We catch the evolutionary resonance much more directly than we once did, which explains all the new emphasis on personal mythology.

Despite the media dominance of economic and political forms, I feel that the most important event in the present whole system transition is the radical incorporation of mythical and archetypal qualities in our lives. Whenever we study myth, we open the gate to this disclosure. And we can begin to examine our own lives as mythic events—events that tell of the unfolding and uncoding of the Soul of the World.

The rise of the goddess Isis and of Gaia, as the personification of our planet, in our consciousness is part of that telling—the immanent image of our soul-directed living. At this point, the tension between soul and world, inner and outer, public and private, begins to disappear as we discover ourselves to be characters in the drama of the world soul, the *anima mundi*. In this mode, ego structures are seen as only one aspect among multiple aspects of the self. Indeed, the most accurate model of human existence reveals innate diversity, both within each individual and among individuals.

The polyphrenic, or multiminded, self is the healthy self. Spiritually, however, as the psychologist James Hillman reminded us, "the soul's inherent multiplicity demands a theological fantasy of equal differentiation."[3] This means that now those psychospiritual potencies whom we call gods—with the neters of ancient Egypt—need to be seen as polyphrenic, multifaceted images of the One.

In the state of partnership that blends into union, we are digested by God and re-formed by God. And, in some sense, God becomes human for us. Meister Eckhart, one of the most powerful conceptual and experiential Christian theologians of the Middle Ages, believed that the mystical union is not the privilege of the few but the very vocation and ultimate realization of humanity. Eckhart, the writer, has God speak to us, saying: "I became man for you. If you do not become God for me, you do me wrong."[4]

In such a statement, our notions of substance and essence begin to shift and vibrate, moving across transpersonal domains. Spirit is infused with matter and matter with spirit. Eckhart believed this entirely because he believed that God is immanent in us all, is in fact our very being. Eckhart said, "If I am to know God directly, I must become completely God, and God I; so that this God and this I become one I."[5]

The "archetype of partnership" is our very reason for being. Marriage to the soul is our raison d'être. Our fears and our limited self-concept keep reducing the sense of the reality and vitality of this union. The quality of our self-hood depends on the presence of that divine image in us, on our communion with this soul, this God self that we contain. Following from that, it depends on the degree of our own immanence in the archetype of soul or God self. This relationship can be experienced as the soul's union with its beloved. By becoming immersed in this archetypal and profoundly loving relationship, we can grow toward our true identity in God.

Exploring the Ancient Versions of Isis and Osiris

With these thoughts held in the background, we now explore aspects of this great myth of marriage to the soul—the drama of Isis and Osiris. We can also do this now that we have read a very full telling of this great story and have experienced the deeper themes of the psychology of ancient Egypt. These themes and that story, essential to the understanding of the ancient Egyptian mind-set, have prepared us to cross the abyss of time so that we can enter in a more personal way into the great root myth of Isis and Osiris. We will now begin an intensive examination and enactment of this myth, not only for what it reveals about the many levels of the hieroglyphic consciousness of the ancient Egyptians but also for the possibilities it offers us for our own personal deepening and transformation.

Egyptian myths demonstrated to the fullest the ability to think hieroglyphically, to illuminate meanings and give explanations on many, many levels. As we begin to consider the relevance of the Egyptian myth of Isis and Osiris to both the soul and everyday reality of ancient Egypt, we discover that its details were so deeply a part of Egyptian culture that scribes apparently felt no need to write down the complete story. Thus we are left with no full account. (The account given in this book is one of the fullest to date, recovered from fragments of the ancient texts.)

We find aspects of the story in the Pyramid Texts, which were carved on the walls of the inner rooms of the tombs of the pharaohs and queens of the Fifth and Sixth Dynasties (2494–2181 B.C.), and the Coffin Texts of the succeeding period. On one visit I led a group to Saqqara to the site of the tomb of Unas. There, we saw these texts, carved on the stone walls, looking as fresh and crisp as if they had been chiseled yesterday. When the guard wasn't looking, several of my students ran their hands over the incised hieroglyphs and claimed that they could feel them as words of power, glyphs redolent of myth and mystery. Without any admonition from me, they quickly withdrew their hands, reporting that they felt "zapped . . . stung . . . burned." Such are the words of power. There on the wall, the power is built into the language of the text; the myth is built into the language:

Heaven shouts, earth trembles in dread of you, Osiris, at your coming. O you milch-cows here, O you nursing cows here, Turn about him, lament him, mourn him, bewail him, as he comes forth and goes to heaven among his brothers, the gods.[6]

The sacred and profane writings of ancient Egypt are filled with allusions to the myth of Isis and Osiris, and portions of the story are found everywhere in tomb and temple paintings and carvings. What we have seen with the Unas text is exactly an example of this partial telling. It remained for the Greek writer Diodorus of Sicily in the first century B.C. and Plutarch in the first century A.D. to provide the fuller accounts.

From these accounts, which are themselves thousands of years later than the initial mythic tellings, we gain a sequential sense of the main episodes of the myth. But remember, both the Plutarch and Diodorus tales are abstractions of abstractions, reductions of reductions, getting the myth down to its essentials. What we tried to do earlier in the retelling of the story was to bring back into it not only the ancient Egyptian sources and texts but also the tones and spirit of the mind and heart of the ancients.[7]

The problem with these interpretations, as with our own here, is that the myth constantly has to be explained in the context of the culture in which it is being retold. The myth itself, however, continues to exist, as perhaps all myths do, in its integrity in the durative realm. We catch only gleamings and inspirations from it in our present. Nevertheless, because of its potency it crosses the barriers of time and culture and awakens in us memories, dreams, and reflections of what was, what is, and what may yet be. That is why I speak of myth as something that never was but is always happening, calling us to wake up to a reality larger than our aspirations, more complex than all of our dreams.

The virtue of a bare-bones version is that it does help us keep the sequence of the myth in mind. So in experiencing this myth, we will be referring to some extent to Plutarch's version,[8] as well as to the fuller and richer story given earlier.

Plutarch's Ancient Myth

Plutarch begins with the birth of the various protagonists in a realm outside time and space:

They say when Nut (the Sky) had intercourse with Geb (the Earth), Ra (the Sun) came to know about it and set on her a curse that she should not give birth in any month or year. Then Thoth, falling in love with the goddess, became intimate with her, and then played draughts against the moon-goddess. He won the seventieth part of each of her illuminations, and having put together five days out of the whole of his gains, he added them to the three hundred and sixty days of the year; these five the Egyptians now call the additional days and on them they celebrate the god's birthday. For they say that on the first day Osiris was born and that, as he was delivered, a voice cried out that the Lord of All was coming to the light of day. On the second day, it is said, Haroeris was born whom some call Apollo and the elder Horus; and on the third day Seth was born, not in the right time or place, but, bursting through with a blow, he leapt from his mother's side. On the fourth day Isis was born near very moist places and on the fifth Nephthys. . . . They say that Nephthys married Seth and that Isis and Osiris, being in love with each other even before they were born, were united in the darkness of the womb.

We hear how since among the Greeks the moon is feminine, Plutarch hellenized the story by making the moon a goddess. In ancient Egypt, however, the moon was ruled by the god Thoth and Thoth is also the ruler of time. One of the evocative teachings of this myth is the story of calendrical time and how the gods are born outside normal time. Indeed, five extra days are created to give them time to be born. What a lesson for today! The calendar of everyday habitual life provides us with no time to gestate and grow. We must discover or create sacred time outside normal time in order that the goddedness within us may come into being.

What would have happened if Joseph had neglected Mary's time for bearing the child conceived of God? For that matter, what would have happened if the busy carpenter, grown-up Jesus, had said, as do some of us, "You wouldn't believe my schedule! I have to build a new barn for Aaron. Then there's the table I promised Sarah. And my mother wants me to strengthen the beams over the kitchen. The days just don't exist for me to develop my inner calling."

Reading a Myth in Our Own Time

If we incarcerate ourselves in habits of filling time with busyness, then our god selves are granted neither space nor time to make entry. We use this busyness and burden of time fatted out to justify our existence while feeling, at the same time, that our true existence is getting away from us. Since few of us continue to live within the festival calendar of feasts and saint's days, we have to create some practice of inserting sacred time into our usual calendar so that we can have the time to recommit ourselves to the gestation and birth of the great forces within us. An hour a day, a day a week, a weekend a month, and, yes, a month a year, would do wonders for most of us. We might even, as in the myth, find the time to enter into marriage with our partner, the soul. Thus the creation of both secular daily time and sacred time is an essential teaching of this myth.

The cultural historian and educator William Irwin Thompson offers another perspective when he states that this myth may have been part of the symbolic science of ancient Egypt, at once anticipating and deeply aware of forces of cosmogenesis, or origins of the universe, which we have just "discovered" in this century. He suggests that

> Geb is not so much the earth as he is a metaphor for the cosmic dust cloud before the separation into the sun and the distinct planets. In other Egyptian myths, Shu, with the aid of the wind-spirits, helps to lift the sky to separate Nut from Geb. . . . Thus, when the Egyptians talk about air or wind, they are talking about the expansion of gases and using the wind, as we still do, as a poetic metaphor. As the primordial gases change, the indistinct cosmic dust of Geb and Nut is transformed, and from these primeval parents new offspring begin to appear, the planets.[9]

This recalls the image in Genesis of God blowing his breath upon the deeps to create form: "And the spirit of God moved upon the face of the waters" (Genesis 1:2).

According to Thompson, there are several other cosmological aspects of this myth that symbolically prefigure a scientific understanding. One of these is that Isis is identified with the earth, while Osiris is her accompanying moon consort:

> When the myth says that Isis and Osiris were making love in the womb we should understand that this represents a conviction that at one time the moon and earth were one and had not separated. And so when the myth speaks of the intercourse of other gods, we can suspect that the formation of the distinct planets and their later astrological conjunctions are being discussed.[10]

Thus, as one part of the story tells the origins of calendar time, another aspect of the story is a symbolic-scientific telling of the origins of the solar system. It also recalls the speculation of astrophysics about the union of the earth and its moon when still in their state as a single fiery ball. Then they may be said to have been together in the womb of fire as a single fetal planet.

In the mythic world and mind it is no great jump from the creation of the world to the creation of agriculture. Thus Thompson also notes the connection between the cosmological myth and the agricultural myth:

> The god associated with the crescent moon is the mysterious force that helps things to grow, *crescere*. (This ancient mode of thought exists to this day in the mystical bio-dynamic gardening practices of Rudolph Steiner,

which call for planting only when the moon is in a favorable position for the variety of plant chosen.)[11]

These ancient knowings continue today in farmers' almanacs as well as in agricultural folklore. Planting is still guided by the beneficent phases of the moon. As a culture hero, Thoth is also the lunar influence helping things to grow and transform themselves from barbaric cultures into civilized, cultivated ones. As we remember how things work on multiple levels of mythic and hieroglyphic thought, as we speak of the growth of solar systems and of agriculture and the growth of life on earth, so we also speak of growing ourselves.

We now enter the myth and prepare to take on all of its cadences and codings. We will experience the passion of Isis and Osiris, of Horus and Seth and Nephthys. But, as is the way with myth, we will also know and come to terms with our past and future selves. We will meet with dimensions of our psyches that have been obscured from us too long— our sun self, our moon self, and most especially our earth self. Our local lives will be taken up in the Great Story, and great can be the consequences for our local life. For we are partaking of a mystery, a myth, a metaphor, a remaking of ourselves from the Mind of the Maker. So we begin.

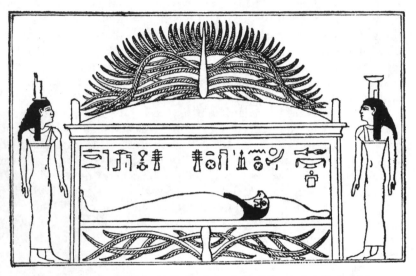

The funeral coffer of Osiris. At the head stands Nephthys and at the foot Isis. From a bas-relief at Dendera.

Entrapment in Life
and Mourning the Lost Beloved

> For every destruction, a creation
> for every creation, a destruction.
> In every birth a death,
> in every death a birth.
> This is the way it has been.
> This is the way it will be.
>> Mayan poem from the *Chilam Balam*
>> translated by Christopher Sawyer-Lauçanno

Most ancient stories are about paradise lost. This one is no exception. Childhood is innocence. The long summer days stretch out upon the throat of the sky like a string of beads. We revel in the tall grasses, lying on our backs watching the parade of clouds. We are eternal creatures in that moment, creating stories, drawings, tree houses, and plays for the sheer joy of creation.

When we become adult, we put away childish things. Not only do we recognize the complexities and ambiguities of our natures—relational, professional, sexual, shadowed, and creative—but we come to understand that it is precisely that which produces life, love, and work in the world that also inevitably produces conflict, confusion, and death. We come to realize that we are trapped in bodies in time, and that our time is limited. The clock ticks away in the background. We scurry to accumulate something that matters—love, career, children, home—before it is all ripped away from us by the inevitable force of death.

And we ask ourselves: Is paradise forever lost or can it come again?

Isis and Osiris as Great Civilizers

This takes us directly into the story. Isis and Osiris are the first king and queen from the days of paradise, a time when giants dwelled upon the earth. Working together, this brilliant couple become partners in civilizing their chosen land and bringing the Egyptians from ignorance to enlightenment, from savagery to civilization. They teach the arts of agriculture and establish the patterns and potentials within which a society may grow.

Osiris, the benevolent king, abolishes cannibalism. He creates a higher ethical code and teaches the people to use grains, to brew beer, and to build houses. Isis gives special emphasis to instituting marriage and the family. She midwives the children and, knowing the ways of gestations and regeneration, teaches the breeding of animals and the cross-breeding of plants. She instructs others in the skills of the weaving of cloth, the making of pots, and the observation of the stars.

Together, Isis and Osiris instruct the people in spiritual realities, teaching the Egyptians the nature of worship and the honoring of the neters both in themselves and in reality at large. With the nation now prosperous and enlightened, they both continue to rule, but occasionally take turns pursuing their missionary roles, traveling to other places, and converting other people to the ways of civilization, not by force but through demonstration and persuasion.

Nymphs and other supernatural beings accompany Osiris on his journey, and they fill the air with music and song. It is music and song, as well as persuasive and reasonable teaching, that cause people to be civilized very quickly. This is a piece of prehistory encoded in the myth, for it indicates that the transition from hunting societies to agricultural ones was often peaceful. However, as we know, not everyone took to agriculturalism, and Seth is the remnant of the hunting, nomadic society. He will not embrace the new culture.

When Osiris is twenty-eight years old (twenty-eight being the completion of the lunar cycle), he returns from his highly successful civilizing activities to resume his kingship of Egypt. Isis then takes up the couple's teaching mission and leaves Osiris in charge of the palace. The pair function very much like a modern couple with dual careers. Each is responsible for a part of the household as well as for the administration of their kingdom.

The Sting of Backlash

It is inevitable that, as the bringer of a new growth in culture and consciousness, Osiris must face the antagonism of the older and more violent hunting culture and its consciousness. The representative of this older order is his brother Seth. While Seth is the exact counterpart of Osiris, he is a being of deserts and tempests and war. He resents the civilizing genius of Osiris and wishes to usurp him. But he is prevented from taking the throne by the vigilance of Isis.

The fact that one of the literal meanings of the name Isis is "throne" reveals the early remnants of a matrilineal culture. Her Egyptian name is Auset, whereas the Egyptian name of Seth is Set. Both names connote an ancient definition of "the foundation" of being. Seth is the foundation of the subconscious mind and the base nature, whereas Isis, as Queen of Heaven, is the foundation of the higher mind of the divine. Osiris, Auser in the Egyptian, is literally the "elevated man," the being who moves between the upper and lower worlds.

But to continue our story, Seth has persuaded seventy-two other persons to join him in his conspiracy (as we will soon see, seventy-two is a number that has both mythical and astrological meanings). He fashions a chest exactly to the measure of the body of Osiris and brings it to the banquet hall where the princes of Egypt have been feasting and celebrating their king's return. The exact measurements of the god are divined by sorcery, the Ethiopian queen Aso having divined them from the dreams of Isis and Nephthys.

As the party becomes more raucous, Seth, playing the clown, promises in a joking manner to give this elaborately ornamented chest to the one whose body most nearly fits it. Each of the princes tries it, but the jeweled chest is found to be too long. Osiris finally lies in it, fitting it perfectly.

Seth yells triumphantly, "Then it's yours!" And the seventy-two conspirators slam the box shut, fasten it with nails, and pour melted lead over all the cracks and crevices. After this they carry the chest to the banks of the Nile and cast it into the river where it joins the sea.

What intrigues me is Osiris's absolute willingness to enter the casket. It's the Last Supper and Seth is playing Judas. It's the last feast of music, beer, and bread, and Osiris gets in the casket. Does Jesus blame Judas? Does he know? Does Osiris? When we are dealing with the hearts and minds of gods or inspirited folk, such a divine power as precognition of imminent death indicates a willing self-sacrifice. Here, the god Osiris—as did Jesus—agrees to be set up for the contact with his own true destiny.

Seth as the God of Time

In Greco-Roman times Seth was linked to the planet Saturn, which astrologers perceive as the planet of limitation and karma.[1] In this story Seth represents the principle of limitation, of measurement, of boundaries. This means that he is not really evil. Rather, he is the force of the inevitable limitation that occurs when our soul wanders too freely. There is no growth without limitation of form. Also, in terms of the creation of macrocosm and microcosm, this moves the myth from the formation of the solar system to the formation of the human body and the soul trapped in time in the body.

Even within ourselves we may feel the painful dualism and dilemma in this tale of a critical turning point in human history—when we stopped depending on the meanderings of the hunt and became tillers of the soil. On the one hand, in a way parallel to the ancient story, we hear the deep self and the evolutionary forces within society calling us to blossom at this critical time of quickening. But we are also greatly influenced by the entrenched and intransigent forces in ourselves and our societies upholding the old familiar and habitual order of things. The sunset effect is in its full technicolor glory—the rays of the sun of the old order blazing out across the horizon with apparent renewal of power and influence before the sun finally sets, and the new sun eventually rises on the opposite horizon.

The Sethian aspect of the story speaks to our psychological entrapment in our habits and customs. Osiris, who is only twenty-eight (again, the number of the phases of the moon), has brought civilization to many in his wanderings but has no one to bring an even higher civilization to him. Who or what teaches the teacher? Often it is the principle of limitation, seen here as Seth.[2]

Seth as Necessary Limitation

When there appears no other way for the depth teachings to penetrate our daily consciousness, then the foundations of the known must be dramatically shaken. We experience a sudden fall, a divorce, a catastrophe, a wake-up call from the universe. This aspect of the myth speaks to the psychological fact that our limitations, although we may see them in a negative light, often become our greatest teachers in a positive sense. This cycle of twenty-eight years is also the cycle of the planet Saturn. Astrologically, through the crisis of limitation its influence brings to our lives, it marks the threshold of transition from our young adulthood into middle age.

Seth is, therefore, the principle of continuity of things as they are, the critical principle of homeostasis. He may represent the memory of what happened when too much and too advanced a civilization occurred in Egypt too quickly. The necessary balancing forces of reaction set in and tried to entrap the soaring soul of the new brilliant Egypt in the chest of tradition.

Once prehistoric ancient Egyptians abandoned hunting and gathering and embraced agriculture, they did so without any awareness of the long-range effects of their agricultural practices. Unwittingly they allowed their cattle to overgraze the land, damaging the delicate ecological balance of the grasslands of the Sahara. The forces of tradition—the Sethian principle—undoubtedly rose to redress this disaster by attempting to curb the spread of agrarian methods.

In modern times, President John F. Kennedy represented Osiris, while Lee Harvey Oswald and Jack Ruby (or even CIA strategists, if you believe recent books and movies) played out the Sethian principle. The thinking of the principal Sethian players was that the man had gone too far in thought and action and had to be stopped. Seth, as the symbol of the older tradition, affirming things as they were, upholds the critical principle of not too much, not too soon.

Yet even though Seth tries to keep things as they are, he actually forces a "transformation" in a dramatic way. It's the case of the unconscious jumping up and biting us from behind. The specter of Death frightens us with its images of physical pain in the dying process and the decay and disappearance of matter. It frightens us emotionally for, having been conscious of both pleasure and sorrow, we cannot comprehend total unconsciousness, annihilation, and loss of the self. Alone in the desert mountains, it frightened Christ, and to us it is only a small consolation that death frightens even the gods and sons of gods.

Yet, as we have learned, there is nothing that dies completely. Energy, light, the essential nature of the soul, simply transmutes. Osiris as matter dies, but Osiris as spirit remains. After the first death, there is no other. Says the ancient Egyptian, "I will not die a second time."

The limitation of Seth actually becomes our highest good, painful as it is to Osiris and, eventually, even to Seth himself. Mortal, we must lose all we have to attain the kingdom of heaven. In their modern translation, the Nordic runes tell us that the great teacher is pain and limitation: "It has been said that only at the point of greatest darkness do we become aware of the Light within us by which we come to recognize the true creative power of the Self."[3] We recall also that later in the myth, after undergoing the initial change of death and mummification in his human form, Osiris becomes the principle of stability as the *djed* pillar in his spiritual form.

Seth and Osiris are twin brothers in the great cosmic womb. They are the dual forces established in opposition, cosmic laws upon which all the forms of the universe are suspended. Seth knows Osiris's inmost nature, as well as his shape. For the ancient Egyptians, knowing the number or measure of a thing was tantamount to controlling its essence. When he hurls the chest containing Osiris into the river of time, Seth changes not only the fate of Osiris, but his own as well.

Loss of Paradise

We see the shadow of this sense of the god entrapped by evil forces in the later Greco-Egyptian Gnostic myths that tell of the physical forms of humans being created by Satan so that their heavenly souls could be trapped in the body of time. Certain Gnostic sects believed that we come from a higher reality and a higher god, and we are living here under the dominion of a lesser reality and a lesser spiritual principle. Throughout the Gnostic liturgies there are exclamations like "I am flung, thrown, hurled into this morass" and "I am an alien in this world, and this world to me. Who has conveyed me into the evil darkness . . . deliver us from the darkness into which we are flung."

In ancient Egyptian terms, we are living under the dominion of Seth and not Osiris. Poets perceive this as the falling away from the perceptions of childhood, as in Wordsworth's nostalgia for that time

> . . . when meadow, grove, and stream,
> The Earth, and every common sight,
>   To me did seem
>   Appareled in celestial light. . . .[4]

Wordsworth intones the Gnostic memory of intimations of immortality in early childhood, the recollection of our true home and truer God:

> Our birth is but a sleep and a forgetting:
> The Soul that rises with us, our life's Star,
>   Hath had elsewhere its setting,
>   And cometh from afar:
>   Not in entire forgetfulness,
>   And not in utter nakedness,
> But trailing clouds of glory do we come
> From God, who is our home . . .[5]

Today the Osirian Gnosticism is seen vividly in the themes of space fantasy: "E.T. phone home!" Or it is felt in the call that one hears from so many noble but overworked souls who, like Osiris, have brought a benign and cultivating influence to their professions and human service and are now weary: "Please! I've been trapped here on this planet and in this time long enough. I did everything I was asked to do. I want to go home now."[6]

What modern jargon might label burnout may have a much deeper origin. For you can't go home, and you do get locked in the claustrophobia of being caught in a precisely measured time and space. The solution—indeed, the heart of the Egyptian, Gnostic, and Christian traditions—is to say, "Ah, but I have depths and dimensions that you cannot even dream of. And in these depths I have the freedom to wander, to explore, to deepen, and then to return and bring the timeless back into time. I am a citizen of two worlds." This is the heart of all mystery religions, and it is expressed most eloquently in *Hamlet*: "I could be bounded in a nutshell, and count myself a King of infinite space."[7]

So the encased Osiris is hurled into the river of time. The soul is trapped in the body and world of generation. William Irwin Thompson makes an interesting point in his pursuit of the calendrical meanings of this myth when he says:

> Only if Osiris can redeem this fallen world of generation can he rise to become the god of growing and generated things.
>
> That we are at the beginning of time and generation becomes clearer when we stop to consider that there are 72 conspirators with Seth. The Platonic Great Year, the time it takes to make a complete circuit through the 12 astrological signs, is 25,920 years; 1/360 of the circle or one degree is 72.[8]

Mourning the Lost Beloved

As soon as Isis receives word of the crime, she cuts off one of her locks, puts on the mourning clothes of widowhood, and sets forth in search of her husband's body. Wandering, lamenting, mourning throughout Egypt, she comes upon some playing children who tell her that they have seen the accomplices of Seth carrying the chest to the Nile. (Perhaps for this reason Plutarch reports that Egyptians regarded the words of children as oracular and paid great attention to them.) The immense poignancy of her love reminds us of an ancient esoteric tradition, common to the Egyptians, Greeks, Mesopotamians, and Druids, that the soul is partnered, and when one part is born into time, the other remains as the Beloved in the spiritual realms, longing for its mate.

In the archetypal realm, the neters of ancient Egypt are created in pairs: Nut and Geb, Shu and Tefnut, Seth and Nephthys, Isis and Osiris. The two form one soul, a soul made of harmonic dualities—heaven and earth, air and fire, light and dark, male and female. In Plato's *Symposium*, Aristophanes says that human beings originally consisted of two persons in one body, and together they were capable of doing miraculous feats. But when the gods saw fit to sunder these creatures, they spent the rest of their lives yearning for their missing half.

By being born into this world, it seems that for a time one dies to the suchness of We. Thus, for the soul, the birth of its partner into the physical body feels like a death, for it is a dying into the body of time. The part now encased in the physical aspect of the "we" is separated from the Beloved. It is now incarcerated in form to serve as the human extension of the Beloved in this theater of space and time. The human part of the pair, however, continues to feel as if someone else exists in a partnership with him or her, giving rise to a sense of loss that is at once both poignant and unclear.

At the beginning of time, Isis and Osiris are twinned. When they become separated from each other, Isis is bereft of her animus, the Osirian nature of her soul. Likewise, Seth, by the sexual deception of Osiris and Nephthys, is bereft of his anima, his wife Nephthys, who even while she lives draws farther away from him into herself. Both Seth and Isis are on a quest to reclaim what has been lost. Isis searches appropriately for her husband-lover, the male complement to her feminine self. Seth, however, misunderstands his loss and searches for a more masculine kingship and domain, rather than for his estranged anima-wife.

It is this deepest wounding of the heart, this yearning for the lost unified soul itself, that will not leave Isis in peace. And it is precisely that wound and sorrow that bring her finally into the full power of her magical being by the story's end. Through her suffering and abandonment, at a deeper level than she is even aware of, Isis has entered the sacred, the sphere of redemption. The wound causes her to lose awareness even of her surroundings, and as a result she wanders into worlds and realms where she has never been in her conscious travels. Byblos, where the coffin of Osiris finally arrives, is not so much a foreign country on a map as it is a foreign state of mind.

Isis has also lost any connection to her former self—the woman who spent her time helping to birth children, tend gardens, build industries. She leaves her home. She puts on the clothes of widowhood. She cuts her hair. By this cloaking of the self and the cutting of the hair, she makes of herself a sexless creature. Her actions are similar to the hair cutting and habit wearing of Catholic nuns, actions that disguise the sexual form as a ritual of purification and submission to the marriage of Christ. And yet what Isis will discover by the journey's end is a deeper sense of herself, a new homeland, which is a land within, a merging of spirit and body, and the creation of new life.

While in the midst of such deep sorrow, a forgetfulness occurs. We forget the self and continue to yearn for who or what we can no longer remember. There is a highly emotional charge to this, which sometimes seems to dissolve altogether, and we fall into a limbo, an emotional and spiritual desert (sometimes called the dark night of the soul). And then, through grace or time or love, something happens and the charge returns.

Many of us have a series of surrogates—noble and, alas, not-so-noble—to fill the in-between spaces of that yearning. Our mistake is that we place on the noble surrogate, the good friend, the spouse, the lover, that sense of twinning that properly belongs only to the Beloved of the Soul. For many, that place is filled by a cultural archetype—Jesus, Buddha, Krishna, Mary, Kwan Yin, or any of the other representations of the Noble One that have appeared through time and myth, scripture, and history.

Isis is consumed by *pothos*; that is, she has entered a stage of utter yearning in which the barriers between herself and the world are torn asunder. James Hillman, a leader in the school of archetypal psychology, has said that there are three kinds of love: *himeros* is the physical hunger for the other, *anteros* is the answering love, and *pothos* is the bridge between the two: "*Pothos* is love's spiritual portion."⁹ This is what drives the wanderer ever onward, the call that forces the hero to undertake his sacred quest. To attain the soul, one must conquer all time and space. In our own lives we may perceive it as a kind of nostalgia for God-Knows-What, and it will not leave us, regardless of how ephemeral its form or how absurd its calling.

The great desire for the Beloved of the Soul, while always present, moves to the foreground when civilizations undergo whole system transitions. In a historical sense, we see the story of Isis and Osiris as a tale of transition from the realm of hunting and gathering to an agricultural lifestyle. In the same way, Mary Shelley's *Frankenstein*, written during the early years of the Industrial Revolution, depicts the horror and grief caused by the separation of the soul from matter during an age of transition to a technological society.

Such eras are also marked by the rise of mystery religions, with their emphasis on dramatic inward journeys and the ecstasy of union with the archetypal Beloved, which provide people with a sense of a deeper identity and belonging. Thus we find the rise of the Egyptian and Eleusinian mysteries in ancient times, and the rise of spiritualism, of theosophy, and of secret societies coinciding with the Industrial Revolution.

Today we are undergoing a profound transition, moving from a cosmopolitan to a planetary culture. Our cultures, beliefs, and practices intertwine one with the other. We are experiencing a revolution in relationships between men and women. We are revising our notions of family and community and experimenting with new forms of ritual in training schools and seminars.

The Self in Each Other

A new natural philosophy based on love as the creative force of evolution is emerging everywhere, and this lure of becoming finds renewed expression in the rising archetype of the Beloved of the Soul. Quite simply we are attempting to figure out how to work together as co-partners, not only in our relationships and jobs and communities, but also with the planet and the cosmos at large. In so doing, we must recognize that in each other, there is the divine being for whom we have searched. The stuff that drives our lives drives the life of the entire planet. Like cells of a single body, we are inextricably intertwined.

That Isis, Nephthys, Osiris, Horus, and Seth are all conceived simultaneously in the same cosmic womb and born of the same mother indicates the eternal law that what affects one part of the psyche, the world, the community, and humankind, affects all parts. In as much as the sorrows of Isis are shared by Nephthys, who helps her to recover and mourn the body of Osiris, so are the sorrows of Nephthys shared by Isis.

One night while looking for her husband, Isis discovers that the timid Nephthys, sitting in the garden in the dark and looking very much like Isis, had been mistaken by Osiris for his wife, and he had made love to her. When the child of their union is born, Nephthys, out of shame, exposes him in the desert. But Isis, learning about the child, discovers his whereabouts, adopts him, and raises him to be her constant guard and attendant. This child is Anubis, who later becomes the guide to the eternal realms.

Anubis is often shown as having the head of a jackal, and it is the way of the jackal in Egypt to bury its carrion in the sands until it has reached just the right time and state for the jackal to digest it. So the rejected infant Anubis, placed in the burial zone of the desert, is brought back at the right time by Isis to become her companion as well as the one who knows the right time to lead the soul through the tests of the underworld. When the gift of love is not accepted, he finds another home, another receiver, another time. Wise Isis isn't upset with Nephthys, for Isis has the ability to receive the gift of the child when the natural mother rejects him.

The Winter of Our Discontent

Part of the process of transformation, and perhaps one of the more painful processes, is that of waiting. The old order has been destroyed, yet nothing new has arisen to take its place. We are in the winter of our discontent. The winters of Egypt (which equate to our springs) are not filled with fluffy visions of white snowflakes. However, the desert nights can be cold, and the days are filled with a dry, desolate landscape cracked by deep fissures as the barren soil turns to dust and blows away.[10]

This is the time of the *khamsin*, when the hot southern winds drive clouds of dense ruddy-yellow sand through the streets. Infection and disease are rampant. At this time, everyday life in Egypt stops. People shut themselves indoors, seal the cracks, and wait out the storm in much the same way that Osiris was shut inside his coffin, or Isis was shut up within the prison of Seth. The ancient Egyptians believed that this evil, ruddy wind was a manifestation of the red-haired god Seth, the personification of the desert and its death, disease, and imprisonment.

During the *khamsin*, it is nearly impossible to see one's hand before one's face. Just so, during emotional winters we are blinded by the storm, blinded by our situation with no remedy in sight, except to submit for the duration of our imprisonment. We must give up that which we cherish. What we cling to must be relinquished, even if that means relinquishing the core essence of our own identities. To resist is to lose one's own soul—a death in life from which one never recovers. To surrender, then, is both courageous and wise.

Even after the storm, the troubles are not over for Isis and Osiris, nor for us. The entrapment of Osiris in his coffin leaves him vulnerable to the destructive powers of Seth. Rescued once by Isis, but nevertheless inert and vulnerable, Osiris is rediscovered by Seth and hacked into fourteen pieces. Bits of the man-god are scattered throughout the Nile. They drift to the far reaches of the land or are consumed by fish. He shall not again be the same man he was before.

Where once Osiris was trapped within his own skin, now the god has been cut asunder and separated from his former self. The fabric of his old life is torn to shreds. In some ways, he has been freed from time. And it is these pieces, these bits that can never be wholly reconstituted that become the touchstones, the relics, the sacred temple sites for future generations.

What King Arthur confesses to Guinevere might be the confession of Osiris to Isis, of Jesus to Mary Magdalene: "I was not born to live a man's life, but to be the stuff of future memory."[11]

So it is with us that the wounding makes us holy, causing us to remember ourselves, to gather together the bits of who we were and make of them something holy, and some wholly other.

✦

PROCESS 5:
Seth's Limitation of Osiris
and Our Casket in Time

One of the keys to this myth is how time seems to trap humanity in its orbit of years, months, days, hours. As Osiris is trapped by the conspiracy of Seth and the seventy-two, so we are trapped by the relentless onslaught of time in our lives. Osiris returns triumphantly from the spreading of civilization. It is a noble task well done, but his story does not end with the triumph: he is soon cut down to size.

Whenever there is a time of growth of self, outer works must cease. The inner voice cries out and the forces of waning rise up and try to set limitations. We often label this wild emotional swing between action and inaction, creation and destruction, a form of neurosis, but it may be the natural cyclical forces of deep transformation at work. It is through reverie, reflection, and dream that we re-member our deepest callings, that we re-member the selves who we once were. How we deepen our relationship to these forces constitutes the mystery.

TIME: 2 hours.

MATERIALS NEEDED: Long sheets of butcher paper or newsprint cut into approximately six-foot lengths, one for each participant; a supply of large markers, one to a couple; and extra markers and other drawing supplies.

MUSIC: Background meditative music from Area 1. A good choice is R. Carlos Nakai, *Journeys: Native American Flute Music.*

INSTRUCTIONS FOR THE SOLO JOURNEYER: This part of the journey can be done alone by taping the instructions for the guide. Establish your surroundings as if you were giving a party. Set out soothing libations; scatter fresh flowers around the room and dim the lights; offer yourself healthy and sensual-looking foods. You may wish to dance a while before you begin.

The consideration of the Osirian and the Sethian aspects of your life can be easily accomplished by writing in your journal, although you may find that facing yourself in a mirror and addressing yourself as Osiris (plus your name) or Seth (plus your name) will deepen the activity.

Ask yourself and respond in writing to such questions as "In what ways am I like Osiris and trying to blossom? What is waxing in me?" After you have written your reflections on this question, ask yourself in your journal, "How am I like Seth and trying to restrain or cut back thoughts or things or people, myself included? What is waning in me?"

Part of the process of re-membering one's self is the act of becoming known and letting one's self be known by others. It is an interesting linguistic trick that the word "render" means simultaneously to tear apart, to give artistic form, to pronounce formally, and to make holy. You may find that you will benefit by rendering what you have written afterward with a friend or with someone to whom you are attempting to draw close.

You should not have too much trouble tracing the outline of your own body. Pin the tracing on a wall and spend some time observing what you have drawn or written there. If the season is right, you may even wish to take the measure of your own body and form of it a garden filled with the herbs, vegetables, and flowers that represent aspects of you. This making of the human garden is reminiscent of an ancient Egyptian rite, wherein the body was buried in the tomb with a "corn mummy." The mummy was seeded with spelt, covered with dirt, and watered. Its sprouting in the tomb signified the process of regeneration. You will have the added benefit of being able to gaze upon the flourishing nature of your life throughout the season and to give physically, if you wish, a part of yourself—carrots, chrysanthemums, or chives—to the others who fill your life.

For the rest of the process, just follow the taped instructions and proceed with the reflections about being carried in the body of time.

SCRIPT FOR THE GUIDE: We are about to look at the confrontation of forces represented by Seth and Osiris in ourselves. You are literally going to take your measure. Your parts are going to be delineated. At the same time, you are going to live out the myth on multiple levels. At this moment you are here, at a certain level of high civilization. You are at a party given for your triumph, but the Sethian forces are saying, "No farther! We've got your measure and you are going to fall."

First, find a partner. Then each of you should take a long sheet of paper—make sure it's as long as you are tall—and one marker for each pair. You will also want to have other markers and drawing materials close at hand.

Turn and face each other. Take each other's hands lightly and begin to breathe together. Feel yourself as Osiris the civilizer, bringing new life, new possibilities into the world.

Take turns talking about the Osiris in you for a few minutes. Speak from the flowering Osiris, and take turns asking and answering these questions: "What is trying to flower in you? How is it trying to blossom? Into what is it trying to grow?" Begin. (Allow ten minutes.)

Now ask each other: "How is the principle of Seth rising in you? What is trying to restrain you, or cut you back into form? What is trying to occur in the waning rather than the waxing of yourself?" This may be either negative or positive. (Allow ten minutes.)

Come to quiet now. Have one person lie down on a length of paper. The one lying down is going to be the Osiris of the pair. You are not going to be particularly conscious of the one who is taking your measure.

Those of you who are going to be taking the measure are Seth. I ask you now to feel deeply your own Sethian power, which you have undoubtedly wielded at one time or another. It is not necessarily evil: a gardener, for example, is often a Seth. You are the one who causes the waning, the conservatism, the restraining, the making of boundaries and limits. Feel the power of the bringer of boundary and limitation. Feel that power moving in you, then take the marker and very slowly, very carefully and mindfully, with full Sethian power, draw the outline of the body lying before you.

Make sure that the arms are distinct from the torso, not drawn as two bumps on the sides of the torso, and that the legs are separated from each other. Articulate the hands and the feet as clearly as you can.

As this takes place, you who are Osiris being measured, reflect on the fact that you are being put into fixed form.

You who are playing Seth, feel the full Sethian power of your being as you do the outlining. Think, as you work, of how you have been Seth in other ways in your life and in the lives of others . . .

(When the drawing is completed, say:)

When the task is completed, it is time to reflect. Those of you who have been drawn, reflect on being measured. Those of you who have been doing the drawing, reflect on your own Sethian power. (Allow two minutes.)

Now, exchange places. Let the Osiris become Seth. Let the Seth become Osiris and lie down on a fresh sheet of paper.

You who are Seth, feel your enormous Sethian powers of bounding, limiting, cutting back. Begin to draw the measure, the exact measure, of your Osiris. Do so without speaking, with great concentration, with great mindfulness.

As this takes place, you who are Osiris being drawn, reflect on the fact that you are being put into fixed form . . .

(When the drawing is completed, say:)

Now I ask each of you to stand up and look at the measurement of yourself. Without speaking, look at that fixed form of yourself. This is the casket that carries you through space and time, the casket that has been hurled into the river of time. This is you. This is your form. There you are, locked into time . . .

This is your form. But it is also the crucible of your transformation, your carriage in time. It is your boat, your vehicle. There it is . . .

Each of you take up markers or crayons. Working very rapidly on your own outline—the outline your partner made of you—draw in the head. You can do it literally with eyes and nose and mouth, or symbolically and hieroglyphically, drawing in the neter of your head. Or you can do a combination of both. Then write your full name on this part of yourself. This is very important, because at a later point you are going to have to find it. Work rapidly. Don't spend time thinking, just draw . . .

Next, your throat. Draw in your throat or the neter of your throat, or both, then write your name on it . . .

Next, the upper part of the trunk, with the heart and the lungs. Be sure your name is there . . .

Next, the lower part of the trunk, with the stomach and the intestines. Draw it realistically or as a neter, or a combination of both. Put your name on this part . . .

Next, any kind of generative organ that you choose, even a kind that nobody's thought of yet. Women may want to include the male organ, and men, the female organs. Don't forget to write your name on this part as well . . .

Next, the right arm. Not the hand, but the right arm. Draw the right arm, or its neter. Put your name on this part . . .

Next, the left arm. Draw that, and add your name when you are done . . .

Next, the right hand, and add your name . . .

Next, the left hand. The process is always the same. Draw in the body part either realistically or as a neter, then write your name on it . . .

Next, the right leg . . .

Followed by the left leg . . .

Followed by the right foot . . .

Followed by the left foot. Make sure your name is on each part . . .

Finally, draw in the liver, a very important organ in ancient Egypt. Draw it on the right side of your torso. Be sure your name is on it . . .

You have now finished drawing the fourteen parts of the body, fourteen representing the time in days it takes for the moon to wax fully or to wane fully. Stand up now and reflect on your body. Stand near your partner with your two drawings side by side on the floor. As you stand looking down on them, reflect to each other on the meanings of what you have drawn. You don't have to comment on each part. Focus on what strikes you most strongly. (Allow five to ten minutes.)

Now, step into your body and lie down on it. This drawing is now much more for you than it was before, for it is you not only in outline but also in the netered parts of you. Step into it, lie down, and become silent . . .

There are two ways that you can experience this, for you are now in your fixed form—locked in, as it were. But instead of feeling claustrophobic and limited, you can, as Osiris did, enter into a period of gestation and germination in preparation for the higher call. For the Osirian part of your self, this is the time of readying for the transmutation. Unless the seed goes into the earth and is bound in limitation, it cannot flower.

Also, time allows for the necessary winter that brings the spring. Time gives the limitation, and that limitation builds up energetic pressure for renewal.

How are you readying yourself in the casket of time? How are you readying yourself in the casket of time? How are you readying yourself in the casket of time?

Feel this form defining you, limiting you. But at the same time all of the parts, the neters, are deepening you, preparing you for the new germination, for a resurrection into experiencing your life much more fully. You are limited in the form of time and lost for a while, but at the same time being prepared for a second birth . . .

"I could be bounded in a nutshell, and count myself a King of infinite space."

You are bounded but germinating, being prepared. In this deep, quiet death, the psyche is preparing itself for its mythic flowering, the flowering of the second life in the casket and the womb of time.

(Quiet flute music is appropriate for this period of reflection, which should last about five to ten minutes.)

Now, having been prepared, stand up for the last time and quietly reflect on your body and soul, limited and yet preparing itself in the casket of your time, in the casket of your own physical dimensions.

You have your measure, and you have your knowing. Take your casket self and line it up with all the others around the edge of the room, or lay them on the floor in rows. Then, just for a few minutes, move around the room and look at the other casket selves lined up like great rows of mummies.

You will see, as you circle the room, that the whole symbolic experience and character of the human race are present in these drawings of mummies.

Think of yourself as being in a chapel, or a cathedral, or an ancient Egyptian temple with all these pictures portraying the effigies of the human being. In quiet, walk among these effigies now. Walk in the room of mummies. (Allow five minutes.)

(Take a break before beginning the next process.)

♀

JOURNAL PROCESS

Osiris trusted Seth. Seth murdered Osiris. Write about a time you lost your trust.

One of the odd advantages of limitation is that we are forced to wait, forced into silence, forced into inactivity. Sometimes that is exactly what we need to do, as when we are brought low by illness and forced into isolation in order to heal. Imagine yourself as Osiris inside the tree, alone, upholding the pillar of the temple of Byblos. Simply there, in that tree, waiting. An inner voice whispers. What do you hear in the silence?

On the other hand, your life may be incredibly busy at this time. Set aside one day. Let your family and friends know of your plans so that you will not be interrupted. Then, alone for one entire day, do not speak, do not read, do not write. Simply listen to the quiet. At the end of the day, before bed, write what you experienced.

Write about a time you were Seth. How have you placed limits on yourself and others? Why? When have you been jealous of another? What was it you really desired for yourself?

♀

PROCESS 6:
Mourning the Beloved

In this myth we find a tender understanding of how the metaphor of Isis, our partner in the depth realm, experiences the event of our birth into the physical realm as a dying into time. And we realize how our spiritual partner takes the initiative of crossing the great divide between the worlds to join us, the mortal Beloved. Part of the supreme mystery of the rites of Isis and Osiris, especially in Greco-Roman times, had to do with how the Beloved finds and reconstitutes the torn body-self. Later Gnostic texts present similar figures, the crucified Jesus being partnered again by his Beloved in Heaven, the Sophia who is the feminine wisdom of God.

The Isis and Osiris myth presents this rending in its extreme form. The mystery concerns how partnership and cocreativity can continue no matter how overwhelming the obstacles. In this myth the most obvious obstacle to union is the aliveness of one partner and the utter deadness of the other.

The following process begins as mourning, but when you take mourning to its depth, it often ends up as yearning for you know not what or whom. When you reach that extraordinary, acute sense of separation—of being a stranger in a strange land—you are at the edge of return to the sacred conjunction.

TIME: 45 minutes.

MATERIALS NEEDED: The guide may want an assistant who will perform a slow, steady drumbeat. Having tissues handy may also be helpful.

MUSIC: Selections from Area 2. The great mood piece *Ignacio* by Vangelis works well here. Add celebrational music from Area 3 at the end if desired.

INSTRUCTIONS FOR THE SOLO JOURNEYER: More than ever, solo journeyers may experience deeply the separation of the self from the Beloved of the Soul. The sense of isolation may at times overwhelm you. It might be useful before you begin the process to call upon your own Nephthys, your sister and companion, to let that person know that you are undergoing a period of mourning for the lost Beloved. Make arrangements to call or meet your friend as soon after the process as possible. Remember that this process will deepen your experience of the sacred in life, calling you to the deepest reaches of your soul and the greatest heights of spiritual union.

This process is readily performed alone by following the script for the guide, which you can put on tape with appropriate music. If you own a drum, you may wish to have it handy, for the drumbeat can help keep your attention focused on the task and provide a ready outlet for emotional expression.

When the moment for the merger with the Beloved has come, you may wish to have sticks of sweet-smelling incense ready, for incense in the temples in ancient Egypt always denoted the presence of the divine. This will also help to clarify the room of any leftover emotional charges and allow you to enter into the union spiritually purified.

The journaling process given at the conclusion of this process is essential here for you who are experiencing this part of the journey by yourself.

SCRIPT FOR THE GUIDE: When the music starts, begin to walk backward slowly with your eyes closed or half-closed. As you do that, remember the mortal Beloved of your life, the noble surrogate . . .

Remember your Beloved. This could be a sister, brother, uncle, grand-parent, father, mother, spouse, friend, dog, cat—the pet you had when you were four years old. Your Beloved may be dead, or gone, no longer here. Your Beloved will have passed out of relationship with you. Mourn now, as Isis did, along the flowing Nile . . .

As you walk backward, you will remember the love, the flow between you at the time of the great flow, even though subsequent years may have become parched and dry. You will remember the flow, the Nile flow of these relationships. You will remember them . . .

With your eyes closed or half-closed, remember the great unions in your life. Remember that great unions often exist on many levels, as Isis and Osiris are both brother and sister, husband and wife, archetypal lover and human beloved . . .

Continue walking backward, remembering, remembering, remembering. Remember the times of feeling special closeness with your mortal Beloved, communion with your mother—perhaps even in the womb. Remember the time of closeness with your father, your brother, your sister, with your part-ner, with your friend, with your dog, with your cat, with your children, with your grandparents, with your grandchildren, your uncles, your aunts, with trees, with the funny man who ran the corner grocery store, the ice cream man who used to stop to talk with you, the teacher who saw your special po-tential, the minister or nun or priest or rabbi who woke something in you. All that remembrance of closeness and communion is present and again with you as you travel back in time . . .

Keep moving backward, remembering, remembering, remembering. Let each memory find its place in the Nile flow of loving communion . . .

Remember the noble surrogates of the Beloved, and the noble time of recognizing the Beloved in others. Remember the loving for its own sake . . .

As you continue to walk backward, feel as if you are harvesting the re-membrance of all that loving. Know that this Nile flow of the moments and times of loving begins to carry you back even farther now, back and back and back to the state of original union . . .

Go back and back and back and back now to that place, carried by the flow of all the Beloveds in your life: teachers, parents, guides, friends, an-imals. Pass through them and with them. Harvest them in their essence. Allow yourself to be carried back to the original union in a different di-mension, the union of unions with the archetypal Beloved, the eternal Beloved, the Isis or Osiris of yourself, your twin, your partner in the deep

realm. Go back now to that place, to that state of your original union . . .
(Allow two minutes.)

Now let yourself feel the sense of loss—the enormity of the loss of your
Isis or Osiris, which occurred when you were born into time. Or feel that
experience that took you beyond the primal bonding with a parent or
friend or loved one. Feel whatever kind of loss you felt. It may be a loss
that goes beyond any loss you've ever known, the loss of original union . . .

And feeling that loss and that aloneness, decide to take action; begin to
come forward now and search for the ones you have lost. Search as you move
forward. Mourn them. Allow yourself to mourn as Isis mourned, as your soul
partner may have mourned for you when you were born into time. But also
search now for the Beloved who has been lost. Search and mourn and, if it
comes out of you naturally, cry and lament. Let the cry rise up out of you.

Let it rise out of you—a great lamentation, that terrible sense of the
loss of connection with the Beloved. Let it rise deeply now as Isis again
mourns. You search the Upper and Lower Egypt of your world, mourning, mourning, mourning, searching, and mourning.

(Here the guide may wish to have a drum beaten slowly.)

Wander, wander, turning around, wander, let the mourning turn you
in circles, sending you here and there as you continue to mourn, wandering, searching without ceasing. Where is the one whom I have loved?
Where and in what place, what reality is the one I have lost? Where are
you, Beloved? You may never have mourned this loss before or in the
same way. Mourn it now . . .

Keep mourning. Keep searching. Mourn the loss. Mourn all the ones
you have lost, both in your own life and in your life before life—the place
and time of your essential union.

(If there is a member of the group who can offer a chant or a ritual
lament, have this done. It might be something like this:)

> So do I yearn for thee, so does my heart tremble, so does the blood drip in
> my veins and remember you and call you to me. So do I yearn to feel your
> arms around me, to look once again into your eyes, to remember who I am
> because you are. O, my Beloved. O, my Beloved, come back. Come back.
> Come back. Come back now. Where are you? Where are you? Where are
> you? Where are you? Where have you gone? Have you gone to other lands
> without me?
>
> Do you remember me? Do you also hold me and remember? Where are
> you? Where are you? Do you remember me? Will you remember me now
> wherever you are? Can you hear me calling? Oh, I love you. I love you.
> Where are you? I have been looking for you forever it seems. Where are
> you now? Do you hear me call you? Oh, oh, listen, wherever you are, I am
> waiting. And I will look for you forever.

Begin to let your mournings blend together. Release the mourning together as one voice. Let the mourning become one voice, one song of

lament, that which has never been spoken, calling, calling, calling, "O, my Beloved, come back, come back, come back."

The mourning becomes a great yearning, and you feel the Beloved yearning for you. You yearn for the Beloved, and the Beloved yearns for you. Open your arms in that great expression of yearning and seeking as the Beloved yearns for you. Feel it. Feel that sense of almost vibrational contact of resonance across the dimensions of being.

You remember, and you are remembered, and the yearning, so intense, goes back and forth between the dimensions.

And the Beloved begins to speak to you and say:

Beloved, Beloved, I have never left you. Don't you feel the connection that has always been there, that will always bind us, will always deepen us? As for the time of seeming separation, this is an illusion, for the love that is between us is what we are made of. This is where we come from. Together. We are always together. I have never, ever ceased to love you, to embrace you. You have never lost me. I am that part of you that you cannot ever lose. Only in your imagination can you lose me, for we are truly together, and this love, which has been with us forever, which has shaped our lives and our yearning, do not imagine that you can lose it. It is not possible.

The love that surrounds you is so immense. Breathe it. Feel it around you. Know my presence, and your presence in me, always twinned, always together, always bigger than imagination. You have only to breathe, and I will be there. Only breathe. Feel my presence. And so let us breathe each other. I have not gone anywhere farther than your own heart. If you can feel your heart, you feel me. If you can breathe your breath, you are one with me, forever.

And breathing into this remembering, breathing, and being breathed into, you inhale, the Beloved exhales. The Beloved inhales, you exhale, breathing together with the Beloved. Taking your hands and crossing them over your heart, embrace yourself as you embrace the Beloved. Feel the Beloved around you, embracing you.

Now all move closer together, eyes closed, so that you feel the connection with all the other Beloveds, embracing your friends here, moving together. Feel the love of the Beloved, reaching back into your memory, bringing deep value, deep loving, deep empowerment to the time of the loving flow, so that it is truly never lost. Regardless of what may have happened subsequently with your human loves, the essential love is never lost. That love flows into the universe of love itself.

Your times of loving become part of the love that moves the sun and the other stars, as Dante says. It becomes part of the love of spirit for nature and nature for spirit, as the Beloved continues in this wonderful time of connection to embrace you. And the spirit of Osiris reaches out and envelops the being of Isis. And the spirit of Isis reaches out and embraces the apparently inert form of Osiris. And the living and the dead Beloveds come together, and that which is lost is now found.

This is the first day of the great time of your life, the time of the renewal, the engagement of your relationship with the Beloved. Through this eternal partnering you may evoke and empower love wherever you are. So be it.

Now, reaching out to whoever is near you, open your eyes and see in him or her the reflection of the Beloved. The great relationship with the Beloved is seen in everyone, and everyone is now seen as a reflection of the Beloved. As you gaze at your partner, see his or her Beloved seeing your Beloved.

Moving into another space and time, begin to stretch, to stretch, and to move, and call out the sound of your connection with the Beloved. From "Aha!" to "Whoop-dee-doo," from "Hooray!" to "Hallelujah," everything is appropriate.

(Play celebrational music, if desired.)

☥

JOURNAL PROCESS

Isis traveled to a foreign land and there confronted herself. As a woman in disguise, without past or future, she was simply present in her moment in time. Write about a similar experience in your life.

List all the times when you lost yourself. This is not a time to analyze, simply to remember quickly. After the list is completed, read it over and respond to any parts that seem to need deepening.

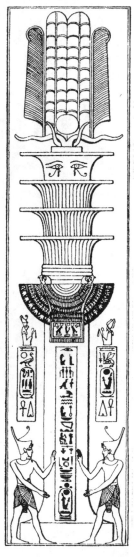

The djed *of Osiris, with the plumes, horns, disk, breastplate, and pectoral of the god. From a bas-relief at Abydos.*

The djed, *from which proceed "Life" and a pair of arms supporting the solar disk. From the Papyrus of Ani.*

II

The Osirian Mysteries, Part 1:
The Raising of the Djed Pillar

> The human being is a living whole in which
> atoms are as alive as he is himself; they form
> his material substance and his organic
> components, which in turn reveal and analyze
> all the functional aspects of the universe.
>
> from *The Egyptian Miracle:*
> *An Introduction to the Wisdom of the Temple*
> by R. A. Schwaller de Lubicz

Abydos, the mythic site of the tomb of Osiris, lies midway between northern and southern Egypt, midway between the barren desert plateaus and the fertile delta. It is here in this in-between realm that pilgrims for three millennia came to mourn the slain Osiris and to celebrate his rejuvenation. The temple that rests there now was built by the devoted pharaoh Seti I during the New Kingdom, but it was based on an older, preexisting temple. That shrine was situated in a grove of trees atop a hill, and it was reached by ascending a flight of steps rising from the Nile waters.

Here, the dismembered body of Osiris was said to have been reassembled. By the time of the Middle Kingdom, the myth was so well known that crowds of people sailed from the farthest reaches of Egypt to attend the rites of Osiris. In ancient evenings, vigils were kept by sacred priestesses who, playing the parts of Isis and Nephthys, reenacted the passion play of Isis and Osiris. Spell 74 of the Coffin Texts duplicates the script of this mystery drama:

> "Ah Helpless One! Ah Helpless One asleep! Ah Helpless One in this place which you know not—yet I know it! Behold, I have found you lying on your side—the great Listless One."
>
> "Ah, Sister!" says Isis to Nephthys, "this is our brother. Come, let us lift up his head. Come, let us rejoin his bones. Come, let us reassemble his limbs. Come, let us put an end to all his woe, that, as far as we can help, he will be weary no more. . . ."[1]

During these night vigils many rituals were performed, in the same way that passion plays of the betrayal, death, and resurrection of Jesus are reenacted during the Lenten season. The weeklong ceremonies began with the "Opening of the Way" into the tomb, a ceremony led by a priest masked and robed as the jackal god, Anubis, the guide for the dead into the next realm. Then followed a ceremony in which an effigy of Osiris was sailed in a boat along the Nile, reminiscent of the sailing of the coffin down the Nile to Byblos. The final sacred act was the "Raising of the *Djed* Pillar," which symbolized the re-membering of the severed backbone of Osiris and the reestablishment of Osiris as the resurrected god, a symbol of strength, vigor, and support.[2]

Religious experience was the life of ancient Egypt. All activities—the hoeing of the ground, the laying of the foundation stones of new buildings, the birthing of children, the weaving of cloth—were invested with the actions of soulmaking. It is no wonder that men and women were ready to lay down their lives for the pharaoh. Every action was a spiritual action, and the king's command was the highest of all. All festivals were public feast days. Although not every ancient Egyptian was accorded the honor of attending the temple spectacle, the shrines of the gods were paraded openly in the streets amid the fanfare of music, the bright costumes of the celebrants, and the riotous noise of merchants selling their wares.

The Secrecy of the Rites

The rites of Isis and Osiris were reenacted until A.D. 400, but during the time of the Roman occupation of Egypt and after the rise of Christianity the old traditions were often mocked and scorned. As a result, the practice went underground, and in some way, this protected the rituals from being tampered with for several hundred years. For those to whom the Osirian mysteries were revealed, the experience was one of total change and radical transformation. It took a great deal of courage to attend these rites when faced by the mocking crowds of Roman officials and upper society. Intellectualism, vanity, and idle curiosity had no place in the initiate's heart.

The kingdom of heaven remained hidden, for its value lay within, not without. Even Apuleius, the author who underwent initiation into the rites of Isis and recorded them in *The Golden Ass*, did not reveal the mysteries. He said simply that he descended to the underworld, saw the midnight sun, and returned to the upper world. He kept the experience of his initiation secret, like a cherished dream too important to be misunderstood.

We are dealing with the transformation of the self from the depths of the sacred realm. Its implications may be universal, but first the transformation must be seeded and take place in the individual self alone. Says the Jungian analyst and writer Marie Louise von Franz:

> One has to stick, with a certain steady uprightness, to one's lonely inner experience and not expectorate it. It has consequences affecting every detail of one's life, and that is always involved with the collective.[3]

The Solitary Wandering of Isis

Haggard, rejected, and scorned for her sorrow, the mourning Isis at last discovers that the chest had been carried down the Nile, cast into the Mediterranean, and tossed up on the coast of Lebanon, at the ancient site of Byblos.[4] There it had lodged in the branches of the tamarisk tree that had miraculously grown around the chest, containing and concealing Osiris within its trunk. The king of Byblos, amazed at this miracle, caused the tree to be cut down and made into a pillar for his palace.

Trees were especially sacred in ancient Egypt, where they were scarce on the desert plains. A tree was always the visible sign of the nurturing power of the neters toward all that they contacted or touched. Because of the hardness of the wood and its perennial green color, the tamarisk was especially sacred to the gods of the dead—Osiris, and the jackal-headed Anubis and Upuaut.

Isis then travels to Byblos. She leaves the boundaries of the known and wanders as a stranger in a strange land. In fact, in the process, she has become a little strange even to herself. The sorrowing and grief have changed her. No longer quite goddesslike or regal, she looks more like a common servant. She enters the palace at Byblos through the back door, very much a goddess-in-hiding. Common as she appears outwardly, she nevertheless attracts the servants and the princesses to her almost in spite of herself, because like most goddesses, she exudes from her inner nature some wonderful-smelling essence.

What did she smell like? We can never know. We are told the gods had a divine fragrance that could never be duplicated. I like to think that Isis smelled like the absolute essence of everyone's favorite odor. Thus for one person it would be the ultimate attar of roses, while for another it might be freshly baked bread, while to yet another it could be the smell of the best-beloved. The miraculous green growth of the tamarisk that contains Osiris and the perfume that pours from the body of Isis tell us that our most primal senses can inform us of the seemingly intangible divine presence—by instinct, by smell, by feel, by the presence of a miracle, by an archaic thrill that raises the hair on our heads.

Because the queen and the servants notice the delicious odor of sanctity about her, and loving her smell—the most primitive and often most accurate of our perceptions—they give Isis the royal child to nurse. So Isis finds something human to love in the palace; thus both the archetypal and the existential loves are served. This is the feminine mystery: that love, devotion, does not serve just one or the other, God or human. Rather, it is both love of the eternal and of the human, of both Osiris and the child. In the agony of her grief Isis finds something to love—a true relationship. This part of the story also shows that the high being never enters through the front door with degrees and titles, but through the side or back door, as the nurse or the beggar. The high being sidles in.

Finding Love Amid Sorrow

Isis soon becomes the much-loved nurse to the children of the king. In a similar and perhaps derivative myth, Demeter, the Greek goddess of agriculture, nursemaids a king's son during her time of mourning her lost daughter, Persephone. Loving the queen's child, Isis decides to give it the gift of immortality. At night, when all the palace is asleep, she thrusts the infant prince into the fire where, through some divine alchemy, his mortal parts will be burned away. While she waits, she transforms herself into a swallow and flutters around the column in which Osiris is embedded, lamenting and bemoaning her fate in strange, sad notes.

The child is the surrogate for her Beloved and expresses her tremendous need to restore life. Or perhaps, in her role as spirit (bird), Isis is trying to lure the essence of Osiris into the body of the child who is being made immortal in the fire. Psychologically, this speaks to our desire to lure the spirit of the archetypal and immortal Beloved into the unprepared body/mind of our existential Beloved. Whenever we try this, inevitably the existential one gets burned, and we experience a double loss, first of the flesh and blood Beloved, whom we damage or terrify through our efforts to turn him or her into a vehicle for the eternal Beloved, and then of the eternal Beloved, who seems to remain inaccessible because our efforts have been inappropriate.

It is a subtle touch of irony that, as Isis tries to free Osiris from the bonds of his rigid existence, she is simultaneously working the same kind of inverse, binding magic upon the child that Seth worked upon Osiris. If her magic had succeeded in making the child immortal, he would have been as stuck in his own timeless time as Osiris, a helpless victim who could only watch all that he loved suffer and die around him, while he could do nothing to save them.

This part of the tale tells us that overgifting or overprotecting can abort the divine possibilities that lie within each of us. When this happens, we are unable to find the higher pattern that is there, nor can we be fully fired into the form and mind that we could have. In both the

Greek and Egyptian versions of the story, the child grows up to be a human being of noble character and many talents, but not a god.

The queen, hearing the noisy swallow, runs in and snatches her child from the fire, thus depriving him of immortality. This represents the frequent refusal of the gifts of the gods as too dangerous; we cannot understand the absurdity of the god's actions. This incident recalls a similar story in the Old Testament in which Abraham willingly prepares to perform the absurd, to sacrifice his beloved son, Isaac, to God, with the result that Isaac is saved by the angel of the Lord and Abraham's people become virtually immortal.

The Pillar of Osiris as Axis Mundi

Having been found out, Isis has no choice but to reveal the glory of who she truly is, to claim the coffin containing her beloved Osiris, and to remove it from the palace pillar. That the trunk of that tamarisk has become a pillar to support the roof of the palace of the king of Byblos contains a mystery of tremendous psychological, physiological, and spiritual richness.

How important is the tree in all the world's religions! It is the *axis mundi*, the center of reality: Yggdrasil in Norse mythology, the tree of knowledge in Genesis, the bodhi tree in Buddhist scripture, the cross in Christianity. The kabbalistic tree of life of esoteric Hebrew thought is itself founded upon esoteric Egyptian practices. In both cultures the structure and pattern of the tree was emblematic for those psychological states and spiritual practices that would eventually bring one into union with the ultimate reality.

In the Eastern world, we have the god-man sitting under the tree in an agony of ecstasy. In the Western world, the god-man is hanging on the tree in an ecstasy of agony. The tree is the place from which new creation is grown.

Osiris is caught in tree and time. Thus he is caught in the *axis mundi*, the center of reality. He completes the Eastern and Western experience, for his is the transcendence of agony and ecstasy within the tree. To extend the metaphor, Jesus does not become fully human until he is nailed on the tree in an irredeemable situation. Buddha, whose disciplines have taken him to the edge of nonbeing, wakes to his full humanity under the tree. And Osiris, "a giant upon the earth," neither god nor man, comes into his own deepened story within the tree. For Osiris, the coffin moving down the waters of life to become embedded in the tree is the final process of incarnation in a physical, terrestrial body. The tree is the vehicle through which the fullness of humanity becomes possible.

Tet with the head of Osiris.

Kundalini Power in the Djed *Pillar*

The tree in Egyptian mythology is also identified with the central nervous system and spine of Osiris. One of the most sacred objects of ancient Egypt was the *djed* pillar, which had as one of its representations the backbone—specifically, the sacrum—of Osiris. Joseph Campbell and many other students of ancient mythology believed that the ancient Egyptians may have known and worked with a system of chakras, perhaps even a kind of kundalini yoga. One could speculate that the symbol of the *djed* corresponds to the location of the fiery serpent, the kundalini energy coiled around the base of Osiris' spine, as well as to the upright Osiris in the coffin in the tree—both important keys to the elevation of the spirit encased in matter.

In various Eastern and esoteric psychophysical traditions, the rising of the kundalini energy activates and releases the powers in the chakras. In Hindu, Buddhist, and Taoist teachings, those centers of psychophysical energy and radiance roughly correspond to major centers of the endocrine system, which then serve to enhance the functioning of the subtle bodies so that the initiate can move in extended realities. In other words, the ascent of kundalini serves as a mode of activating the chakras as doors to the intradimensional and durative worlds, where the subtle bodies can travel and function.[5]

In the descent of kundalini, which occurs as Osiris is encased in a tree, the Soul or *ba* incarnates, is caught in matter, and sets its wheels of influence spinning in the chakras located throughout the body. The effect of this descent, then, is to code and activate the spiritual centers in the body. In the Egyptian mysteries the ascent of the kundalini energy, indicated by the "setting up of the *djed*," represents a state of illumination attainable during one's lifetime; the descent of spiritual energy represents a similar state of illumination occurring at the moments of birth and death.

In texts of ancient Egyptian magic, we read time and again that the magi can "straighten the serpent." In the Old Testament we have several accounts of Egyptian priest-magicians turning a waving, curling serpent into a straight rod. The magician-trained Moses, however, is portrayed as doing the opposite and commanding Aaron to turn his rod into a serpent. The noted Egyptologist R. T. Rundle Clark observed that

> during the early stages of Osiris's underworld development, Mehen (the serpent) keeps the god closely enfolded; but when Osiris begins to revive, the serpent is an opponent to his recovery as a positive, active force. If Osiris is to rise up the serpent must be straightened out. The serpent is both protective and retarding.[6]

Many schools of training in spiritual wisdom emphasize the importance of the spine and spinal exercises. The spine and the brain are the

repositories of what is most ancient and most future about us—
hundreds of millions of years have their messages coded there. As a spiritual model for the process, we may look to the words of the great medieval mystic Meister Eckhart, who wrote, "When the higher flows into
the lower, it transforms the nature of the lower into that of the higher."

As a scientific model, we may look to the work of Paul MacLean and
his associates and their study of the three different developmental brains
contained in the human organism. Many of the conclusions that they
reached are shared by research teams under the direction of leading neu-
rophysiologists such as Karl Pribram and Wilder Penfield.[7]

Working with the Three Brains

MacLean, who was formerly chief of the Laboratory of Brain Evolution and Behavior at the National Institutes of Mental Health,
has presented evidence that our neurological equipment has evolved
over time into what he calls the "triune brain." This refers to the three
major neural systems that emerged sequentially in evolutionary history.
Through them we inherit the many developments of the species that
preceded us and, perhaps, the latent potential that has yet to unfold. In
the accompanying diagram, note the placement and evolutionary development of the three brains within the one brain, from the earliest *reptilian* brain, through the *paleomammalian* system of the old animal brain,
to the present human *neomammalian* brain.

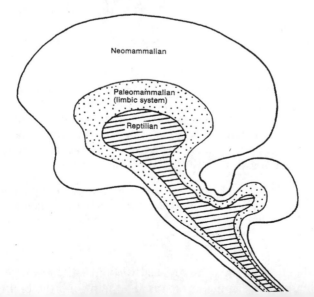

These three brains operate in a nested fashion with the earliest, the reptilian brain or R-complex brain, providing the foundation for the more advanced structures of the old mammalian and the new mammalian brains to build upon. Each of these three brains in the human system continues to have its own specific tasks to perform as well as its own characteristic behaviors.

For example, in the recesses of the reptilian brain are the fish, the reptile, and the amphibian. To some extent, these still govern our survival attitudes as well as those patterns that relate to habitual behavior, continuity, and stability. Responsible for our sensorimotor system, as well as for those physical processes that keep us awake and aware in the world, the reptilian brain is also our automatic pilot, storing those learnings about operating in the world that come to us from the higher brain functions. We can blame our reptile, then, when we get into obsessive-compulsive behaviors or find ourselves stuck in a tiresome devotion to details and routine. But we can thank our reptile when we realize that it provides needed unconscious protection to help us maintain stability within an ever-changing world. Being as ancient within us as it is, this reptilian brain also provides us with a great deal of primary energy and life-support systems.

Stages of Osirian Initiation into the Power of the Djed

It's not likely that the Egyptians had this specific neurological knowledge. Nevertheless, they managed to understand and utilize the power of this reptilian complex in esoteric ways. Thus, in both ancient Egyptian and various Eastern models, the reptilian brain was symbolized as the primal serpent power of kundalini—specifically, for the Egyptians, as the *djed* force of Osiris. Initiates had to enter a phase of training in which they became acutely aware of these primary energies of the reptilian level in order to raise the serpent, that is, to set up the *djed* pillar of Osiris. This would involve working with the body and its knowings (a kind of ancient Egyptian yoga), as well as orchestrating the release of a variety of physical energies. In psychological terms, it possibly involved tapping into ancient subconscious trace memories and allowing the initiate to identify with the neters of the snake or reptile within.

A second stage of initiation may have been learning to raise the serpent power along the spine to the paleomammalian brain. This second brain is the site of the midbrain and limbic system (from *limb*, which means "to wrap around"). Not only does it wrap around the reptilian brain, but it offers a far more adaptable and inventive intelligence, as well as many more openings to the nature and function of reality.

Within this second brain, trace memories of the mammalian beast continue to survive. Here reside the species' prodigious preparations for partnership and procreation, which in turn give us the emotional impetus for the development of family and clan, and thus the early basis for civilization. The paleomammalian brain, or limbic system, therefore, contains the cranial endocrine glands, which govern sexual development, sleep, dreams, desire, pleasure, and pain—the full spectrum of our emotional life. It is the seat of intuition and grounds the fantasies and inventiveness that come from its relative above, the neocortex. But since the limbic also works to combine the three brains, it can direct the intellectual powers of our highest brain into the service of the lowest defense system in an emergency or survival mode, whether real or imagined.

Dangerous as well as desirous, this early mammal brain also contains the neurochemistry that makes for war, aggression, violence, dominance, and alienation. When activated and amplified, this part of the brain can be experienced by the unprepared as inflation of the ego and a stupendous emotional passion for willing one's way. It also seems to activate a destructive charisma.

It has been said, for example, that Genghis Khan studied the ways of activating these kinds of power. When he reached this stage, he killed his teacher because he wanted to stay at this place of emotional and charismatic power over others. Adolf Hitler, a student of esoteric practices, may also have experienced this stage.

Some even suspect that, like Georgy Malenkov, Joseph Stalin was a member of the Skopsi or Bogomil cult, which practiced certain disciplines distantly related to ancient Egyptian mysteries. Certainly, both men also had an abundance of charismatic, but negative, emotional power, which some biographers suggest may have been derived from these practices.

In the prepared person, however, the experience is just the opposite, for it seems to give one a deep sense of emotional compassion for all beings. The bodhisattva state is the result of an amplified, but spiritualized, limbic system. One may have power in this state, but one uses it to serve others, rather than to wield power over them. At this stage of deepened compassion, the enlightened initiate in the ancient temples was given the scepter of Osiris to hold.

The third stage of initiation had to do with the neomammalian brain—the neocortex and the frontal lobes. The neocortex is divided into right and left hemispheres, each of which has its own specialties. The left hemisphere is concerned with temporal, linear, objective, analytic data processing, with language and logic. The right hemisphere of the neocortex is more involved with visual, spatial, intuitive, subjective, and analogical thinking. These parts of the brain, the last to develop and five times larger than the earlier two brains, work in an integrated manner to control conscious thought and activities—reason, will, analysis, logic, calculation, voluntary movement, creativity, and, when developed, altruism, empathy, identity, compassion, and higher orders of love.

The frontal lobes make possible the development of the visionary and the higher mind, the mind that can enter into causality itself. The activation of this brain, with its enormous powers of reflection, self-awareness, and conscious orchestration of other functions, means that its development allows for the integration and conscious orchestration of the other brains. It thus can use the simpler systems of the earlier neural structures to its own higher purposes. As the writer and theorist Joseph Chilton Pearce has observed:

> Our lower order intelligences become refined when incorporated into service of our neocortex. Our R-system is the seat of sexuality, for instance, but what humans do with that basic instinct is different from a black snake's (or should be). Our high, neocortical system transforms this crude reproductive impulse into Tristan and Isolde, or Romeo and Juliet. As [horticulturalist Luther] Burbank observed, the simple system incorporated into the more complex opens vistas of possibility. Same instinct, different setting.[8]

However, as I have written, the neocortex is also

> a Pandora's box of ideas and inventions, idiosyncrasies—not the least of which is its often tentative and ambiguous relationship to the two earlier brains from which it has sprung. Part a cold calculating computer, part the home for paradox and a vehicle for transcendence, the neocortex is that aspect of ourselves that apportions our fate and determines whether as a species we will grow or die.[9]

Because it is a brain more given to higher frequency patterns, it has the ability to consciously enter into macrophasic wave functioning. This means that in states of deep meditation or contemplation, certain spiritual exercises, high creativity, mystical or unitive experience, this part of the brain enters into a frequency resonance with higher orders of reality. Since it is more connected to the realms of psyche, it is possibly the neurological doorway to the great archetypal and creative patterns of existence. It has the capacity to tap the source levels, to hear the music of the spheres, and to see the architectures of creation and consciousness.

This was a critical experience for Egyptian initiates, for when they came back into the world of time, space, and form, they brought with them the sacred geometries of the depths that may have been the inspiration for the great temples and pyramids. It was these experiences, I think, rather than any visitors from Atlantis or from other planets, that were responsible for the rapid development of the high, sacred culture of ancient Egypt.

Thus the *djed* pillar of Osiris is telling us, in mythopoeic form, a very great secret concerning Egyptian origins. It is the secret that has to do with stages of initiation in which developmental patterns in the spine and the brain are accessed to yield the power, purpose, and pattern we need to evolve consciousness and to cocreate higher civilization.

PROCESS 7:
Straightening the Spine and Raising the *Djed* Pillar

To return to the story, the king of Byblos takes the coffin lodged inside the tamarisk tree and uses it to prop up the ceiling of his own palace. This is a clear symbol that the divine spirit in each person can hold up the temple of his or her own life. In ancient Egypt on the occasion of the Osirian festival at Abydos and elsewhere, the *djed* tree-pillar, which symbolized the axis of the world, the spine of Osiris, and the initiation of the adept, was raised at the high moment of illumination, dramatizing for the populace the myth and meaning of this theme. The following scenario is a physiological preparation for "raising the *djed.*"

TIME: 2 hours.
MATERIALS NEEDED: An exercise mat or soft rug for each participant.
MUSIC: For Part 1, use serpentine music with a theme that continually returns to itself, like Ravel's *Bolero.* For Part 2, employ evocative music from Area 2 that builds to a climax, like Samuel Barber's *Adagio for Strings* (repeated several times). Portions of the tone poem *Finlandia* by Jean Sibelius could also be used here.

A CAUTIONARY NOTE: The ancient Egyptian and Greek neophytes to the Osirian mysteries were guided through these incredibly powerful steps by trained initiates who assisted them in "Opening the Way" and "raising the *djed.*" The neophytes were schooled in what to expect. Even in the Hebraic tradition, the student of the kabbalah who asked his teacher to instruct him in the inner mysteries was twice refused before he was admitted to higher study.

In *The Time Falling Bodies Take to Light,* William Irwin Thompson likens the process to a bad LSD experience, and cautions:

> In a trained student of yoga this experience, though frightening, does not generate a psychotic break; in a neurotic person taking LSD, the sudden opening to subconscious material can . . . generate a psychotic disintegration of the personality. Because the brain is what Aldous Huxley called "a reducing valve" for shutting out the million signals a second that we re-

ceive, the brain shuts us into the few signals a second that we prefer to call "reality." When that function of suppression is suddenly suspended, and the individual is flooded with sensory signals and repressed psychic contents, he is overwhelmed by the serpent.[10]

Raising the *djed* pillar is a critical step for the voyager into the Egyptian mysteries. Yet, it should be noted, the raising of kundalini energy is not the mark of an accomplished adept. If anything, it means the neophyte has only just begun. Nevertheless, it is not a work to be taken lightly or to be boasted of. Discipline is the key to this work. Self-control is at the center of this task and self-discipline will be the saving grace. Enlightenment is not an end product, it is a lifelong process.

For inexperienced groups and solo travelers, there are attendant risks. The raising of kundalini energy is a sacred, time-honored tradition that has always involved working under the tutelage and watchful eye of a practiced spiritual master. One may find oneself frightened by the intensity of the experience, or disoriented, or agitated. The experience affects different people in different ways.

Commonly, extroverted people find that their emotions and passions are extremely heightened. They may find that they draw to themselves a complex charge of awareness reflecting issues, emotions, and ideas that had up to now remained unconscious.

Introverted people may experience a sudden opening between the realms of the physical and imaginal worlds, experiencing a loosening of the boundaries between what is real and what is imagined. At times, insomnia and anxiety can occur following the raising of the kundalini because it zaps the entire energy system. The effect lasts more than a day, for one has opened a door into a new land.

In general, the practice of raising the *djed* should not be undertaken by very young or inexperienced or unstable people, but rather by those who have the wisdom of life experience behind them and the physical health to withstand the high-powered energy charges that result from the raising of the kundalini. The ideal candidate is physically healthy and emotionally stable. Those with fragile constitutions, arthritis, back trouble, or similar physical conditions should be cautious about attempting some of these exercises without the proper instruction and practice in yoga movement, modern dance, or the like.

Those with unhealed emotional wounds may wish to perform this process with a trained master in yogic studies, a spiritual counselor, or even a good therapist. It may behoove you to keep in mind when examining yourself or a guide to the mysteries that, although the experience of raising the kundalini is one of intimate contact with enormous power, the attainment of power is not the aim. Compassion is the aim—the recognition that the power of the Self derives from the One.

We warn you that those who have had little or no experience in working with subtle energies may find themselves in deep waters. Nevertheless, this changed energy pattern is a typical occurrence. Relaxation is essential to the work. But again, if you are in a group but do not feel ready for this process, by all means stand aside. Take on the role of High Witness, honoring the experience of others and knowing that you will take the journey only when you feel confident that you are ready.

Also know that you can safely experience something of the power and depth of the process just by reading it to yourself a number of times.

INSTRUCTIONS FOR THE SOLO JOURNEYER: First of all, do not attempt to do this process alone. Reread the cautionary note above as well as the script for the guide and do not enter into this experience unless you are certain that it is right for you. If you do not feel ready for this process, then just allow yourself to experience it by reading the instructions. In this way, you can safely avail yourself of the power of its content. Should you decide, however, to undertake the full experience, make sure someone knows your intention and is available to work with you, since this experience requires that you have attendant emotional, physical, and spiritual support. *Do not do it alone.* Remember, be certain that you are in good physical health before you begin. It certainly won't hurt to have already established an exercise program. This will also provide a healthy outlet for you to burn off any excess energy.

During the week before you begin this process, you may wish to perform several centering and clearing rituals for yourself. For example, finish up or set aside any demanding work for the rest of the week. Put your house in order and get any bill paying out of the way. Then purify yourself with an Epsom salts or Dead Sea salt and baking soda bath, or an aromatic bath in orange blossom essence or some other substance good for the nerves. Purify your sacred space with incense or other sweet-smelling herbs and spices. Enter the process with a ritual affirmation that you will be safe and protected throughout the *djed* process. Ask that the energy and light will become available in a manner that is appropriate for you.

Make a recording of the script, with appropriate musical background. Leave sufficient pauses to do the exercises and processes indicated. Because the second part of this process is extremely powerful, it is wise to have someone nearby to look in on you from time to time over the next few weeks. Be sure to avoid driving or operating machinery right after finishing the process because you may become disoriented for some minutes or hours following the experience. Before you resume your normal activities, walk around the room, clap your hands, stamp your feet, and do a number of simple daily things that will ground you in "ordinary" reality.

♁

PART I

SCRIPT FOR THE GUIDE: Make enough room for yourself in your sacred space so that you can lie comfortably stretched out on your back. You will be lying down for a while, so if you think you might be cold, add a layer of clothing. You will probably also want to take off your shoes. Close your eyes and allow yourself to relax.

Let us now enter into the mystery of the *djed* of the spine. Osiris is being prepared for immortality. The child, the beloved Horus, is soon to be conceived. The depths have been broached, the entrance to the other reality is available. The engendering of a new form of being is taking place. And now the spine is to be straightened so that the primary restorative and creative energy, the kundalini energy, may be raised.

First, allow yourself to wriggle along your spine on the floor like a serpent. Scan your body; notice how it lies on the floor. Be especially aware of your lower back, the place of the *djed* . . . Without moving, do you sense that there is space beneath your lumbar spine (the small of your back)—the place of the *djed*—and the floor? How large is that space? Feel with one of your hands and determine if the space is what you sensed it to be. Then use your other hand to check this from the other side. Note whether the sides of the back lie equally, or whether one side lies lower or higher than the other . . .

We are going to change and straighten your spine. This will allow your body to lengthen, and for some to allow the spine to lie flat on the floor, often for the first time in years. In ancient Egyptian parlance this is called "extending the serpent."

Sense how you lie. See if you are more aware of your back. Be aware of the curving of the back, the upper and lower spine, the neck and the head . . .

Now sit up, close your eyes, and place the soles of your feet together. Extend your arms to the side and behind you, placing the palms on the floor to give you support . . .

In this position rock your pelvis forward and backward, so that you are moving from your tailbone to your sitting bones, and from your sitting bones to your tailbone. Keep your hands in back of you on the floor to support you. Continue the rocking . . .

The movement can be increased if you push out your abdomen as you go forward, and suck it in as you come backward. Make the movement as large as you can without discomfort. Push out your abdomen as you go forward. Suck it in as you come backward . . .

Be aware that this involves a considerable curving of the spine in the lower back. As you come forward the back is arched. As you go back the spine curves in the opposite direction. So you are going from an arch to a curve as you go forward and backward. Forward and backward, arching and curving like the great serpent that your spine is. Arching and curving. Curving and arching. Going forward, pushing the abdomen forward. And backward, sucking it in. Arching and curving. Curving and arching . . . Arching and curving . . . Curving and arching . . .

Continue rocking for a while, pushing the abdomen out and then sucking it in, being aware of the movement in the hip joints, and the movement in the knees and the legs as well. But keep most of your awareness focused on the lower back and spine. There is also, of course, some movement in your upper back and shoulder joints and throughout your body. Do not ignore these sensations, but keep your main focus on the lower spine and pelvis . . .

Now, once again, lie on your back and scan your body. Are you lying the way you were before? Notice this. Is the space under your spine smaller or larger? Notice. What other changes do you note? . . .

Bend your legs so that your feet are flat on the floor, and gently raise and lower your pelvis a number of times. Each time you lower your pelvis, try to place your entire lower back flat on the floor. So you raise your pelvis, and you bring it down to the floor. Just raise your pelvis a little bit off the floor, then down. A little bit off the floor, and down. A little bit off the floor, and then down.

Make a light rapping noise with the small of your back on the floor as you raise and lower it. Rap, rap, rap, with your pelvis. Rap, rap, rap . . . rap, rap, rap.

Stop and rest, keeping your feet flat on the floor. Notice whether your spine has straightened even more . . .

Bring your thighs back toward your chest. Keep your knees spread apart and your feet together. Now perform the following movement very gently. Exercising care, swing your feet and legs lightly from side to side. Make it a light, flowing movement, so that you can clearly feel the contact of your lower spine with the floor as the sides of your pelvis alternately move up and down along the floor. Swing your feet and legs gently from side to side . . .

Whenever you feel like it, leaving your knees up, stop and rest. You may hold on to your knees with your hands if you like, to ease the effort of lying in that position.

Continue the side-to-side movements, but vary them somewhat. Varying the movements helps the brain to stay interested and focused. For example, you can do some movements with the right foot on top of the left. Then you can reverse that, doing some movements with the left foot on top of the right. Also, move with the sides of the feet together. Always concentrate your main awareness, however, on the contact your lumbar spine, your lower spine, is making with the floor . . .

Now stop. Take hold of your knees for a minute, keeping your spine as flat on the floor as you can, and gently lower your legs so that your feet are flat on the floor. Gently. Gently. Then raise and lower the pelvis a few more times until you can place the lower spine fully on the floor, or as close as you possibly can at this time, as you straighten the lower spine, the place of the *djed* . . .

Flex your ankles and while exhaling through your mouth, very gradually extend your legs while trying to keep your lower back and spine on the floor. Slide your heels along until the legs are extended, trying to keep the lower back on the floor . . .

Bring your legs back up so that the feet are again flat on the floor. And lift the pelvis up and down, repeating the whole process. Place the spine on the floor as fully as you can, flex the ankles, exhale through the mouth, extend the legs, and only release the tension in the ankles when the legs are extended . . .

And rest. Sense how your body is lying. Does it feel longer or different in any way? . . .

Now bend your legs again so that your feet are flat on the floor, and roll your legs and lower back from side to side a little. Don't go all the way over, just enough so that you are rolling over your spine and lower back and sensing their contact with the floor. You can put your feet and knees closer together and continue . . .

Expand the movement a little so that the knees come closer and closer to the floor on each side, even making contact with it. Sense clearly what happens in your lower back and spine. Be sure that somewhere in the movement your spine and the lower back are making contact with the floor . . .

Your head can remain stationary or turn in the same direction as the knees. Or, while your legs go in one direction, your head goes in the other. Your head goes right; your legs go left. Your head goes left; your legs go right. Experiment with all possibilities to determine how your head movement affects the leg movement, the flexibility of the lower back and spine, and the contact your back and spine are making with the floor . . .

Now stop. Leave your feet flat on the floor. Let your knees sink just a little bit to the left, then push gently with the right foot so that the right buttock and the right side of the body leave the floor, then bring them back to the floor again. Keep doing that, pushing with the right foot so that the right buttock and the right side leave the floor gently, and lower it to the floor again. Continue doing this, sensing how the lower back and spine are moving. Be sure that you return the entire back and spine to the floor each time . . .

And stop. Now let your legs sink slightly to the right, and push gently with your left foot so that the left buttock and left side of the body leave the floor and then return. Push with the left foot so that the left buttock and left side of the body leave the floor, then come back, lying flat on the floor . . .

Let both legs sink left again, and press a little with both feet, arching the back and curving the spine, which then returns to the floor. Legs sink over to the left, pressing a little with both feet, arching the back, curving the spine, which then returns to the floor . . .

Now bring the legs over to the right and do the same thing. Arching, curving, down. Arching, curving, down . . .

Next, feet flat on the floor, raise and lower your pelvis a few times. Leave your lower back on the floor after you have done that. First raise and lower your pelvis a few times, then leave your lower back on the floor. Flex your ankles, exhale through your mouth, extend your legs straight out in the air, then begin to lower them to the floor. When you reach the floor, release the ankles . . .

Bring the legs back so that your thighs once again approach your rib cage. Feet together, very gently move your pelvis left and right. Left to right, but gently. You can do it with the right foot on top of the left, or with the left foot on top of the right . . .

Note how your back is contacting the floor. Lift your legs into the air a little and use their weight to swing yourself up to a sitting position. Keep your eyes closed . . .

Put the soles of your feet together, hands behind you on the floor, and again rock your pelvis back and forth. Extend your abdomen as you go forward, and suck it in as you go back; let the movements in the lower spine and back be as large as possible. Does the movement feel any different now than it did at the beginning? . . .

Slowly lie down on your back, leaving your feet flat on the floor for a moment, with some space between your feet and between your knees. Then let your knees go a little to the left, and then to the right. Left and right. Sense the rolling of the lower back and spine across the floor . . .

Elevate your pelvis for a moment. And with the pelvis elevated, rock your body up and down along the floor so that your shoulder blades and shoulder joints move. Feel the movements very clearly on the floor.

And stop. Raise and lower your pelvis a few times until your lower back rests entirely on the floor, or as close as possible. Then extend your legs and sense how your body is lying. Note the feeling of length in your spine. Notice how your back is in contact with the floor, and especially how it is lying in the region of the lower spine . . .

Roll your head lightly from side to side several times. Then, one last time, bend your legs and push and pull with your feet, rocking your body up and down along the floor, so that when you push up with your feet, your head moves away from your body, and when you pull down, your chin approaches your chest. Your pelvis stays on the floor as you do this. Try to feel the entire length of the spine, the *djed*, straightening, the serpent straightening as it moves along the floor . . .

Good. Now rotate both your head and your pelvis together. Your pelvis is rotating clockwise, along with your head. First in one direction, then in the other . . .

Rotate just your pelvis, so that the small of your back makes circles on the floor, with as much of the lower back as possible circling on the floor. Now extend your legs and observe how you lie. The straightened spine. The serpent extended. What do you notice?

Roll slowly to one side and slowly, gently, come to a standing position. While standing, take note of how you feel, especially any feelings of height you may now have. See if you feel taller. You actually are taller. Your lower spine, where you've been compressed, is now expanded. Now begin to move, slowly, gently. Be aware of that expansion. Standing and moving, observe that your body is longer and lighter, that your posture has significantly changed for the better, and this brings feelings of more pleasurable and effective functioning in areas that perhaps have not been able to function this well or easily.

Walk around. Are you more erect? Now that your posture is improved, are you looking at more things? Instead of looking at the floor, are you looking in different directions—the ceiling, the walls—perhaps perceiving them simultaneously? Your enlarged perspective probably means that your eye muscles are freer than before . . .

Increased awareness, increased height, improvement in your posture and how you carry yourself—these are all very objective facts. They mean that your skeletal alignment—what the ancient Egyptians called the *djed* raising—has changed. Your muscular organization has changed because the organization within your brain and nervous system has changed.

Return to your place and sit down, with your legs extended and your feet together.

For a few minutes, we're going to attempt to prime the kundalini energy. In Part 2 of this process we are going to enter the early stages of the raising of the *djed* pillar, an internal process that was celebrated overtly and dramatically in ancient Egypt.

♣

PART 2

Closing your eyes, follow your breath. Inhale up the spine—from the base of the spine up through the top of the head to what has been called the transpersonal chakra about a foot above your head, where you will meet the Beloved, the Isis or Osiris of your soul. Then exhale down the front of the body, down the chakras. The crown, the brow, the throat, the heart, the solar plexus, the second chakra, the root, and down through the knees and the feet . . .

Inhale up the back. Up the back of the spine from the root, the chakra at the base of the spine, up the spine, all the way to the top of the head and farther above to the transpersonal chakra, where you will meet and feel a sense of interchange and communion with the Beloved. Then exhale down the chakras on the front. The crown, the third eye, the throat, the heart, the solar plexus, the second chakra, the root . . . And up the spine, up the chakras, on the back. All the way up, until you reach the top of the head. Above the head you'll meet the Beloved. Then exhale down the front, passing through the chakras.

Keep doing this as I talk to you. Inhale up the spine, meeting the Beloved at the top of the head in the transpersonal realm, then exhale down the front, down the chakras. Then up the spine, meeting the Beloved, then down the front, down the chakras to the root . . .

You are finding yourself becoming aware, gradually at first, of rays of white light reaching down to you, the descent of kundalini. Sparkling white light, a cone of that light, from the Beloved at the transpersonal realm, descends your being . . .

This light is entering you now, and growing brighter and brighter, sparkling and shimmering. Brilliantly white, it cascades through you, washing through you and warming you with its radiance. It washes over and through you, suffusing your whole body, changing in appearance from one moment to the next, sometimes white, sometimes golden light. It comes down from the Beloved as a gift of grace through the different chakra centers of your being . . .

Wonderful golden white light, perhaps unearthly, perhaps dazzling, moves down through your body. And your body becomes more and more a part of it, merges with it. Your body, which has just been rendered taller, is becoming still taller. It is feeling more and more elongated, for the serpent is straightened. Your body is becoming taller and receiving this light . . .

Continue to breathe up the spine to the Beloved from whom the light comes. Then exhale down the chakras. And back up the spine to the Beloved from where the light comes, then breathing down and receiving . . .

You are experiencing a feeling, a spiritual feeling perhaps, something more than human. Experience what your body is feeling as you sit there so tall, so *djed*-like, your serpent spine extended, elongated, with the golden white light now passing through you . . .

It may seem that your body is becoming more of light than of flesh. That light continues to grow and deepen, passing down through you. Your whole body becomes light. Perhaps you're aware of yourself as showers of sparks descending, descending to become a pool of light there on the ground where your awareness is, where you are. You are a pool of light, for that is truly what you are made of. A pool of light. A pool of energy about to be released . . .

Energies, forces are gathering. The light now goes upward from your spine, rises upward. A column of white and golden fire reaches up and up and up, through that long spine, a column of golden white flame. You have no awareness beyond that column of golden white fire that reaches down through you, that reaches up through you.

The column is growing whiter and whiter. You are a part of a column of white fire, reaching upward from the very center of the earth, surging, flowing upward and upward, bursting out through the opening of the earth's surface and surging upward far, far up into the sky.

You are that light, surging from the depths of the earth high up into the sky. You are the pillar of light rising from the earth's center, soaring outward endlessly into the black vastness of space, as if its power would allow you to penetrate the universe. You know the feeling of awesome power, of sublime power, and wonder and energy, as you partake of that great column of fire that you are . . .

Now feel yourself sinking back, back and down again, back past the earth's surface, down and down, until only a small white flame is burning, available to you whenever you need it. And you rise out of the fire.

Become aware of your body, a body of flesh, but somehow changed. It's as if your body has passed through some kind of important catharsis of fire; as if it has been made new by that experience; as if you have been given access to more vital energies and powers than your body could draw upon before. This is your Osirian body now, your body of resurrection. The *djed* body . . .

Go deeper and deeper. Able to go still deeper and deeper, yet at the same time find yourself here in this place with all of us together. Know that you have access to some very potent energies within you . . .

Focus your consciousness now on the base of your spine, your *djed*, wholly focused on the base of your spine . . . Become aware of a pool of gently swirling but potentially powerful energies there. The *djed* pillar is trying to rise. Focus on that pool of energy . . .

Begin to experience a tingling sensation, perhaps slowly at first near the base of the spine . . . then experience increasingly stronger sensations as you direct that energy to rise along your spine. Be aware now of its power growing and growing, and feel it as it gains momentum, slowly, as it gains more power, as it rises . . .

Know that the *djed* has the capacity to surge with enormous power all the way up the spine, through the chakras, amplifying them, up to your brain. It triggers an unfolding of the reptilian brain, to give you the power of survival. It enters the old mammalian brain, to give you the amplification of the energies of compassion. It travels to the neocortex, to transform you into a citizen of two worlds, one who has access to both the great creative sources and the powers of the universe. The *djed* mind gives you access to powers only latent within you . . .

Be conscious again of that energy system rising up along your *djed* spine. Restrain it so that its energy can accumulate, but do not prevent its movement. Allow only as much movement as you are willing to take. Hold that movement to a slow, steady progress up your spine. And observe it closely.

The *djed* is rising. The *djed* is rising. The *djed* is rising. Allow the *djed* to rise, but not with such a force as to be overwhelming, only as much as you can contain . . .

You will know when to stop holding back, and when you do release that power, it will rise upward to your brain. There it will trigger the activation of the old brain, the brain of survival. It will amplify the emotional brain, the brain of compassion. It will enhance the brain of high creativity, the new brain, liberating all those powers within you . . .

Now concentrate on the task of directing those energies, the Osirian energies, the *djed* energies, the kundalini energies, up and along your spine. Breathe up the spine, directing the energies upward, until you feel their accumulation, until you feel that by letting go you can send those energies into the activation of your brain, into the initiation of your higher nervous system, into partnership with the Osiris within yourself. Let that happen now. Let the *djed* rise . . .

(Allow a period of silence at this point in the experience.)

Now let the *djed* energy come back down. Coming down. Extending through the chakras and down the spine. Coming down, and down, and down, and down, and down, and down, and down. The *djed* flows into the pool of light, which is always there to be sourced, in the pool that is the great vortex of creation. The pool is there at the base of the spine, the base of the pool of life. The *djed* is always ready to rise and resurrect and bring you to the next stage of evolution, ready to rise from the pool of light . . .

You are able to stand up now gently, easily. You are able to walk around. Notice the world and let the world note you, one whose walk and manner express the risen *djed*. Stand tall and walk forth. Know that much is going on, felt or unfelt, and it will continue through the hours and days and weeks to come.

NOTE: Before leaving, all participants should walk around the room, clap their hands, stamp their feet, talk to each other, have a cup of noncaffeinated tea and a bite to eat, and do a number of ordinary things in order to ground themselves again in reality. Also, it is not advisable for participants to operate a car or other machinery for some hours following the second part of this process. The guide should check participants' state of alertness, being sure not to let anyone go who may still be in an inward or trance state.

♣

JOURNAL PROCESS

Write about what you have just experienced in your body and mind. Are your perceptions the same? What is your mood and your sense of reality? Do you feel as if your possibilities are changed? Do you note a difference in the way you sense your energy systems, your basic vitality, your life force? How does your charged and flexible spine affect your way of seeing and feeling the world? What does the raising of the *djed* now mean to you?

The body is a sacred instrument, an adytum, an alchemical vessel. It is the temple of the spirit. It is the ball of earth from which the golden soul of Ra transforms as Kheperi. Notice how your body feels now when you pray, meditate, or engage it spiritually. What does it do? What intentions are manifested in which parts of your body?

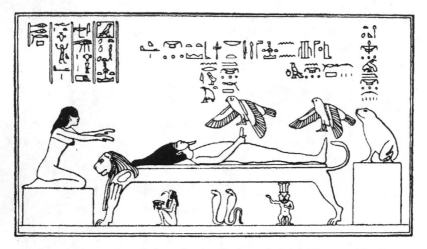

Osiris begetting Horus by Isis, who is in the form of a hawk. The second hawk is Nephthys. At the head of the bier sits Hathor and at the foot the frog goddess Heket.

The Osirian Mysteries, Part 2: The Spiritual Insemination of Isis and the Rending of Osiris

Here is magic. In this sphere of spells
the common word is exalted . . .
and really is still like the call of the male
crying out to the invisible female dove.

from "Magic"
by Rainer Maria Rilke

The cries of Isis, who has disguised herself in the form of the mourning swallow, bring the queen. The frightened woman snatches her baby out of the fire. Isis is forced to reveal her own divine nature and the mission that has brought her to Byblos. She is given the pillar and cuts out the chest containing her husband.[1] Taking Osiris away from Byblos and returning to Egypt, she animates him to the point that she raises up his phallus and inseminates herself with the child Horus.

In a frieze at the Seti temple of Osiris in Abydos, Isis is shown as a falcon hovering over the body of the partially animated Osiris and receiving the spirit of insemination. The ancient text reads:

> She shaded him with her feathers and gave him air with her wings. She cried out for joy and brought her brother to the land. She revived the weariness of the Listless One and took his seed into her body, [thus] giving him an heir. She suckled the child in secret, the place where he was being unknown.[2]

The imagery recalls that of later Christianity, almost as a reverse annunciation. In this myth, it is the immortal Isis who conceives in the form of a bird, which in Egypt can also represent the Holy Spirit. Possibly, too, in the mystical rising of the generative organ of Osiris there is a relationship to the rising of the *djed*-kundalini.

Conceiving the Heroic Child

Thus the union of Isis and Osiris is at once magical and spiritual, involving the intercourse of the essences of their subtle bodies—a kind of ancient Egyptian tantra. It can also be seen as a union between the *ka*, the double or etheric body of Osiris, and the *sahu*, or spiritual body of Isis. Thinking hieroglyphically, this can be taken to mean that the spirit of the Beloved of the Soul—our higher essence hovering over us—can in union with us engender a great being, a great creative action in time. In Egyptian myth, this is the eternally renewing king of Egypt, Horus.

Mortal children are born of physical sexuality, but in this tale Isis conceives her child by magic. He is a divine child born of a union of the psychic and the spiritual. The heroic child exists beyond the boundaries of karma, beyond the borders of ego and personality. The heroic child is born to a great task—the raising of the consciousness of an entire community. Such was the task of Christ, the son miraculously born of a physical woman and an immortal father.

The mystery of the conception of the divine child becomes even more mysterious when we ponder why Isis—the goddess of fertility, the surrogate mother of Anubis, and the midwife to so many other children—has previously birthed no child. In fact, she conceives no child until her husband Osiris is dead. Joseph Campbell pointed out that in many pagan stories, as well as in Christian myth, the Divine Matrix, the womb of the mother, remains fallow until the birth of the heroic child. The womb is not sterile; it is fallow, like a field waiting for seed. It represents the symbolic imitation of the primordial abyss waiting in readiness for the resurgence of the original power from which the world was first created.[3]

The divine creative principle is always inherent, even though it may seem comatose or dead—it just needs to be awakened and called forth. Horus had been conceived in spirit already by the lovers in the womb. The possibility of him existed in the spiritual memory of Isis, and she calls him forth into actuality, even though her husband is dead.

This suggests that each of us comes into being already coded with individual creative possibility, which, if we choose, we can—with passion and commitment—bring into world and time. Should we choose not to pursue the remembrance of this creative potential, because we believe it unlikely, then we are left with unspecified yearnings that we tend to project on to almost anybody. And almost anybody is just what we get. How many of us have been overwhelmed at times by a yearning for who or what we know not? Or, if we do sense its cause, we soon deny its validity because it isn't practical, or because it would take too much time, or because we're not sure it's real. Thus we deny our birthright and settle, like Esau, for a mess of peas.

The Dance of Seth and the Rending of Osiris

To return to our story, once Isis has been given the pillar, has returned to Egypt, and has received the gift of spiritual insemination, she hides the chest containing the dead or comatose Osiris. Yet once again, Seth discovers it and, knowing of Isis's magical powers, hacks his brother's body into fourteen pieces and scatters them over Egypt. The scattering of the parts of Osiris is as rich in meaning as it is evocative of our own sorry state. For as the Sufi teacher and writer Kabir Edmund Helminski reminds us:

> We are forever in parts and yet wish to be whole. We are distracted and yet wish to concentrate; we are scattered and yet wish to be gathered.
>
> We are scattered to the extent that we yield our "I" to every impulse. We say "my" likes or dislikes, "my" feelings and "my" pain, and we diminish that "I" to the proportions of our personal pain. This "I" becomes enfeebled and absorbed in all these things. At one time it is absorbed in a compulsive, unconscious act, at another in a vague anxiety. From one moment to the next it moves through likes and dislikes, through various motives and preoccupations. Its attention quickly shifts from being occupied with what is in front of it to entering a daydream. Some sense of "I" is identified with each of these events.
>
> We are fragmented when we wander from our own center. When our attention is merely reacting to outer events, or when it is being dominated by something, it loses contact with its own source. Attention is a sacred faculty, but when it is drawn to whatever pulls strongest, it has no force of its own; it is passive. If attention is not connected to will, a human is not fully a human being.[4]

Not only does Seth kill the spirit by trapping it in time in the coffin of Osiris, but now he rends the body into bits. These fragments are the scattered pieces of the self, the lives not yet lived, the personalities that, stunted, do not reach their full potential. It is our task, said William Irwin Thompson, to "gather up the bits and pieces of our lives on the astral plane and fuse them into one integral being who sees beyond the limits of the life of one ego."[5]

Isis is joined by her sister in mythic sorrowing, and together she and Nephthys go looking for the pieces. Now Nephthys is the lady of dreams, of hidden places and mystic knowings, and always of the background. She contrasts with her sister Isis, the lady of light and enlightenment, an active foreground presence. In partnership, then, of light and dark, of the background and the foreground of consciousness, they can discern the places in which to find the hidden parts of Osiris, the fragmented self. By helping her sister through her time of gestation of the new child Horus, Nephthys is also healing her loss of Anubis, redeeming perhaps her act of abandonment.

Isis fashions a boat out of papyrus and, with Nephthys, travels throughout Egypt searching out and gradually finding the scattered parts of her husband. This is what happens when we agree to renew our lives and engage in the needed reconstruction of who and what we have been. This is the finding and putting together of all the pieces of the self, those that have been mislaid through distractions, or lost, or forgotten, before we move ahead toward our reweaving and eventual rebirthing of the self.

With each found piece of Osiris, the rite of mummification takes place. These various bodies of Osiris are buried with high funerary rites, echoing the Neolithic ritual in which the king at the end of his life or his power was sacrificed, and his dismembered body was spread across the fields to fertilize them.

In one version of the myth, Isis buries each piece after first encasing it in a magical mummy composed of water, incense, and grain seed. To us this can mean the replanting of each of the fragmented mental, physical, emotional, and spiritual parts of ourselves into the greening ground of mindful attention.

An important Egyptian ceremonial practice included planting mummy effigies of Osiris with grain that would become green with new shoots when watered. What a good idea, and an easy one to apply to our own situation. What would change in us if we planted a garden with each section devoted to some aspect of ourselves that we would like to see sprout again with new life and vitality? In taking care of this garden, we would find that we would attend to those parts of ourselves that need to be regrown and nourished in consciousness. As our garden grew and flourished, so would we.

The Missing Part of Osiris

In other versions of the story, Isis pieces the parts together to make one complete mummy. Only the phallus is not to be found since it has been eaten by a fish. Isis honors the lost generative organ by making one of gold, symbolizing that the essential part of ourselves, which has been consumed, can be alchemically changed into another kind of form.

The phallus, as organ of generation, disappears on a physical level for it has performed its task in the conception of Horus. But it is regenerated in gold on a spiritual level, where it inspires the conception of immortal thoughts. Isis thus gave the Egyptians their first sacred funeral rites, and in Osiris their first mummy.

The all-important child has already been conceived, so the organ has served its purpose and is no longer needed. This is a somewhat curious version of the doctrine of transubstantiation that deals with changing the nature of one state into another. In the more familiar Christian version the bread and wine of the Mass are transubstantiated into the body and blood of Christ. Here, in the ancient Egyptian version, the vital essence of the spirit of Osiris inseminates the mortal womb of Isis.

Isis and Nephthys have done their part well. By establishing the temples to the god, they have ensured the resurrection and rejuvenation of Osiris in the hearts of all Egyptians in rites that would last some three thousand years. By symbolically burying and reviving the god in a newly erected temple in every city in Egypt, they secured the continued knowledge of Osiris for generations to come.

In just this way, repeated ritual maintains our continuing attention to the powers of the divine. The death of Osiris and the suffering of Isis represent the symbol of the great human drama that was later enacted by the historical Jesus—the union of spirit and matter, and the assurance of survival after death.

PROCESS 8:
Spiritual Insemination

Taking the coffin to a desert place, Isis performs a magical rite by which the body of Osiris, whether he is dead or in a coma, is temporarily animated by the passionate yearning of Isis. She literally calls life into him. He responds enough so that she can conceive of him a son, Horus. So, too, do we call into the depths of the self for the power to create, to regenerate, and to transform in an effort to birth the divine gifts within.

In ancient Egypt fire represented the generative, spiritual powers. As in ancient Greece with Hestia, the goddess of the hearth, woman was seen as keeper of the flame, holder and receptacle of the sacred fire. In this process you will perform the insemination by fire by moving and dancing around the flame. It is a ritual act, but because it is being done in sacred time and space, the ritual creates a venue through which the durative realm of generative, spiritual powers can enter the realm of the here and now.

This is the time of conceiving new life within ourselves. We choose what is to be conceived out of the passion for the possible. Just as we die many deaths during our lives, so we conceive again and again the possibilities for new ideas, projects, relationships, ways of knowing, ways of being. In this way, we always have the opportunity to choose what is going to be engendered within ourselves. Hopefully, after completing the processes in this book you will have realized your Horus—

your passionate child of wonder and opportunity—in the journey of your life.

TIME: 90 minutes (for Processes 8 and 9 combined).

MATERIALS NEEDED: Each participant will need a small votive candle and the large paper drawing of Osiris in the casket of time made in Process 5. The guide will need assistants to help direct this ritual enactment. This scenario needs to be performed in a large, uncluttered space. A drum can be used by the guide's assistant to encourage the rhythm of the chants and to heighten the energy. The person chosen to play the particularly awful fish should have created an amusing and original "fish costume" to wear over a bathing suit. This costume will not be seen by the participants until the part where they journey to the fish. The fish is to be kept as a surprise.

MUSIC: Selections from Area 2. It is best in this process that the music be made or sung or chanted by the group with the help of drumming. However, strong, pulsing, rhythmic music, such as Olatunji's *Drums of Passion*, can be very effective. Another piece that we have found stirring, if somewhat comical under the circumstances, is The Doors' rendition of "Light My Fire."

INSTRUCTIONS FOR THE SOLO JOURNEYER: This entire process can be done alone by taping the script, including the drumming and chanting, and by following the instructions. For the part involving the particularly awful fish that swallowed the generative organ of Osiris, you should make out of paper and other materials such a fish. At the appropriate time find a place to put it in water—whether a lake, river, pool, or even bathtub—and follow the instructions. Because you're doing this process by yourself, you won't have sufficient "organs" to make a substantial mummy. Therefore, feel free to stuff your "mummy" with whatever materials (cloth, cotton, wads of paper, etc.) you choose. Make a splendid mummy and decorate it with flowers, rocks, gems, whatever you need to know this mummy for your own.

SPECIAL NOTE: The following rituals in Processes 8 and 9 are part of the same sequence and should be performed as one long process with only a short break between the two.

SCRIPT FOR THE GUIDE: In this enactment you will go on a psychological journey through the myth of the discovery of Osiris and his partial reawakening. It is a ritual journey involving both movement and action, reflection and psychological discoveries, as you find the parts of the myth that relate to you. Let us begin with the divine insemination.

In the first part of this mystery play, Isis finds the body of Osiris. Find your coffin, your casket, the long sheet of paper on which your form has been outlined. Make a circular arrangement with these caskets on the floor in this room, leaving as much space as possible between them. Remembering the Egyptian's exquisite sense of proportion, take time to make the arrangement beautiful, to be sensitive to the geometry of this room.

Take your lighted candle, and place it on the form at the place of the generative organ.

You will now be Isis, flying over that part, taking in from the fire the Essence, the Spirit of that fire. You will dance around it. You will sing to it. And you will be inseminated by the depth level of yourself. You will be made fertile by the depths, by the Osirian flame, by the inner Beloved of the Soul, with whatever kind of spirit child you now need to take into yourself.

Whether you are male or female, at this point in the myth everyone is Isis, as everyone has already been Osiris in the casket. What is the Horus that you need to deliver? What is the nature of this child of your spirit that you need to conceive? Is it a creative principle? Is it a book? Is it a change or growth in your profession or a relationship? Is it a quality of life? Is it a movement in consciousness? What is it that you desire to have cocreated in you by the fiery seed of the depths?

Stand now so that you may see the whole of the Osiris body on the floor before you. Stand so that you can behold this Beloved one . . . Stand and behold the Beloved. Begin now the Ritual of the Divine Insemination. Dance around the flame. (Allow five to ten minutes for this dancing, then continue with Process 9.)

♣

PROCESS 9:
The Dance of Seth and the Rending of Osiris

Isis has conceived the holy child, but her troubles are far from over. Seth, hunting with his tribe one night, finds the body of Osiris and in a fury cuts it into fourteen pieces—the dismembering of the phases of the moon. Seth, the principle of limitation, entraps the self in time. Psychologically this represents our own limitations, which cut us into pieces. Like the moon in its fullness, that which seems whole never stays whole, but is always turned into pieces of itself, which then require a cosmic power, a loving partner or friend, or a source of inspiration to be brought again to fruition or wholeness.

MUSIC: Continued strong drumming, or drumming and music from the previous exercise.

SCRIPT FOR THE GUIDE: Form groups of from three to seven members. Begin to dance in a circle, leaving a space in the middle. Feel the energy of Seth begin to move in you. Seize your paper Osiris "body" and dance with it, shaking and rattling the large piece of paper to evoke the raging glee that Seth felt when he found the body of Osiris.

(The chants given here are only suggestions, although the directions need to be followed in terms of sequence. The guide must get into the spirit of the chanting and feel free to improvise Sethian chants and meter. The reference to the 7, 7, 7, 7 refers to a group in which the circles are composed of seven members. One could as easily refer to the circle of the 3, 3, 3, 3 if that is the number of people in the circles. Participants should be urged to take on the energy of Seth, to speak as Seth, as they rend the paper bodies.)

RIP OFF THE RIGHT FOOT,
and throw it in the circle of the 7, 7, 7, 7.

RIP OFF THE RIGHT HAND,
and throw it in the circle of the 7, 7, 7, 7.

RIP OFF THE RIGHT LEG,
and throw it in the circle of the 7, 7, 7, 7.

RIP OFF THE RIGHT ARM,
and throw it in the circle of the 7, 7, 7, 7.

RIP OFF THE LEFT FOOT,
and throw it in the circle of the 7, 7, 7, 7.

RIP OFF THE LEFT HAND,
and throw it in the circle of the 7, 7, 7, 7.

RIP OFF THE LEFT LEG,
and throw it in the circle of the 7, 7,.7, 7.

RIP OFF THE LEFT ARM,
and throw it in the circle of the 7, 7, 7, 7.

RIP OFF THE LIVER,
and throw it in the circle of the 7, 7, 7, 7.

RIP OFF THE LOWER TRUNK (but not the genitals),
and throw it in the circle of the 7, 7, 7, 7.

RIP OFF THE UPPER TRUNK,
and throw it in the circle of the 7, 7, 7, 7.

RIP OFF THE THROAT,
and throw it in the circle of the 7, 7, 7, 7.

RIP OFF THE HEAD,
and throw it in the circle of the 7, 7, 7, 7.

RIP OFF THE GENITALS,
and *don't* throw it in the circle of the 7, 7, 7, 7,
crumple it up and put it in your pocket.

What shall we do, do, do, do.
The fish will make it stew, stew, stew, stew.
Oh, my friends, don't you dare mock it.
Crumple it up and put it in your pocket.

Now Isis searches for the pieces of Osiris. (The guide chants something like this:)

Rent apart. How now!
Rent apart. Holy cow!
Rent apart everywhere.
Osiris is strewn without a care.
Now listen. Now listen. Now listen. Now listen.
The search begins.
Isis is mourning.

Isis is longing.
Isis is yearning.
Isis is seeking.
Isis is searching.
Isis is finding.

You will now find each individual piece of your body from the pile of body parts made by the members of your circle. As it is called for, bring each piece to the center of the room. There, we will form a huge paper body of Osiris from everyone's paper body fragments.

Go in the circle of the 7, 7, 7, 7.
Find all the right feet.
Find all the right feet.
Find all the right feet.
Find all the right feet.
Go in the circle of the 7, 7, 7, 7.
Find all the right feet.
And place all the right feet right here.
Here we're going to build the Temple of the Right Foot.

Right here.
Right here.
Take the right foot.
Put it right here.
Searching through Egypt . . .
Searching through Egypt . . .
Searching through Egypt . . .
Picking the right foot. Putting it here.
Picking the right foot. Putting it here.

(Guide should allow a few minutes for the process of searching.)

Now look for the left foot.
Look for the left foot.
Go to the circle of the 7, 7, 7, 7.
Where is the left foot?
Where is the left foot?
Go in the circle of the 7, 7, 7, 7.
Find all the left feet.
Searching through Egypt . . .
Searching through Egypt . . .
Picking out the left foot. Putting it here.
Finding the left foot. Putting it here.

(The chanting continues through the rest of the body parts—right hand, left hand, right leg, left leg, right arm, left arm, liver, lower trunk, upper trunk, throat, head—until all except the generative organs have been found and added to the huge paper Osiris that takes shape on the floor. The guide and the assistants have placed each body part approximately where it would come on the body.)

Step back and look at the form that has been created on the floor from all the pieces of the body.

All the pieces have been found.
We'll make a temple on the ground,
From an arm, a leg, a hand, a foot,
Osiris will be put to root.
Osiris has been found.
The world can now go round.
For Osiris has been found.
The world can now go round.
(Repeat . . .)

(This kind of chant can go on for a long time and become quite ecstatic, if time and place and participants are willing. Allow a few more minutes before continuing.)

Leave now the land of the dead. Earlier you were Osiris bounded by Seth. As Isis, you found Osiris and were inseminated by the Beloved. As Seth, you ripped Osiris apart. And again as Isis, you collected the precious pieces of the body of Osiris.

Your next act is a personal one to be done ritualistically. Take the generative symbol and together gather in a procession as we go now to the waters to give this symbol to the fish.

(It is most effective here to be actually able to take the participants to an indoor pool or, preferably, an outdoor body of water. Have one of the participants costumed outrageously to resemble a particularly hideous fish. Aluminum foil and paint work well. Be as wildly inventive in creating this costume as you can. We have found that it is most effective if this part of the process is done at night when the "fish" is seen in the dark with only a small amount of light cast upon it so as to heighten the comic mystery. The fish should make outrageous noises and remarks as it pretends to devour the pieces of paper representing the genitals—it helps to have a waterproof bag or a net hidden in order to do this.

The walk to the body of water is done as solemnly as possible with an accompanying drumbeat. Once there, encourage each participant to throw his or her "genitals" to the fish.

The guide will say words like the following:)

Thus give back your vitality to the world, to the Nile, the great river, the place of fertility. So may you fertilize the world, fertilize the planet, with the essence of your own creative, generative power.

(While the guide is leading the participants to the water, the assistants should stay behind to arrange the newly re-created body of Osiris. The head can be wrapped in a white sheet to give it more definition, as can the whole form if there is time. A large candle should be placed at the site of the phallus and the form decorated and sweetened with flowers, as the mummy in ancient Egypt was made aromatic with sweet-smelling herbs and spices. When the participants next see the figure of Osiris, which occurs during the remaining processes, it should have taken shape and be lovely to behold.)

☥

JOURNAL PROCESS

Imagine that you are an Isis or an Osiris looking down upon the world and about to fill it with beauty. Number the lines of a journal page from one to fifty. Now quickly write down the things that you have created in your life.

On a new page, number the lines from one to fifty. As fast as you can, jot down as many things as you can think of that you're going to create in the future.

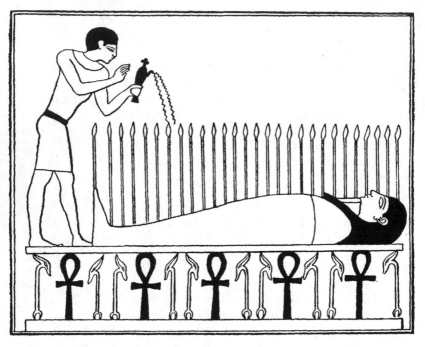

Osiris with wheat growing from his body. From a bas-relief at Philae.

13

Spinning the Genes of New Life

In the dark of the moon, in flying snow in the dead
of winter,
war spreading, families dying, the world in danger,
I walk the rocky hillside, sowing clover.
> from "February 2, 1968"
> by Wendell Berry

Isis has conceived the child, but Osiris is dead. The old order has passed away and the new one has not yet appeared. Seth finds Isis and imprisons her in his spinning mill. This is a fitting circumstance, for it is while spinning that the child is gestated. Isis is spinning the threads of new life. It is while spinning that she has time and place to go within, to reflect as well as to gestate.

Pregnancy of any kind, whether with a child, a work of art, or an idea, requires us to focus inward. On the surface it may not look like much is going on, even to the one who is pregnant, since much transpires at the unconscious level. But new life and new forms are taking shape all the same, being spun out of the silence and darkness of the inner world into the shapes of things to come.

During much of her pregnancy, Isis allows herself to be the captive of Seth. While she spins, what thoughts or inner work does she do as she reflects on the holy child she is carrying? Prenatal studies indicate that the thoughts and reflections of the mother during pregnancy have very definite effects on the life and talents of the child. Too often, pregnancy becomes an unconscious process, with the mother offering little in thought *to* the child. Rather, she tends to think *about* the child.

Communing with the Inner Child

With Isis, however, there is sufficient reason to believe from the poetics of existing texts that she communes with Horus during the pregnancy. Indeed, perhaps the gods commune with each of us during our prenatal period of development before we emerge from the womb of time as fully human. But gestation, like so many things in life, is always recurrent in one way or another. We are always given opportunities to renew our gifts and to glimpse again those that are lost or are waiting to be developed.

A wonderful metaphor for this uncoding occurred in the film and book *2001: A Space Odyssey*. One of author Arthur Clarke's themes concerned ape and human intelligence reaching certain levels of development, then being exposed to a cosmic rectangular pillar, not unlike a *djed* pillar, which, when touched, releases the next stage of evolutionary coding. This visual metaphor owes its power to the truth it expresses—that we get to places in our lives where we've gone about as far as we can. Then, either through triumph or tragedy, crisis or commitment, we touch the *djed* pillar of the next form in our own mind, and the depth-level DNA goes into action. Suddenly, we find ourselves making a leap of growth, a *metanoia*—a leap of mind—or an *enantiodromia*—a big turn around.

The use of the DNA metaphor is perhaps more accurate than it might seem at first. Barbara McClintock's Nobel Prize–winning work in genetics showed how genes are not fixed in the DNA, but are, in fact, dynamic explorers who travel to other genes and mix and match with each other. This means that they do not have the fixed qualities we used to think they had. Indeed, many genetic patterns of brain, body, and, therefore, mind and psyche can cross-generate for new qualities. What is fascinating, too, about McClintock's work is how she played Isis to the Horus of her research. She actually communed with the genes she was studying; she had, as it were, a "feeling for the organism." Having a mother-mind for the genes, she found it natural that the genes "spoke" to her in an ongoing conversation. "If you'd only just let the materials speak to you," she said. "I actually felt as if I were down there and these were my friends."[1]

Shape-Shifting on a Molecular Level

Contrary to present sociobiological faddism, you are not necessarily stuck in cultural or genetic forms. How might you choose to be using all those wandering genes on the one hand, and all that cross-fertilizing culture on the other? The work and disciplines of human transformation receive a deep confirmation from the findings of McClintock and others exploring the nature of genetic transposition. It suggests a scientific basis for the age-old practice of consciously altering and evolving the patterns that limit or liberate us through the training and reeducation of the body, mind, and spirit.

I would like to suppose that modes of self-transcendence are built into the very essence of our wandering genes—as Michael Murphy has suggested in *The Future of the Body*, his brilliant study of the further possible evolution of human nature:

. . . each of us to some extent can realize our own evolutionary transcendence, our own exceeding of genetic endowment. In a manner analogous to the large jumps in development that occurred during earlier stages of evolution, we are sometimes lifted to new levels of excellence. The fact that such transcendence is not wholly predictable from what we know about genes and culture precludes our specifying the limits of anyone's potentials for growth.[2]

I believe that dynamic evolution is actually the conscious orchestration of physical, mental, and spiritual latency, which then changes the nature of body, and mind, even of culture itself. As Elizabeth Janeway, a Pulitzer Prize–winning author and literary critic, reminds us:

Any existing culture can only reach and develop a certain amount of human creativity. The rest is suppressed because the terms of life don't demand its use, or are even hostile. In times of change, however, the old repertory of action will turn out to be insufficient; then the untapped reservoir of creativity belonging to hitherto overlooked groups and classes of society may be called on.[3]

These overlooked groups, I might add, include classes of potentials previously ignored but now desperately needed by individuals and by society as a whole.

The Crystallizing Moment

After a while, this long period of spinning ceases to be appropriate. In fact, in her withdrawn and inward state, Isis may be forgetting who she is and what she has yet to do. Such is always the peril of too much inwardness. It is then that Thoth, the principle of law and wisdom, the one who knows the right time for things to happen, comes to her assistance—unbidden and quite unexpected. He appears not in his own guise, but in the guise of two other women who assist Isis in her escape from lethargy.

In the life of every artist, scientist, educator, and anyone who has ever achieved anything, there comes a moment when outside forces appear to deliver almost oracular statements about that individual's destiny. These transformative, crystallizing moments serve to reshape the individual's concept of the self and of that person's life work. In his brilliant analysis of the alchemical process of creative thinking, *Fire in the Crucible,* John Briggs quotes the artist Louise Nevelson as she recalls how her crystallizing moment came when she was a child. The town librarian asked her a simple question:

There was a big plaster of Paris Joan of Arc in the center of the library, and I looked at it. Sometimes I would be frightened of things I said because they seemed so automatic. The librarian asked me what I was going to be, and of course I said, "I'm going to be an artist." "No," I added, "I want to be a sculptor. I don't want color to help me." I got so frightened, I ran home crying. How did I know that when I never thought of it before in my life?[4]

What allows us to take advantage of these moments is precisely that we have been busy on the interior. All the deep work has been done previously, gleaning bits and pieces of this and that, allowing the mind to play upon the fragments of thought, literally gathering, weaving, and knitting together a new life. Thus, when the crystallizing moment appears, we allow ourselves to take advantage of it and to move forward with determination toward the awaiting destiny.

Tapping the Cosmic Womb

The myth tells us that while Isis is gestating and birthing Horus, Osiris is in the underworld communing with Atum, the darkness, the void, the hidden potentiality. There in the subconscious underworld of the self, a place prior to conception, prior even to inwardness with its teeming images and patterns, there in that hear-nothing, see-nothing, feel-nothing state, one can commune only with what is inner, with the Atum—the atoms of self and cosmos, where even these distinctions as to what is self and what is cosmos disappear.

On several occasions I have rented the Great Pyramid for my students for a night-long vigil in the King's Chamber. One by one during the long dark night of silence and reflection they came up and were helped to enter the great stone sarcophagus of the king. Lying there for several minutes they communed with what is inner, with the Atum, with that which is. For many, the two minutes in the tomb seemed hours, years, forever. For some, it was a dying, a dissolution of all they had been, and with their return, a renewal of all they could be. There were those who felt that they had reclaimed their inner world and could now help in the reclamation of the dying biological and spiritual world of the planet. For me, watching this from a mythic cast of mind, it was the union of the inner experience of both Isis and Osiris, the inner worlds of time and eternity coming together within the ancient womb-tomb of an early pharaoh.

Re-Creating the Old Order

And so Isis, near the fullness of her term, escapes from Seth's prison and goes away to have the child in secret. She knows that if Seth learns of the infant's existence, he will destroy Horus as surely as Herod tried to destroy Mary's infant, Jesus. In those times when the status quo no longer suffices, when the controlling forces of society have been debased, when people have been brought to their knees and yearn for something or someone "other," then the child is born whose destiny will be to combat the misgoverning, tenacious ego. As Thoth prophesied, the child is born and he is the spiritual warrior, Horus, who will sit upon the throne of his father to rule the double empire of Egypt.

Isis hides her infant son among the rushes of a papyrus swamp (another familiar and influential motif), saving him from the wrath of Seth. The papyrus swamps were part of the ancient Egyptian symbol for the beginning of the world. The papyri were the first plants to appear at the dawn of creation; therefore, the site of the birth of Horus is the beginning of a new dispensation.

Although Seth appears to be in control of Egypt, Isis continues to perform her duties as queen in secret. She establishes temples to Osiris and works with the men and women in fields and homes. She comes from and goes to the papyrus swamp where Horus, the child, is being protected and tended by the loving hands of other goddesses. All the while, Seth is seeking the holy child in order to kill him.

One day Isis returns to her son in the papyrus swamp, arriving there in the nick of time to save him from certain death from the stings of scorpions. But he is already dying and swollen with poisons. She cries out in her frenzy and begs Thoth to halt the barge of the sun and make time stop in its course. To save her child, she needs to move from mortal time to immortal time. This means stepping into *kairos*, the loaded moment, in which the categories of time are strained by the tensions of eternity.

Entering Kairos *Time*

Kairos is the potent time when transformation can happen. In early Greek usage, *kairos* also referred to that moment in weaving when the two sets of warp threads are opened and the weft thread, carried by the shuttlecock, can be passed through—the moment when the new fabric (lives, fate, cloth, living and dying) is actually being created.[5]

Kairos is the loaded, sacred space between durative and local time. The urgency and/or opportunity of *kairos* time can allow for local, solar time to be suspended and the re-creative powers of durative time and space to reign. This is where the world stands still, and you have the option to change the story. Then you have the capability of becoming *kairotic*—meaning, having the passion of the loaded time.

Refusing to accept the fallen state of local reality with its debacles and disasters, people stop the world and rise to incredible feats of strength, agility, wild courage, and magical insights. In *kairos* time, mothers rescue children by lifting cars; scientists and artists solve problems and create new works in weeks or months that would normally take years; the fearful become intrepid; and the stone that the builders rejected becomes the cornerstone of whole new enterprises.

Words of power fill one's mouth with blood and one is no longer afraid of the living Logos. Thus in *kairos* you regain your powers, as Isis, to save her child, sought the words of power. These she learned from Thoth and with them was able to heal her desperately sick son.

We have come a long way on our journey. Where once we were stuck in transition and uncertain about the future, we have now brought forth the new order and gained the ability to protect it by speaking its truth.

♀

PROCESS 10:
Isis Spins the Genes of Horus/Hieroglyphic Clustering of Genetic Possibilities

Isis, pregnant with the child Horus, has been kept captive in the spinning mill of Seth. Gestation, like so many things in life, is recurrent in one way or another. We are always given opportunities to renew our gifts and to glimpse again those that are lost or not developed. As we play both Isis and her unborn child, we will refer to these as the latent codings for our own unexpressed possibilities.

What follows is a process that uncodes our psychogenetic storage systems. This opens us up to making use of the untapped reservoir that awaits us. It allows us to discover new ways of being, to begin to live the life we are given. You will be drawing maps of your psychogenetic possibilities and spinning them together into new capabilities. You will begin, like Isis, to reflect upon and spin a finer, more realized person from the threads of possibility, the "genes" you already contain. Your earlier work in Process 2—in which you learned to think and write hieroglyphically, to make the abstract concrete, and to map your creative process— has prepared you for this future spinning of the genes.

You will decide what qualities you desire, then transform them into hieroglyphs with pictorial or symbolic associations. As you draw these pictures and symbols, you will also be symbolically depicting and naming your own potentialities, just as Isis learned the "secret" and potential name of Ra.

This is a deep process of magic-making, and as in the ancient Egyptian tradition of protecting the sacred name of the king with a cartouche, you will draw the cartouche around your own "secret names" by drawing a box around each image.

You will weave these associations and names together, to develop a cluster or network of hieroglyphs that may give you still further associations. The more concrete and specific the hieroglyphic clustering of your needs and intentions, the more readily you will be able to spin them into existence.

Like hieroglyphic thinking, hieroglyphic clustering for genetic spinning can be practiced as a regular form. It will require only a few minutes of your time to become proficient. As with hieroglyphic thinking, you will find that your customary, conditioned modes of existence break up. This will allow you to acquire the new modes needed to sustain this enhancement in everyday life.

TIME: 1 hour.
MATERIALS NEEDED: Drawing materials and paper.
MUSIC: Quiet and reflective music, such as that found in Area 1.

INSTRUCTIONS FOR THE SOLO JOURNEYER: Follow the instructions given here. For the partnering sections of the process, you may try viewing the hieroglyphs through the eyes of Ra, then again through the eyes of Isis, or through the eyes of several particular neters to whom you feel drawn. This will offer you the unique perspective of being able to shift personal time and space, to enter deeply into the durative realm, and to see your own life through the eyes of a larger vision.

SCRIPT FOR THE GUIDE: If you were to enter into a period of being gestated again, spun once more on the loom of possibility so that the codes that comprise you could change or even cross-generate, what would you wish for yourself?

Take your drawing paper and materials and begin to create a hieroglyphic map of your latent possibilities. Use images, hieroglyphs. It does not have to be in words. What capacities, skills, and potentials do you need to be a better functioning human being?

Don't put down the obvious things, like acquiring word-processing skills or developing counseling techniques or statistical knowledge. Ask yourself which of your own latent capacities you need to gestate. It might be your capacity to be a more compassionate person. Perhaps it's understanding ways of reaching people and institutions now closed down to new ideas. Perhaps you need to gestate your capacity for greater spiritual understanding, or you need to develop your sense of the patterns of history to realize your unique place in helping to make the world work. You may need the capacity to think in different modalities—in images as well as in words or in music, or even kinesthetically.

Just know that there are enormous latent powers within you, pure potentials that you have never lost, no matter how little you may have recognized or used them up to now. This is your chance to remember and record these potentials. Spend the next few minutes doing this while some quiet music plays.

Take one of the things you would like to realize in your life and draw it symbolically in the middle of your paper. Do it as a picture, as a hieroglyph. Circle it. Now begin to cluster drawings around the circle that portray the association or network of skills or training you feel that you need to accomplish your goal. These are the hieroglyphic clusters. Think of these pictures or hieroglyphs as helpful genes, the deeper imaginal genes that can help you in your realization. Be as inventive as you can. Do this quickly now, without thinking too much about it. Allow yourself to create a free-flowing association of ideas and pictures.

Begin now. Tap into the depths . . . Tap into the depths . . . your latent possibilities . . .

Remember that you can respond in pictures, for your answer may transcend words.

Tap into the depths . . . your latent possibilities . . . your possible selves . . . (Allow at least ten minutes.)

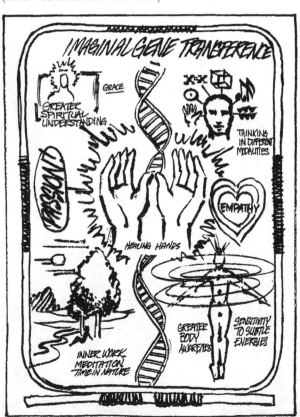

Are you getting a sense of the patterns of possibility that you feel you need? Suppose you asked to access the capacity for healing hands. You would have drawn a symbol for healing hands. Around that symbol you would have drawn a hieroglyphic cluster of associations and other potentials needed to release your healing gifts—greater body awareness, sensitivity to other people's energy fields, and the requisite inner work and empathy so that the healing is not ego related. You have drawn these associations symbolically wherever possible.

These clusters represent multiple transferences of the psychophysical "genes" of the latent potentials you need.

Think of the "gene" transference as hieroglyphs of pure possibility that you can now transfer out of the dormant "file" of your coding into the active one. (Allow five to ten minutes.)

Now find a partner. Sitting together, examine each other's sheet of hieroglyphic clusters. Begin to breathe deeply as you look intently at your partner's picture . . . When you're ready, begin to speak of what you see, remembering to think and read hieroglyphically. Allow several minutes for each partner to speak of what he or she sees. (Allow eight minutes.)

Now that each of you has spoken of the other's hieroglyphic expression of desired training in the depths, take a few more moments to relate what you actually intended with your drawing. Speak about how this has been enhanced or otherwise affected by your partner's interpretation or reflections. (Allow five minutes.)

You have begun something here that is very important. Later today, or now, if you have the time, do this process again, in full color and in even more detail. Do it on a very long sheet of paper. After a while you'll find that your drawing is beginning to look like a DNA spiral, and it is. It's the spiral coding of your own genetic reorchestration. Study it carefully, for in the next exercise you'll have the opportunity to work with these "genes" of possibility at still another level. And this time, you'll have the help of some extraordinary allies you'll find within yourself.

♣

JOURNAL PROCESS

What parts of yourself have you not been using to reach your goals? Why have you disowned these parts? How can you integrate them with your conscious self? If you let the opposites inside you exert their power, what do you think would happen?

COSMOS

URGODS

DIVINE METAEIDOLONS

SPIRITUAL ORDER

sahu
khu
haidit
ka
aufu

DISORDERED PARTICLES

DEMONIC METAEIDOLONS

URDEMONS

CHAOS

14

The Way of the Five Bodies

Is he of our world? No, out of both
realms has his vast nature grown.
He bends the willow's branches with the skill
of one who knows equally well the willow's roots.
  from "The Sonnets to Orpheus"
  by Rainer Maria Rilke

The next part of the myth turns to the activities of Osiris in the underworld. Osiris, who had brought civilization to the earth, now becomes the king of the underworld and, following his earthly activities, brings civilization there. Now, the underworld, which had been the place of wasteland and shadows, becomes instead a fertile, well-cultivated country. Once the dead have been given the prescribed funeral rites and have answered the questions of the forty-two Assessors, they, like Osiris, enjoy perfect happiness in the midst of perfect nature.

The heavenly site of eternal life was a place the ancient Egyptians called the Field of Reeds, a place similar to the Greek Elysian Fields. There the souls of the dead lived in abundance. It was always harvest season in the Field of Reeds. There was no more want or drought. In fact, the ancient image of heaven was exactly the image of Egypt on earth, with its Nile waters, delta plains, animals, and plant life.[1]

It is evident that this myth also has a strong basis in geographical and climatic conditions. According to Plutarch, the Egyptians saw the inundation of the Nile, which began in September, as the essence of Osiris, and the earth as the body of Isis. Thus, in the yearly flooding of the Nile, Osiris seeds Planet Earth, Isis. The most enlightened of the priests, according to Plutarch, specify that Osiris is the principle of all that is humid, the power and cause of all generation, the substance of every seed, the definitive symbol of all death and rebirth. Seth, on the other hand, is the principle of all that burns and consumes. He has red hair, for he represents the desert rocks and the aridity and sterility of the desert.

Plutarch says that the ambush Seth laid for Osiris represents the intensity of dryness, which evaporates the Nile's waters and narrows them to a riverbed. Also, the stifling of Osiris in his coffin represents the low water mark of the Nile. It was the time when the people could allow themselves a colossal collective depression. When the flood comes, it symbolizes Osiris's annual resurrection and the restoration of the people's hopes. In this interpretation we see how the Greek Plutarch attempted to provide a linear, rational explanation of the myth within his own alphabetic culture—a culture from which much of our own derives.[2]

The Birth of Harpokrates

After his resurrection in the underworld, the spirit of Osiris visits Isis and, in consequence, she gives birth to another son—Harpokrates, or little Horus. He is generally depicted with a shorn head, adorned by a single curling lock on the right side, this being the Egyptian symbol of youth. His finger is often shown held to his lips, like a hungry child. Throughout Egypt, even now, one sees children standing barefoot by the side of the road with a delicate finger touching their lips. The modern gesture is one of begging, but even in ancient times the finger to the lips indicated that a child wanted food.

Modern mothers are aware that, when their infants need to suckle, a finger in the mouth will momentarily serve to halt their fretting and crying. The Greeks, however, interpreted the action of Harpokrates more symbolically. From this grew the Greek and Roman custom—and thus our own—of placing a finger to the lips to indicate the need for quiet or secrecy. Statues of little Horus were placed in Greece and Rome before the entrance to temples where the mysteries were to be performed.

The Power of the Dream

Isis's firstborn, having grown up, longs to avenge his father's murder. Osiris appears to Horus in a vision and shows him how to defeat Seth and his allies. The story is reminiscent of the ghost of Hamlet's father, who urges the prince of Denmark to avenge his father's "foul and most unnatural murder."

It is important to note that Osiris contacts Horus in a dream. When the god has been removed from earthly physicality, it is only at the dream level that Horus is able to receive instruction.

Training in dreams is an ancient and honored practice, still prized in the various psychotherapies, as well as in shamanic and spiritual disciplines. We see this in the way we dream of dead friends and relatives, receive messages and orders from dream guides, invoke in prayer the presence of a higher power while we sleep perchance to dream. The way that pregnant mothers present their babies to be blessed in the dream, or adolescents dream of their fathers when they need male energy, the way the psyche reconstructs its contents to give us dramatic tellings of our nature and destiny—all these events tell us that we are sustained on a level in dream that goes far beyond what we imagine on a conscious level. Somehow, we get it more easily in the dream because it comes in directly, avoiding the baffles and obstacle course of our everyday mind.

We find that we are available to be trained by our parent, our patron, our finest life pattern in the depth world, our partner in the archetypal realms when we are ready to take on the great tasks of our lives. Yet we often have to alter our consciousness in some way to enter into this amplified or changed learning and listening mode. This alteration of consciousness is necessary. It tricks us out of our conditioned mind-set, which has very specific ideas concerning the nature of appropriate training.

Our "training" for normal life teaches us linear and analytic ways of knowing. This certifies us to act in the "normal" world with one mind-set and one way of being in the body—a ridiculously narrow point of view, and a very thin reality base. Inevitably, the time comes when the true scope of reality exceeds our limited ideas of normality. That's when we go back to school in our depths, the repository for rich patterns of skills we have forgotten or never realized we had. This, then, is a training that accesses other levels of ourselves—other "bodies"—so that we learn the new ways of being necessary to perform these deeper tasks.

The need to educate ourselves for sacred stewardship of the planet is patterned, mythically, through the education of Horus. He is trained in the depths, through dreams and visions of his father, to take on the rising of Seth and the principles of limitation, stagnation, and recalcitrance. In our time of rising Seth and the threat of worldwide destruction, we have no choice but to listen to the once-and-future genesis that calls to us in dreams, visions, voices in the dark, jokes, seminars, peculiar books, visitors ambling in from the side door, and other announcers of ways of training for evolutionary governance.

Quite simply, we need to be able to use our full equipment and operate on more levels if we are to rise to the challenges and complexities of modern life. The training of the five bodies is one such way of operating on various levels. It offers an equivalent to the kinds of learning that Horus received in the dream time "between the worlds" from his father.

The Five Bodies of the Egyptians

According to an extremely ancient tradition, such as the mystery schools of pharaonic Egypt, the human being encompasses five bodies, each of which has its own characteristics, realms, and unique capacities. These bodies and realms range from the subtle or etheric bodies to actual physicality. Proper training in ancient Egyptian esotericism involved a mastery of all five bodies. In ascending order, from the most physically tangible to the least, they are:

1. *Aufu*—the physical body.
2. *Ka*—the double.
3. *Haidit* (sometimes called the *Khabit*)—the shadow body.
4. *Khu*—the magical body.
5. *Sahu*—the most subtle, etheric spiritual body.

To perceive these five bodies, one must develop a level of consciousness that can simultaneously distinguish each of the five, while still experiencing them as an integrated whole. The easiest way to begin is to become deeply aware of the physical realm first, then move up through the increasingly subtler realms.

My husband, Robert Masters, has offered a metapsychology and methodology for doing this in his work *The Goddess Sekhmet: Psycho-Spiritual Exercises of the Fifth Way.*[3]

Aufu. Masters describes the *aufu* realm as "the gross material or physical body," or "what most people think they mean by 'my body.' This body, however, has a brain, but no mind and is, therefore, not the body of most experience."[4] It perceives images, sound, sight, smell, and touch, and sends these signals to the brain. The mind interprets the meanings of these signals, but the *aufu*'s function is to be mobile, to perceive, to provide a form to contain the other bodies of more subtle perception. In Osirian terms, it is the coffin in which we have been ensnared.

Ka. The second, more subtle body is the *ka*, what some people call the "etheric double." This is the body as experienced by the mind of that body. In other words, the *ka* is our body image. The *ka* is similar to the *aufu* in that it has a form, but its form is what the theosophists have labeled the "astral body." Its sensations and images are more or less symbolic representations of an imagined reality, rather than a physical reality. It is associated with the functioning of the heart. In some ways, the *ka* distorts what it perceives through its lens of desire.

Haidit. The realm of the shadow, or *haidit*, is more subtle than that of the *ka*. The *haidit* operates in an altogether mental—and mostly unconscious—world. One enters the world of the *haidit* during dream, trance, and drug-induced states. As Masters says, "It can be a world of either the personal or the collective or transpersonal unconscious, a world that is the source of many works of art [or] other sorts of creativity."[5]

Khu. Most of us may experience the three previously mentioned physical or subtle bodies when the doors of perception slide open momentarily. However, the ancient Egyptian *khu* and *sahu* are rarely experienced accidentally. Contact with these realms is usually reserved for the trained priest-magician or shaman, who has experienced the purposeful movement of his soul through the subtle layers of manifestation in an effort to gain closer contact with the realm of the neters.

Although the realm of the *khu*, or magical body, is only rarely consciously experienced, the *khu*, nevertheless, shapes that "work of art" or "myth" in which the *haidit* dwells. The force of this realm is then imposed on the realm of the *ka*, which, in turn, lives out the same myth, but almost always unconsciously.

There may be brief, spontaneous experiences of being out-of-body—most often triggered by unusual stress that produces an alteration of consciousness. Also, in some less technologically developed societies, shamans, witch doctors, and similar persons may still attain to some kind of fragmentary knowledge of the *khu*. As a result, they can generate some "paranormal" effects, but these fall far short of what is possible. Says Robert Masters:

> In ancient times when such matters were better understood, the *khu* was not thought of as "magical," but as magical-spiritual—the line between magic and religion being artificial and imposed on human thinking by religions. . . .[6]

Nevertheless, the *khu* remains one of the most important of the five bodies, for through it, one can experience the power to serve either Cosmos or Chaos. Since the temptation to abuse such power is great, the teachings of this realm have been, by and large, shrouded in mystery for the last few thousand years. Nevertheless, the *khu* is a realm to which any of us may ascend. Each of us is to some extent an unconscious magician, affecting our world, and the people in it, by telepathic, psychokinetic, and other means.

Sahu. The highest and most subtle body is the *sahu*, or spiritual body. This is the world of authentic "religious experience" as it has been attained by lamas, adepts, masters, and rigorous practitioners of the world's great "spiritual disciplines." The realm of *sahu* leads one toward complete consciousness—to the knowledge and use of all five of the bodies and their respective dimensions. It is the body of light that returns to its source, the Great Body of Light.

Sahu was a state that all ancient Egyptians longed to attain in the afterlife; but it was always available to the high priest-king or adept of ancient Egypt through rigorous spiritual discipline and practice. Osiris's greatest gift to human beings was the gift of the *sahu*, for having died once, there was no other death.

PROCESS 11:
Training in the Depths

Osiris returns from the underworld and visits Horus, now a young man, in a dream or vision in order to train him on many levels to be able to face his responsibilities and attain his victory. The training of Horus by his father through dream reenacts the depth teachings of shamans by the divine beings in all magical traditions.

The ancient Egyptian training involves more than an intellectual understanding. It requires the tangible integration and bringing to consciousness of all one's selves and all five bodies. Exercising these bodies enables us to develop our capacities to accomplish the Great Work—the task of becoming, with Horus as our model, the spiritual warrior.

We will now begin to learn how to both contact and be gifted with some of the qualities of each of the five bodies.

TIME: 90 minutes.
MATERIALS NEEDED: Mats.
MUSIC: Vital celebratory music from Areas 2 and 3.

INSTRUCTIONS FOR THE SOLO JOURNEYER: Tape the script for the guide, with appropriate music at the indicated places. Be sure to allow yourself enough time to do the processes as completely as possible. Because you will be sitting a long time, you may need some support for your back, so seat yourself next to a wall or in a comfortable chair.

SCRIPT FOR THE GUIDE: Seat yourself so that you can remain comfortable for a period of time with your back straight.

Close your eyes. Be aware of your physical body, what the Egyptians called the *aufu* body, the body that houses all of your physical functions . . . Scan this body, this *aufu*, and bring it as much into awareness as you can . . . Then begin following your breath all the way in and all the way out . . . All the way in and all the way out . . . Relax . . . Relax . . . as we begin to shift levels . . .

Now, you are going to meet your *ka*, your double. In order to get a sense of sitting opposite yourself, actually get up physically in your *aufu* body and sit opposite yourself . . . You may image this second self as your kinesthetic body.

Good. Now, go back to your original place and sit there in your *aufu*, your physical body . . . Get up and sit opposite yourself again. Really have a strong sense of sitting opposite yourself . . . Then go back to your original place.

With your eyes closed, sense sitting opposite yourself. Don't move. Simply sense yourself sitting opposite yourself. We will call this opposite self the *ka*, what the Egyptians referred to as the etheric double of your physical body.

Reach out with your physical *aufu* body and sense the field of life, the field of energy, around the *ka*. Just as you had interesting experiences with your own body outline in the process where your body was outlined on paper, now sense the *ka* body in front of you. Does it tingle? Is there a slight electric feel to it? Or do you sense a subtle structure there, like the feel of butterfly wings? Sense these things . . .

Reach over to it now and embrace it, so that you actually have a sense of that body. Begin to breathe together, your *ka* body and this, your own physical body, what the Egyptians called your *aufu* body. Breathe together. Breathe together, so that you feel as if some part of your breath of your *aufu* body is flowing into the *ka* and is animating the *ka*, or is animating your awareness of the *ka* body . . .

Breathe even more deeply, so that the two of you are breathing together . . . Now feel yourself actually being in the *ka* body, which is embracing your *aufu* body, your physical body, and breathing with you . . .

Now let the *ka* body get up and sit directly in front of you with its back toward you . . . With it sitting in front of you, we will work now in the *ka* body.

Sense the *ka* body in front of you. Sense especially the right knee and ankle of the *ka* body in front of you. Let the *ka* body's right ankle just sort of fall over to the side and back, so that the knee goes over to the side and back. The right ankle and knee of the *ka* body to the side and back. To the side and back. To the side and back. To the side and back. Increase the movement in the *ka* body. To the side and back. To the side and back. The *ka* body, side and back. You are working only in the *ka* body, the imaginal body. You are making no actual physical movements.

Rap with the right heel of the *ka* body. Rap, rap, rap, rap, rap, rap, rap, rap, rap. The *ka* body is sitting in front of you. Rap, rap, rap, rap, rap.

With the ball of the right foot of the *ka* body, rap, rap, rap. Rap, rap, rap, rap, rap, rap, rap, rap, rap, rap, rap, rap.

Make circles with the right foot of the *ka* body. Make circles, around and around and around in one direction. And around and around and around in the other direction. Go round in one direction. Then go round in the other direction . . .

Raise and lower the right knee toward the chest of the *ka* body. Raise it up to the chest. Really sense your chest as the knee approaches. Now lower the knee. Raise it up, approach, and lower. Raise it up, approach, and lower . . .

Raise and lower the right shoulder of the *ka* body sitting in front of your *aufu* body. Raise it and lower it. Raise it and lower it. Raise it and lower it. Circle in one direction with the shoulder of the *ka* body, then circle in the other direction.

Scrunch up and release the right part of the face of the *ka* body. Scrunch it up, and release. Scrunch it up, and release. Scrunch it up, and release.

Make circles in the air from the elbow on down, with the whole right lower arm and hand of the *ka* body. Make circles in the air with the lower arm and hand of your *ka* body. Circle, circle, circle in one direction. Circle, circle, circle in the other direction . . . And release.

Now, just sort of shake and dance while sitting on the floor, with the whole right side of the *ka* body. Shake it and dance it. Shake it and dance it. Shake it and dance it. Shake it and dance it. Shake it and dance it. Shake it and dance it. And even increase the shaking. Shake it and dance it. Shake it and dance it. Shake it and dance it. Shake it and dance it. Shake it and dance it. Shake it and dance it. Shake it and dance it. Shake it and dance it. Shake it and dance it. Keep shaking and dancing while sitting on the floor with that whole right side of the *ka* body. Shake it and dance it. Shake it and dance it. Shake it and dance it. Shake it and dance it. Shake it and dance it. Stop.

With your *aufu* body, your actual physical body, stand up. Walk around a little bit. What do you notice? Walk around. What else do you notice? Walk again. What else do you notice? Now, sit down again. Just notice how working only on the *ka* body has affected the definition, the flow, the vibrancy, the energy feeling on the right side of the body. Are you feeling as though you'd been born on the side of a hill? Don't worry. We're going to restore the other side now.

Close your eyes. Follow your breathing all the way in and all the way out . . . Reach out and embrace the *ka* body in front of you. It is sitting with its back to you. Reach out and embrace the *ka* body in front of you.

Come back and work now on the left side of the *ka* body. Let your left ankle fall over to the side, and the left knee. Let the left knee fall in the *ka* body over to the side and back. Over to the side and back. Over to the side and back. Over to the side and back. Over to the side and back. Over to the side and back. Very good. Over to the side and back.

Begin to flex and extend the left foot of the *ka* body. Flex it and extend the left foot. Flex it and extend it in the *ka* body. Flex and extend. Flex and extend. Flex and extend. Flex and extend. Flex and extend.

Now, rap with the ball of the left foot of the *ka* body. Rap, rap, rap, rap, rap, rap, rap, rap, rap, rap, rap, rap, rap, rap. Rap with the heel. Rap, rap, rap, rap, rap, rap, rap, rap, rap, rap, rap, rap, rap, rap.

Bring the knee up toward your chest, the left knee up to the chest of the *ka* body. Up to the chest and down. Up to the chest and down. Up to the chest and down. Circle with that knee in the air. Circle in one direction. Stay very focused. In one direction. Circle in the other direction. Circle and circle. And bring the knee down.

Begin to circle with the left shoulder. Circle, circle, circle, circle in one direction. Circle, circle, circle. Now circle in the other direction. Circle, circle, circle, circle in one direction. And circle, circle, circle in the other.

With the lower part of your left arm and hand, circle and circle and circle and circle. Now circle in the opposite direction, staying very focused on the *ka* body, on the left side of the *ka* body.

Scrunch up the left part of the face of the *ka* body. Scrunch it up, and release. Scrunch it up, and release. Scrunch it up, and release. Scrunch it up, and release.

Let both right and left sides of the body shake and dance in the *ka* body. Shake it and dance it in the *ka* body. Shake it and dance it in the *ka* body. Shake it and dance it. Shake it and dance it. Now let the *ka* body—just the *ka* body—stand up and begin to dance in this room.

The *ka* body, of course, has a great deal of flexibility to become different things. The *ka* body begins to become a dancing dolphin, diving in the sea. Find yourself in the body of a dancing dolphin . . . The dancing dolphin begins to change form, and the *ka* body now becomes a dancing elephant. You are a dancing elephant in your *ka* body . . . The dancing elephant begins to change form, and you now become a little puppy, prancing and dancing . . . You change again, and you become a prancing, dancing high priest or priestess of ancient Egypt, having a merry time with the myth of Isis and Osiris in the *ka* body . . .

You release that image, and the *ka* body becomes your own Higher Self, your entelechy, your center of dynamic purpose, your deepest coding with all its possibilities and transferences. In this body you are whirling and whirling and whirling and whirling and whirling and whirling and whirling. And the body is whirling down and around and around and down. It is as if in whirling it is penetrating through the earth. Whirling down and around and around and down, and deeper and deeper and deeper and deeper. And whirling down and around and around and down.

The *ka* body finds itself passing through levels and layers, not just through the earth, but through levels and layers and images of your life. And through colors in the *ka* body: magenta, blue and pink, purple, silver and gold, white, black, gray. Children you went to school with. Past people that you knew. Places that you've been. Knowledge that you've learned. Teachers that you've had. Houses that you've lived in. Rooms that you have known. Books that you have read. Experiences that you have had, funny, sad, tragic, triumphant, trivial, profound. All manner and kind of experiences. Pass through them . . .

The *ka* body, now as your Higher Self, goes down and down and down and down. Now you seem to be passing through various Western civilizations: Renaissance Italy, perhaps, medieval France, Celtic Ireland. Down through time, through the civilization of ancient Rome, and now of ancient Greece, and the complex and beautiful civilization of ancient Crete. And now you are passing through ancient Egyptian civilization, now through the Mesopotamian and Sumerian cultures. You find yourself in ancient India and Tibet. And now you are passing the strange and interesting peaked roofs of Far Eastern civilizations, past civilizations of China and Japan and Korea. Down . . . down . . . down . . . past great ruined temples, down past symbols of many societies. Down, down, down.

You see below you a crystal mountain. You descend to the crystal mountain, and as you stand there, you see reflected just below you, inside the mountain, another body. That other body seems to be like you, but it seems to have an even clearer substance. And you know that this is the body of what the ancient Egyptians referred to as the *haidit*, or the Shadow. This shadow figure holds the memories that you have forgotten. It holds the memories of all your ancestors, your culture and community, your DNA. The *haidit* holds the generational stories and myths in its deep, deep knowing of the inner patterns of reality.

Seeing the *haidit* body reflected there within the crystal mountain, you lie down with it face-to-face. As you lie there, you begin to become conscious of the *haidit* by moving your right hand in the *ka* body and feeling a connection with the right hand of the *haidit* body underneath. Feel your own consciousness expanding to include the knowledge of the right hand of the *haidit* body.

As you move the right arm of the *ka* body, lying there on the crystal that contains the *haidit*, you feel an awareness and a communion with the arm of the *haidit* body. You move the right shoulder of the *ka* body, and you feel a knowledge of it in the *haidit*. You move the right leg of the *ka* body, and you feel a communion as you begin to feel the movement in the right leg of the *haidit* body. The right foot of the *ka* body is moving on the crystal and communicating back and forth across the crystal with the foot of the *haidit* body.

Now do the same thing on the left side. Guide yourself. Move the *ka* body as it is lying down there on the crystal. Feel the reflection of the *haidit* body moving and experience the two of you tuning, tuning, tuning, tuning to each other.

Now feel the internal organs, the heart of the *haidit* moving into the heart of the *ka*, the lungs of the *haidit* moving into and joining with the *ka*. The intestines, the liver, the generative organs, the spleen, the stomach of the *haidit*, all move into the heart of the *ka*. The mind field is moving.

Suddenly, you discover that you are now integrated, that you contain both the *ka* and the *haidit* bodies. In the *haidit* body you can begin to feel that you have access to so many images and archetypes, and to a formidable capacity to tap into the collective unconscious . . . With this body of wisdom you can attain to deep knowledge of the creative patterns behind things to the degree that you allow your consciousness to shed light upon it.

You are in the *haidit* body now, along with the *ka* body. But the *haidit* body is now the dominant one. And you begin to journey. You rise and notice a path leading deep into the crystal mountain.

You begin to proceed joyously, in your *haidit/ka* body, filled with the mind of the *haidit*, the images and archetypes, the myths, symbols, metaphors, and knowings of many places and many times. As you move down the path, you feel yourself able to access the many varied realms of creativity—the realm of music, perhaps, where all music abides; the realm of art filled with the masterpieces of artistic creation; the realm of science—science past and science yet to come; the realm of literature and poetry; and now the myriad realms wherein the soul of humanity touches the sky and god-stuff is brought into time. This you have in your journey with the *haidit*.

You continue to travel in this *haidit* body through the mountain as the music begins to play. (Play music from Areas 2 or 3 here.) Proceed joyously, not moving the physical body, but proceeding, in a grand procession, down into the great crystal mountain, which is the place of the meeting with your great teacher, parent, patron, Osiris of the depths. Proceeding now, the *ka* and the *haidit* bodies move together. The *aufu* physical body is so very quiet, but it serves as ground control for it all.

Go into the depths together.

(Play vital celebratory music here.)

You find yourself in a place where you find the neters, the great archetypes and principles of creation all around you. They're saying, "Welcome! Welcome Home! Come, meet your Osiris of the depths, your parent and your teacher in the archetypal world."

You continue to travel joyfully in the school of becoming.

As you move closer, you see in the distance a great *djed* pillar, a pillar through which higher knowledge and initiation into who and what you really are may come. You move toward that pillar, filled with a sense of wonder for what is waiting for you there.

Reaching the *djed* now, you embrace the pillar, and as you do, sensing its charge and energetic presence, you begin to feel the pillar take form. For the pillar is both the *khu* and the *sahu*. It contains both the *khu*, or magical body, and the *sahu*, or spiritual body, of the great teacher of the depths.

Feel yourself now in the *haidit/ka* body, embracing and receiving knowledge from the wise one of the depths contained within the *djed* pillar. For within the *djed* pillar, which you are embracing, is contained the magical knowing and spiritual knowing of the *khu* and the *sahu*. You are being filled with the knowledge and the training. You perhaps begin to feel a surge of life and thought and possibility. This is happening now, either consciously or unconsciously. You are being filled with this knowledge and possibility as the training continues.

In the next two minutes of clock time, equal in the depth realm to all the time you need, you will continue to receive this knowledge and training that is being imparted to you. You may sense it in images, you may sense it in words, or even as an energy charge. You sense it happening now. (Allow two minutes.)

You and your great teacher, your own particular Osiris, begin to have a sense of the unique mapping of the codes of your possibilities. The DNA of all that you contain is pure potential. You can actually feel it. It is tangible. You feel little balls of energy, of awakening possibilities. These codings are now writ large in this place of amplified space and time, so that what had been there as the tiniest minutia in the cellular structure, you now feel as substantial energy balls of possibility . . .

Aware of all your bodies—the *aufu* body, the *ka* body, the *haidit* body—and with your teacher in his or her *khu* or magical body, and in the *sahu* or spiritual body, begin in this place of amplified experience to weave and cross-generate the genes of awakening possibilities that you need. Perhaps you see them as energy balls or as hieroglyphs. Remember what you learned about this in our previous process of genetic reorchestration. Begin the reweaving now. You have three minutes of clock time, equal subjectively to all the time you need, to do this reweaving in the depths. (Allow three minutes.)

Now go back to the *djed* pillar in the fullness of your five bodies. You go together in your *aufu*, your physical body; your *ka*, your etheric double; your *haidit*, the deep unconscious. Reaching out to your teacher who contains the *khu* and *sahu* bodies, stand there and embrace the pillar. Feel a column of white light rising up through the pillar and through you. Allow it to rise without fear or worry, for this is the source of deep knowledge that has no name.

Feel yourself merging with the pillar, which is your magical and spiritual body. In your more subtle bodies you can merge with these magical and spiritual bodies. Feel yourself pass into them. Feel the light begin to rise through you—the light of knowledge and of becoming and of evolution and of transformation. The DNA coding of God. This is the deeper coding beyond even your chosen, or rechosen, coding that rises like kundalini, rises as energy or as light. It is the light to overthrow the darkness of the troubled times in which we live. It is the light that Osiris, the parent of the depths, gave to Horus that he might overthrow the darkness of Seth. Feel the white light rising through the pillar of the *djed*, the body of Osiris, the body of the depth realm.

Feel yourself flow with it. The flexibility of the *haidit* and *ka* bodies allow you to be one with this light. Its energy and knowledge are rising through you, refining you, tempering you, strengthening your purpose and will, giving you greater access to your own coding, your own possibilities. This energy, this light will continue to be available to you in a manner that is safe and appropriate for you. Safe and appropriate . . .

Now bid good-bye to the *khu/sahu*, to the *djed* pillar of deep learning, to the Osiris body of your teacher of the depths. Know that you can always return to it, especially as you make your physical body more receptive by working with the subtle bodies to receive and integrate these subtle interchanges of knowledge.

Embodied now in your *ka* and your *haidit*, begin to look upward, up the path of the crystal mountain.

Begin to move upward, up into this world. Moving upward and upward, toward the world of space and time, celebrate what you have done and what you have begun in the depths. A procession of celebration up the crystal mountain. Up and up, until you reach this world and this body, the body of the *aufu*. But this is an *aufu* physical body that has now been enhanced and to some extent integrated with the other bodies.

When you reach this world and this body, begin to stretch, to feel something of the integration of your five bodies in the stretching . . . Enjoy that special charge of vitality. Feel what has happened in the reweaving and the reforming of the self.

Now, stand up and dance! Feel the dancing of all the bodies. Feel the teaching moving in you! Feel the fullness of the light that can defeat the darkness.

(Play celebratory music here, preferably the same music used earlier in the process.)

In the ancient Egyptian mystery play, at this point Horus says:

> *I am Horus.*
> *Great God, Lord of the Sky.*
> *Lord of the Upper Egyptian Crown.*
> *Prince of the Lower Egyptian Crown.*
> *King of the Kings of Upper Egypt.*
> *King of the Kings of Lower Egypt.*
> *Beneficent Prince, Prince of Princes.*
> *I receive the Crook.*

> *I receive the Flail.*
> *I cross my hands.*
> *For I am the Lord of this Land.*
> *I take possession of the Two Lands.*
> *I assume the Royal Diadem.*
> *And I am ready to overthrow the Foe!*

(Repeat this several times, and have the participants echo it.)

☥

JOURNAL PROCESS

Aufu. Using the stream-of-consciousness technique, write about your relationship to your body. What changes do you want to make? How do you use your body to prevent you from attaining your goals? How has your body helped you to attain your goals?

Ka. Write down the kinds of things you fantasize about or imagine doing and being. What kinds of imaginings feed your body, mind, and soul?

Haidit. Color an entire page of your journal black. Then, in white ink, write about the possibilities that lie in shadow within you. Write about the things within you that seem to exist between the borders of unconscious and conscious thought. If you can't quite grasp what they are, then just let yourself draw images of the feelings you have about them, or turn them into hieroglyphs. It may help to do this with your left or nondominant hand (right hand for lefties). This is often the hand that is less conditioned to avoid blocks from the unconscious. It may give you some revealing news from the shadowed part of your inner self, the other side of the moon of yourself.

Khu. Define your concept of magic. Then, using the stream-of-consciousness technique, beginning with the words "I remember," recall the times in your life when you felt magic or witnessed miraculous happenings. Now go to the next page of your journal. Again, beginning with the words "I remember," recall the magical properties of the earth. As if you witnessed them happening, describe the creation of the cosmos, the birth of our planet and what the newborn earth looked like; describe your own birth and/or being in the womb.

Sahu. Color an entire page of your journal sky blue—either the day or night sky. Then, in gold or silver ink, with your nondominant hand, write what it is that is shining in you. Let your Higher Self tell you what your good qualities are. Copy these positive statements onto colorful pieces of paper, paste them on tinfoil stars, then paste the stars on the ceiling above your bed for a week. Fall asleep meditating on your Higher Self.

In another entry write about a time when you stopped thinking so hard and simply allowed the higher spiritual reality world to contact you. What sacred message was given? Allow another such message to come to you now. Add it to the stars on your ceiling.

Horus and his four sons, each armed with a knife, standing before Osiris and Serapis.
The animal-headed man, with knives stuck in his body and bound by his arms to a
forked stick, represents Seth, conquered.

15

The War in Heaven

He has illumined the path with rays of splendor. He has destroyed all evil defects of the body. He has made the two Horus brothers to be at peace within. He has destroyed the storm wind and the hurricane. He has made the Two Combatants to be gracious, and the Two Lands to be at peace. He has put away the wrath that was in their hearts and each has become reconciled to his brother.

from the Book of Breathings
translated by Normandi Ellis

Osiris, having trained Horus in dream, returns to the underworld. Unlike other myths in which the underworld is reached through the descent of the hero or heroine, Osiris rises from the depths through the vehicle of vision and dream.

The solar Horus is a much more individuated being than the lunar Osiris. A dynamic man of action, he wants to fight the principle of limitation, his uncle Seth. The warrior-hero is the only one who has enough gall, enough galloping chutzpah, to challenge the principle of entrapment and limitation.

This is much like what happens to us when we become so trapped, so bound by the demands of our lives, that there seems no way out. It takes this active, activating muscular will of the Horus within us to stand up to our own self-limitation, to that form of recalcitrance and fear of action that sometimes seems both pathetic and pathological. A dubious recalcitrance can sometimes be found in those who serve the status quo and brook no innovation—whether they are boss, supervisor, principal, parent, spouse, preacher, or president. Often they have a formidable relationship with the reptilian brain.

When this situation occurs, we need to apply the visionary training we received in the depths. We need to become a spiritual warrior in the world of space and time. The lunar, passive, reflective, wise Osiris within can get us only so far. If we want to advance the world, then the individuated, willful Horus must emerge.

The Battle between Horus and Seth

A terrible eighty-year-long battle ensues, with Horus and Seth inflict-
ing horrible wounds on each other. They shape-shift and fight each
other continually as men, as hippos, as lions, as bears, as snakes, and as
mythic creatures never before seen. The battle is interrupted at times for
councils of the gods, but the gods themselves are in chaos and disagree.
So the war goes on. There is war in heaven as well over the battle, with
the gods taking sides and the earth suffering the consequences.

This is what ensues whenever the guiding principles of a culture become ambivalent and ambiguous. Our twentieth century stands as a major testament to what occurs when the guiding principles of hundreds,
even thousands of years become outmoded and dubious to both individuals and societies. Things fall apart. Widespread war and violence become the way out, replacing the lost principles with the illusion that
something forceful is being done to make the world work again. Ma'at,
the essential principle of truth, goes underground and becomes unconscious. She lives with Osiris now, leaving the gods to their chaos.

Finally, Seth and Horus take the forms of hippopotamuses and sub-
merge themselves in the Nile waters. In their shape-shifting they have
taken on the traits of one another and have become nearly indistinguish-
able, even to Isis. Standing on the riverbank, she tries to spear Seth but
strikes Horus instead. She releases him and spears Seth, but when Seth
cries out, she is overcome with compassion and releases him, infuriating
Horus.

The Uncrowning and the Recrowning of Isis

With the help of his mother, Horus finally achieves victory and presents Seth to Isis for custody. Being the sister of Seth, and deeply
understanding the need for polarity, Isis cannot bind him. She lets him
go again. Enraged, Horus pulls the royal crown from his mother's head—
or in some versions, he actually tears off her head.

So much anger constellates here—the son against the mother; the patriarchy against the matriarchy; the child against the parent. Only Isis is
wise enough to embrace both points of view, for she understands that
existence requires each, rather than just one or the other heroic stance.
But this honoring of the polarities through the freeing of Seth makes no
difference to the adolescent Horus.

Thoth, however, shares the wisdom of Isis. In an effort to stabilize the
division of power between the positive and negative energies, he, too,
stops the battle when either Seth or Horus is about to win. Seth plucks

out the eyes of Horus, while Horus tears off the testicles of Seth. In Plutarch's version, Horus loses one eye (perhaps the origin of the emblem of the eye of Horus), which is restored by Thoth, the god of wisdom and magic. However, in the Egyptian version, the goddess Hathor, the feminine principle, heals Horus, the completely blinded warrior. Thereupon, Thoth presents Isis with a new crown in the shape of a cow's head.

Some commentators suggest that the uncrowning of Isis indicates the end of matriarchal rule and the beginning of the patriarchy. This is an elegant and convenient explanation. But it overlooks the rest of the incident, which tells us that Thoth, the god of wisdom, immediately places the new cow-headed crown on her. This is the most ancient crown of all, the one associated with the Great Goddess, who survives all gods, all cultural changes, all combats. Isis is integrated now with animal, human, and divine natures—the above and the below and the great in between. Virgin, mother, and crone, she now owns all time and all things.

The patriarchal theory also ignores the fact that it is Isis, not Horus, or even, for that matter, Osiris, who continued to be honored and worshiped thousands of years later in Greece and Rome, and then had many of her qualities integrated into the Christian mystery in the guise of the Virgin Mary.

The Continued Honoring of Isis

Thoth's recrowning of Isis speaks of the supreme importance and continuity of the Great Goddess throughout time and space. This is expressed most powerfully in *The Golden Ass* (*Metamorphoses*) of the second century A.D. by the Latin novelist Apuleius. In this story, the protagonist, Lucius, has been tampering with magic, which has caused him to be turned into an ass. Eventually, after many strange adventures, he is changed back into human form through the compassion of the goddess Isis. After he purifies himself in the sea seven times and prays with fervor to the Queen of Heaven, the goddess reveals herself as the original Great Goddess, the source of many different goddess names and traditions, then tells Lucius her true name:

> But scarcely had I closed my eyes before a god-like face emerged from the midst of the sea with lineaments that gods themselves would revere. Then gradually I saw the whole body, resplendent image that it was, rise out of the scattered deep and stand beside me.
>
> I shall now be so brave as to attempt a description of this marvelous form, if the poverty of human language will not altogether distort what I have to say, or if the divinity herself will deign to lend me a rich enough stock of eloquent phrase. First, then, she had an abundance of hair that fell gently in dispersed ringlets upon the divine neck. A crown of interlaced

wreaths and varying flowers rested upon her head; and in its midst, just over the brow, there hung a plain circlet resembling a mirror or rather a miniature moon—for it emitted a soft clear light. This ornament was supported on either side by vipers that rose from the furrows of the Earth; and above it blades of grain were disposed. Her garment, dyed many colors, was woven of fine flax. One part was gleaming white; another was yellow as the crocus; another was flamboyant with the red of roses. But what obsessed my gazing eyes by far the most was her pitch-black cloak that shone with a dark glow. It was wrapped round her, passing from under the right arm over the left shoulder and fastened with a knot like the boss of a shield. Part of it fell down in pleated folds and swayed gracefully with a knotted fringe along the hem. Upon the embroidered edges and over the whole surface sprinkled stars were burning; and in the center a mid-month moon breathed forth her floating beams. Lastly, a garland wholly composed of every kind of fruit and flower clung of its own accord to the fluttering border of that splendid robe.

Many strange things were among her accoutrements. In her right hand she held a brazen sistrum—a flat piece of metal curved like a girdle, through which there passed some little rods—and when with her arm she vibrated these triple chords they produced a shrill sharp cry. In her left hand she bore an oblong golden vessel shaped like a boat, on the handle of which, set at the most conspicuous angle, there coiled an asp raising its head and puffing out its throat. The shoes that covered her ambrosial feet were plaited from the palm, emblem of victory.

Such was the goddess as, breathing forth the spices of pleasant Arabia, she condescended with her divine voice to address me:

"Behold, Lucius," she said, "moved by your prayer I come to you—I, the natural mother of all life, the mistress of the elements, the first child of time, the supreme divinity, the queen of those in hell, the first among those in Heaven, the uniform manifestation of all gods and goddesses—I, who govern by my nod the crests of light in the sky, the purifying wafts of the ocean, and the lamentable silences of hell—I, whose single godhead is venerated all over the Earth under manifold forms, varying rites, and changing names. Thus, the Phrygians that are the oldest human stock call me Pessinuntia, Mother of the Gods. The aboriginal races of Attica call me Cecropian Minerva. The Cyprians in their island-home call me Paphian Venus. The archer Cretans call me Diana Dictynna. The three-tongued Sicilians call me Stygian Proserpine. The Eleusinians call me the ancient goddess Ceres. Some call me Juno. Some call me Bellona. Some call me Hecate. Some call me Rhamnusia. But those who are enlightened by the earliest rays of that divinity the sun, the Ethiopians, the Arii, and the Egyptians who excel in antique lore, all worship me with their ancestral ceremonies and call me by my true name, Queen Isis.

"Behold, I am come to you in your calamity. I am come with solace and aid. Away then with tears. Cease to moan. Send sorrow packing. Soon through my providence shall the sun of your salvation rise. Hearken therefore with care unto what I bid. Eternal religion has dedicated to me the day which will be born from the womb of this present darkness."[1]

Chaos in the Court of Heaven

Meanwhile, a truce is called. Seth invites Horus to a party as he had done for his brother, Osiris. When they are besotted, Seth cajoles Horus to lie down with him, the way he first seduced Osiris to lie down in the casket. Horus escapes seduction by Seth but takes his petition again to the gods. As in myth, so in actuality. One continues to meet one's obstacles and limits again and again, always the same issues coming up to be worked on at increasingly richer and more complex levels. It would seem that we are given our failings as a perpetual stimulus to self-transcendence.

As in many myths of the ancient Greeks, Sumerians, and others, this explicit scene raises many questions about the ancient Egyptian view of sexuality. Unfortunately, this is a question that cannot be fully answered since most of what we know about ancient Egypt deals with their views of life after death. We know less about their day-to-day social mores.

It seems best to interpret the scene as an ancient treatise on the seduction of war and the male pejorative. The terror of Horus resides in the fact that he has been almost seduced by the masculine principle of Seth, which knows no feminine side, Seth having been estranged from Nephthys, his anima, for a long time.

The gods agree to meet in council in the "island in the mist," a time-out-of-time sort of place. To this Seth agrees, but he insists that Isis cannot be present. Indeed, as we have come to see, she must be there, and well she knows it. So she disguises herself as an old woman bringing food to her shepherd son. After royally bribing the ferryman, she is rowed out to the island.

In ancient tales of both the East and the West, there is this recurrent theme of bargaining with the ferryman. To get to the other side of one's nature or opportunity, one tricks one's stolid self with bribes and disguises. The ferryman goes back and forth between the worlds, and cunning must be she who would get to the other shore.

The Revelation of Seth

Upon arriving at the distant shore in the time out of time, Isis disguises herself as a beautiful young woman who lures the smitten Seth with her own kind of seduction. Where Seth attempted to seduce Horus and persuaded Osiris to enter the casket, Isis leads Seth on by making up a story of injustice that parallels their own family story. She gets him to agree that it is a terrible thing for an uncle to steal the land of his nephew. Bitten by his own shadow, Seth has been seduced by the very anima principle he has denied. The gods say that he has spoken his own verdict.

Seth is ordered by the gods to make his body into a barge to carry the coffin of Osiris in the funerary rites. An exquisite irony exists in this. The first vessel Seth fashioned was the coffin that bore Osiris to his death. Now from that very wood—metaphoric of the pharaoh's wooden sarcophagus—he takes his power of limitation and crafts the boat that carries the high spirit of Osiris into the depth world. Thus Seth is re-mythologized from the principle that traps us in time to the vehicle that carries us into eternity. He becomes the vehicle that can transport us to our deeper, spiritual place.

Resurrection and Redemption

In this new peace in heaven, Horus becomes the orchestrator of the physical world; Osiris becomes the evocateur of the spiritual world; and Seth becomes the principle of appropriate limitations, which can help us deepen our understanding of reality. The Fall has been reversed. In the symbolically similar Christian story, the single God enters into time and space in a human body, which becomes the vehicle for the resurrection. In the tale of Isis and Osiris, however, it is a divine quarternity—the symbol of completion—that is required to make this possible: Isis and Osiris, Seth and Horus. Together they express the very requirements of the transformational journey of the human being, that is, fertility, inspiration, limitation, and growth.

The fact that Seth moves from creator of the coffin to bearer of the coffin is the same movement, the *enantiodromia*, the big turnaround, by which the Fall becomes the resurrection, and the nature of Osiris moves from earthly civilizer to civilizer of the depth realm. In our own lives that which has apparently been killed in us may not live itself out in existential space and time. Rather, it may have been transmuted into a deepened interior quality. It is the *djed* being within.

This was the basis of the great mystery cult of Egypt, the transformational journey of the Egyptian soul, celebrated by initiates as a tremendous and intensive psychophysical and psychospiritual voyage of the self to the Self. This same transformative journey was also experienced with a different power by the ordinary person at the magnificent and fascinating annual reenactment of the ritual drama at Abydos. There one was able to play all the parts, take sides, battle with Seth or Osiris, and have a marvelous funeral and resurrection before the fact of one's own death.

In a hellenized mode, the mysteries of Isis and Osiris were celebrated throughout the Greco-Roman Empire. Some elements even found their way into the Christian mystery: the drama of the pregnancy of the mother made pregnant by the father in the spiritual world; the birth of the holy child and the forces that seek to destroy him; the contention with the forces of darkness and limitation; the destruction by these forces; the importance of the tree to the dead or dying god; and the full drama of death and resurrection, with the Christ figure continuing to guide and lead from the spiritual world. The New Testament offers many other textual parallels as well. For example, when Mary Magdalene, like Isis before her, finds the empty tomb and says, "They have taken away my Lord, and I know not where they have laid him."

So does a great story of the journey of the eternal soul in time continue to guide the soul's journey in ongoing historical time.

PROCESS 12:
The Battle of Seth and Horus

The battle between Horus and Seth rages for a long, long time, with both parties suffering awful wounds. Horus has his eye (or eyes) plucked out, and Seth has his testicles ripped away. But both are cured by Thoth. Back and forth they go between winning and losing, shifting shapes, becoming warring birds, hippopotamuses, even men.

When Horus finally wins, he hands the bound Seth over to his mother Isis, who immediately releases him. This can be taken to mean that Isis is expressing the higher feminine wisdom that Seth and Osiris are not opposites, but polarities that are necessary and essential to each other. To bind one or the other would be to freeze the universe and block all creative striving.

Horus, as a highly individuated consciousness incarnate in a body, could not have come into being unless Seth had opposed Osiris and killed him, bringing Isis to such a place of mourning and yearning that she could receive the insemination of a creative principle. If she had had a child of the ordinary body of Osiris, she would have had an ordinary child. She would not have had Horus, whose genes are cross-generated from several realms. So it is often the principle of opposition that forces you to go to your edges and receive the seeding and teaching of the depths.

TIME: 20 minutes.
MATERIALS NEEDED: None.

INSTRUCTIONS FOR THE SOLO JOURNEYER: This process, of course, is best done with another person. If this is not possible, then imagine that you're sitting opposite someone who is giving you a hard time as either the Seth or Horus principle. You might want to use your kinesthetic body as your sparring partner. You will need to simulate a fight and to speak very loudly and with much passion about the Seth point of view to your imagined Horus partner. Then, after about five minutes, change roles and do the same for the Horus self within you.

Try working with two tape recorders during this process, one to play the tape you made in advance of the script for the process, and a second to record your own dialogues between your Seth and Horus selves. This will give you the freedom to become physically active, to fight with your Horus and Seth, who may take the shape of pillows or even punching bags. The intense physicality of this process is part of the emotional power of this process. You will want to be dressed as comfortably as possible and pick a time and place where shouting, screaming, raging, and jumping up and down will not cause a disturbance.

SCRIPT FOR THE GUIDE: Find a partner, then form a double circle around the figure of the Osiris we constructed. Sit facing each other, with one partner in the inner circle and the other becoming part of the outer circle. Pay attention to the shape of the circle, making it as perfectly round as possible. Sit fairly close together.

In this battle those in the inner circle take the part of Horus; those in the outer circle play the role of Seth. You will get to change places and roles later. Those of you who are Seth, in the outer circle, will scream and yell from your core the principles of limitation, of constriction, of being bound. Say the things that you usually say when you're the one who limits and constricts. Say those things loudly and belligerently.

You can yell in English, or any other known language, even make animal sounds. If you do not want to speak in English, yell in glossolalia— word sounds or gibberish with no apparent meaning—knowing full well, however, who you are and what you really mean. Those of you in the inner circle, who are playing Horus, will answer back with equal fervor, expressing the sense of power and possibility, of vision and opportunity, of "wanting to get on with it." Say the kinds of things you usually say when you're in an expansive and creative mood. You who are Horus can express your sentiments also in English, or in glossolalia, or in any other language—human or animal—that you choose . . .

Each pair should now join hands and prepare for a real battle, with real give-and-take. If you want to have a genuine physical struggle, tell your partner so that he or she is willing to offer real resistance. Remember, you don't have to destroy each other. If you want a gentler "battle," then inform your partner of that also. You may need to find another partner if your wishes vary too much about how much physical struggle you require. If you wish to stand to do battle, then stand. Decide these things among yourselves. No pinching, no tickling, no hitting—just hands locked together and pushing while you yell at each other.

All right. Get ready. Are the Horuses ready? Are the Seths ready? Begin. (Allow four or five minutes.)

Stop! Stop! Come to quiet. Thoth is coming to heal the wounds and restore the organs . . . And now reflect. You who have been Horus, you who have been Seth, reflect on the powers that you have just experienced. Reflect on the power of the Seth in you and how it is represented in your life. Reflect on the power of the Horus in you and how it is demonstrated in your life. Allow these reflections to show you something of the range and scope of these powers that you contain within you. Ask yourself what you need to do to bring the power of limitation or expansion that you have been enacting into the world in a creative and constructive manner. Feel the power and the possibilities of both, and let them take hold in you.

Now change roles. Change places in the circles. You who were Seth become Horus, the principle of blossoming, of expansion, of extension. You who were Horus become Seth, to enact the Sethian aspects of your life. Feel them in your body/mind. Feel the principle of the carving back, the limitation, the setting of boundaries, of rules, but also of cutting back excessive growth.

Grasp your partner's hands. Are you ready, Horus? Are you ready, Seth? Let the battle begin! (Allow four or five minutes.)

All right. Stop! Stop! Close your eyes. Reflect . . . Reflect on the Horus qualities in yourself, the strength, the individuation, the expansion. Reflect on the Seth qualities, the power of the conservative, the power of limits, the keeping of the traditions. Reflect on these . . .

Having played both, reflect on the necessity of having both in your life. Reflect, too, on the continual opposition that goes on in your soul between these two qualities. Reflect on how they can be used to deepen and complement each other . . .

Just sit quietly together for a few moments. Speak with each other of what you have discovered about those qualities in your life and how they can be brought together in a fruitful complementarity. Speak about this complementarity together. (Allow five minutes.)

Come to quiet now. Come to silence. Know that now, as a result of playing the battle of Seth and Horus, you have within you a greater knowledge of your own polarities as well as their complementarity.

♣

JOURNAL PROCESS

Without thinking about them or detailing them, make a list of your current fears. When you are finished, go back over the list, noting every fear that spins on a particular theme, the ones that really get you on a gut level. Ask yourself whether each fear belongs to the Seth or the Horus within you.

When you have finished with the list, take a look at your main fears. Write a prayer to your Heroine Within (your own inner Isis). Ask her to tell you how to fight your fears one by one, or how to have them complement each other.

Anger is the fire that moves us or burns us. Think about some injury, some event, some relationship that has not healed. As fast as you can, without stopping, write down what you're so angry about. Write for ten minutes with absolute fury. Then stop. Relax.

Now, turn your focus inward. Make contact with your heroic self, your own Horus. Reflect on what it is that you're really being asked to battle. What lesson does the universe insist that you learn? Write quickly for ten minutes.

PROCESS 13:
Recrowning Isis and Being Gifted by the Goddess

With the help of his mother, Horus finally achieves victory and presents Seth to Isis to keep in custody. However, being the sister of Seth and also having knowledge of the need for polarity, Isis cannot bind him. She lets him go. This makes her son so enraged that he pulls her royal crown from her head. In some versions, he actually tears off her head.

Many times in our lives we have been given a gift that we did not understand, and we have rejected that gift. There may have been times, too, when we made some gesture of peace, an offering that was overlooked or ignored. But now we've come to recognize that the oppositions in ourselves, and in others, are simply the manifestations of polarity.

Through Isis we learn the wisdom of embracing both points of view, that compassion is the key to resolution. This is the numinous power of Isis as it is still felt three thousand years after the devotions to her began, through a ritual celebration that was itself written two thousand years ago.

TIME: 45 minutes.
MUSIC: Music from Area 1.

INSTRUCTIONS FOR THE SOLO JOURNEYER: This process is readily done by making a tape recording of the script for the guide. Just be sure to give yourself enough time to experience each of the areas of history, as well as the full three minutes of clock time for the goddess to gift you. You may wish to do this process in a room filled with the scent of fresh flowers, perhaps in brilliant sunshine, or in full moonlight to give yourself a sense of deeper connection. This process is also well adapted for the out-of-doors, perhaps in a remote wooded area, a nearby mountaintop, or an isolated stretch of beach.

SCRIPT FOR THE GUIDE: Here we become Thoth, the wise aspect of ourselves, and we recrown the goddess.

Select a partner and sit back-to-back, or in a position that keeps your back supported and straight, as we journey to the goddess and give her the crown.

Hold your hands in your lap as if you were carrying the crown. Envision the crown being made of the material that is the most sacred or appealing to you so that your gift to Isis will be unique to you. Is it gold, is it silver? Is it jeweled or enameled? Is it made of moonbeams? What does it look like, feel like? Is it heavy? Is it gossamer? Have a sense of the material and the beauty of this crown. Now, begin to hum gently. You're going to hum as you travel the path to the goddess.

See yourself in the foothills of a mountain. As you climb this mountain, you'll find yourself passing through the realms of history.

In the foothills you pass early human beings. You see them worshiping a maternal figure of stone. Her body is very full, but her facial features are as yet uncarved. You pass by them, heading up this mountain on a spiral path until you see people of the Neolithic Age, planting seeds along with effigies of the goddess to ensure fertility. These are full-figured goddesses, but now they have faces, some with birds' heads.

And you pass up and you pass through the great high civilizations of Egypt, see temples built to Isis and Hathor and Sekhmet and all the other representatives of the Great Goddess. Passing still upward, you enter the Tigris and Euphrates valley and observe the rites of Inanna, Astarte, and Ishtar. Climbing farther, you witness a simple fisherwoman in China praying to Kwan Yin, hoping for the goddess's infinite compassion to shine upon her. Traveling upward now through civilizations of South America, you pass the Aztec temples and see the worship of the goddess Tonantzin. Later, in the same place you see how she has been transformed into the Virgin of Guadalupe. In Africa you find people worshiping the goddess in her manifold guises, especially the thrilling and life-giving Oya. In North America you discover the goddess as she unfolds in the Corn Mother and Spider Woman and White Buffalo Woman.

Continuing up the mountain, you find yourself in Greece, where you visit the temples of Aphrodite and observe the Panathenaea festival to Athena. You join in the Eleusinian mysteries and participate in the drama of Demeter and her daughter, Persephone. In Rome you partake of the mysteries of Isis. While farther north you reverence the Celtic Bridget.

You pass onward and upward to Glastonbury and the isle of Iona, where you encounter the rites of Cerridwen and her Holy Grail that contains every good thing. You observe the Druid priestesses who come under the name of Morgana. You pass through the Crusades and see the devotion given to the Black Madonna, hearing the sounds of *Salve Regina*. Going up and up and up. You pass through the Middle Ages and you see and hear the sound of stone being hewn. You are in the midst of the creation of the great cathedral of Notre Dame—Isis raised in a later form.

And you pass up and up and up. You move through Renaissance Italy, seeing the glory of Leonardo painting Isis in the form of the Mona Lisa. Climbing up and up, you see Queen Elizabeth of England as Isis Astarte.

As you rise up and up and up, you see all the guises and variations—across time and through many cultures—of the Great One, the Beautiful One, the goddess in history. Finally, you reach our own time at the top of the mountain.

There you find a shining temple and you go into it, still carrying the crown. You know that you are in the realm of the goddess. The art and architecture here are very strange. They are both very ancient and very new, a blending of the distant past and the distant future. The ceiling contains star maps of other places in the universe where the goddess's presence is honored and felt.

You find yourself approaching a throne, and you sense the presence of the Great Goddess on that throne. You approach her reverently and give her the crown, saying, "Great Isis, here is your crown."

She bows to you with grace and elegance, and she thanks you for acknowledging who she truly is.

And then, here in her presence, she gives you a gift. It is a gift that in some way contains the essence of that which you require. It is a great gift, and only you will know what it is. It fills an emptiness; it fulfills a need. You have three minutes of clock time, equal subjectively to all the time you need, to receive the gift of Isis, the Great Goddess, the Great Creative Universal Principle. Receive your gift now. (Allow three minutes.)

Having received her gift, leave the great hall of the goddess, knowing that she is always with you in whatever form she takes in your life.

Leave the shining temple and begin to go down the mountain, past all the civilizations and all the forms of the goddess. Through the present civilizations . . . through the Industrial Revolution . . . then the Renaissance . . . the Age of Exploration. Down and down, past the Crusades, past the Celtic times. Down, down, down, through all the empires and cultures in which the goddess has reigned. South America, North

America, Africa, the Far East. Down past Greece, Babylonia, Egypt. Down past the Neolithic era. Past the early cave people. Until you reach the bottom of the mountain of time and stand once again in its foothills.

Now, open your eyes and sense your gift. Sense its value and importance in your life. Know that part of what happens in the gifting and in this myth is that you are given the essence of what you need as well as the courage to accept new challenges and opportunities. But above all, know yourself to have been recognized, honored, and gifted by that principle of creativity, kindness, and renewal that sometimes goes under the name of the Great Goddess.

⚶

JOURNAL PROCESS

Write about how you have gifted others—not about presents that you have given, but rather about gifts of heart or courage or empowerment that you have brought into other people's lives.

Next, write about how others have gifted you in a similar manner. Write especially about gifts that have come to you unexpectedly, out of the blue, as a grand surprise.

Finally, write about some gifts that you plan to give to others.

⚶

PROCESS 14:
Creating the Barge of Seth

Horus regains the kingdom of his father and is regarded as an actual incarnation in the physical realm of Osiris. In reparation for his crimes against Horus, the gods have Seth turn his body into a barge to ferry the mummy of Osiris to the other world. Thus, in an unconscious way, the principle of limitation has yet again acted as an agent of transformation. But now it is being made conscious, and we begin to understand the function of limitation as a vehicle of transcendence.

By creating a barge of Seth within ourselves, we fund the energy to provide a new structure through which we can manifest the creativity of heaven and direct it into a new, redeemed form.

TIME: 20 minutes.

MATERIALS NEEDED: The decorated mummy of Osiris in the center of the room.

MUSIC: Celebrational music from Area 3. Also, if desired, environmental sounds of the sea, or of the passage of waters (Area 1).

INSTRUCTIONS FOR THE SOLO JOURNEYER: Make a tape recording of the script, with suitable music added. When the time comes to dialogue with your own personal Seth and Osiris, you may wish to do some journal writing. Let one write through your right hand, the other through your left hand. Experience them as your two hands writing in opposition to each other. As you listen to the previously taped instructions for this process, put yourself at the prow of the Boat of the Millions of Years and imagine a circle of friends behind you. You may want to go through a photo album in advance, selecting pictures of your loved ones. From those pictures, create the outline of the boat in which you will sit. And in that boat, carry your own Osiris into the Other World.

SCRIPT FOR THE GUIDE: As the concluding act of this mystery drama, you're going to take on both Osiris and Seth—the creative negative.

Ask yourself which quality in your life up to now has been your receptacle for negative or depressing emotions. Recast it into a creative quality that can be used to carry you more deeply into your life and depth.

For example, let's consider a quality that many people experience as a negative: the Sethian quality of excessive vulnerability and sensitivity. At a deeper level, many of those who suffer from this sensitivity also have a complementary positive quality. This shows itself in the capacity to be sensitive, empathic, and understanding about where other people may be in their life journey, as well as being sensitive to the larger possibilities and qualities in each person.

This doesn't make the vulnerable quality any less excruciating, but it does allow us to make use of the deeper and more positive value of the seemingly negative quality. We can view a negative quality as a constant detriment in our life, or we can see it in terms of its deeper potential—remaining sensitive to others.

As another example, take anger. People who tend to be angry often have as their creative corollary a rich and diverse emotional palette. They are capable of expressing many emotional colors and shadings. But too often their unexpressed emotional genius is locked up inside them and rises to the surface as rage. The issue, then, concerns allowing themselves to focus on the great range of emotional coloration and express this rather than the anger.

Your Sethian quality is your foremost negative quality seen in its full positive potential. Seth's negative quality of wanting to cut back, to contain and limit, becomes his creative quality of being able to serve as the container, the barge that carries Osiris to the Other World.

What is your Sethian creative negative quality? Think about it now. What is the deeper positive aspect of this quality—the creative Seth quality? Reflect on it. In twos or threes sit down and discuss your creative negative quality. Talk first about what you believe to be your most negative quality, then go deeper. Try to perceive what the depth quality of this apparent negative quality really is. (Allow ten to fifteen minutes.)

Now, take that creative Seth quality and form a boat around this mummy of Osiris. Form a boat or a barge, holding on to each other. Form the boat with the prow in front and the stern in back. Make it look like a real boat.

(Music plays.)

The Nile is flowing past you. You have only to be the boat. Sway together as a boat. You are here in this place of the Reality of This Time and That Time, in this present moment and in ancient Egypt in 2000 B.C. Both times are. They are flowing here now . . .

This was known as the Boat of the Millions of Years. In the middle of it we place the mummy of Osiris that we have made. This body represents all our parts that have been recast in the depths . . .

Now we are carrying it into the archetypal world of ourselves. And our Seth, our creative negative, forms this boat . . .

Begin to make the sound of the boat moving through the waters of the Nile as you carry Osiris. As you float down the Nile, the sound of the water is joyous, as this is a merry processional boat. Feel the creative Seth quality rising as you carry Osiris to the depth realm, as you enter the depth realm with both your Osiris and your Seth . . .

And the Boat of the Millions of Years floats through all time and all space . . . as we join ancient Egypt now. We are in the realm of eternal Egypt, and its great patterns charge us and give us the power to re-create our time . . . Here, Osiris brings our deep world into bloom and Isis graces us with love.

SO BE IT. THUS ENDS THE PASSION PLAY OF ISIS AND OSIRIS.

(Once the entire passion play is complete and all processes ended, it is important that participants carefully and reverently dismantle the mummy of Osiris, and that several people take responsibility for burning the paper parts representing the fourteen parts of the sundered body.)

♣

JOURNAL PROCESS

Write a creation myth of your own. Now, reread your creation myth from the beginning of your journal. How does this story differ? Write a myth about ending. Make a ritual of leave-taking.

Celebrational orchestra.

16

The Marriage of
Body and Soul

The seeker marveled, for a new world was revealed, neither within him
nor without, but with no separation between the two.

Then the Fire of the depths awoke; intense heat filled his whole
body like a tide of superabundant Life, and Joy flooded him, for all his
doubts disappeared, his obstacles melted away, and he perceived the
treasure that he had found, which by its power is both end and means,
the source of Life, the Living Fire, the One Thing Necessary.

from *The Opening of the Way*
by Isha Schwaller de Lubicz

This, then, is the mythical tradition of the good king Osiris, the first victim, the first mummy, and the first resurrection. He dies and is reborn in
three forms: first, as god of the underworld, where he rules the just and
honorable dead; second, as the first Horus, in whose form he battles for
his honor; and third, as the younger Horus, the silent child. The Horus-
Osiris union led to the famous Egyptian ritual words "I and the Father
are One." Osiris exists, however, independent of these two incarnations
as the judge of the dead and the lord of the resurrection.

The Deceased Become Osiris

In the Old Kingdom (circa 3100–2181 B.C.), the dead pharaoh was
aligned to the spirit of Osiris, and the whole drama of the mortuary ritual was modeled on the death and resurrection of Osiris. In the Pyramid
Texts of the Old Kingdom (2494–2181 B.C.) the dead king was ritually
assimilated into the body of Osiris. The following text equates the dead
pharaoh Unas with the fallen god Osiris, and his resurrection as the
brightest star of the constellation Orion—the shining body of the god
Osiris. This was the Dog Star, or Sothis, whose appearance indicated the

rising of the Nile. This mythic drama depicts the power of the goddess Isis who will raise the dead pharaoh as she raised the fallen Osiris.

> Truly, this Great One has fallen on his side,
> He who is in Nedyt¹ was cast down.
> Your hand is grasped by Re,
> Your head is raised by the Two Enneads.
> Lo, he has come as Orion.
> Lo, Osiris has come as Orion. . . .
> You shall live!
> You shall rise with Orion in the eastern sky,
> You shall set with Orion in the western sky.
> Your third is Sothis, pure of thrones
> She is your guide on sky's good paths
> In the Field of Rushes.²

By the New Kingdom (1700 B.C.), the royal mortuary ritual had been democratized, and all people who could afford it could hope for revivification through ritual assimilation to Osiris. Ritual papyri were made available in a standard fill-in-the-blank format, leaving room to insert the dead man or woman's name by simply calling the deceased "Osiris (Name)." This text appearing below was one of the most well-documented in the Book of the Dead. It is taken from the Papyrus of Ani.

Behold Osiris Ani. He saith: I am in thy presence, O Lord of Amentet. There is no fault in my body. I have not spoken lies with knowledge. I have not acted with double intent. May I be like the favored ones who are about thee, an Osiris favored greatly by the beautiful god, beloved of the Lord of the World, the veritable royal scribe who loves him, Ani, triumphant before Osiris.³

In the tombs and temples of Egypt you find many funerary scenes with Osiris as a mummy with a green or dark face. The green face suggests the growing of the spirit of Osiris, and the dark face suggests that he is the fertilized one, as the black land is fertilized by the Nile. He holds the royal insignia of flail and scepter, indicating his dominion over both the earth and the underworld.

Judgment in the Underworld

The dead are presented by Anubis or Horus to Osiris, who presides at the weighing of the heart in the Hall of Judgment. It was here that the deeds of a lifetime were recounted by the scribe god Thoth. It was here that the heart was weighed in the scales of Ma'at, the scales of truth and justice. If the heart was heavier than the feather of truth belonging to the goddess Ma'at—that is, if the human passions were too strong, or iniquity lurked within the heart—the heart and its owner would be tossed to Ammit, the Eater of Hearts, known as the Great Devourer.

In this Hall of Ma'at, as the deceased, we determine whether or not our individual consciousness matches the consciousness of the cosmos at the moment of creation. Before our heart is weighed we stand before the forty-two Assessors who accompanied Osiris in the underworld, at which time our soul declares our purity and innocence before each of the Assessors, who bear such names as He Who Eats Shadows and He Whose Strides Are Long. Rather than confess our sins, we cite our merits, or at least tell each Assessor one negative thing in our life that we have not done. The forty-two statements made before them became known as the Negative Confession.[4] Examples of this list of deeds one must not commit in thought, word, or action were:

> *I have not robbed with violence.*
> *I have not slain man nor woman.*
> *I have not made light the bushel.*
> *I have not carried away food.*
> *I have not laid waste the lands that have been plowed.*
> *I have not pried into matters of other people.*
> *I have not defiled the wife of a man.*
> *I have not struck fear in any one's heart.*
> *I have not been a person of anger.*

As well as the above list of avoided sins were the following misdeeds left undone—which, if literally accomplished, would have been quite amazing feats:

> *I have not eaten my heart.*
> *I have not taken vengeance upon the god.*
> *I have not fouled the water.*
> *I have not wagged my jaw too much. . . .*[5]

Parts of the very ancient Pyramid Texts, as well as the later Coffin Texts and the Books of the Dead, were used as "crib sheets" to help the dead say the right things to Osiris so that he could help them move on to the immortal realms. Some of these critical notes were placed as papyrus sheets in among the mummy wrappings of the corpse.

The Cults of Osiris and Isis at Abydos

The main center of the cult of Osiris was at Abydos, and beginning in circa 3000 B.C. devotees would come there, sometimes even bringing their mummified dead with them to be blessed by Osiris. The festivities at Abydos were renowned for the wild democratized ritual enactment of the myth, in which all the visitors would be engaged in the enactment of the story, especially in the battle between Horus and Seth.

The great feast of Osiris was held in Abydos toward the end of the second month of inundation, approximately September 2. A great many feasts were held at this time, primarily because the entire land was flooded and not much work could proceed. It was best to celebrate the coming new year through festivals and ritual dramas.

The plays were rich in costume and commanded performances by select noblemen in the community. They began with a great procession under the leadership of a high priest wearing the mask of Anubis or Upuaut, the Opener of the Way. It was necessary for a slight struggle to ensue with the crowds. The Way was not to be easily opened, and like the Catholic congregation who play the crowd screaming for the release of Barabbas in the passion play of Christ during the Lenten season, the ancient Egyptian crowds took the part of the negative forces standing in the way of the will of the gods by attempting to prevent the procession from entering the temple. This was the dramatic physical realization of enacting one's own Sethian nature as an obstructor to the god's sacred transformation.

During the second act, the god Osiris was ritually murdered by Seth. The audience displayed unrestrained grief, wailing, tearing their hair, smearing themselves with dirt. Then the entire procession moved out of the temple toward the sacred tomb of Osiris for the ritual interment. The voyage to Byblos was probably enacted on the sacred lake of the temples, or by boats launched upon the waters of the Nile.

Still other parts of the play involved the ritual slaying of the enemies of Osiris, which usually included a stick fight, often a drunken brawl, and a few broken bones in the process. The play concluded with the reemergence of the risen god Osiris, embodied in the *djed* pillar, which was drawn upright by the tugging of ropes. At this point, the crowd sang out with joy, and another round of drinking, dancing, and feasting ensued.[6]

Following the rowdy male demonstrations of heroic struggle at Abydos, the priestesses of Isis held their own pageant and drama in the temples of the goddess during the following month. At this time two high priestesses impersonating the goddesses recited the moving and sorrowful text called the "Lamentations of Isis and Nephthys." The ritual drama recalled the loss of the god, the long search for his body, and the subsequent resurrection by the twin goddesses. One can imagine the pilgrims gathered outside the temple chanting the passionate words of the play of Isis:

> Come to your house, come to your house.
> You of Anu,[7] come to your house.
> Your foes are not!

O good musician, come to your house!
Behold me, I am your beloved sister,
You shall not part from me!
O good youth, come to your house.
Long, long have I not seen you.
My heart mourns you, my eyes seek you,
I search for you to see you!
Shall I not see you, shall I not see you,
Good King, shall I not see you?
It is good to see you, good to see you

You of Anu, it is good to see you!
Come to your beloved, come to your beloved![8]

One of the main dramatic lines included words saying, in effect, "I am the resurrection and the life. He who believeth in me shall have eternal life."

Beneath this ritual cult of the dead there flourished, beginning at the time of the New Kingdom, another more philosophical mystery cult of Osiris. It was in this form that the rite of Isis and Osiris spread throughout the Greek world and then the Roman Empire. Its overt emphasis was on the passionate and compassionate Isis, leaving Osiris something of a background figure. Indeed, so extensive and intensive became the expanded mysteries of Isis in the second and third centuries A.D. that they threatened to oust other gods from popular worship. Plutarch, himself, was a priest of the Isis mysteries.

Entering the Mysteries

And so, the myth of Isis and Osiris became the basis for a great religious drama and mystery. The underworld of Osiris is not the sphere of the dead alone: it is the realm of the mysteries, the realm of the depths. Osiris presides at the temple of the depths, where initiates seek truth and resurrection or transformation. His throne is not in the objective world, but in the subjective sphere, which is the inner life of the human.

Osiris's wife, Isis, is the mother of mysteries, the guide of mystery religions from the time of the New Kingdom and later Egypt and throughout the Greco-Roman world. This could have happened only after the Old and Middle Kingdoms waned and the political and spiritual power previously centered in the pharaoh began to decline. This released the mystery to be assumed and democratized among many people.

Isis' search for Osiris, and her diligent efforts to resurrect him, are the symbol of the initiates' journey to restore the parts of themselves that have been forgotten or abandoned. Through our reenactment of the mystery, we actually create the new body and soul. These are finer instruments, more involved with the depths of reality than the ones that have been lost. In the Isis and Osiris mystery, we die to a part of ourselves and are reborn into a deeper and richer self in which that which lies within is no longer hidden, and that which lies without is understood on many levels.

This mystery greatly influenced the ancient Greek mysteries of Eleusis; of Demeter searching for her daughter, Persephone, after she had been abducted into the underworld; and later, in the Christian world, of

Mary mourning over the body of her son brought down from the cross before there was any hope of resurrection.

Osiris the king lives only twenty-eight years.[9] Osiris as mummy and resurrected one lives forever in the durative realm of archetypal time and space. He becomes the lunar pharaoh of the inner life, whereas Horus becomes the solar pharaoh of the outer life. In every exploration of the Egyptian mysteries, the sun, dramatic and stark in its arrival and departure in the Egyptian sky, assumes central importance. It is an enormous presence, an enormous ego of nature, assimilated to the living pharaoh as Horus.

In all the Egyptian mysteries, as the sun rises and falls in its path across the sky, so does consciousness develop in every individual as the ages of life unfold, and individuation is the end of the diurnal arc. The metamorphosis of the Horus (sun, ego) ends in the death of the sun's course where Osiris, the fully achieved self, receives and Osirifies the ego/Horus/sun, transforming him into the Higher Self. When the sun-son goes down, he enters the underworld where the individuation of life is complete.

Thus the pharaoh was thought in life to be identified with Horus. But when he died, he moved down into the underworld of the Higher Self and became Osiris. The mystery of mysteries—"I and the Father are One"—is the key to the final phase of the transformation, the unfolding of the netered self. This culminates in the death of the old existential ego and the assumption of a higher, deeper self—one that in some sense, like Osiris, dwells in both worlds and pulses both the punctual and durative realms with new meaning. The human being who has entered into his "Osirification" is thus able to be a citizen of two worlds, assuring the god world its continuity and its greening.

The Reality of the Soul

What we have attempted in this long journey into myth is to effect something of a conscious reunion of soul in body and body in soul, in addition to discovering some of the capacities that emerge once this reunion is effected. The ambivalence that most people feel toward their own bodies is perhaps the key to the history of humankind on this planet. That you and I exist by reason of being embodied—that we are incarcerated in flesh, encased in our bodies like Osiris in his tomb, that we see through its veiled portals oh so dimly, that we feel as if we are quite literally grounded in this protein-based biocomputer—is the source of much of our frustration, most of our confusion, and a good deal of our resentment. We often feel that our soul could soar and visit many worlds, many realities were it not pinned like a butterfly to the flesh of our mortal form.

The myth of Isis and Osiris points up the sense felt by so many people in many times and cultures of being betrayed or tricked into life, of falling or being exiled from the realms of pure light and grace, of therefore feeling shame, dismay, anger, fear at being trapped and imprisoned in the body. These feelings, universal as they are, are all grist for the soul's mill, its purpose being the deepened experience of life in the world. Our task, as the myth tells us, is to reconcile the body and soul, to remember that they are together in this time and space for a purpose that involves the growth of both ourselves and that which lies beyond us that we are yearning to discover.

It has been a major purpose of the journey of this book to explore and experience this great myth of the marriage of body and soul to call forth the yearning to know the soul's reality for our own. For the soul is not a no-thing. It is textural, tactile, a very touchy thing. When we're in touch with our soul stuff, we have access to extraordinary capacities that otherwise lie dormant.

The soul may initially be felt as a feather on the breath of god, rising to a humming in the heart, a vibration, a frequency that soars until it sings through our bones like a flute and beats its drum on our brain pan. A great connection occurs in this mind and body made music, made soul. The body is filled with extraordinary capacities and a vitality that seems to extend well beyond healthy functioning. There are many ways of opening up those capacities and maintaining them. We've explored and experienced some of these openings of the ways through the story of Isis and Osiris.

The Ultimate Union

We are living in mythic times, and our lives often contain dimensions as mythic as those enshrined in the stories of the gods. We seek an archetypal identity, for we instinctively require a larger context, a richer formulation to account for our experience. Yet, ultimately, we may be even more than that. I believe that we are a particular rendering of the God stuff in space and time that allows us to embody the many levels and varieties of experience. This permits us to engage in training to further our skills as cocreators, as godseeds, and to gradually become responsible in our time for evolutionary governance. Perhaps our experience as embodied soul stuff sends messages back to the metaworlds—the home regions of soul and spirit, of higher orders of civilization and existence. Perhaps we communicate with those mythic beings remembered as Isis and Osiris. We tell them what it is like to be in flesh on this planet. This allows for improvements to be made, changes to be incorporated, and the entire creative process of world- and soulmaking to be enhanced.

If this sounds like metaphysical science fiction, it is. But it just may be the basis for a whole new mythology, one that we badly need. We haven't had any evocative new mythologies of the soul in the body for a long, long time. This has added to our dilemma of diminished awareness of the soul's place and powers both within the body and without; within the earth and without.

At this point in time, when we're about to join the larger universe and venture out into space—as well as redesign and reinvent ourselves—it is critical for us to gain a broader view of who we are and what our place is in the order of things. To do this, we need to regain in contemporary terms something of the understanding we had in ancient times of our more cosmic aspect. For without this enriched understanding of the soul in its double life in time as well as in eternity, we'll just go blundering along, foisting our diminished history onto other planets. We see this impoverishment in the myths of space operas in the movies and on television, where we project this soulless dimension onto other humanoid species. They become our shadows writ large—the weird flash and face of soulless humanity.

This is why we have looked back through the ages to an ancient myth to tell the tale of our times. It speaks of a world rent apart yet trying to come together again in a form that allows for larger and more soulful living, for a new order of partnership between men and women, different cultures, and the many varieties of conscious experience. It tells, above all, about the marriage to the soul. This ultimate union is our birthright, our destiny, our lure for becoming.

The bark of Osiris sailing over heaven, which is supported by four pillars, in the
form of goddesses. On the right are three hawk-headed spirits, and on the left are:
1. Three jackal-headed spirits; 2. The eight primeval gods of Khemennu, frog-headed
and snake-headed; 3. The four-headed ram of the North wind; and, 4. The ram-headed
hawk of the East wind.

Alphabetical List of the Neters of Ancient Egypt

The names appearing here represent a process of symbolic thinking, a historical development of religious thought, and the advancement of consciousness as it developed in ancient Egypt over a five-thousand-year period.

In general, the ancient mind seldom deleted a neter's power from its repertoire. When encountering a similar god, one generally incorporated the unknown god's qualities into the list of attributes of the known gods. Thus myths intertwine, gods and goddesses intersect.

You may find yourself confused. Don't let that stop you; even Egyptologists get confused. Some gods predate others, who later take on the same functions of their predecessors. Some gods perform similar functions, but represent the native gods of either the north or the south prior to the unification of Egypt in 3000 B.C.

You will find a helpful list of the cosmogonic and protective neters at the end of this appendix. Some attempt has been made to separate the list into the predominant neters of a particular region. Refer to the map in Appendix C for clarification of the temple precincts for each neter.

In addition, know that the Greeks—to whom much of ancient Egypt was arcane and unfamiliar and to whom we owe a debt of gratitude for trying to record the ancient history and life of the Egyptians—added a patina of their own to the interpretations. By and large, their interpretations are all that remain.

In essence, let there be duality. Dual thinking is the sacred task of learning to think, to be, and to do in two places and on several planes at the same time. Nevertheless, as you read, some gods may appear more familiar to you than others. Hear those who speak to you. Don't worry if the other gods are silent. Their time to speak will come soon enough.

Aker The twin lion god of the underworld, personification of Earth. Sometimes he appears as a strip of land with a human head. More often he's seen as two sphinxes seated back-to-back—one facing east, the other west. The sphinxes guarded the entrance and the exit to the underworld. In later traditions each lion of Aker received a name: the eastern lion was called Sef, meaning "yesterday"; the western lion was called Tuau, meaning "today." The book of Aker documents the journey of the sun from sunset to sunrise. The cult of Aker was located in the delta nome of Leontopolis.[1]

Amaunet The hidden goddess, feminine form of Amun. One of eight primordial deities in Hermopolis, she represented the unmanifest before creation. Her husband, Amun, had the head of a frog, she the head of a snake. Her cult was not long-lasting and she went through various manifestations, first as Opet or Tauret, the hippo wife of Amun in Thebes, and later as the vulture goddess Mut. She was also identified with Hathor as the goddess of the underworld. Her name means "what is hidden."

Ammit The demonic, fearsome lion, hippo, crocodile goddess of Ament, the hidden underworld. She is called The Eater of Hearts, The Great Devourer, or The Great Death. Seated beside the scales of justice in the Hall of Osiris, she devours the souls of evildoers. Her mouth is filled with flame and smoke.

Amun (also Amen, Ammon) The primordial blue-fleshed sky god who creates and sustains the universe. In Hermopolis he is associated with Amaunet as one of four divine pairs. He represents the unmanifest. His name means "the hidden one," but may also relate to the Libyan word *aman*, meaning "water." The neterworld, Amentet, was his body. During the Twelfth Dynasty, Amun gained prominence in Thebes as the great unseen, all-pervasive deity. Merged with Min, as a phallic god, and with Ra, as a solar god, he was also a deity of creation. He was called He Who Abides in All Things and he becomes the essence of soul, or *ba*. His name abides even on the lips of Christians who end their prayers by intoning his name, "Amen." In the temples of Luxor and Karnak he appears as a handsome man with a curved, pointed beard, wearing two plumes as a headdress. At other times he appears as a ram, the *ba*, whose horns curve in toward the sides of his head, indicative of inner hearing and that voice that speaks within.

From *The Hymn to Amun* by priest Montemhet:

> *Hail to you, Amun,*
> *Maker of mankind,*
> *God who created all beings!*
> *Beneficent king,*
> *First one of the Two Lands,*
> *Who planned the eternity he made.*
> *Great in power,*
> *Mighty in awe,*
> *Whose forms are exalted above other gods . . .*
> *I bow down to your names.*

Amun-Re (also Amen-Ra, Amun-Ra) A combined form of the gods Amun of Thebes and Ra of Heliopolis. The two gods merged as the epitome of the great creative power of the universe manifesting as Light, both in the visible and invisible realms. The effort was also due in part to an attempt to unify the similar but competing priesthoods of Upper and Lower Egypt. In his most common image, the god is shown as a man wearing the double plumes—identical to the god Amun.

Anubis (also Anpu) The son of Osiris and Nephthys, raised by Isis. He appears with the body of a man and the head of a black jackal. His qualities are not devouring, but steadfast and devout as those of a hunting dog. Most often he is found in the necropolis surrounding Abydos. The origin of his name suggests "putrefaction," a possible link to his functions as lord of the dead. Skilled in the arts of embalming, he guards the body in the tomb and performs the intricate process of mummification—packing the body with spices, binding the bones, wrapping the body in linen, and casting protective spells that guarantee immortality. He leads the dead into the Hall of Judgment for the weighing of the heart ceremony.[2] He also acts as a messenger between the worlds and functions as a god of intuition. In archaic times he appeared as one of two jackal gods, the other being Anpu or Upuaut.

From *Address to Anubis* from the Pyramid Text of Unas:

> *Unas stands with the Spirits.*
> *Get thee onward, Anubis*
> *into the Underworld. Onward,*
> *Onward to Osiris!*

Anuket (also Anukis, Anqet) Goddess of Elephantine and Nubia. She is associated with the gazelle and accompanies the ram-headed god Khnum and her sister Satis, with whom she shares many attributes as the goddess of the chase and the flood. Her name means "to surround" or "embrace," as the Nile waters surround the islands of the cataracts and embrace the fields along the river. When Satis is identified with Isis, then Anuket is identified with Nephthys. She wears a tall, many-feathered African crown and carries a papyrus scepter.

Apis Not a god, the sacred bull of Memphis was revered as a fertility symbol. On its head appeared the solar disk and uraeus.[3] Variously associated with the rites of Ptah, Osiris, Min, and especially the Nile god Hapi (from whom his name is derived), the Apis bull could be identified by a white crescent moon on its side, a white triangle on its head, a black lump under its tongue, and a flying vulture on its back. Apis bulls were kept in sacred temple stables and used by the priests as oracles.

Apophis (also Apep) The snake enemy of the sun, the embodiment of darkness and chaos, a companion of Seth. Born from the spittle of the primeval snake goddess Neith, his name means "he whom she spat out." This underworld serpent demon is equivalent to the Babylonian monster Tiamat, but it also represents the dark power of the crone. Apophis attacked Ra at sunrise and sunset, thus smearing the skies red with blood. It was said that Ra assumed the form of a cat and finally slew the serpent beneath the sacred sycamore. Apophis lived in the waters of Nun, and the coils of its body formed the labyrinthine maze of the underworld.

Aten Sole creator god of the monotheistic pharaoh Akhenaten. The word *aten* meant "the disk." As a god, Aten took the form of the sun with human arms and hands stretching forth the symbol of life, the ankh. Aten worship temporarily replaced the worship of Amun in Thebes. When the priests of

Amun refused to cooperate with him, Akhenaten moved his temple to Tel el Amarna, the city he built exclusively for the worship of the sun.

From *The Great Hymn to Aten* by the pharaoh Akhenaten:

> *You are the one God,*
> > *shining forth from your possible*
> *incarnations*
> > *as Aten, the Living Sun,*
> *Revealed like a king in glory, risen in light,*
> > *now distant, now bending nearby.*
> *You create the numberless things of this world*
> > > *from yourself, who are One alone—*
> > *cities, towns, fields, the roadway, the River,*
> *And each eye looks back and beholds you*
> > . *to learn from the day's light perfection.*
> *O God, you are in the Sun-disk of Day,*
> > *Overseer of all creation.*

Atum (also Temu) The demi-urge, primeval creator of the universe, the nothing from which everything sprang and to which everything will return. He was the first self-generated neter and lord of all. In Heliopolis he was known as the bisexual originator of the *paut*, the nine great neters who came after, including Shu and Tefnut, Geb and Nut, Osiris, Isis, Horus, Seth, and Nephthys. He was called The Completed One. Atum is sometimes depicted as the hillock rising above the sea, or the ourobouric serpent biting its tail. When Ra became supreme sun god, Atum was relegated to the position of an aspect of Ra—the setting sun depicted as an old man leaning on a stick.

From the Book of the Dead (in the spirit of the god):

> *I am Atum in his rising. I am the only One.*
> *I came into being in Nu, his primeval waters.*
> *I am Ra who rose in the beginning.*

Bastet (also Bast) The cat goddess who was the tame form of the lioness Sekhmet. In Bubastis she was adored for her sensuality and loving nature. Sekhmet's voracious thirst for blood was said to have been pacified by Thoth when he tricked her into drinking red wine instead. Bastet then became the goddess of festivals and intoxication. The sistrum held in Bastet's hand was emblematic of pleasure in music and dance. Called Lady of the East, she was a daughter of Ra, and her solar nature embodied the sunlight, whereas Sekhmet embodied destructive solar power. Other texts give Bastet a lunar nature, whereas Sekhmet possessed a solar nature. Her name is thought to derive from the combined words *ba* and *Ast*, meaning "soul of Isis." She appears as a woman with a cat's head, surrounded by kittens, a sign of her nurturing nature.

Bes The dwarf god with a beard, lion's mane, and monstrous face, his tongue pressed between his teeth as if laughing or frightening evil spirits. He wore a lion skin robe and a plume of feathers on his head, indicative of his African origin. A companion of the goddess Hathor in Dendera, Bes was fond of dancing, music, and jubilation. Like Hathor, he came from the land of Punt. He played the lyre, tambourine, and sistrum and danced to please the gods. One of the favorite household gods of Egypt, he protected women in childbirth, frightened away the bad dreams of children, strangled snakes, and brought good luck and fortune. Bes means "fire," perhaps a reference to his lion's mane and tail, sharing the lion's solar characteristics.

From *The Metternich Stela* (identification of Bes):

> *The Old Man who renews his youth*
> *and the Aged One who maketh himself a boy*
> *Once again.*

Duametef See Four Sons of Horus.

Four Sons of Horus In an elaborate mortuary ritual in the New Kingdom, the human organs of the dead were placed in four canopic jars. Four organs in particular had a specific mystical function. These organs were protected by four gods called the four sons of Horus. Each patron god protected a particular organ. The jar containing the liver was protected by Imset, a bearded human god. The jar containing the lungs was protected by Håpy, a baboon god. The jar containing the stomach was protected by Duametef, a jackal god. The intestines were protected by Qebehsenuf, a hawk god. Like the four cherubim in the vision of Ezekiel, each god commanded a particular cardinal point and was linked with one of four protective goddesses. Imset was linked with Isis and the west. Håpy was linked with Nephthys and the east. Duametef was linked with Neith and the north. Qebchsenuf was linked with Selket and the south.

Geb (sometimes Seb) The primeval earth god in the Heliopolitan tradition. He appeared as a hill, the first land to emerge from Atum. On his back grew the vegetation of the earth. Like Aker, he also ruled the underworld. A consort of the sky goddess Nut, he was called father of the gods and sired not only Ra, the sun, and Thoth, the moon, but also the five epagomenal neters: Osiris, Isis, Horus, Seth, and Nephthys.[+] In human form he is depicted as a man lying beneath the sky goddess, phallus erect, or with his legs above his head, indicating the roundness of the earth. At other times he appeared as a goose, was known as The Great Cackler, and was said to have laid the egg of the world from which Ra emerged. After the death of his son, Osiris, he abdicated his throne as ruler of the underworld.

From the Book of the Dead:

> *The doors of heaven are opened for me.*
> *The doors of Earth are opened for me.*
> *The bars and bolts of Geb are opened for me . . .*

> *I am decreed to be the divine heir of Geb,*
> *Lord of the Earth and protector therein.*

Hapi The fecund neter of the river, his name means "inundation." Linked with
Nun as the primordial water and with Osiris as a fertility god, his home was
a watery cavern hidden beneath the first cataract of the Nile near Elephantine. He also presided over the river of the underworld. He appears as a long-
haired, naked man with blue-green skin and pendulous breasts. From these
breasts flow the twin sources of the Nile, the Blue Nile and the White Nile.
He appears seated before a table of offerings, which indicate an abundant
harvest. At other times he holds two water jars from which the Nile waters
pour forth, the first image of the zodiacal sign Aquarius.

From *The Hymn to Hapi:*
> *May your countenance shine on us*
> *Hapi, god of the moving River,*
>   *who comes forth from Earth*
>   *returning to save the Black Land.*
> *His features are hidden, dark in the daylight,*
>   *yet the faithful find him fit subject for song.*
> *He waters the landscape the Sun god has formed,*
>   *giving life to every small creature. . . .*
>   *for his is the rain, as it falls from heaven;*
> *Loved by the waiting Earth*
> *He nurtures the newborn Grain. . . .*
> *Man cannot know the place where he is,*
>   *nor his grotto be spied in the writings. . . .*
> *He descends to the netherworld, rises again,*
> *Revealer, returning with news of the mysteries. . . .*
>
> *O Hidden god, be it well with you!*
>   *may you flourish and return!*
> *Hapi, river-spirit, may you flourish and return!*
> *Come back to Egypt*
>   *bringing your benediction of peace . . .*

Håpy See Four Sons of Horus.

Harakhty (fused with Harmachis) The falcon-headed sun god who wears a solar
disk. His name means "Horus of the two horizons." An early form of the elder Horus as the personification of light, he was identified with Ra. As the
Greek Harmachis, he was linked with Kheperi, the scarab, as a symbol of
eternal life. As a man with a lion's head, his most common manifestation is
as the Sphinx. Because he continually watched sunrise and sunset, the loss
and return of light, and because he himself was completely covered by sand,
then uncovered through the eons, he was said to be the wisest creature of all.
In his Sphinx form, Harmachis was the most famous oracle in Egypt.

From *The Pyramid Text of Unas:*
> *The sky's reed floats are launched for Harakhty*
> *That Harakhty may cross on them to Ra.*

> The sky's reed floats are launched for Unas
> That he may cross them to lightland, to Ra.
> The sky's reed floats are launched for Unas
> That he may cross them to Harakhty, to Ra.

Harpokrates Literally, "Horus the child," son of Isis, the threatened infant savior who was cherished and protected by his mother. Often shown with the youthful sidelock of hair, he appears with his finger to his lips, a gesture of suckling. As the embodiment of the rising sun, he is associated with Nefertum, the child seated on the lotus.

Hathor Most ancient goddess of the sky. Hathor was the prehistoric prototype from which the later Isis emerged, and confusion between the two goddesses, common even in ancient times, was perpetuated by ancient Greek historians. During predynastic times, Isis was the Great Goddess of the Delta, whereas Hathor was the Great Goddess of Upper Egypt. The worship of Hathor, however, predates nearly all other goddess worship in Egypt and stems from an early matriarchal culture. She was the mother of the elder Horus, the hawk who was both her son and lover; her name means "dwelling place of Horus." In later times she was linked with Horus the younger as his wife and mother of his son, Ihy. As mother of the universe, her powers were as a triple goddess. She bears the characteristics of the lover, mother, avenger, and comforter of the dead. In the Nile Delta she merges with the sky mother. Like Nut, she wears a disk of the sun, which she uplifts with her cow horns. At other times, she appears completely cow-headed. She also took shape as a lion, the daughter of Ra, and her twin solar aspects were Sekhmet and Bastet. When she takes beautiful human shape as goddess of love, beauty, and dance, she exhibits small cow ears. In Upper Egypt she appears as a birth goddess linked to Khnum, the ram-headed creator god who shapes the souls and bodies of men on his potter's wheel. In Dendera, her archaic cult site, Hathor is sky mother and patroness of astrology.

From *A Hymn to Hathor*:

> All hail, jubilation to you, Golden One
>   sole ruler of the world
> Mysterious one who gives birth to divine beings
>   who forms the animals, molds them as she
> pleases
>   who fashions men and women.
> O Mother, luminous one who thrusts back darkness,
>   who illuminates every human creature with her
>   rays
> Hail, great one of many names. . . .
> It is the Golden One! Lady of drunkenness, music,
> dance,
>   of frankincense and the crown, of women and
> men
>   who acclaim her because they love her.
> Heaven makes merry, the temples fill with song,
>   and the Earth rejoices.

Heh One of eight primeval gods in Hermopolis. Along with his wife, Heket, he represents the endlessness before the first creation. His name means "millions." Later he became the god of eternity, depicted as a man seated on a perch and holding notched palm branches in his fists. He wears a reed upon his head and carries the ankh, the symbol of long life.

Heket (also Heqet) The goddess with a frog's head who heralded abundance. Associated with Khnum, who molds the child and its soul from clay, she assisted in childbirth and in processes of transformation. In Hermopolis she was one of the eight primeval neters. Linked with Heh, she symbolized endlessness.

Heru-Khuiti The god of the month of Mesore in the Egyptian festival calendar. Heru-Khuiti is a god combining the aspects of Horus (or Heru) as the solar god and Thoth (or Khuiti) as the lunar god. He is a god of dualities.

Hike (also Heka) The companion of Ra at the moment of creation, along with Sia and Hu. These three gods were essential in any form of magic-making: where Sia signified the ritual (or intelligence) and Hu signified the magician (or divine authority), Hike was literally the "magic" of the spell, or the power of creative utterance. The Memphite priests linked these three with Ptah's creation of the world through the divine word.

Horus (also Heru) The embodiment of day, the heroic combatant of Seth in his personification of darkness. Two forms of Horus are known; both of them assume the solar form of a hawk. Horus the elder was the son of sky mother Hathor and was called The Distant One. Later he became the son of Geb and Nut, the brother to Isis and Osiris. His eyes were the solar and lunar orbs. He embodied the heroic temperament, his name being associated with "heroism." During his battle with Seth, the evil god poked out the eye of Horus, but the god Thoth healed him and replaced his sight. Thereafter the blue-green eye of Horus the elder was one of the most powerful healing talismans in Egypt. The younger Horus, or Harpokrates, was born in the delta papyrus swamps as the lame child of Isis and Osiris. Healed and nurtured by his mother, Isis, guarded by her attendants who were cobras, he became the avenger of his father's murder by waging a battle against his uncle Seth. The living pharaoh who protected his kingdom is equated with Horus, and every pharaoh was given a sacred "Horus name," a name of power. Horus Behdety was yet a third spiritual form of the god, appearing as the winged sun disk often seen sculpted over temple doorways or as a falcon hovering near the pharaoh in battle, grasping an ankh in his claws. Originally a god of southern Egypt, his main temple site was at Edfu.

From *The Hymn to Horus-Min* on the Stela of Sobekiri:
> *Tall-plumed, son of Osiris, born of divine Isis.*
> *Great in Senut, mighty in Akhim.*
> *You of Koptos, Horus, strong-armed,*
> *Lord of awe who silences pride.*
> *Sovereign of all the gods! . . .*

Hu One of three gods (along with Sia and Hike) who accompanied Ra in his solar boat and participated in creation and magic-making. Literally, he was "the command," or "utterance." In Heliopolis, Hu and Sia were said to have sprung from the drops of blood on Ra's phallus. The Memphite priests linked the trio with Ptah's creative utterance.

Ihy Child of Hathor and Horus, his name means "jubilation." He was the royal bearer of the sistrum and god of music. He usually appeared naked, wearing his hair with the sidelock of youth and touching his finger to his mouth. At times he was called Lord of the Bread and Bringer of the Beer, part of his duties in the celebrations of intoxication at Dendera.

Imhotep The architect of the pyramid of Saqqara for King Djoser during the Fifth Dynasty. During his life he was a fabled scholar and medicine man. In later dynasties he became the patron of all priests and scribes, the only historical, nonroyal person in Egypt to attain the stature of a god. He was regarded as the son of Ptah and Sekhmet, a lord of learning and healing. He held in common many of the attributes of the Greek god Asclepios and the Egyptian god Thoth.

> From *The Hymn to Imhotep* at Karnak:
>
> *Hail to you, kind god, Imhotep, son of Ptah. . . .*
> *Men applaud you; women worship you.*
> *One and all exalt your kindness.*
> *For you heal them; you revive them.*
> *You renew your father's creation.*

Imset See Four Sons of Horus.

Isis (also Ast, Auset, Iausas) Queen of Heaven and Earth, wife of Osiris, mother of Horus, and daughter of Nut. Her cult lasted from prehistory into the Christian era. She was wife, widow, mother, protectress, savior, comforter, and destroyer—the ultimate female in the Egyptian tradition. She assumed Hathor's attribute as triple sky goddess, wearing Hathor's crown of cow horns. She also wore the vulture wings of the mother goddess Mut. Isis was revered as a doting mother, faithful wife, and devout mourner. Nearly all goddesses were identified with her, including later versions of Mary, the mother of Jesus. Her life was full of difficulties, among them the loss of her husband, her incarceration by Seth, and the near death of her infant son. But she was also Great of Magic, having been taught the words of power by Thoth. Among her talents were the resurrection of the dead, shape-shifting, commanding snakes and scorpions, and tricking Ra into revealing his secret name. The *tat* talisman, or knot of Isis, was a symbol of her womb and represented her generative powers. Where Osiris was the fertilizing Nile water, she was the dark fertilized flood plain. Said to have civilized the barbarians, she taught them to weave, plow fields, heal with herbs, marry, build homes, and rear children. Her Egyptian name, Auset, literally means "seat" or "throne," and her identifying hieroglyph is a throne. Because matrilineal descent determined a pharaoh's right to rule, and because the queen mother embodied Isis, the living pharaoh embodied the god Horus. The child who sat upon Isis's lap was guaranteed the right to rule. Her temples stretched from southern to northern Egypt, from the island of Philae near Nubia to Sebennytos in the Nile Delta, and to Greece and Rome.

From A *Hymn to Isis*:
> O *Thou holy and eternal savior of the human race.*
> *Thou bestowest a mother's tender affections*
>   *on the misfortunes of unhappy mortals.*
> *Thou dispellest the storms of life*
>   *and stretchest forth Thy right hand of salvation*
>   *by which Thou unravelest even the*
> *inextricably*
>   *tangled web of Fate.*
> *Thou turnest the Earth in its orb.*
> *Thou givest light to the Sun.*
> *Thou rulest the world.*
> *Thou treadest Death underfoot.*
> *To Thee the stars are responsive.*
> *By Thee the seasons turn*
>   *and the gods rejoice*
>   *and the elements are in subjection.*

Khentamenti The universal name of Osiris as lord of the underworld and judge of the dead. Khentamenti means "chief of the Hidden Place." The living pharaoh embodied Horus as the protector of Egypt, whereas the mummified pharaoh embodied Osiris. Since the dead were buried in the sandy hills west of Thebes, this name indicated that Osiris was the first god-man to enter Ament, the world of death. His attendants were the jackal gods Upuaut and Anubis.

Kheperi The scarab or dung beetle. God of transformation, the word *kheper* means "to become." Ra as the morning sun was said to have emerged from a ball of dung pushed by the beetle. In other texts, the sacred beetle pushes the solar barge of Ra through the underworld. He was said not only to create life but to restore life, and thus is always associated with the idea of resurrection. He is sometimes a form of Atum.

Khnum The ram-headed god whose name means "to create." In Upper Egypt, he was Maker of Heaven and Earth and All Things Therein. At Esna, he was Creator of All Things, father of fathers and mother of mothers. As one of the principal birth deities, he was known as Lord of Destiny. From the clay of the Nile River he molded the bodies and souls of children on his potter's wheel and placed these in the mothers' wombs. The rams' horns on his head extend in a wavelike pattern resembling the lapping waves of the Nile, one stream of water feeding northern Egypt, the other stream feeding southern Egypt. As such, he was associated with the Nile god Hapi. His two wives were the sister goddesses Satis and Anuket. On the island of Elephantine, his temple appeared side by side with a temple to the Hebrew god Yahweh.

From *Hymn to Khnum*:
> *God of the potter's wheel,*
> *Who settled the land by his handiwork. . . .*

Who drenches this land with Nun,
While round sea and great ocean surround him.
He has fashioned gods and men,
He has formed flocks and herds;
He made birds as well as fishes,
He created bulls, engendered cows.
He knotted the flow of blood to the bones. . . .
He makes women give birth when the womb is
ready.
So as to open the flood gates of life. . . .

Khonsu (also Khensu) The moon god, child of Mut and Amun in Thebes. He wears the moon disk and crescent on his head, as well as the sidelock of youth. Often he appears riding on the back of a crocodile. He was called The Wanderer, and like Thoth was a messenger for the gods. He assisted Thoth as a healing god by holding the crook, flail, and *djed*, emblems of power, authority, and stability. His crescent moonlight was said to fertilize women, cattle, and the germ in the egg.

Kuk One of eight primeval gods who preceded creation. In Hermopolis, Kuk and his consort, Kauket, represent eternal darkness.

Ma'at Goddess of truth, justice, balance, morality, and cosmic law, she appears as a winged woman wearing an ostrich feather. When Isis and Nephthys sometimes appear in winged form together, they are called the *ma'aty*, or the Double Ma'at. Present at the time of creation, Ma'at was called daughter of Ra, his food and drink, and the heart and tongue of Ptah. Dual in nature, she was the balance between good and evil, light and dark. Atum created the world by setting Ma'at in the place of chaos; thus her symbol was the foundation stone. Upon their coronations pharaohs were "given *ma'at*," that is, the right to rule and the duty to preserve cosmic order, for the duration of their reign. Upon his death the pharaoh handed *ma'at* back to the gods. Her presence in mortuary ritual was essential. In the Halls of Osiris her feather, placed on the scales, was weighed against the heart to measure the lightness or heaviness of the soul. It was the heart that remembered all the deeds of life.

Mehen Literally, "the encircler." This serpent of the underworld was also known as Nehaher (Fearful Face) and Wer (Most Ancient One). In the underworld, Mehen contains Osiris and works as his guardian, rather in the same manner that the encircling womb protects a growing fetus. But as Osiris grows stronger in the underworld, Mehen becomes a constricting, confining force that keeps him locked in its embrace. At that point, Mehen takes on a Sethian aspect, becoming an opponent, rather than a protector.

Meretseger Goddess of the necropolis in the Valley of the Kings. Called Lady of the Peak, meaning the western hills where the dead were buried, she sometimes appeared as a lion, snake, or scorpion with a woman's head. Those who disturbed the tombs of the dead were attacked by her until they begged forgiveness. To the righteous, she was a beneficent deity who assured the dead their peace. Her name means "she who loves silence."

From *Hymn to Meretseger*:

> *Behold, I say to the great and small. . . .*
> *Beware the Lady of the Peak*
> *For there is a lion within her.*
> *The Peak strikes with the stroke of a savage lion.*
> *She is after him who offends her.*
> *I called on my Mistress*
> *And found her coming to me as sweet as a breeze.*
> *She was merciful to me,*
> *Having made me see her hand.*

Meshkhent The birth goddess identified with Hathor in Upper Egypt, Edfu, and Dendera. On her head she wears a brick, emblematic of the bricks on which women squatted to deliver their children. Her name literally means "birth dancer." In the birth chamber she appeared as four dancing women who inscribed the fate of the child on the cracks in the birthing bricks. At the birth of Horus in the papyrus swamps, she delivered the child to Isis and foretold his great future. She also assisted Isis in the funerary rites of her husband. A goddess of reincarnation, she petitions for the rebirth of the dead in the Halls of Osiris. She was married to Shai, god of destiny.

Min The most ancient fertility god, the consort of Hathor, and a sky god. He manifested as the lightning bolt of life at the moment of sexual union. A creator god, he was linked with Amun in the Temple of Karnak and wore the twin plumes on his head. As the embodiment of renewal, abundance, procreation, and sexual power, he appeared as a one-armed man with a large, erect phallus. His name means "to be firm." The orgiastic festivals at Coptos, his cult center, were designed to fertilize the fields and impregnate females. The Greeks equated him with Pan.

Montu (also Menthu) An ancient warlike solar god. His name means "the wild one." Originally a god of the desert, he personified destructive solar heat and was linked with the Asian bedouins. He appeared with the head of a hawk surmounted by a sun disk and uraeus. His early sun cult in Hermon-this depicted him spearing the enemies of Ra, just as Horus spears the enemies of Osiris. He embodied the solar soul as Ra-Harakhty. In later times he was called Buchis, the white bull with the black face.

Mut Vulture goddess of Thebes, wife of Amun, and mother of Khonsu. Her name means simply "mother." It was said that vultures lifted their tails to the winds to fertilize themselves, and that when their fledglings were starving the vultures plucked at their own breasts to feed them with their blood. Mut embodies self-sacrifice, nurturing, and caring. The wings of the vulture, which appear clasped around the heads of Isis and other goddesses, signify the qualities of motherhood. At Karnak, Mut is linked with Sekhmet as the eye of Ra. At other times she appears as the primeval birth goddess Opet, the big-bellied hippo with pendulous breasts. The proof of her ancient aspect is the fact that she was said to have given birth to many, but to have been born of no one but herself.

Nefertum Son of Sekhmet and Ptah, he appears as a bald, serene child emerging from a lotus flower and represented the dawn of creation. His name means "beautiful perfection." He was seen as the young Ra or Atum in Hermopolis. A healing god, he brought perfume to Ra to ease his suffering. Patron god of aromatherapy, Nefertum often appears holding a lotus to his nose.

Neith (also Neit) Goddess of creation, goddess of the hunt. On her head she wore a set of crossed arrows or the shuttle of a loom. Near the delta city of Sais she was the archaic goddess who took form as a cobra and was the patroness of weaving. From her name come such words as "net" and "knit." As the creative matrix, she reached into herself when she was still the watery chaos and withdrew the forms of the world, such as frogs and fishes. The crocodile god Sobek was said to be her son. In the underworld she wove the mummy cloth for the dead. In the tomb she joins Isis, Nephthys, and Selket as a guardian of the dead. Like a female Anubis, she uses her strength as a warrior to open the way for the dead. She joined Seth as patroness of war and hunting, but she also loved creation and light; therefore, she became the final judge in the quarrel between Horus and Seth.

> From *A Hymn to Neith*:
>> You are shielded!
>> She is coiled upon your brow.
>> You are shielded!
>> She is draped about your temples.
>> You are shielded!
>> All you gods of the South, North, West, and East
>> All nine gods who follow you
>> Let their spirits, their kas rejoice over this king
>> As Isis rejoiced over her son Horus
>> When he was but an innocent in Egypt.

Nekhebet Vulture goddess of el-Kab who ruled southern Egypt while her sister, the cobra Wadjet, ruled northern Egypt. She was the right eye of Ra, whereas her sister was the left eye. With Wadjet she inhabited the watery abyss before creation. As the vulture appearing on the king's diadem, she symbolizes strength and warriorship. Her name means "she of Nekheb," the archaic city of Upper Egypt. However, the hieroglyph *nekheb* means "to tear open" and may refer to her vulture nature. During the early Old Kingdom dynasties, she became fused with the vulture goddess Mut, whose name means "mother." By New Kingdom times, Mut's maternal power had overshadowed the more warriorlike powers of Nekhebet.

Nephthys (also Nebhet) Daughter of Nut and Geb, mourner and lover of Osiris, and sister and comforter of Isis. Married to Seth, Nephthys did not take part in the death of Osiris or in Seth's battle with Horus. Called The Dark Isis, The Hidden One, she had no cult of her own. Her name means "mistress of the house." Her emblem is a house with a wicker basket. As wife of the arid, sterile war god Seth, she bore no children, but she was mother of Anubis by Osiris. Whereas Isis embodied light feminine power, Nephthys embodied the dark feminine. Together, she and Isis appear as a pair of kites or swallows mourning the dead Osiris. In the tomb, she appeared at the head of the coffin, and Isis stood at the foot.

Nun (also Nu) One of eight primeval gods who existed before the world was made. In Hermopolis he was called The Nothingness, The Nowhere, The Abyss, The Dark Deep. Along with his female double Naunet, Nun represents the charged cosmic soup. Like Hapi, he is associated with the flood, the well, and all watery depths, such as seas, rivers, and caverns. He was the heavenly water along which the solar barge of Ra floated.

Nut (also Nuit) The sky goddess often appears as a cow. One of the most an-cient deities, her name means simply "the goddess." She is akin to all the other ancient archaic goddesses, including Neith, Mut, and Hathor. As the feminine part of the cosmic soup, she was depicted as a woman with a water pot on her head. At other times, because she was mother of all things, the emblem was said to represent a womb. In Heliopolis she appeared as a woman arching over the earth god Geb from whom she was separated by Shu. She gave birth to five divine siblings—Isis, Osiris, Seth, Horus, and Nephthys—during the five epagomenal days that Thoth won for her from the sun god. As mother of the sun, she births Ra at dawn and swallows him at dusk. The stars are all the unmanifest souls and neters within her body awaiting birth. She was called The One with a Thousand Souls. At death and in dreams one entered the body of Nut. The pharaohs' coffin lids and tomb ceilings are lavishly illustrated with pictures of Nut reaching down to embrace the dead.

From A Hymn to Nut:

> O Great One who became sky, you are strong and
>   mighty.
> Every place fills with your beauty. The whole world
>   lies down beneath you. You possess it.
> As you enfold Earth and all creation in your arms
> So have you lifted up me, a child of the goddess,
> And made me an indestructible star within your
>   body.

Opet (sometimes Apet) Protective goddess of childbirth, she is similar to the ancient predynastic goddess Tauret. She is depicted with the big belly and face of the hippopotamus. Like Ammit, she also appears with the feet and mane of a lion, as well as the head of a crocodile. In one hand she carried the *sa* amulet, symbol of the womb, and in the other hand she carried the knife used to cut the umbilical cord.

Osiris (sometimes Ausir) Husband of Isis, brother of Seth, and son of Geb and Nut. He was the original sacrificial god of Egypt. He twice suffered death at the hands of his brother—once by drowning and once by dismemberment. Ensnared in a tamarisk tree, he was lost and found by Isis, only to be lost again. Mourned by his sisters, Isis and Nephthys, he was resurrected into the next world. His symbol was the *djed* pillar, representing either the sacred tree of Byblos in which his coffin came to rest or the reconstituted backbone of Osiris. As cult object, the *djed* symbolized stability and strength. His hieroglyphic sign was the throne surmounted by an eye. The meaning of his name is obscure, but "place of the eye" has been commonly suggested. He organized agriculture on earth and civilized the barbarians. But his major contribution was his complex role as ruler of the dead and judge of souls in Amentet, the underworld. His earthly forms were as the barley, grains, seeds, floodwaters, black soil, and phases of the moon. As the embodiment of the flood, he is equated with Hapi. In human form, he wears the tall *atef* crown with its twin feathers and appears inert and mummified, holding the *waz* scepter and the flail and crook in his hands. His original cult site was Busiris in the Nile Delta, but throughout Egypt he appears in every necropolis and tomb. At death the pharaoh becomes Osiris, but as the living pharaoh he embodies the warrior Horus. Osiris fathered Horus, his hawk son, first when he lay with Isis in the womb of Nut, and again when Isis magically resurrected him after death. He also fathered the jackal Anubis by Nephthys.

From *The Hymn to Osiris*:

> *Turn your face gentle upon us, Osiris!*
> *Lord of life eternal, king of the gods,*
> *unnumbered the names of his protean nature,*
> *holy his manifold visible forms,*
> *hidden his rites in the temples. . . .*
> *God who remembers still*
> *down in the halls where men must speak*
> *true,*
> *Heart of the inexpressible mystery,*
> *lord of regions under the Earth,*
> *Worshiped in white-walled Memphis,*
> *power that raises the Sun,*
> *whose earthly form rests in Heracleopolis. . . .*
> *Lord of forever, first in Abydos,*
> *yet far off his throne in the red land of death.*
> *His tale endures in the mouths of men:*
> *god of the elder time,*
> *Belonging to all mankind—*
> *he gave Earth food,*
> *Finest of the Great Nine,*
> *most fruitful among the divinities. . . .*

Ptah The Memphite god who created the world by speaking its name. His own name means "to incise" or "chisel." Author of the world, he was patron of all artists and craftsmen. His power resounds in every musical note, vowel, and heartbeat. He made the world through *ma'at*, or truth, and the goddess Ma'at was his heart and tongue. As Atum closed the day, so Ptah opened it. Father of fathers, power of powers, he was said to be a great magician. He appeared in human form, but inert and nearly mummified, grasping the *waz* scepter and wearing a skullcap. Husband of the goddess Sekhmet, he fathered Nefertum, the child of dawn.

From the *Hymn to Ptah*, Stela of Neferabu:

> *I am a man who swore falsely by Ptah, Lord of Ma'at,*
> *And he made me see darkness by day.*
> *I will declare his might to the fool and the wise,*
> *To the small and great:*
> *Beware of Ptah, Lord of Ma'at.*
> *Behold, he does not overlook anyone's deed.*
> *Refrain from uttering Ptah's name falsely,*
> *Lo, he who utters it falsely, lo he falls! . . .*
> *Righteous was Ptah, Lord of Ma'at, toward me,*
> *When he taught a lesson to me.*
> *Be merciful to me, look on me in mercy!*

Qebehsenuf See Four Sons of Horus.

Ra (often Re) Most well known of the solar gods, the child of the goddess Hathor or of Nut, who births him at dawn and devours him at dusk. His cult arose late in the Fifth Dynasty in Heliopolis. Eventually, he assumed all the attributes of earlier solar deities, including Horus, Sokar, and Harakhty, the hawk forms, as well as other creator gods: Atum, Amen, Aten, and Ptah. As child of dawn, he appears in the form of Nefertum on his lotus. Initially, his cult provided a golden age for Egypt called the First Time. At times a petulant god, he once asked Sekhmet to devour the world because he was disappointed with his creatures. Later, tired of humankind, he withdrew, leaving the upper world for Horus to rule and the lower world for Osiris. Ra was the sun at high noon, whereas the morning sun was Ptah and the evening sun Atum. By day, Ra sailed his boat across the sky accompanied by faithful servants. On earth he was sunlight itself and sustainer of life. By night he either traveled the underworld in his boat along the back of a snake or was enclosed in a ball of dung and pushed along by the beetle Kheperi. The phoenix, or *bennu*, symbolized his ability to continually regenerate.

From *A Hymn to Ra*:

> *I give praise when I see thy beauty.*
> *I hymn Ra when he sets.*
> *O august, beloved, and merciful God*
> *Who hearest him that prays,*
> *Who hearest the entreaties of him who calls upon*
> *thee,*
> *Who comest at the voice of him who utters thy name.*

Raet The feminine form of Ra, a female sun goddess with cow horns. She was a precursor to Hathor and akin to Tefnut. She was said to be the soul or feminine half of Ra.

Renenutet (also Renenet) The birth goddess whose name means "snake who nurtures." She is goddess of good fortune and fertility. In Faiyum, she assured abundant harvests and was associated with Sobek, the crocodile. According to the Nile Delta legend, she was nursemaid to Horus, suckling him and guarding him in the papyrus swamps. A snake-headed form of Isis, she was especially fond of children.

Satis (also Sati, Satet) The flood goddess who wears a tall crown between two antelope horns. In many ways she was an Upper Egyptian version of the goddess Neith. Her name means "to shoot forth" or "eject." Associated with whatever was swift, she was both goddess of the hunt (symbolized by her arrows) and goddess of inundation. With her sister Anuket and the ram god Khnum, she shared a home on the island of Elephantine near the first cataract. Identified with Isis when she appeared as the Dog Star, Sothis, Satis was patroness of women in love.

Sekhmet (also Sakhmet) Goddess of magic, wife and sister of Ptah, mother of Nefertum, and child of dawn. According to Memphite tradition, Ptah was intuition and will, while Sekhmet was will and action. At times she appeared with an erect phallus, symbolizing her powerful, magical, and creative forces. Where Ptah was linked with Thoth as author of the universe and creative intelligence, Sekhmet was linked with Ma'at as one of the seven wise beings who assisted in world creation. As a form of Hathor, she appears as a woman with a lion head wearing a red dress and a sun disk surmounted by a cobra. The lion goddess was noted for her strength, courage, and protective instincts. Her name means "the most powerful one." She defended divine order, destroyed the king's enemies, and caused pestilence as well as cured disease. As Lady of Flame, she was the sun's fire-spitting eye, a world devourer, and bloodthirsty warrior for the sun god Ra. When pacified, however, she was linked with the cat goddess Bastet. Where Bastet was goddess of the eastern rising sun, Sekhmet was goddess of the western setting sun.

Selket (also Serqet) The scorpion goddess who protects the child at birth and the pharaoh at death. In death, she joins Isis, Neith, and Nephthys as guardians of the tomb. Among the living, she was associated with medicine men and magician priests. Her name means "she who allows the throat to breathe." A powerful ally or terrible foe, her scorpion's sting could arrest breathing, restrict the throat, and cause instant death. In the underworld she defends Ra from the serpent Apophis and binds the unjust in chains. In Saqqara, her site of earliest appearance, a headless scorpion is her identifying crown.

Seshat Heavenly consort of Thoth, she records man's fate, measures the length of his days on notched palm branches, and writes the book of life on leaves of gold. Her leopard skin robe designated her role as high priestess, and her palette and ink pot identified her as scribe. Her name means "the scribe," and she was linked with prayer as well as with all forms of writing, painting, building, and meditation as a spiritual discipline. In Abydos, Karnak, Edfu, and elsewhere she was mistress of libraries and books, keeper of akashic records, and goddess of scribes, priests, and architects. Because of her knowledge of geometry and math, she was invoked during the ceremonial groundbreaking of each new temple. Her headdress was a seven-pointed star or a seven-petaled flower beneath the down-turned crescent horns of the cow goddess Hathor.

Seth (also Set or Sutekh) God of the desert, sandstorms, rainstorms, and any restriction. Originally Seth was the Lower Egyptian equivalent of the Upper Egyptian hawk Horus. God of the hunt, he was a beneficent deity of strength. His bones were the iron ore of the earth. In some myths he defended the sun god Ra against the serpent of darkness. Later, when agriculture dominated Egyptian life, he was known for his violent, destructive nature. Too impatient to wait for his birth, he burst through the side of his mother, Nut. He murdered his brother, Osiris, in order to usurp his land, then battled with his nephew, Horus, in a dispute over the throne. Married to his sister Nephthys, he was sterile, and she birthed a child by Osiris. His origin may have been as a sky god of Libya. As a god of foreign lands, his harem included the mythical Ethiopian queen Aso, the Asiatic goddesses Anath and Ashtoreth, and the warrior goddesses Neith and Anuket. He appeared in human form with an animal's head, perhaps that of an ass, jackal, or okapi. His companions were odious creatures such as snakes, scorpions, pigs, crocodiles, hippos, and creatures of the hunt, such as jackals, dogs, and antelope. Because he was god of the red desert land, any people with red skin or hair belonged to Seth. His Egyptian name was Sutekh, meaning "instigator of confusion."

From the Book of the Dead:

> *[He is] the great god who carries away the soul,*
> *Who eats hearts and who feeds upon offal,*
> *the guardian who is in the darkness,*
> *the guardian of the Seker boat.*
> *Who is this then? It is Seth; it is the soul of Geb.*

Seven Hathors These goddesses of fate appear at the moment of birth and act in a similar fashion to the Greek fates or European fairy godmothers. As aspects of Hathor in her role as goddess of sensuality, ecclesiastic dance, and astrology, they signify good fortune and appear as women dancing with tambourines. They correspond to the seven visible planets, as well as the seven notes of the harmonic scale. In the night sky they appear as the constellation Pleiades. Sometimes they are the seven points of the goddess Seshat's crown in her manifestation as celestial biographer of the pharaoh. Their images appear in the birth houses of Philae and Dendera.

Shai God of destiny and good fortune. No one could ignore Shai; his name means "what is fated." At birth he appears as a guardian angel and continues to follow a person throughout life. However, Shai also determined the length of one's life and the manner of death. Usually depicted as a man, sometimes as a goat, he was husband of the birth goddess Meshkhent.

Shu God of air and twin of Tefnut. The priests of Heliopolis said he issued from the phallus of Atum. Whereas Tefnut was the moisture of her father's lips, Shu was the breath of his father's nose. His domain was the cloudless, waterless sky. He appears in three forms: as a lion, as a man with lion's haunches, or as a man wearing an ostrich feather. An onomatopoeic word duplicating the sound of wind, *Shu* also means "feather." On orders from Ra, he separated heaven from earth, uplifting his mother. Shu and

Tefnut possessed one soul between them, yet the two halves made up the entire soul (male and female) of Ra.

From *Address to Shu* from a text at Edfu:

> He has gone forth from thy mouth.
> He has become a god
> And brought thee every good thing.
> He has toiled for thee. . . .
> He has labored for thee in these things
> And for thee he bears up Heaven on his head.

Sia God of perceptive mind or divine intelligence. Sia, Hu, and Hike made possible the world's creation. In Heliopolis Sia and Hu were born from the blood of Ra's phallus. The trio appeared at Ptah's creative word and accompanied Ra in the solar boat.

Sobek (often Suchos) The primeval crocodile god. Some texts claim that Sobek emerged from the waters of Nun at the moment of creation; other texts say he was the son of Neith, drawn from her body's fluid depths. He combined the dualistic natures of good and evil. Whereas in many nomes he was equated with the destructive god Seth as the devourer of the phallus of Osiris and enemy to the child Horus, in other cities he helped Isis to gather the parts of Osiris, which were lost, and he assisted Osiris in his role as god of the flood. Some scholars believe the meaning of his name is "to collect," or "to bring together." His gaping jaws symbolized the great abyss, but linked with Ra, it was his fierce nature that was admired. Sobek ruled great stretches of water, including the Nile, canals, and oases. His cult centers were Kom Ombo and Faiyum.

From the Pyramid Text of Unas:

> Unas is Sobek, green-plumed, wakeful, alert.
> The fierce one who came forth
> From the shank and tail of Neith, the Great Green.
> Unas has come to his streams
> In the land of the great flowing flood . . .
> Unas rises as Sobek, son of Neith.
> Unas eats with his mouth.
> Unas spends waters, spends his seed. . . .
> Whatever Unas wishes, his heart urges.

Sokar (also Seker) A solar god depicted as a hawk-headed man. Originally the spirit guardian of the tomb and god of the desert, his domain was the underworld and his boat ferried the god Osiris through the darkness. One ancient etymology of his name says that Sokar (or Sy-k-ri) was the cry of the dying Osiris to Isis, meaning "come to me." As a god of craftsmen in Memphis, he was associated with Ptah.

Sothis (also Sopdet, Sept) Isis as the Dog Star, Sirius. Every July she rose with the sun in the eastern sky to herald the inundation of the Nile and the reappearance of Osiris as the fertility god. Sopdet means "to make ready." She is depicted as a woman with a star for a crown or as a cow with a star between her horns. Her home was the distant hills of central Africa, source of the Nile waters. Sothis is sometimes called the soul of Isis.

Tauret (also Thoeris, Opet, or Apet) The predynastic hippo goddess of creation. Predominantly Upper Egyptian, her followers spread far and wide. Although she had no central cult, she was one of the oldest and best-loved fertility goddesses. Like Hathor and Isis, she wore the disk and cow horns. As protectress of pregnant and child-birthing women, her life-giving symbols were the ankh and the *sa*.⁵ Her name means "the great one," and she stood at the center of heaven as the pole star. In her beneficent form, she held Seth fettered by a chain and assisted in the rebirth of the soul in the underworld. At other times she was identified as Seth's destructive consort, the monster Ammit, the terrible devourer of sinful hearts.

Tefnut The lion goddess, first daughter of Atum. She and her twin, Shu, emerged from the fluids of her father's body. Her name means "moisture of the lips." She personified the eye of the sun, was called Lady of Flame, and was associated with the goddess Sekhmet. Her cult city was Leontopolis. Upset with her father, the sun, she once left Egypt and entered Africa, intending never to return, but the god Thoth convinced her otherwise.

Thoth (also Tehuti) God of wisdom and divine intellect. Like Hermes, he was the emissary of the gods. He attended the world's creation, and the eight primordial deities of Hermopolis—or the ogdoad who were called The Souls of Thoth. A moon god, he was called The Silent Being and Beautiful of Night. The crescent horns and full moon disk he wore represent the lunar phases. As moon god, lord of time, and measurer of years, he took a part of each day of the lunar year and created five epagomenal days in which to allow for the birth of Nut's children. This accounted for the 365 solar days of the year. A divine magician, he taught Isis the words of power that let her heal the sick and raise the dead. He invented writing and speech, penning forty-two books of magic that explained the universal mysteries; thus he was patron of scribes, physicians, and priests. A lover of truth, law, number, and order, he was linked with the goddesses Ma'at and Seshat. In Hermopolis his common manifestations were as an ibis, a baboon, or an ibis-headed man carrying a scribe's palette and pen.

From *The Hymn to Thoth*:

> *Praise to Thoth . . . the Moon beautiful in his rising*
> *Lord of bright appearances who illumines the gods.*
> *Hail to thee, Moon, Thoth, Bull in Hermopolis*
> *Who spreads out the seat of the gods*
> *Who knows the mysteries . . .*
> *Who recalls all that is forgotten,*
> *The rememberer of time and eternity*
> *Who proclaims the hours of the night,*
> *Whose words abide forever.*

Unnefer Osiris in the underworld. The name means "the beautiful one" or "the good being." In this fertility aspect, he is associated with the Nile god Hapi as lord of abundance. At times he appears as a mummified man wearing the high white crown and holding the *waz* scepter and the crook and flail as emblems of power. Other times he appears as a seated hare whose favorite food, lettuce, was considered an aphrodisiac.

Upuaut (sometimes Wepwawet or Apaut) Jackal god of the dead. His name means "the opener of the way." This warrior god in jackal or wolf form joins the jackal god Anubis as attendant of Osiris in his aspect as Khentamenti. He was invoked as guardian of the necropolis, and in some texts he pilots the solar barge of Ra. Whereas Anubis is the opener of the roads to the north and personification of the summer solstice, Upuaut is opener of the roads to the south and personification of the winter solstice.

Wadjet (also Uatchit and Uto) Fire-spitting cobra of the delta, she was called The Great Green One and may have originally personified the Mediterranean. Linked with Isis as one of the guardians of the infant Horus, she defended all pharaohs and protected innocent children. She appears as the uraeus on the king's crown, was called Lady of the Papyrus, and was the counterpart of the vulture goddess Nekhebet in the south. Where Nekhebet was a protective motherly influence spreading her wings, Wadjet was a fierce defender thrashing her head and tossing venom.

From the Book of the Dead:

> *The goddess Wadjet comes to thee in her form of*
> *the living uraeus, to anoint thy head with her*
> *flames. She rises up on the left side of thy head, and*
> *she shines from the right side of thy temples*
> *without speech. She rises on thy head during each*
> *hour of the day, even as she does for her father, Ra.*
> *And through her the terror that you inspire in the*
> *holy spirits is increased. . . . She will never leave thee;*
> *awe of thee strikes into the souls, which are made*
> *perfect.*

Cosmogonies of Neters

HELIOPOLITAN COSMOGONY

Atum

Shu (Air)	Tefnut (Fire)
Geb (Earth)	Nut (Watery Sky)

Osiris   Horus   Isis   Seth   Nephthys

HERMOPOLITAN COSMOGONY

Nun and Naunet	(Primordial Waters)
Heh and Hehet	(Infinite Space)
Kek and Keket	(The Darkness)
Amun and Amunet	(That Which Is Hidden)

Ra

MEMPHITE COSMOGONY
Ptah   Sekhmet
Nefertum
Attendants: Thoth, Ma'at, Hike, Sia, and Hu

THEBAN COSMOGONY
Old Kingdom
Min   Hathor   Horus
New Kingdom
Amun   Mut   Khonsu

NUBIAN (ELEPHANTINE) COSMOGONY
Khnum   Anuket   Satis

OTHER PRIMORDIAL DEITIES
Aten (a form of Amun and Ra)
Kheperi (a form of Ra)
Harakhty (a form of Horus)
Hapi (a form of Osiris and Nun)
Seshat (linked with Thoth and Ma'at)
Aker (Yesterday and Today)

Protective Deities

PROTECTORS OF THE PHARAOH
Nekhebet (Upper Egypt)   Wadjet (Lower Egypt)
Montu   Sobek   Horus
Neith   Sekhmet   Bastet

PROTECTORS OF WOMEN IN CHILDBIRTH
Bes   Hathor   Khnum   Heket   Meshkhent
Opet   Tauret   Mut   Renenutet
The Seven Hathors   Shai

PROTECTORS OF THE DEAD
Anubis   Upuaut   Sokar   Horus
Four Sons of Horus   Neith, Selket, Isis, and Nephthys
Osiris   Khentamenti   Unnefer

Enemies

Seth   Apophis (Apep)   Ammit

Glossary of Words, Phrases, and Place Names

It should be noted here that current researchers do not know the precise pronunciations of ancient Egyptian words. Like Hebrew, the language was not written with vowels, since the breathy vocalization was considered the sacred breath of god. There are hard *a* sounds and *e* or *ee* sounds, perhaps an *o* that is closer to an *ou* or *w*. However, we cannot assert this with any accuracy.

This confusion of the pronunciation was by direct intent. The ancient Egyptian scribes did not want strangers to their mysteries to be able to speak the words of power. Thus the writing preserved the magic of the hieroglyphic language, but it has also caused a great deal of befuddlement among scholars. The remnants we have of the language may well be Coptic.

Egyptologists resorted to simply placing an *e* sound wherever they believed a vowel was needed, or they tried to duplicate the sound as it appeared in Coptic. This has resulted in a variety of spellings. Those who wish to work further with the ancient language should consult Sir Alan Gardiner's *Egyptian Grammar* (see the bibliography).

ab The human heart. Rather than the brain, the heart was the seat of memory, emotions, and intellect. It kept the record of one's life on Earth. The heart was weighed against the feather of truth in the scales of *ma'at* in the Halls of Osiris. The primeval god Ptah was said to have produced the universe with the words of his tongue and the desire of his heart. The goddess of truth Ma'at was said to be the heart and tongue of Ptah.

Abusir The ancient desert necropolis of the Fifth Dynasty located between Giza and Saqqara. Here, the pharaohs Sahure, Kakai, and Neuserre built their small but elegant pyramids.

Abydos (also Abtu) A city north of Dendera, capital of the eighth nome of Upper Egypt. It was devoted to the worship of Osiris as Khentamenti, the god of the dead, and was considered the greatest of cemeteries. Many pharaohs had their tombs here next to the burial place of the god Osiris. A sacred, cavernlike healing temple, or Osireion, was said to be found here.

acacia Trees were rare in the dry desert plain of Egypt; therefore, whenever they appeared, they were viewed as bearing the life-giving, nurturing properties of the goddess. The gods were said to have been born in Heliopolis beneath the sacred acacia. The acacia was thought to possess a mystical healing power.

agon A Greek word meaning "contest," or "to drive forward against all obstacles"; a test of the will, strength, and endurance. *Agon* is the root of the word "agony."

akashic records The memory the cosmos has of itself, and that we have of our soul's journey through its many lives. From the Sanskrit word meaning "pure space." The goddess Seshat was said to be the keeper of the akashic records.

akh The spiritual part of the soul that becomes linked with the circumpolar stars in the night sky. Akhakh was the name of the "imperishable stars" in the body of Nut.

akhet The season of the inundation (or winter). It was considered the first of three seasons of the year. Traditionally, it began with the rising of the Dog Star, Sirius, during the third week of July.

Ament (or Amentet) Originally the place where the sun set. Thus it became the hidden world of the god Amun. It was the site of return to the gods after death. Synonymous with necropolis, it became any stony plateau or mountain on the western bank of the Nile where the dead were buried.

Amratians Predynastic, Neolithic peoples of Upper Egypt from 4000 to 3500 B.C. Their oval huts were found from Abydos to Nubia, and they were well known for their pottery.

analogical thinking Thought patterns that use comparative modes. Thinking that centers on the similarities of things and moves toward unification of the parts.

analytic thinking Thought patterns that use reasoning to separate the parts from the whole. Thinking that centers on differences in things and moves toward individuation.

ankh Symbol of life eternal. The hieroglyph is perhaps a sandal strap, perhaps a magical knot. In the Coptic tradition this cruciform shape is called the *crux ansata*.

anthropocentric thinking A manner of thinking that regards the human being as the central rationale for and aim of the creation of the universe. In anthropocentric thinking, human values and experience are attributed to all of reality.

Anu The city of Heliopolis was the site of the early predynastic sun cult and was located at the southern edge of the Egyptian delta. Also called On by the Hebrews, it was the capital of the thirteenth nome of Lower Egypt. It was known as the place of the Eye of Osiris. Here was found the body of The Aged One, or Osiris himself. Here, also, the deceased made his way to join his soul with his body and live eternally.

aor Light. In Heliopolis it was the radiance of the sun, of the human aura, of the phoenix on its *benben*.

archetypal The structure or the model of the universe. In this instance it refers to the powers of the divine creator, author of gods and goddedness, who creates the patterns of existence that we experience as psychological and spiritual states. The neters themselves may be thought of as archetypal patterns of divine thought.

Assiut (also Lykopolis) Cult center of the wolf god Wepwawet. This thirteenth nome of Upper Egypt is located south of Hermopolis. The tombs here date from the Ninth and Tenth Dynasties.

Aswan (also Sunnu) The city built along the first cataract of the Nile. Aswan was the site of extensive trade with Nubia, the location of the island of Elephantine where the gods Khnum and Yahweh were worshiped side by side.

atef Crown with disk and plumes. (See also crowns.)

aten The disk of the sun. The pharoah Akhenaten said the *aten* represented the sole true god.

aufu The living physical body. The *aufu* has bodily sensations of pain and pleasure, but it lacks a form of consciousness except through the *ka*.

axis mundi The world pole. It is the geographical site nearest to heaven where the sacred spirit, word, or cosmic energy of the gods may be received. It may be thought of as the sacred mountain of Moses, the oracle of Delphi, or the primordial hill of the Egyptians. It is any place within the world where the self aligns itself with the divine.

ba The soul, the active divine and immortal self. The *ba* sometimes appears in the hieroglyphic form of a ram, but more often it hovers near the dead in the form of a human-headed hawk. The phoenix was the *ba* of Ra. The fourth-century Greek writer Horapollo believed that the *ba* was similar to psyche and acted as a psychic force. An eternal state, the *ba* could come and go in and out of heaven or earth. It possessed imperishable powers and could assume any form it wished.

Babylon The ancient civilization that arose in the southwest Asian country of Mesopotamia along the Euphrates River. It superseded the Sumerian culture and preceded the Assyrian. Babylonian culture arose around 1900 B.C. In Babylon the Sumerian goddess Inanna became incorporated into the goddess Ishtar. The Babylonians were reputed to be great astrologers.

Badarians Predynastic, Neolithic peoples living in Upper Egypt from circa 4500 to 4000 B.C. Essentially a nomadic people who wore animal skins, they returned to their camps along the Nile to collect herbs, wild grains, and so on.

bedouin A nomadic people of the desert plains.

benben The obelisk. The primordial stone on which the *bennu* bird, or phoenix, rested in its manifestation of the rising sun. Gilded *benben* stones were erected in many temples, then burnished to catch the sun's golden rays.

bennu **bird** The phoenix. This sacred bird of Heliopolis was a form of the heron. It was said to be a shining soul, a manifestation of the *ba* of Ra.

birth brick Ancient Egyptian women in labor squatted to deliver their children into the hands of a midwife. In order to raise the woman high enough off the ground for the midwife to deliver the child, the birthing mother stood upon two freshly made mud bricks. Having no birthing chair, she was also supported by several other midwives. The midwife embodied the goddess

Isis, and the mud bricks were symbols of the god of the flood and fertility, Khnum, who sculpted the child and its *ka* on his potter's wheel. The cracks in the bricks were caused by the pressure exerted during childbirth. These cracks were interpreted by the sorceress-midwife as omens for the health and prosperity of the new child.

Book of the Dead A New Kingdom compilation of ancient spiritual texts dating from 3000 B.C. The Book of the Dead was comprised of many older texts, including the Book of Two Ways, the Coffin Texts, The Chapters of Coming Forth by Day, The Book of What Is in Duat, and the Pyramid Texts. The spells and incantations, designed to assist the dead in their journey through the underworld, were written on papyri and placed in the tomb.

Books of Thoth The forty-two magical texts used by the priests and kept in the sacred library. The texts were said to have been written by the god himself with his own fingers. The texts contained ritual instructions for the priests, books of healing, astrological data, philosophy, and the history of creation.

Bubastis Delta cult center for the cat goddess Bastet. The Egyptians called it Per-Bast, "house of Bastet." It was a metropolis of the eighteenth nome of Lower Egypt.

Busiris A central delta town, also called Djedu or Per-Aser, meaning "house of Osiris."

Buto A delta town, south of Tanis, where the snake goddess Wadjet was worshiped. The Egyptians called this district Pe.

Byblos The mythical site where the coffin of Osiris landed after it floated down the Nile, left Egypt, and entered Syria. It is in Lebanon on the coast of the Mediterranean.

calendar The Egyptians kept three separate calendars: the lunar calendar, the solar calendar, and the Sothic calendar. The lunar calendar was based on the worship of the goddess and related its festivals to the phases of the moon. The lunar calendar is 360 days per lunar year. The solar calendar adds five epagomenal days (see entry) to the lunar calendar, for a total of 365 days. The solar calendar preserved the yearly planting festivals. The Sothic calendar dates specifically to the rise of the Dog Star, Sirius, which yearly heralded the inundation of the Nile. It is said to be the most accurate calendar in the Egyptian system.

canopic jars The four jars that stored the wrapped viscera of the mummy. The jars were named Håpy (the baboon who ruled the lungs), Duametef (the jackal who ruled the stomach), Imset (the man who ruled the liver), and Qebehsenuf (the hawk who ruled the small intestine). These four minor gods were called the sons of Horus.

cartouche The hieroglyph in the shape of a rope that surrounded and magically protected all proper names and the names of the king.

cataracts The dangerous white water of the Upper Nile caused by a multitude of rocks and islands. In all, the Nile has seven cataracts. The first is located in Aswan at the island of Elephantine. Most of the cataracts occur in the domain of Nubia.

cenotaph A mortuary complex where rites for the dead were performed, but no bodies were buried.

chakras In the tantric system, the chakras are those seven magical wheels of spiritual power held in the body. These are contacted by the uncoiling of the energy held in the spine, the so-called kundalini energy. Each chakra represents an ascending step toward enlightenment.

companions of Horus The supernatural, mythical descendants of the god Horus. They were the godlike people who ruled Egypt before the pharaohs. *Shemsu* means "companions." Thus the Egyptians called themselves the *Shemsu-Hor*.

Coptic The Christian Egyptian religion, also the language of its priests. The word "Copts" derives from the Greek *aiguptos*, through the Arabic word *qubt*. Also the last remnant of the ancient Egyptian tongue. Coptic language and script arose around the third century A.D. Its usefulness to students of the hieroglyphs is that the Coptic language retains the unwritten vowel sounds of the ancient language.

Coptos (also Koptos) The city south of Dendera, capital of the fourth nome of Egypt. Sacred to the god Min and the goddess Hathor, it provided an important caravan route to the Red Sea through the eastern desert by way of Wadi Hammamat.

cosmogenesis The magical creation of the universe by the cosmic ray.

cosmogony Creation legends of the various religion centers of ancient Egypt. A study of cosmogony provides insight into the diverse and unified spiritual vision of ancient Egypt. The main centers of study were Heliopolis, Hermopolis, Memphis, and Thebes. The Heliopolitan tradition gave rise to the legends of Ra, Atum, Isis, and Osiris. The Hermopolitan tradition gave rise to the creation legend of ogdoad (see entry). The Memphite tradition stressed the creation of the world by the word of Ptah. The Theban tradition stressed the creation of the world by the god Amun. Cosmogony also applies to the scientific study of the creation of the universe.

Crocodilopolis The ancient city of the Faiyum oasis in the Libyan desert where Sobek and Neith were worshiped.

crook The symbol of authority for the shepherd king. Its possession gave the pharaoh the right to rule.

crowns The royal crowns of ancient Egypt signify various functions. The *deshret*, or red basket crown, was the sign of rulership of Lower Egypt, whereas the *hedjet* was the white war helmet of Upper Egypt. When the pharaoh wore both crowns—the *wereret*, or double crown—he signified his domain over both Upper and Lower Egypt. The *khepresh*, or the electrum war helmet, was used specifically for military functions. The *atef* crown was a tall white war crown with two plumes on either side; it also bore the horns of the ram, and the *uraeus* (see entry). It was a ritual crown worn only on solemn occasions connecting the king with Osiris and Ra through ritual.

cult center Any site where one or more of the neters were honored.

cuneiform The ancient writing of the Sumerians. Cuneiform originally began as a phonetic and pictographic script similar to the hieroglyphs of the Egyptians. Because cuneiform was written on clay tablets with reed styluses, however, the script soon developed into a more abstract language, losing its pictographic elements.

Dahshur The necropolis around Memphis where many of the Old Kingdom pharaohs are buried. Sneferu built his famous pyramid here during the Fourth Dynasty.

Deir el-Bahri The holy of holies (see entry) mortuary complex of Queen Hatshepsut built during the Eighteenth Dynasty. In her temple, designed by the architect Senenmut, Hatshepsut established chapels for the god Anubis and the goddess Hathor. Here, she also recorded her successful expedition into the land of Punt. The site is located on the opposite side of the mountain range from the Valley of the Kings.

delta The huge triangle of waterways and marshes that mark the end of the Nile's long journey. It extends to the north of Cairo, between Lake Mareotis in the west and the Suez Canal in the east, forming a wide arc along the Mediterranean coast. This region offered much better conditions for agriculture than the Nile valley because of its alluvial soil, annually inundated by the flooding of the Nile. Because of the narrow range of temperature change over the year, a factor that influences the choice of crops to be grown, cultivation would have been possible year round.

demiurge The name used by Plato to signify the creator god. In Gnostic creation the demiurge is the creator of the world.

demotic The popular or business script form of the ancient Egyptian language. Demotic originated circa 700 B.C. as a shorthand variation of hieratic (see entry) and lasted as late as the Roman era. Demotic and hieroglyphic scripts, with the ancient Greek inscriptions of Ptolemy, made possible the translation of the Rosetta Stone.

Dendera Cult site of the worship of the goddess Hathor. The Egyptians called it Iunet, and it was the sixth nome of Upper Egypt, just south of Abydos. The temple was well known for its zodiacal ceiling and its celestial observations. Once a year the cult statue of Hathor sailed down the Nile from Dendera to the temple of Edfu, where it spent several nights with the cult statue of the god Horus.

***djed* pillar** (also *tet, djet*) A prehistoric amulet that represented either a leafless tree in which the body of Osiris was enclosed or the reconstituted backbone of Osiris. A symbol of the supporting pillar of creation, the function of the *djed* in the underworld was to turn human flesh into spiritual form. It was a symbol of fertility, energy, stability, and strength. The ceremony of raising the *djed* began in Memphis as a ritual to bring full health and power to the reigning pharaoh.

Duat (or Tuat) A common name for the land of the dead or the world beyond. It was through the halls of the underworld Duat that the dead needed to travel, passing through various pylons and addressing the gods of the underworld by name. It was in this place that the soul sought transformation.

durative realm Eternity, as well as that whole complex of the time/space continuum. In the durative realm, all of history exists, all thoughts, feelings, forms, actions. It is in the durative realm that the akashic records (see entry) exist.

dynasty A succession of rulers from the same family line.

Edfu Cult center of the elder hawk god Horus, north of Aswan and south of Thebes. Ancient temples to Horus were established here in the second nome of Upper Egypt. Edfu's temple library contained forty-two texts of sacred writings, including information on astrological dates, medicine, ritual, and the history of creation.

electrum A metal alloy of gold and silver; called *tjam*, or white gold, by the Egyptians. It was highly prized as the gleaming finish on the apex of the obelisk because its reflective surface caught the rays of the sun.

Elephantine The large island at the first cataract of the Nile near Aswan. Elephantine was the cult center for the god Khnum and his consorts, Satis and Anuket. The nilometer (see entry) placed at Elephantine in the temple of Satis yearly measured the rise of the flood.

Eleusinian mysteries The ancient rites of death and renewal celebrated in the Greek temple at Eleusis. The mysteries were devoted to Demeter and her daughter, Persephone, who was kidnapped by the god of the underworld. The myth of the mourning Demeter bears a marked resemblance to the sorrows of Isis.

enantiadromia "The big turnaround." One might think of it as the point at which the ouroboros (see entry) eats its tail. It is the charged moment of transformation.

ennead Earliest group of nine gods. The ennead of Heliopolis contained Atum, Shu, Tefnut, Geb, Nut, Isis, Osiris, Seth, and Nephthys.

entelechy In Aristotelian thought, this is the culmination of possibility. It is actuality as differentiated from potentiality. The entelechy is the vital force that urges the individual toward self-realization. Entelechy is derived from the Greek words meaning "complete perfection." In Egyptian terms, it may be thought of as the Nefertum, the Ra in the lotus.

epagomenal days The five days at the end of the lunar year, making a total of 365 days a year. During these five days, the goddess Nut gave birth to Osiris, Horus, Seth, Isis, and Nephthys. The epagomenal days were added to the calendar by Imhotep, the brilliant scribe, physician, and architect who lived in the Third Dynasty.

Esna The site of a Ptolemaic temple, north of Aswan. Called Enit by the ancient Egyptians, it was a cult center for the god Khnum. Yearly the temple was flooded by the Nile and the silt deposited to such a degree that when the temple was finally excavated, the town of Esna was found to be built on top of it.

esoteric That which pertains to the mystery traditions. Esoteric wisdom is that which is gained by only a few. It is a hidden tradition of teaching.

etheric body The astral state, the body as light, a combination of heavenly cosmic gases. The etheric body may be the Egyptian *khu* or the *akh*, that which is invisible and immaterial, but immanent.

existential That which has to do with the individual's unique experience and isolation in the universe. Existentialism oftentimes defines experience as ultimately uncomprehendable and random, without divine intervention. Yet it affirms the empowerment of the individual through freedom of choice and responsibility for right action.

exoteric That which is public, external, and popular. As related to the religious and spiritual traditions, it implies the general and accepted understanding of common people.

eye of Horus The moon. As a talisman, the eye of Horus had healing properties, since it was said that Thoth healed Horus's eye when it was injured in the battle with Seth.

eye of Ra The sun.

faience Glassy beads imitative of turquoise. The beads were made of a quartz crystal base, covered with a vitreous alkaline compound with calcium silicate to provide the colors and glassy finish.

Faiyum (or Fayyum) The great oasis outside Cairo in the western desert. A salt lake, Lake Qarun, is nearby. The oasis is fed by a channel, called Joseph's Canal, and a water wheel that draws water from the Nile River to the oasis sixty-five miles away. It is one of the most beautiful and fertile areas in all of Egypt. In ancient times it was known as the site of the city Crocodilopolis (see entry), where the god Sobek was worshiped. It was also in nearby Hawara that the Twelfth Dynasty pharaoh Amenemhet III built his temple and labyrinth.

Faiyum A culture The Neolithic agricultural peoples who lived in the Lower Delta in the area of the Faiyum oasis circa 5000 B.C. They worshiped a cow goddess similar to Hathor.

fallahin A peasant worker.

false door An offering niche in a royal tomb that led into the *serdab* chamber, where a statue of the dead pharaoh, enlivened by its *ka*, was kept. Through this stone doorway the *ka* of the dead entered and exited to receive the gifts of food and libations left for it.

Field of Reeds Equivalent to the Greek Elysian Fields. After the trauma of the trial in the underworld and the treacherous journey through the gates of the Duat (see entry), the dead arrived at last in the Field of Reeds, where they lived happily, ate well, worked little, played much, and communed with the gods.

flabellum The sun shade of ostrich feathers. It often represented the shadow, or *khabit*.

flail The fly whisk or whip that was a symbol of authority. The flail was also used in the threshing of grain. Often seen in conjunction with the crook (see entry), it was associated with Osiris in his role as king of agriculture and animal husbandry.

forty-two Assessors The divine judges of the soul who assist Osiris in the halls of the underworld.

four sons of Horus The four gods who presided over the canopic jars (see entry) that held the internal organs of the mummy. They were Hâpy, the baboon-headed god of the lungs; Duametef, the jackal-headed god of the stomach; Imset, the human-headed god of the liver; and Qebehsenuf, the hawk-headed god of the small intestine.

galibeya The traditional dress of the Egyptian peasant. The galibeya is a long linen shift worn by both men and women.

Gerzeans Predynastic, Neolithic peoples who lived in Upper Egypt after the Amratians, from circa 3500 to 3000 B.C. They were known as potters, traders, and travelers. Kings Scorpion and Narmer were from the Gerzean culture.

Giza The western plateau just outside modern Cairo where the Sphinx is and the Great Pyramids were built in the Fourth Dynasty of the pharaohs Cheops, Chephren, and Mycerinus.

gnosis Intellectual and spiritual wisdom. A group of early Christians was known as the Gnostics. Many of their sacred texts on the teachings of Christ, some of which incorporate Egyptian influences, have been found in the Egyptian desert near Nag Hammadi.

golden ass Related to the Roman worship of the goddess Isis. The second-century Roman writer Lucius Apuleius penned a satirical documentation of the worship of Isis. In his tale a young man is turned into a donkey and not released from his torment until the goddess Isis takes pity on him. *The Golden Ass* recorded many of the intimate beliefs of the Greco-Roman worship of Isis.

Greco-Roman period That period of Egyptian history spanning the years 300 B.C. to A.D. 300 in which the Greeks, then the Romans, ruled Egypt. During this period the native ancient Egyptian religion was heavily influenced by the thinking of Greece and Rome.

haidit (also khabit) The shadow, or the Green *umbra*. The *haidit* freed itself at the moment of death and entered an entirely independent existence. We might think of it as the personal unconscious that joins the collective unconsciousness at death.

Hawara An ancient burial site in the Faiyum oasis where Amenemhet III built his labyrinth and pyramid circa 1800 B.C.

heb sed The festival of the pharaoh's spiritual and physical renewal. The *heb sed* festival marked the anniversary of the king's thirtieth year of reign. Thereafter, it was celebrated every three years. Rameses the Great attended more *heb sed* festivals than any other pharaoh.

heka Magic, the words of power. An important aspect of religious rites, *heka* was the prayer, invocation, and intonation of the sacred names of the gods. The rule of *heka* was that an effective magical prayer had to be spoken with the right words in the proper order, with the proper intonation, and with the proper intent. *Heka* was the way Ptah created the world. *Heka* was the way Isis healed Horus and raised Osiris from the dead. *Heka* was intimately linked with knowing the names of the gods, most of whose names were hidden, written without vowels, and therefore unpronounceable by anyone other than the priest-magician.

Heliopolis Chief cult center of the god Ra. Originally called Anu, it was called On, Aven, or Beth-Shemesh by the Hebrews. It was capital of the thirteenth nome of Lower Egypt.

Herakleopolis Called Ninsu by the ancient Egyptians, this ancient city was located on the edge of the Faiyum oasis. It was a popular cult center of a ram-headed god during the Ninth and Tenth Dynasties.

hermetic Pertaining to sacred writing or secret wisdom. The hermetic teachings of ancient Egypt are related to the god Thoth as the magician of words of power, as well as in later Ptolemaic dynasties to Hermes, messenger of the gods.

Hermopolis Cult center of the god Thoth and the site of the origin of the ogdoad (see entry). The Egyptians called their city Khemenu. It was a metropolis of the fifteenth nome of Upper Egypt.

Hierakonpolis Cult center of the hawk god Horus. This was the town of origin for the predynastic King Scorpion.

hieratic The cursive script form of the hieroglyph. Hieratic developed nearly simultaneously with the hieroglyph, but it was more commonly used in day-to-day writing. During the Late Period, the hieratic script became the language of priests, while the demotic (see entry) became the common language.

hieroglyph The sacred written language of the ancient Egyptians. Hieroglyphs, because they were developed by the god Thoth, were the words of gods and used primarily by the priests. They incorporate phonetic signs and symbolic (or determinative) signs, as well as internal puns and plays on words.

Hittites Nomadic, warlike Indo-European peoples who settled in eastern Asia Minor circa 2000 B.C.

holy of holies The inner sanctuary of a temple where the shrine of the neter was placed. Only the priests might go there to attend the needs of the god or goddess and to offer ritual food and prayer.

Horus name The first of the pharaoh's royal names. Rather than the birth name, the Horus name relates to the aspect of the hawk god that the pharaoh embodies.

hotep Peace and offerings.

Hyksos The princes of foreign lands. They were a mixed race of Semites and Hurrians who arrived in Egypt from the northeast circa 1633 B.C.

ichneumon Called the "pharaoh's rat," this African mongoose was known as a fierce fighter with keen powers of observation and rapid reflexes. Pharaohs often kept ichneumons in the palace as protection against poisonous asps. The ichneumon was so swift it could pounce upon a reared cobra before the snake had a chance to strike.

irit The eye.

ithyphallic The manifestations of neters who have erect penises, indicative of their fertilizing aspects. The god Min, the god Amun, and, on occasion, the goddess Sekhmet are depicted as ithyphallic.

Judgment Hall of Osiris (Hall of Judgment or Hall of Osiris) Located in the underworld, the hall where Osiris sits in judgment of the souls. The dead person is escorted into the hall by either Anubis or Horus and is presented to the goddess Ma'at and the forty-two Assessors (see entry). Here, his heart is weighed in the balance in the scales of *ma'at* (see entry). Here, he makes the negative confession (see entry) stating the sins he has not committed in his lifetime.

ka The creative and preserving power of life. The symbol of the *ka* was the arms upraised in prayer. Some people believe it to be similar to the double, or the doppelgänger. The *ka* is associated with one's image, the mental attributes, and personality. Differences of opinion exist over whether these represent an intellectual or astral state. It is possible that the *ka*'s true function is mind exerting a force on matter, the electrical charge of thought and desire. We are born with our *ka*, fashioned by Khnum on his potter's wheel. When we die, our *ka* lives on so long as it is offered sustenance.

el-Kab Cult center for the goddess Nekhebet, the town was also called Nekhen. It was the capital of the third nome of Upper Egypt.

kairos A Greek word meaning "the loaded time."

Karnak The great temple in Thebes, called The Throne of Two Lands. Built over a period of two hundred years by a multitude of pharaohs, it was the cult home of the god Amun.

khamsin The desert storms of Egypt, a destructive force of sand and wind, an aspect of the god Seth. These hot desert winds blow mainly in the spring.

khat The physical body, that part of the person which decays. Its symbol was a corpse and a fish.

Khemt The land of Egypt itself. It means "the fertile black soil." All things black were thought to be in the process of transformation and renewal. From *khemt* are derived the words "alchemy" and "chemistry."

khenti An African word, meaning "chief." The name of Osiris as Chief of the Hidden Place or Chief of the Dead is Khentamenti.

kheperi An ancient word meaning "to become." Its symbol was the dung beetle. (See also scarab.)

khu The shining intelligence, that part that is glorious and communes with the gods. Sometimes called "the magical body," it is a shimmering, translucent, intangible sheath around the body, perhaps akin to the aura. During one's lifetime it functions as part of the intuition. Rather than soul, it might be defined as spirit.

kings' list A compilation of names of the various rulers of Egypt in chronological order. Throughout the history of Egypt various scribes attempted to document the names of the pharaohs. The official lists occasionally deleted the names of unpopular rulers or those who had fallen from favor. Among these are the Abydos List, the Saqqara List, the Karnak List, and the Turin Canon. All of these lists were used by Manetho, the priest scribe of 30 B.C. who compiled a history of Egypt.

kites The goddesses Isis and Nephthys as they appear during the mourning of Osiris. The sisters transformed themselves into a pair of kites or hawks and flew round and round, lamenting.

knot of Isis (also *tet*) The knot of the goddess's girdle. Knots were connected with the magical power of binding and releasing. The *tet* resembled the *ankh* (see entry) with arms folded downward, rather than jutting out. It was said to represent the womb and tomb of the goddess, and it was red in color. A symbol of the hidden force of life, its powers were especially regenerative.

Kom Ombo Cult center of the dual worship of the gods Horus and Sobek. The city is located north of Aswan.

labyrinth The maze of the temple complex outside the pyramid at Hawara (see entry). The shafts, corridors, and shifting walls were designed to obscure the central burial site of the pharaoh.

ladder of Osiris A talisman of resurrective power. The ladder of Osiris assisted the god in his ascent from the underworld to his eternal kingdom within the body of the sky goddess Nut. It was said to have been made of iron, in other words, from the bones of Seth. In some texts the goddess Isis is depicted holding the ladder of Osiris.

Leotopolis Cult center of the worship of the lion god Aker. The ancient city existed near the area of modern Cairo.

lunar calendar The lunar calendar was the calendar of the goddess based on the phases of the moon. The cycle from new moon to new moon was completed every 29.5 days. Thus, after following the lunar calendar, the seasons began to shift. During the first dynasties of the Old Kingdom, the year consisted of only 360 days, or twelve months with thirty days each. Imhotep revised the calendar during the Third Dynasty to reflect 365 days a year by adding five epagomenal days (see entry).

Luxor The modern name of the ancient city of Opet, in the area of Thebes in Upper Egypt. The worship of the god Amun was predominant here. Prehistorically, Luxor was the site of the worship of the hippo goddess Tauret in her manifestation as birth mother. The Temple of Luxor was part of a longer complex that stretched to the Temple of Karnak and was connected by a double row of ram-headed sphinxes and lions. The annual feast of Opet was celebrated by both temples with a gala of ritual parades between the two temples in which the gods Amun, Mut, and Khonsu were honored.

Ma'adi The predynastic delta peoples who lived in the area of modern Cairo. They were descended from the Merimda culture. The Ma'adi lived circa 3400 to 3000 B.C., exhibiting a sedentary, agricultural lifestyle.

ma'at Truth, justice, and cosmic order as a principle. *Ma'at* was the spiritual ideal. Without it, life was impossible. Most Egyptians made a sincere effort to be honest, upright people. Their literature is filled with maxims and instructions for daily living. They believed *ma'at* was the true essence of creation, that it was a part of every human life, and that, at the end of life, *ma'at* was returned to the gods.

ma'aty The winged goddesses Isis and Nephthys, who protect Osiris in the underworld.

Macedonia An ancient kingdom of Greece that extended into parts of southeastern Europe, what is now Bulgaria, and the former Yugoslavia. Alexander the Great was a Macedonian king who conquered Persia, Greece, and, in 332 B.C., Egypt.

mammisi The "birth house." In these chapels to the goddess and her son the sacred rebirth of the god was annually celebrated. Later, the *mammisi* became associated with the birth of the pharaoh as the son of the goddess.

mastaba The stone tombs of the early Old Kingdom dynasties. These were flat-topped, private burial places with sloping walls resembling a bench. When piled one on top of the other, the *mastabas* gradually developed into the Step Pyramid shape.

Megiddo The ancient city northwest of Palestine where the Twenty-sixth Dynasty pharaoh Necho battled the Syrians and won. He later lost to Nebuchadnezzar of Babylon.

Meidum A city south of Memphis where Sneferu built his "bent" pyramid during the Third Dynasty.

Memphis Cult center of the worship of the god Ptah. The Egyptians called the city Het-Ptah-Ka, or The House of the Spirit of Ptah. It was a metropolis of the first nome of Lower Egypt and the original site of the delta capital. It was also called the City of the White Wall.

menat A roped, beaded necklace with a long, knobbed counterpoise that hangs down the wearer's neck. It was the favored jewelry of the goddess Hathor in her aspect as the goddess of love and fecundity. The *menat* was a symbol of joy, sexual power, and fertility. It was also imbued with healing powers.

Merimdan A culture of the western edge of the delta that flourished from circa 4300 to 3700 B.C. The Merimdans lived in pole-framed huts and were among the first agricultural peoples.

Meshwesh The Libyan people during the Nineteenth and Twentieth Dynasties of the New Kingdom. Twice the Egyptians defeated attacks by the Meshwesh peoples, but in 1070 B.C. they were overcome by these foreigners and Egypt endured a dynasty ruled by Libyans.

metanoia Literally, a "changed mind."

monotheism The worship of a sole god, creator of heaven and earth and all things therein. Aten worship, a short-lived phenomenon established during the reign of the pharaoh Akhenaten, was the only ancient Egyptian experiment with monotheism. The people of Egypt did not easily abandon the worship of the multitude of neters from whom they had received so many benefits and abundances. They incorporated as many gods as possible into their own polytheistic notions, and a jealous sole creator god simply did not fit their notion of creative imagination in nature.

muu dancers A professional group of male and female dancers and musicians.

At the grave sites in the Valley of the Kings they waited for the funerary procession, then danced in an elaborate ritual of drama, music, and song intended to duplicate the mourning of Isis and Nephthys for Osiris.

myrrh An aromatic gum resin exuded from myrrh trees that grew in the land of Punt. Myrrh was sacred to the goddess Hathor. It was highly prized, as its resin was used in the process of mummification, as perfume, and as incense in temple rituals.

mythopoeic thinking Thinking in terms of myth, the producing and making of myths. Recalling one's life and experience as a deepened fiction related to the "Great Story."

naos The shrine or tabernacle where the statue of the god or goddess was kept within the temple chapel.

Naqada A predynastic burial site north of Thebes where Narmer and several other kings of the First Dynasty were buried.

natron A natural mineral substance appearing in the valley and wadi near Cairo. A mixture of sodium bicarbonate and salt, it was used in embalming, in herbal medicines, and as a detergent. The use of natron was essential in temple rituals of purification.

neb All things.

necropolis The city of the dead. These burial sites were used by a number of pharaohs and royal families.

Nedyt An ancient Egyptian word meaning "to fall down." As a place, it symbolizes the land of the dead.

nefer Beautiful, good, complete, and perfect.

Negative Confession A part of the ritual of purification recited by the dead in the Judgment Hall of Osiris (see entry). The negative confession proclaimed the soul's innocence from all despicable and foul deeds, such as stealing, plundering, murdering, lying, cursing, and fornicating, as well as such minor but burdensome crimes as gossiping and eavesdropping. The forty-two Assessors (see entry) passed judgment on these nondeeds before the heart was weighed in the balance of Ma'at.

neter A god or goddess, a natural divine essence.

neterworld The residence of the gods. It is to this place that one goes after death. It is not envisioned as beneath the earth, but as a part of the heavens. The neterworld is the star-filled body of the sky goddess Nut, or the home of the hidden gods.

nilometer These pillars, slabs, or staired wells were used to measure the depth of the inundation at its height to determine the prosperity of the coming harvest and to estimate the expected future income from the yearly taxes.

nome Any state, province, or administrative area of ancient Egypt. The nomes originally began as independent tribal communities in predynastic Egypt, gradually merging with one another, then joining as a nation. Each nome had a capital city, an overseer, a sacred god, an animal, and an object associated with it. The nomarch was the ruler of that nome, a position that often passed through the successive generations of a single family. During times of strong central authority, the nomarch was of less importance and was usually appointed by the pharaoh.

Nubia The land beyond the first cataract of the Nile, in particular Wawat and Kush. Nubia marked the entrance into Africa, and trade with these peoples was essential for ivory, gold, amethyst, carnelian, wood, gums, oils, ostrich feathers, leopard skins, cattle, and exotic animals. Throughout their history the Egyptian people and the Nubians were intimately linked, but their relations were not always amiable.

obelisk A monolithic pillar with four sides, topped by a gilded, triangular apex. The Greek word means "spit." The earliest obelisks were much smaller and were equated with the *benben* (see entry) stones of the sun god Ra. In later times, large obelisks were erected within the temples to commemorate the festivals and activities of the pharaoh.

ogdoad The first eight gods of creation worshiped in Hermopolis. They existed in male and female pairs of darkness, infinite space, invisibility, and primeval waters. The male members of the ogdoad had the heads of frogs, while the female members bore the heads of serpents.

ontogeneic Relating to the development of the individual organism.

Opening of the Mouth A ceremony performed by the priest on behalf of the dead during the process of mummification so that the deceased has the power of speech and the magic of *heka* in the underworld.

Osirian mysteries The ceremonies held in honor of the god Osiris. In Abydos, the Osirian mysteries recounted the god's life and death, and his resurrection and ascension to the throne as lord of eternal life. The Osirian mysteries viewed the soul as seed and life as vegetation. They recalled the battles of the soul between Horus and Seth, the making of the spiritual warrior, as well as the transformative power of grief embodied in the goddess Isis.

ostraka Broken limestone tablets or potsherds. Because papyrus was expensive to make and highly prized, *ostraka* were used for writing practice by scribes.

ouroboros The serpent that bites its own tail—the cosmic cycle of life in which the end is also the beginning. The serpent illustrates how life feeds on itself.

oxyrhynchus The hideous fish that ate the phallus of Osiris and thus became a forbidden food. The capital of the nineteenth nome of Upper Egypt was also called Oxyrhynchus, and the remains of many Greek papyri were found there.

Palette of Narmer A schist palette that documents the victory of King Narmer of Upper Egypt over the delta peoples led by a chief named Washi. The palette documents the early worship of the solar hawk Horus and the cow goddess Hathor. Although the palette is primarily illustrative of the battle, the hieroglyphic names of the contestants prove that writing developed well before the First Dynasty.

passion play The reenactment of the dual deaths and loss of Osiris, and the lamentations of the goddesses Isis and Nephthys.

paut An ancient word meaning "the first time." The *paut* refers to the origin of creation, the appearance of the first gods.

Peak of the West The name of the highest hill in the Valley of the Kings, under which the pharaohs of the New Kingdom were buried. It was understood to represent the primeval hillock that arose from the waters of Nun at the beginning of creation. It was also said to be an embodiment of the goddess Hathor, who was called Lady of the Peak.

per-a'a "Pharaoh" in ancient Egyptian, originally meaning the "house of the king."

peret (also *proyet*) The season of the sowing (or spring). Peret was the second of three agricultural seasons in ancient Egypt following the inundation. During this time the plants were set. Peret began around the end of November or the beginning of December.

persea tree A sacred tree of ancient Egypt, perhaps an avocado. It was said to be the sacred tree in Heliopolis (see entry) beneath which the serpent Apep was slain by Ra in the form of a cat.

Philae An island south of Aswan. Philae is the mythic site where Isis returned each year to await the resurrection of Osiris at the annual inundation. When he appeared, she heralded his coming by rising as the star Sothis. The temple of Isis located here was the last bastion of the Egyptian religion.

phylogenic Pertaining to the historical origin of the group or tribe, as opposed to the growth of the individual.

polyphrenic Literally, "multimindedness." Polyphrenic thinking is that which exists on many levels at different times and merges the actual, the mythical, the psychological, and the spiritual states.

predynastic Any of the organized but isolated cultures that arose in ancient Egypt before the dawn of recorded history prior to the unification of Egypt by King Narmer around 3000 B.C.

prenomen This was the first name within the king's cartouche (see entry), usually the name by which historians recognize the pharaoh.

priests The scribes, magicians, and servants of the neter (see entry) in the temple. In ancient art priests and priestesses were identified by their leopard skin robes. The Egyptians had various kinds of priests. The *wab* priest's function was purification of the temple for the rites, and the *kheri-heb* priest was the lector. The *heri-shesheta* headed up the mystery rituals. The *hem-ka* priest performed the funerary rites; the *hem-neter* priest acted as prophet; while the *ka* priest brought the ritual offerings to the tombs of the dead. The high priest of the temple was known as the *shem* priest. *Ounits* were "priests of the hours."

primeval The original time, an era that exists at or just before creation.

primordial The first appearance, the original occurrence of an entity from which all else sprung.

psychospiritual The way in which the mind and spirit work together to interpret experience.

psychostasis The soul in the balance, the weighing of the heart.

Ptolemaic Dating from the time of the Greek rulers of ancient Egypt circa 300 B.C. Most of these rulers bore the name Ptolemy.

Punt The mythical homeland of the goddess Hathor and her attendants. Punt was a tropical district to the south and east of Egypt. It may have been part of the Arabian peninsula or part of the coast of Somalia.

pylon The gateway into the temple or into the halls of the underworld.

pyramid The tomb of the Old Kingdom pharaohs that developed from the early *mastaba* (see entry) tomb. The pyramid was a four-sided structure that duplicated the primeval hill and was linked with the worship of the sun god Ra. The entrance and exit faced north, situated around the circumpolar stars called the *akhakh*, or Imperishable Souls. Within each pyramid lay the king's central chamber, which faced west, the land of the dead. Few pyramids have been found with the bodies intact, and it is believed by many that some pyramids, the Great Pyramid in particular, may have been used purely in a ritual enactment of death and rebirth.

Pyramid Age The Old Kingdom, especially the Third, Fourth, and Fifth Dynasties, during which the majority of the pharaohs built their pyramids. The Pyramid Age is synonymous with the golden age of ancient Egypt.

Pyramid Texts The first occurrence of hieroglyphic texts inscribed on the tombs of the dead. The best-known Pyramid Text, found in Saqqara, is that of the Fifth Dynasty pharaoh Unas. The Pyramid Texts were chiseled in stone and were the precursors to the later Book of the Dead, which was written on papyri.

Qadesh Site of the battle of Rameses II against the Hittites in Syria circa 1290 B.C. The illustrious battle was recorded on the walls of the Temple of Luxor as the poem of Pentaur. In fact, however, Rameses II nearly lost the battle.

Rameseside era The Twentieth Dynasty of Egypt. The entire dynasty was peopled by pharaohs named Rameses. In fact, Rameses III was the only son and heir of the Nineteenth Dynasty pharaoh Rameses the Great.

ren The name of a person. It was possible for the name to be as immortal a part of a man as his *ka*. All people had secret names, and those who knew a god's secret name were said to have his power.

Restau The hidden passages in the tomb that lead from life in this world to life in the next.

Rosetta Stone The large black basalt stela found in 1799 by one of Napoleon's men in the delta city of Rosetta. The stela itself is of little importance, since it commemorates only a minor activity of one of the Ptolemaic rulers. But because it was written in three languages—hieroglyphic (see hieroglyph), demotic (see entry), and Greek, it enabled the French scholar Champollion to crack the hieroglyphic code.

sa A rolled shepherd's shelter of papyrus. The *sa* symbolized protection from the chaotic elements.

sahu The spiritual body that emerged after death, the spiritual germ. The *sahu* exists in closest proximity to the neters (see entry). Released through the process of mummification, it would live for all eternity. It was equivalent to the potency released in the seed as the seed dies and the plant is born.

Sais Cult center of worship of the goddess Neith. The Egyptians called this metropolis of the fifth nome of Lower Egypt Sa.

Saqqara The desert plateau overlooking Memphis where King Djoser of the Third Dynasty built his mortuary temple and Step Pyramid. Saqqara has a large necropolis used consistently throughout the history of Egypt. The serapeum to the north was the burial site of the Apis bulls during the Greco-Roman period (see entry). The large festival temple and courtyard were the site of the *heb sed* (see entry) festivals for the renewal of the king.

sarcophagus Literally, "eater of the flesh." It was the stone receptacle for the mummified remains of the deceased. The pyramids and tombs were built around sarcophagi. They were used during the Old and New Kingdoms.

scales of *ma'at* In the underworld, the balance in which the heart of the deceased was weighed against the feather of *ma'at* (see entry). If the heart was light and had committed no wrong, harbored no ill will, or remembered no evil thoughts, then the deceased was allowed to enter the Judgment Hall of Osiris (see entry), where he or she was given eternal life. If the heart was heavy, it was thrown to the monster goddess Ammit, who devoured the person's heart and soul.

scarab The sacred dung beetle was the image of Kheperi. As a talisman, scarabs were symbols of transformation and self-generation.

sebbakh The fertile soil found in mounds of rubble marking ancient sites.

sekhem Literally, "power" or "form." This characteristic was a manifestation of divine power and the vital principle of the human being. It was a passionate power related to strong emotional states, particularly protection and love, but also (wrongly used) violence and avarice.

senet An ancient board game, similar to chess. It was based on the travels of the soul as Osiris through the underworld. The difficulty was in reaching the end of the game without being overcome by the Seth game pieces.

serdab chamber The room behind the false door in which the statue of the dead pharaoh was kept. The *serdab* chamber had a slit in the wall through which the eyes of the statue might look out and observe its own funerary rituals. These statues were the dwelling place of the *ka* (see entry) or spirit of the dead, which received the food and drink offered it.

shadow As much a spiritual part of a man as his body and soul. The shadow appeared as a black outline of a person seen leaving the tomb, accompanied by the *ba*. (See also *haidit*.)

shemu The season of the harvest (or summer). Shemu was the third of the three agricultural seasons in ancient Egypt before the inundation resumed. Harvest began at the end of March or the beginning of April.

sistrum A musical instrument that was the divine emblem of Hathor. The sistrum was an essential part of the dance ritual. It was a sticklike object with a U-shaped frame and rows of small metal disks that made a "shushing" sound when shaken. The head of Hathor was often depicted on the base of the frame. It was said to drive away snakes and darkness.

solar barge The boat of the sun god Ra. As it sailed through heaven, it was called the *mandet*; as it passed through the underworld at night, it was called the *mesektet*. The solar barge carried the sun and was made of gold. Solar barges were found in burial sites for the benefit of the pharaoh in his neterworld (see entry) manifestation as Ra.

Sothic calendar The calendar that began the true New Year's day festival with the helical rising of the Dog Star, Sirius, on July 17. As an aspect of the goddess Isis, this star was called Sothis. The day marked the beginning of the inundation and was celebrated by the festival of Hathor. The Sothic calendar was more reliable than the solar or lunar calendars (see entry). The lunar calendar lost five days every year, whereas the solar calendar lost one year every 1,460 years. Because the helical rising of the Sothic star was always predictable and always heralded the inundation that brought the planting season in its wake, it was used as the official religious and state calendar.

sphinx Statues of crouching lions with the head of either a man or a ram. The ram-headed sphinx was the symbol of the god Amun. The human-headed sphinx was the symbol of the sun god, either Ra or Horus of the horizon. The Great Sphinx on the Giza plateau was originally thought to be the construction of the pharaoh Chephren, but recent excavations suggest that it is much older than originally thought, apparently predynastic. The Sphinx as an oracle was said to have predicted the reign of Thutmose IV in the Eighteenth Dynasty. Periodically, the Sphinx was covered over by sand and disappeared. It is amazing that Herodotus, who traveled extensively throughout Egypt and who marveled at the Great Pyramid, failed to mention the Sphinx. Apparently, it was covered in sand when he was there.

Sumerian The ancient Near Eastern civilization that developed in Mesopotamia along the Euphrates River. It preceded the Babylonian and Assyrian cultures and arose circa 3000 B.C. The goddess Inanna and the god Dumuzi were similar agricultural deities to the Egyptian neters Isis and Osiris. The Sumerian written language was cuneiform (see entry).

sycamore Sacred tree of the goddess Hathor. It grew at the edge of the desert near Memphis. The souls of the dead were believed to take wing and rest there in its branches. In the underworld, Hathor appeared in the form of a sycamore and offered the dead a cool drink of water.

tachyon A hypothetical particle that travels faster than the speed of light.

Tanis Cult site for the worship of the god Set. A nome capital of the eastern delta, Tanis was the site at which Hyksos and the Hittites entered Egypt.

Tasian The predynastic, seminomadic culture of the Neolithic African peoples living in Upper Egypt circa 5000 B.C. The Tasians preceded the Amratians by about five hundred years.

Tel el Amarna (also Akhenaten) The city built by the Eighteenth Dynasty pharaoh Akhenaten exclusively for the worship of the sun god Aten. Tel el

Amarna was located along the cliffs of a desert plain north of Thebes and Assiut. It was reputed to be a large center for scribes and artists, who had their own villas. The palace of Nefertiti, the queen, was also said to contain beautiful gardens. Called the City of the Solar Disk, it lasted little more than two decades and was destroyed by the pharaoh Horemheb, who attempted to wipe out any memory of the monotheistic heresy.

Thebes Cult site of the worship of Amun. This capital city of the New Kingdom is now the modern city of Luxor, located halfway between Cairo and Aswan. In ancient times it was the "great hundred-gated city of the gods" with at least two large temple complexes, an abundance of mortuary complexes, and two huge necropolises, as well as all the attendant shops necessary to keep the priests and royal retinue busy. Originally it was the site of the city of Twaset.

theocentric That which centers on god as its prime concern. The study of cosmogony (see entry) is theocentric; theocentric thinking is that which continually examines the divine state in all things.

Thinite dynasty The early Old Kingdom pharaohs who arose before the Third Dynasty. Not much is known about these archaic warrior kings who were said to have been natives of the ancient city of Thinis, near Abydos.

transmigration of souls The passing of the soul into another body. The ancient Egyptians believed that the soul moved from one state to the next. The idea is akin to Eastern notions of reincarnation, but the Egyptians believed that the soul does not always move from one visible form to another. The certainty of the transmigration of souls allowed the ancient Egyptians to compile their massive Book of the Dead, filled with words of power, incantations, food for the afterlife, and so on.

transsubstantiation In essence, transformation. Transsubstantiation deals with changing from one state to another, although the movement may not affect the physical composition of the first form. In Christian terms the bread and wine are transsubstantiated into the body and blood of Christ. To the ancient Egyptians, transsubstantiation was a movement from the mortal to the immortal, from the physical to the spiritual state.

triad Similar to the Christian trinity. The Egyptian triad usually consisted of male and female parents and a holy child. Among the better known triads were Amun, Mut, and Khonsu in Thebes (see entry); Hathor, Horus, and Ihy in Dendera and Edfu (see entries); Khnum, Satis, and Anuket in Elephantine (see entry); and Ptah, Sekhmet, and Nefertum in Memphis (see entry).

underworld The term refers to Ament as it appears as the land in the west, and to Duat as it appears as the Judgment Hall of Osiris (see entries), as well as to the necessary darkened channel through which the solar barge (see entry) must pass at night. It varies from the neterworld (see entry), since the neterworld was a realm of the gods alone and was believed to lie above rather than below Egypt.

uraeus Meaning "she who rears up." The *uraeus* was the royal cobra, the protector of the pharaoh, who spat fire at his enemies. A symbol of the *uraeus* appeared on the headdresses of the king, usually in conjunction with the head of a vulture, manifestations of the goddesses Wadjet and Nekhebet.

ushabti A magical figure placed in the tomb, which could be called to life to perform the bidding of the pharaoh in the underworld (see entry).

utchat (also *wedjat*) The sacred eye, a healing talisman.

Valley of the Kings The site of the elaborate burial tombs of the pharaohs of the New Kingdom, located in the western desert hills across from the temples of Amun in Thebes. The Valley of the Kings is located directly beneath the Peak of the West (see entry). The pharaohs and their royal wives were buried separately during the New Kingdom era. The burial ground of the queens lies on the opposite side of the hill and is called the Valley of the Queens.

vizier Equivalent to the prime minister for the pharaoh. The chief vizier often became the next pharaoh if the king died without an heir. Many viziers became the initiators of later dynasties.

wadi In Arabic, a dry riverbed. This was often the only passage through and into the desert hills to the east of Egypt. Wadi Hammamaat led from Coptos to the Red Sea. Wadi Maghara on the Sinai Peninsula was the site of extensive copper and malachite mining.

waz scepter A talisman of uncertain origin. The top of the staff was designed as the head of a jackal, and the bottom was two-pronged. It appeared as a symbol of dominion and was sometimes seen as a support for the sky.

weighing of the heart See scales of *ma'at*.

words of power See *heka*.

Map of Ancient Egypt

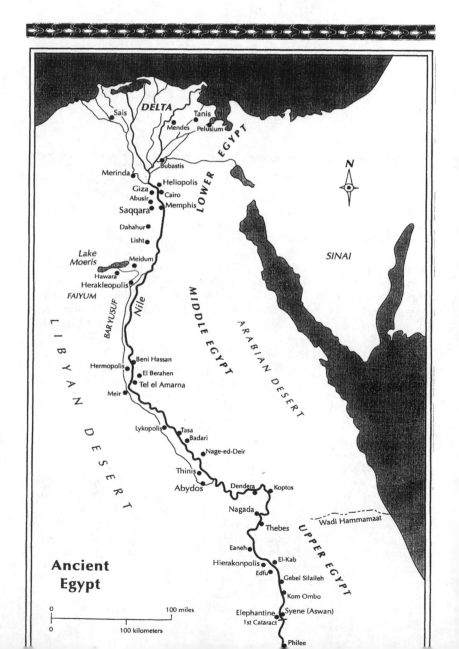

APPENDIX D

Historical Overview with Principal Kings and Queens of Each Dynasty

Prehistoric Egypt   c. 10,000–3150 B.C.

Human settlement appeared near Luxor about two million years ago. These Paleolithic peoples employed crude stone tools. During this time Egypt was said to have been ruled by gods and demigods. Around 7000 B.C., the Neolithic peoples evolved from hunting and gathering tribes to agricultural societies. By 5000 B.C., during the time of the first building of the temple at Jericho, the Faiyum A culture arose in the Nile Delta, marked by simple pottery and basket weaving. By 4000 B.C. the Upper Egyptian Badarian culture had spread from Nubia. Meanwhile, in Mesopotamia, the Sumerian and later Babylonian cultures gained prominence. The Badarians gave rise to the Amratian and Gerzean cultures, which preceded the early Thinite dynasties of Egypt.

Dates	South (near Luxor)	North (delta and oasis)
5000–4500 B.C.	Tasian and Badarian	Merimda and Faiyum A
4500–3600 B.C.	Amratian (Naqada I)	
3500–3000 B.C.	Gerzean (Naqada II)	Ma'adi

Thinite Dynasties (or Predynastic)   c. 3150–3050 B.C.

Rapid development in writing and metal working marked this era. Multiculturalism was evident, including influences from Africa and Mesopotamia. Civilization made huge leaps during this time as foreign peoples moved into Egypt, bringing their culture with them. Meanwhile, the Sumerians in nearby Mesopotamia were establishing the first dynasty of Ur. Also, northern and southern Egypt were in contact with each other, each having its own regent. The dates and names of these kings are uncertain. The central authority of the lower delta peoples lay in Buto, while the Upper Egyptian capital was at Hierakonpolis. King Scorpion of Hierakonpolis led a campaign to join Upper and Lower Egypt. Toward the end of this period, Upper and Lower Egypt were indeed united by King Narmer. Memphis became the capital city. (The names of the most important rulers are in **bold face**.)

King Scorpion
King Narmer

First Dynasty (Old Kingdom Begins)   c. 3100–2890 B.C.

After a time of war, Upper and Lower Egypt united under Menes. It is possible that Menes and Narmer are the same person, or that Menes and Aha are the same. Nevertheless, a united Egypt was brought about by Narmer, an Upper Egyptian king who conquered the delta peoples. He ruled from Abydos, where the first two dynasties kept their capital, but he also established a royal city at Memphis.

Menes
Aha
Djer
Djet
Den
Anedjib
Semerkhet
Qaa

Second Dynasty   c. 2890–2686 B.C.

All pharaohs from Menes on associated themselves with the god Horus. However, for reasons unknown, Peribsen associated himself with the god Seth. His mortuary complex was built at Abydos.

Hotepsekhemwy
Raneb
Nynetjer
Peribsen
Khasekhem

Third Dynasty   c. 2686–2613 B.C.

The Third Dynasty marked the true beginning of the glory of Old Kingdom Egypt, beginning primarily with the pharaoh Djoser. Art and architecture flourished. Djoser moved his capital city from Abydos to Memphis, near Cairo. On the nearby plains of Saqqara, he and the brilliant architect Imhotep built the first Step Pyramid and a large temple complex. During the end of the pharaoh Huni's reign, the famed scribe and philosopher Kagemni wrote his maxims.

Sanakhte
Djoser
Sekhemkhet
Khaba
Huni

Fourth Dynasty   c. 2613–2494 B.C.

This era was known as the Pyramid Age. During this period many pyramids were built on the plains of Giza and Dahshur. Sneferu inaugurated a period of extensive military and artistic projects. He built his pyramid at Meidum and waged campaigns against both the Libyans and Nubians, who were threatening Egypt's borders. Sneferu also established trade on the Mediterranean. His son, Khufu (or Cheops), built the Great Pyramid at Giza, followed by the second pyramid built by Cheops' son, Khafre (or

Chephren), and the third, smaller pyramid by Menkaure (or Mycerinus). The Sphinx was originally thought to have been built by Chephren as part of his mortuary complex, but recent findings indicate that the structure existed long before the pyramids were erected.

Sneferu
Khufu (Cheops)
Djedefre
Khafre (Chephren)
Menkaure (Mycerinus)
Shepseskaf

Fifth Dynasty   c. 2494–2345 B.C.

During this period the pyramids built at Abusir were of shoddy construction; however, elaborate sun temples and mortuary temples were built. The Fifth Dynasty began the reign of pharaohs associated with the sun god Ra. Apparently unrelated to the pharaohs of the Fourth Dynasty, they were the children of a high priestess in the cult of Ra at Heliopolis. Around this same time, the early Minoan culture in nearby Greece was established. At Saqqara, pharaoh Unas constructed his pyramid tomb, inscribing the walls for the first time with the hieroglyphic texts that became known as the Pyramid Texts, a precursor to the Book of the Dead.

Userkaf
Sahure
Neferirkare Kakai
Shepseskare Isi
Neferefre
Neuserre
Menkauhor
Djedkare Isesi
Unas

Sixth Dynasty   c. 2345–2181 B.C.

Teti, the first pharaoh of the Sixth Dynasty, was apparently unrelated to Unas, but had married his daughter. Teti was murdered by his own guards. His son Pepi I was a great military strategist, but like his father, his domestic instincts were not always reliable. His first wife vanished after becoming involved in an intrigue to overthrow him. Internal strife, the rise of local chieftains, and unnaturally low Nile floods made this era precarious. Art and building skills diminished, even though trade was extended into the Upper Nile and to Syria.

Pepi II attained the throne when he was but six years old. His mother, Ankhnesmeryre, coruled. Pepi II was known to have sent trading expeditions to Nubia and Punt, especially to obtain a pygmy for his entertainment. Ptahhotep, a scribe of Pepi II, looked back from the late Sixth Dynasty and called the Fifth Dynasty a golden age, the likes of which would never be seen again.

Teti
Userkare
Pepi I

Merenre
Pepi II

Seventh through Tenth Dynasties
(First Intermediate Period) c. 2181–2040 B.C.
Central authority collapsed. Several regional monarchies overlapped, but
the kings of the Seventh, Eighth, Ninth, Tenth, and the beginning of the
Eleventh Dynasties were ineffectual, ephemeral, and relatively unknown.
It is possible that the Seventh and Eighth Dynasties continued to rule at
Memphis; but by the Ninth Dynasty, the capital city had been moved to
Herakleopolis. The only true art of this period was a flowering of literature
during the reign of King Khety III, who penned the famous ethical instruc-
tions for his son, Merikare.

Ninth Dynasty c. 2160–2130 B.C.
Khety I
Khety II

Tenth Dynasty c. 2130–2040 B.C.
Khety III
Merikare

Eleventh Dynasty (Middle Kingdom Begins) c. 2133–1991 B.C.
During this period Mentuhotep established Thebes as the capital city of
Egypt. The princes of Upper Egypt regained control of Egypt. Massive for-
eign trade efforts were initiated, arts and literature again flourished, the
country extended its borders, and building was resumed.
Mentuhotep I
Sehertowy Inyotef I
Wahankh Inyotef II
Nakhtnebtepnefer Inyotef III
Mentuhotep II
Mentuhotep III
Mentuhotep IV

Twelfth Dynasty c. 1991–1786 B.C.
The Twelfth Dynasty represented a return to prosperity. Sesostris III ex-
panded his land holdings far into Nubia and consolidated the delta land.
He constructed his pyramid at Dahshur. His son, Amenemhet III, built the
famed pyramid and labyrinth at Hawara. Although pyramids and large
complexes were still being built, Egypt experienced periods of internal
strife. Extensive effort was put into the arts and crafts; for example, jewelry
making reached a pinnacle.
Amenemhet I
Sesostris I
Amenemhet II
Sesostris II
Sesostris III

Amenemhet III
Amenemhet IV
Queen Sobekneferu

Thirteenth Dynasty (Second Intermediate Period)   c. 1786–1633 B.C.
Once again, centralized government broke down, especially during the reign of Sobekhotep III. Nubia withdrew from Egypt and was established as an independent state.
Sobekhotep III
Neferhotep
Mentuhotep

Fourteenth Dynasty   c. 1786–1603 B.C.
Many ephemeral and regional kings arose during this period; some ruled for only a few months. Few names are recorded. Internal strife was rampant, and Egypt was unable to resist the arrival of foreign kings. The Hyksos invaded around 1633 B.C. During this same period the Babylonian Empire fell.

Fifteenth Dynasty (Hyksos)   c. 1674–1567 B.C.
Called the shepherd kings, the Hyksos were probably of mixed Semitic and Hurrian origin. They moved quickly into the delta from the Near East and eventually took over all of Egypt. Little is known of this period, but the Hyksos were responsible for introducing the horse-drawn chariot to Egypt.
Mayebre Sheshi
Meruserre Yakubher
Seuserenre Khyan
Apophis I
Apophis II

Sixteenth and Seventeenth Dynasties   c. 1684–1552 B.C.
In Palestine the tribe of Abraham rose to importance, and Hammurabi ruled the Babylonian Empire. By the end of the Seventeenth Dynasty, Theban princes ruled Egypt, primarily as vassals of the Hyksos. However, several strong princes resolved to return Egypt to its rightful owners. In 1560 B.C. Seqenenre and his sons, Kamose and Ahmose, rebelled against the Hyksos king Apophis I. In 1552 B.C. Kamose defeated the Hyksos; one year later, Ahmose expelled the last of the intruders from the delta.
Nubkheperre Inyotef VII
Senakhtenre I (the Elder)
Seqenenre II (the Brave)
Kamose

Eighteenth Dynasty (New Kingdom)   c. 1551–1320 B.C.
Native rulership gradually returned. The empire again prospered, began extensive trade, and expanded its territories. Riches abounded as enormous tributes from other countries flowed in. A kind of Renaissance emerged, with Egypt as a powerful kingdom. The temples that had fallen into disrepair during the Second Intermediate Period and the reign of the Hyksos were restored.

The necropolis of the New Kingdom pharaohs was established in the Valley of the Kings on the western bank of Thebes. Queen Hatshepsut, wife of Thutmose II and royal heir, defied tradition and kept the throne rather than relinquish the royal title to the son of Thutmose II by a minor wife. Nevertheless, after her suspicious death, Thutmose III succeeded her as pharaoh and his influence extended through Syria into western Asia. At this time a predominance of Asian influences appeared in the art.

Amenophis (or Amenhotep) IV became known as the heretic king after he refused to worship the god of his fathers, Amun, and began a monotheistic religion devoted to Aten. He changed his name to Akhenaten and moved the capital city to Tel el Amarna. His reign lasted less than twenty years. After a brief rule by the boy king Tutankhamen, the royal line was lost. By the close of this dynasty, the Hittites were rampaging through Syria and threatening Egypt's possessions.

Ahmose I
Amenophis (Amenhotep) I
Thutmose I
Thutmose II
Queen Hatshepsut
Thutmose III
Amenophis (Amenhotep) II
Thutmose IV
Amenophis (Amenhotep) III
Amenophis (Amenhotep) IV (Akhenaten)
Smenkhare
Tutankhamen
Ay
Horemheb

Nineteenth Dynasty   c. 1320–1200 B.C.
The New Kingdom's material prosperity continued. Grand building plans were begun and war campaigns waged. The boundaries of Egypt were extended. The dynasty opened with two strong rulers, Seti I and his son, Rameses II. Seti returned briefly to the worship of the warrior god Seth. He campaigned against the Libyans, the Syrians, and the Hittites.

His son, Rameses II, continued to wage war against the Hittites, narrowly winning the Battle of Qadesh. He reigned sixty-seven years, but several weak and ineffectual rulers ended the dynasty, turning over their thrones in rapid succession. Although scholars have long debated the exact dates, we now believe that the Exodus of the Hebrews from Egypt took place during the reign of Rameses' son, Merenptah, or soon thereafter. The priesthood exerted a heavy influence on these pharaohs, disturbing their authority. In Greece the Trojan War was fought, while in Palestine, King Solomon reigned.

Rameses I
Seti I
Rameses II
Merenptah

Sethos II (Seti II)
Amenmesse
Siptah
Queen Twosret

Twentieth Dynasty   c. 1200–1085 B.C.

Although unrest and poverty plagued the country, Rameses III continued to make elaborate and expensive gifts to the gods, thereby increasing the wealth of the priests of Amun in Thebes. After his murder, his successors fell under the influence of decadent priests. Marked by a loss of funds and gradual internal breakdown, the Rameseside era became a time of increasing unrest. Tombs were robbed with impunity.

Sethnakhte
Rameses III
Rameses IV
Rameses V
Rameses VI
Rameses VII
Rameses VIII
Rameses IX
Rameses X
Rameses XI

Twenty-first through Twenty-fourth Dynasties (Third Intermediate Period) c. 1085–712 B.C.

The Third Intermediate Period was again a time of unstable rulership. Control of Egypt was passed from one usurper to another. The priests of Amun and the native delta rulers battled for control of Egypt for nearly 150 years before the invasion of the Libyan chiefs, who ousted them both and ruled the country for nearly two centuries. Following that time, the Nubians ousted the Libyans in what appeared to have been a battle between Upper and Lower Egyptians for authority. Thereafter authority alternated between Nubia, Sais, and Thebes.

Twenty-firs Dynasty   c. 1085–945 B.C.

Around 1085 B.C. new rulers in the delta attempted to overthrow the priests of Amun in Thebes. Their attempts were weak and ineffectual. The priesthood of Thebes remained a kind of mini-reign and began to usurp the central authority

<u>Rulers of Tanis</u>	<u>Priests of Thebes</u>
Smendes	Herihor
Amenemnisu	Paiankh
Psusennes I	Pinudjem I
Amenope	Masaherta
Siamun	Menkheperre
Osorkon I	Pinudjem II
Psusennes II	

Twenty-second Dynasty (Libyan) c. 945–715 B.C.

Libyan chieftains of the Meshwesh tribe settled in the delta. They assumed control, ruling first from Bubastis, then from Tanis. Sheshonq I (the biblical Shishak) captured Jerusalem and plundered the Temple of Solomon. The chieftains divided the rulership into local principalities.

Sheshonq I
Osorkon II
Takelot I
Sheshonq II
Osorkon III
Takelot II
Sheshonq III
Pami
Sheshonq IV
Osorkon IV

Twenty-third and Twenty-fourth Dynasties c. 818–712 B.C.

By 878 B.C. the Nubian kings had assumed control of Upper Egypt, ruling from both Nubia and Thebes. Around 730 B.C., during the Twenty-third Dynasty, Tefnakhte, prince of Sais, attempted to regain control of the delta, but he was defeated by King Piankhi of Egypt. Tefnakhte's son, Bocchoris, regained control of the delta for a mere three years.

Pedubastis I
Osorkon V
Peftjauwybast
Tefnakhte
Bakenrenef (Bocchoris)

Twenty-fifth Dynasty (Late Period) c. 747–656 B.C.

Egypt was now ruled by Nubian kings. The last delta usurper, King Bocchoris, was overthrown by King Sabakon of Kush, son of Kashta. The Nubians preserved much of the ancient culture, although they were strict rulers, insisting on the validity of their native right to rule.

Piankhi
Sabakon
Shebitku
Taharqa
Tanutamun

Twenty-sixth Dynasty (Saite) c. 664–525 B.C.

The Nubians battled with the delta kings. Eventually Psammetichus of Sais drove Tanutamun back to Ethiopia. Again Ethiopians and Nubians were separated from Egypt. As trade with Greece arose, Egypt enjoyed another brief period of prosperity and flourishing art. But greed at home and war in the Near East disturbed the national harmony. Necho II engaged in a successful battle against the Syrians at Megiddo but was conquered by Nebuchadnezzar of Babylon. The Egyptians lost their outposts in Syria. Naucratis was ceded to the Greeks, and at last Psammetichus III was defeated by the Persian king Cambyses.

Psammetichus I
Necho II
Psammetichus II
Apries
Amasis
Psammetichus III

Twenty-seventh Dynasty (Persian)   c. 525–404 B.C.
Although Persian kings succeeded the native rulers, there was no interruption of the national religion. King Darius built a canal from the Nile to the Red Sea. The Greeks attempted to assist the native Egyptians in overthrowing the Persians, but to little avail. During this time the Greek historian Herodotus visited Egypt.
Cambyses
Darius I
Xerxes
Artaxerxes I
Darius II
Artaxerxes II

Twenty-eighth Dynasty   c. 404–399 B.C.
A brief dynasty of one native Egyptian king, Amyrtaeus of Sais, who maintained his authority for little more than five years.

Twenty-ninth Dynasty   c. 399–380 B.C.
Increasingly weak Egyptian kings relied on Greek support.
Nepherites I
Psammuthis
Hakoris
Nepherites II

Thirtieth Dynasty   c. 380–343 B.C.
This was the last native Egyptian dynasty before the Greeks took total control. A strong ruler, Nectanebo, rebuilt the temples as far as Philae. Campaigns into foreign lands, however, led to disaster. The last native ruler, Nectanebo II, who was said to be a great magician, foresaw the ruin of Egypt in one of his oracles. After his vision, he fled to Ethiopia, leaving Egypt vulnerable. Invading Persians plundered its temples.
Nectanebo I
Teos
Nectanebo II

Persian Kings   c. 343–332 B.C.
The Persians briefly controlled Egypt but were ousted by the Greeks.
Artaxerxes III
Arses
Darius III

Macedonian Kings   c. 332–305 B.C.

After conquering Palestine in 332 B.C., the Macedonian king Alexander the Great went on to conquer Egypt. He appeared at the temple of Amun, where the oracle declared him a divine ruler, son of the god. He founded the delta city of Alexandria and developed the area as a vast commercial site. After his death, Macedonian rule quickly degenerated. Alexander's son (Alexander II) attempted to help Alexander's half-witted brother, Philip, rule the country, but his efforts failed.

Alexander the Great
Philip Arrhidaeus
Alexander II

The Ptolemies   c. 305–30 B.C.

Art, commerce, and personal wealth revived under the Ptolemies, who were Egyptian-born Greek rulers. In 280 B.C. Ptolemy II engaged the scribe-priest Manetho to pen a history of Egypt from its beginning. The Ptolemies waged extensive and expensive rebuilding campaigns to preserve the ancient temples. Nevertheless, their thinking was largely influenced by Greece. The heirs fought among themselves and three centuries were marked by intrigue, controversy, and greed. Eventually, they relied more heavily on Roman support, until at last Rome easily overpowered the dynasty in an intrigue with Queen Cleopatra, which has gone down in history as one of the most sordid stories of corrupt love and power

Ptolemy I (Soter I)
Ptolemy II (Philadelphus)
Ptolemy III (Euergertes I)
Ptolemy IV (Philopator)
Ptolemy V (Epiphanes)
Ptolemy VI (Philometor)
Ptolemy VII (Neo Philopator)
Ptolemy VIII (Euergertes II)
Ptolemy IX (Soter II, Lathyros)
Ptolemy X (Alexander I)
Ptolemy XI (Alexander II)
Ptolemy XII (Neos Dionysos, Auletes)
Cleopatra VII (Philopator)

Roman Emperors   c. 30 B.C.– A.D. 323

Roman rule was harsh. However, the ancient religion became popular in Rome, and the practice of it in Egypt continued uninterrupted. Under Caligula, violent disturbances between the Greeks and the Jews rocked Alexandria. During Nero's reign, Egypt became a center of trade between Rome and India. In the second century A.D., Lucius Apuleius wrote *The Golden Ass*, which described the rites of Isis in Rome.

Augustus
Tiberius
Claudius
Nero

Vespasian
Titus
Domitian
Nerva
Trajan
Hadrian
Antoninus Pius
Marcus Aurelius
Septimus Severus
Geta and Caracalla
Diocletian

Byzantine Emperors   c. A.D. **323–642**
With the rise of Constantine the Great, the Christian emperors banned
the worship of the neters. The temple at Philae continued the worship of
Isis until it was closed during the reign of Justinian. The earliest Coptic
translations of the Bible were done during this period. In A.D. 622 Mo-
hammed fled from Mecca to Medina, beginning the chronology of Muslim
influence in Egypt.
Constantine
Theodosius
Justinian

Festival Calendar of
the Ancient Egyptians*

THUTHI   Akhet (Winter)   Season: Inundation
     God of the Month: Thoth   God of the Season: Hapi

Egyptian Calendar	Gregorian Calendar	Festival Day
1	July 19	Month of Thuthi begins
		Feast of Thoth
		Opet festival: marriage of Isis and Osiris
3	July 21	Birthday of Aten
7	July 25	Feast of Anket: welcoming the rise of the Nile
9	July 27	Queen Hatshepsut's birthday
10	July 28	Festival of the goddess of weaving (Hedjihotep)
17	Aug. 4	Festival of the dead: sunset ceremony
19	Aug. 6	Festival of Nut and Ra
		Chief festival of Thoth
25	Aug. 12	Day of Sekhmet's repulsion of Set
		Osirian mysteries: feast of lights of Isis
26	Aug. 13	Day of the battle between Horus and Seth
		Isis gains the horns of Hathor
27	Aug. 14	Day of peace between Horus and Seth
30	Aug. 17	Rituals in the temples of Ra, Horus, and Osiris

PAOPI
     God of the Month: Ptah

Egyptian Calendar	Gregorian Calendar	Festival Day
1	Aug. 18	Month of Paopi begins
2	Aug. 19	Procession of Horus to Neith
3	Aug. 20	Thoth orders the healing of the eye of Horus
		Thoth in the presence of Ra

*This calendar was compiled by the Reverend Harold Moss, for the Festival Calendar of the Church of the Eternal Source in Boise, Idaho. It is drawn from a compilation of ancient Egyptian sources and is used here with his kind permission.

PAOPI (continued)
God of the Month: Ptah

Egyptian Calendar	Gregorian Calendar	Festival Day
5	Aug. 22	Feast of Mont
6	Aug. 23	Great feast of the gods and goddesses
9	Aug. 26	Day of jubilation in the heart of Ra
10	Aug. 27	Procession of Bastet
		Birthday of Nut
12	Aug. 29	Birthday of Hathor
13	Aug. 30	Day of satisfying the hearts of the Ennead
14	Aug. 31	Day Horus received the white crown
16	Sept. 2	Feast of Osiris
18	Sept. 4	Ceremony of transformation through Anubis
19	Sept. 5	Ceremony of raising the *djed*
21	Sept. 7	Neith goes forth to Atum
27	Sept. 13	Festival of lighting the fires of Neith
30	Sept. 16	Land in festival for Ra, Osiris, and Horus

HETHARA
Goddess of the Month: Hathor

Egyptian Calendar	Gregorian Calendar	Festival Day
1	Sept. 17	Month of Hethara begins
		Feast of Hathor
5	Sept. 21	Autumn equinox
		Honors to Hathor
6	Sept. 22	Ritual of the neters of the Two Lands
7	Sept. 23	Honors offered to Atum
8	Sept. 24	The going forth of Isis
12	Sept. 28	Osiris goes forth to Abydos
		Purification of the hearts of the gods
		Feast of Hapi: cresting of the Nile
15	Oct. 1	Contemplation of the fertility of Min
16	Oct. 2	Day of the appearance of the eight Great Gods
17	Oct. 3	Landing of the Great Gods in Abydos
		Lamentations of Isis and Nephthys for Osiris
18	Oct. 4	Festival of Hathor
20	Oct. 6	Bastet appears to Ra
21	Oct. 7	Feast day of Ma'at
23	Oct. 9	Ra judges the dispute between Seth and Horus
24	Oct. 10	Isis goes forth
		Nephthys celebrates
26	Oct. 12	Black Land given to Horus
		Red Land given to Seth
28	Oct. 14	Festival of establishing Horus as king

HETHARA (continued)
Goddess of the Month: Hathor

Egyptian Calendar	Gregorian Calendar	Festival Day
29	Oct. 15	The appearance before Ptah Feast of the three noble ladies

KOIAK
Goddess of the Month: Sekhmet

Egyptian Calendar	Gregorian Calendar	Festival Day
1	Oct. 17	Month of Koiak begins Feast of Sekhmet
2	Oct. 18	Gods and goddess in festivity
4	Oct. 20	Festivals for Sobek
5	Oct. 21	Hathor goes forth to her people
7	Oct. 23	Feast of Selket Ceremony of Thoth
11	Oct. 27	Feast of Osiris in Abydos
12	Oct. 28	Day of transformation into the *bennu* (phoenix)
13	Oct. 29	Going forth of Hathor and the Ennead
14	Oct. 30	Celebrations of the goddess of weaving and fate Coming forth of the *bennu* transformed
15	Oct. 31	Feast of Sekhmet, Bastet, Ra
17	Nov. 2	Festival of Hathor The people and the gods judge the speeches of the crew of the solar barge in Heliopolis
21	Nov. 6	Raising the *djed*
22	Nov. 7	Ploughing the earth
27	Nov. 12	Isis seeks the body of Osiris
28	Nov. 13	Isis grieves the loss of Osiris
29	Nov. 14	Isis rejoices as she finds Osiris
30	Nov. 15	Ennead feast in house of Ra, Horus, and Osiris Invocation and offering to the spirits *(khu)*

TYBI
Peret (Spring)   Season: Sowing
God of the Month: Min   God of the Season: Kheperi

Egyptian Calendar	Gregorian Calendar	Festival Day
1	Nov. 16	Month of Tybi begins *heb sed* festival Festival of Bastet
5	Nov. 20	Day of Sekhmet and the purifying flame
9	Nov. 24	Day of offerings to Sekhmet Feast of burning lamps for Isis and Osiris

TYBI (continued)   Peret (Spring)   Season: Sowing
God of the Month: Min   God of the Season: Kheperi

Egyptian Calendar	Gregorian Calendar	Festival Day
13	Nov. 28	Feast of Hathor and Sekhmet
		Day of prolonging the life and goodness of *ma'at*
18	Dec. 3	Going forth of the gods of Abydos
20	Dec. 5	Bastet goes forth from Bubastis
21	Dec. 6	Bastet guards the Two Lands
		Day of offerings to the followers of Ra
23	Dec. 8	Feast of Neith
28	Dec. 13	The day of Thoth's taking the oath
29	Dec. 14	The appearance of Hu and Sia
		Thoth sends Bastet and Sekhmet to guide Egypt
30	Dec. 15	Day of crossing before Nun in the temple of Hapi

MECHIR
God of the Month: Rekhur

Egyptian Calendar	Gregorian Calendar	Festival Day
1	Dec. 16	Month of Mechir begins
		Festival of the Little Heat
		Day of Ptah lifting up Ra with his hands
2	Dec. 17	Day the gods of Heaven receive Ra
3	Dec. 18	Seth goes forth
6	Dec. 21	Winter solstice
		Feast of Isis
		Raising of the *djed* pillar of Osiris
8	Dec. 23	Festival of the Great Heat
		Feast Day of Hathor
10	Dec. 25	Birth of Horus, the child of Isis
		Going forth of Wadjet singing in Heliopolis
		Day of elevating the goddess
11	Dec. 26	Feast of Neith
		Birth of Sobek
13	Dec. 28	Day of Sekhmet going forth to Letopolis
16	Dec. 31	Feast of Sekhmet
17	Jan. 1	Day of keeping the things of Osiris in the hands of Anubis
20	Jan. 4	Day of Nut and Raet proceeding southward
22	Jan. 6	Feast of Ptah and Horus
23	Jan. 7	Festival of Isis
24	Jan. 8	Festival of Isis
		Birth of Aion
26	Jan. 10	Going forth of Min to Coptos

MECHIR (continued)
God of the Month: Rekhur

Egyptian Calendar	Gregorian Calendar	Festival Day
26	Jan. 10	Isis sees Osiris's face
27	Jan. 11	Feast of Sokar

PAMENOT
God of the Month: Amunhotep

Egyptian Calendar	Gregorian Calendar	Festival Day
1	Jan. 15	Month of Pamenot begins
		Feast of entering heaven and the Two Lands
5	Jan. 19	The brilliant festival of lights as Neith goes forth from Sais
6	Jan. 20	Going forth of Anubis
		Festival of jubilation for Osiris in Busiris
8	Jan. 22	Day of making way for Khnum
9	Jan. 23	Day of Hathor
10	Jan. 24	Day of the coming of Thoth
13	Jan. 27	Thoth and the *khu* go forth
16	Jan. 30	Day of opening the doors and courts at Karnak
18	Feb. 1	Feast of Nut
19	Feb. 2	Birthday of Nut
22	Feb. 5	Birthday of Apophis
23	Feb. 6	Feast of Horus
26	Feb. 9	Day of unseeing in the underworld
28	Feb. 11	Feast of Osiris in Abydos
30	Feb. 13	Feast of Osiris in Busiris
		The doorways of the horizon are opened

PARMUTI
Goddess of the Month: Renenutet

Egyptian Calendar	Gregorian Calendar	Festival Day
1	Feb. 14	Month of Parmuti begins
2	Feb. 15	Geb proceeds to Busiris to see Anubis
7	Feb. 20	Min goes forth in festivity
8	Feb. 21	Day of counting the parts of the eye of Horus
13	Feb. 26	Day of Nut
16	Mar. 1	Going forth of Kheperi
17	Mar. 2	Going forth of Seth, son of Nut
19	Mar. 4	Feast of Ra in his barge in Heliopolis
27	Mar. 12	End of the world by Sekhmet
29	Mar. 14	Adoration of Unnefer
30	Mar. 15	Offerings to Ra, Osiris, Horus, Ptah, Sokar, and Atum

PACHONS

	Shemu(Summer)	Season: Harvest
God of the Month: Khonsu	God of the Season: Khonsu-Ra	

Egyptian Calendar	Gregorian Calendar	Festival Day
1	Mar. 16	Month of Pachons begins
		Feast of Horus and his companions
5	Mar. 20	Feast of the good soul for sexual fertility
6	Mar. 21	Spring equinox
		Harvest festival
		Festival of restructuring the heavens
		Coming forth of the Great Ones from the house of Ra
8	Mar. 23	Festival of Isis
10	Mar. 25	Day the Shining Ones of heaven move upstream
14	Mar. 29	Day of cutting out the tongue of Sobek
17	Apr. 1	Day of Hathor
18	Apr. 2	Day of joy for the Ennead and crew of Ra
19	Apr. 3	Day of the counting of Thoth who heard Ma'at
20	Apr. 4	Ma'at judges the souls before the gods
30	Apr. 14	Celebrations in the house of Ra, Osiris, and Horus

PAYNI
God of the Month: Horus

Egyptian Calendar	Gregorian Calendar	Festival Day
1	Apr. 15	Month of Payni begins
		Festival of Horus
		Festival of Bastet
2	Apr. 16	Holiday of Ra and his followers
7	Apr. 21	Feast of Wadjet
13	Apr. 27	The Ennead sails throughout the land
18	May 2	Osiris goes forth from his mountain
21	May 5	Day of the living children of Nut
25	May 9	The Akhet eye pleases Ra
26	May 10	Going forth of Neith along the water
28	May 12	Day of purification of all things
30	May 14	Thoth appears with Shu to bring back Tefnut

EPIPI
Goddess of the Month: Wadjet

Egyptian Calendar	Gregorian Calendar	Festival Day
1	May 15	Month of Epipi begins
		Festivals of Hathor and Bastet
		Great feast of the southern heavens

EPIPI (continued)
Goddess of the Month: Wadjet

Egyptian Calendar	Gregorian Calendar	Festival Day
2	May 16	The goddesses feast in their temples
5	May 19	Hathor returns to Punt: the gods are sad
7	May 21	Sailing of the gods after the goddess
12	May 26	Holiday of the receiving of Ra
15	May 29	Horus hears prayers in the presence of the neters
16	May 30	Ma'at is taken to Ra in Heliopolis
18	June 1	Ma'at and Ra go forth in secret
29	June 12	Festival of Mut: feeding of the gods
30	June 13	Ceremony of Horus, the Beloved

MESORE
God of the Month: Heru-Khuiti

Egyptian Calendar	Gregorian Calendar	Festival Day
1	June 14	Month of Mesore begins
2	June 15	Ma'at unites as one with all the gods in heaven
3	June 16	Feast of Raet
		Feast of Hathor as Sirius
4	June 17	Day of procession of Sopdu, the Warrior
5	June 18	Day of appearance of Min
7	June 20	Anubis travels to every necropolis
8	June 21	Summer solstice
		Wadjet ceremony
10	June 23	Anubis ceremony
13	June 26	Holiday for the followers of Horus
15	June 28	Ra goes forth to propitiate Nun
19	July 2	The Wadjet eye has returned complete
22	July 5	Feast of Anubis with the children of Nut and Geb
28	July 11	Feast of Min
29	July 12	Holiday in the Temple of Sokar
		Festival of the estate of Ptah
30	July 13	Birthday of Ra

THE EPAGOMENAL DAYS

Egyptian Calendar	Gregorian Calendar	Festival Day
1	July 14	Birthday of Osiris
2	July 15	Birthday of Horus the Elder
3	July 16	Birthday of Seth
4	July 17	Birthday of Isis
5	July 18	Birthday of Nephthys

NOTES

Introduction

1. Joseph Campbell, *The Hero with a Thousand Faces* (Princeton, N.J.: Bollingen, 1972), 3–4.
2. Joseph Campbell, *The Masks of God: Creative Mythology* (New York: Viking, 1964), 4.
3. Campbell, *Masks of God*, 4–6 passim.
4. Ibid.
5. Campbell, Hero, 4.
6. Lawrence E. Cahoone, *The Dilemma of Modernity: Philosophy, Culture and Anti-Culture* (Albany: State University of New York Press, 1987), 223–234.
7. Rainer Maria Rilke, "Letter to Hulewicz," in Danah Zohar, *The Quantum Self* (New York: Morrow, 1990), 188.

How to Use This Book

1. These suggestions are drawn from the work of Joseph Jochmans, who conducts tours of as well as research on ancient Egyptian sites. He is an esoteric scholar whose radical but always fascinating interpretations of the meaning of these sites is to be found in several of his books. See, in particular, Joseph R. Jochmans, *New Lights along the Nile*, vols. 1–3 (Rock Hill, S.C.: Alma Tara Publishing, 1990).
2. For practical approaches to journal keeping, see Natalie Goldberg, *Writing Down the Bones* (Boston: Shambhala, 1986).
3. Patricia Hampl, as quoted in Christina Baldwin, *Life's Companion: Journal Writing as a Spiritual Quest* (New York: Bantam, 1990), 146.

Chapter Two

1. Duat is the neterworld. For more information on this and other Egyptian terms, see the glossary in Appendix B.

Chapter Four

1. Sir Alan Gardiner, *Egyptian Grammar*, 3d ed. (Oxford: Griffith Institute, 1957), 219.
2. Octavio Paz, *The Bow and the Lyre*, 1st ed. (Austin: University of Texas Press, 1973), 54. The second edition of this text has been substantially revised and this quote does not appear.

3. For more information on the ideas of cyclical and durative time in the ancient cultures of Egypt and the Near East, see Theodor H. Gaster, *Thespis: Ritual, Myth, and Drama in the Ancient Near East*, 2d rev. ed. (Garden City, N.Y.: Doubleday/Anchor Books, 1961).

4. For more information on the calendars of ancient Egypt, see the section on astrology and the cycles of time in Chapter 7, "Magic of Magic, Spirit of Spirit, Part 1." Further information on the festival calendar of the ancient Egyptians can be found in Appendix E.

5. Sirius (or Sothis), the brightest star in the constellation Canis Major, does not move uniformly through the heavens. It sometimes appears either ahead of or behind its mean position in an apparent elliptical orbit. This helical rising is caused by an unseen double star that affects the star's apparent spiral-like motion.

6. Herodotus, *The Histories*, trans. Aubrey de Selincourt, rev. ed. (New York: Penguin Books, 1972), 135. Herodotus states that many of these protodynastic peoples "moved down into the new territory and many remained where they originally were." The implication is that the culture arose around the area of Thebes in southern Egypt, or even farther south in Africa.

7. Ibid., 186.

8. See R. A. Schwaller de Lubicz, *Sacred Science: The King of Pharaonic Theocracy*, trans. André and Goldian VandenBroeck (Rochester, Vt.: Inner Traditions, 1982), 86. Source for the kings' list is the Royal Papyrus of Turin mentioned by Schwaller de Lubicz. It should be noted that, according to some historians, these time frames may be based on lunar cycles rather than on solar cycles, since the lunar cycle was the predominant calendar of choice during the prehistoric matriarchal cultures.

9. Ibid.

10. Irmgard Woldering, *The Art of Egypt* (New York: Crown, 1967), 15.

11. Martin Bernal, *Black Athena: The Afroasiatic Roots of Classical Civilization*, vol. 1 (New Brunswick, N.J.: Rutgers University Press, 1987), 11. Bernal suggests that these Africans likewise moved into Chad and Morocco, across the Strait of Gibraltar, and perhaps into the Arabian peninsula across Ethiopia.

12. Leonard Cottrell, *Queen of the Pharaohs* (London: Evans Brothers, 1966), 13.

13. For approximate dates of prehistoric cultures, see Cyril Aldred, *The Egyptians* (London: Thames & Hudson, 1961).

14. V. Gordon Childe, *New Light on the Most Ancient East*, 4th ed. (London: Routledge & Kegan Paul, 1952), 26. The earliest known Egyptian sheep was the *ovis longipes*, a relative of the long-tail sheep found today only in Afghanistan and the Punjab.

15. Aldred, *Egyptians*, 33.

16. Lucie Lamy, *Egyptian Mysteries: New Light on Ancient Spiritual Knowledge* (New York: Crossroads Publishing, 1981), 66.

17. Childe, *New Light*, 34.

18. The burial grounds in the western hills were called Amenti by the Egyptians, meaning "the hidden place." Later, Amenti became synonymous with "the land of the dead." One of the appellations for Osiris as Lord of the Dead is Khentamenti, meaning "chief of the hidden place."

19. Childe, *New Light*, 36.
20. A. Rosalie David, *The Ancient Egyptians: Religious Beliefs and Practices* (London: Routledge & Kegan Paul, 1982), 12.
21. Ibid., 20.
22. Heru is the Egyptian name of the god whom the Greeks called Horus. Some linguists believe that Heru is origin of the word *hero*.
23. Egyptologists disagree as to Punt's exact location. Some place it on the African continent, others in Asia. Most believe that Punt lay to the east, bordered by the Red Sea—traditionally thought to be Somalia. Yet several of these historians say it ran on both sides of the Red Sea and as far north and east as Arabia. It appears to be the land from which the "dynastic race" appeared, bringing with them their god, Horus.

    The ancients tell us that they traveled to Punt extensively and that it was a place filled with incense-bearing trees, including myrrh, and a variety of animals, such as emu, ostrich, panthers, and baboons. Queen Hatshepsut went to great lengths to bring back from her expedition to Punt live myrrh trees, which she planted in the desert in front of her temple at Deir el-Bahri. Her temple was dedicated to Hathor, the goddess of love and beauty, who was said to have arrived in Egypt from her homeland in Punt.
24. Alan W. Shorter, *The Egyptian Gods* (London: Routledge & Kegan Paul, 1937), 47.
25. Quoted in Mircea Eliade, *Myths, Dreams, and Mysteries* (New York: Harper Torchbooks, 1975), 32.
26. Schwaller de Lubicz, *Sacred Science*, 13.

CHAPTER FIVE

1. Peter Tompkins, *Secrets of the Great Pyramid* (New York: Harper/ Colophon Books, 1971), 375. Pharaoh Djoser's Step Pyramid and temple complex built at Saqqara duplicated in stone the natural harmonics of number, the thirty-six-degree triangle being one-tenth of the full circle. The Greek mathematician Pythagoras emphasized the importance of the right-angle triangle in his philosophies, and the five-pointed star that was the symbol of the Pythagorean sect was composed of just such triangles.
2. Alan Honor, *The Man Who Could Read Stones* (New York: Hawthorn Books, 1966). This text provides an excellent account of Champollion and his process of learning to read the hieroglyphs.
3. For a fuller accounting of the life of R. A. Schwaller de Lubicz, see André VandenBroeck, *Al-Kemi: Hermetic, Occult, Political, and Private Aspects of R. A. Schwaller de Lubicz* (Great Barrington, Mass.: Inner Traditions/Lindisfarne Press, 1987).

    For a further study of the theories of Schwaller de Lubicz, refer to his works: *Symbol and the Symbolic*, trans. Robert and Deborah Lawlor (Brookline, Mass.: Autumn Press, 1978); *The Temple in Man: Sacred Architecture and the Perfect Man*, trans. Robert and Deborah Lawlor (New York: Inner Traditions, 1981); *Nature Word*, trans. Deborah Lawlor (West Stockbridge, Mass.: Lindisfarne Press, 1982); *Sacred Science: The King of Pharaonic Theocracy*, trans. André and Goldian VandenBroeck (Rochester, Vt.: Inner Traditions, 1982); and *The Egyptian Miracle: An Introduction to the Wisdom of the Temple*, trans. André VandenBroeck (Rochester, Vt.: Inner Traditions, 1985).

4. Quoted in VandenBroeck, *Al-Kemi*, 82.

5. Kenneth Patchen, *Selected Poems* (New York: New Directions, 1957), 74.

6. Everything in ancient Egypt centered on religion, including the activities of the day and the language itself. Both hieratic and demotic Egyptian were used in writing the language of business. But both scripts were derived from the sacred hieroglyphs, which was the domain of the artisan-scribe-priest. The position of scribe—and with it, the more priestly functions—was reserved for the upper class, as academia has often been.

    The hieroglyphs of the Middle and New Kingdoms were always accompanied by illustrations, so that both upper and lower classes could understand them, in the same way that unlettered European peasantry in the Middle Ages could understand the minutia of Christian symbolism in the stained-glass windows of churches.

7. J. J. Bachofen, *Myth, Religion and Mother Right*, trans. Ralph Manheim, Bollingen Series 84 (Princeton, N.J.: Princeton University Press, 1967), 49.

8. For more information, see Loren Eisley, *The Immense Journey* (New York: Harcourt Brace Jovanovich, 1957) and *The Star Thrower* (New York: Harvest/HBJ, 1978). See also Lewis Thomas, *The Lives of a Cell* (New York: Viking, 1975).

9. Quoted in VandenBroeck, *Al-Kemi*, 82.

10. Brian and Esther Crowley, *Words of Power: Sacred Sounds of East and West* (St. Paul, Minn.: Llewellyn Publications, 1991), 47.

11. Rudolf Steiner, *Eurythmy as Visible Speech* (London: Rudolf Steiner Press, 1984), 13.

12. Octavio Paz, *The Bow and the Lyre*, 2d ed. (Austin: University of Texas Press, 1987), 4.

13. John Anthony West, *Serpent in the Sky: The High Wisdom of Ancient Egypt*, 2d ed. (Wheaton, Ill.: Quest Books, 1993), 123.

14. Ibid., 136.

15. The discovery of the Rosetta Stone and Champollion's translations of Egyptian hieroglyphs had an abiding spiritual effect on the writers of nineteenth-century America, including Poe, Hawthorne, Melville, and Whitman. For more information, see John T. Irwin, *American Hieroglyphics: The Symbol of the Egyptian Hieroglyphics in the American Renaissance* (New Haven: Yale University Press, 1980).

16. Schwaller de Lubicz, *Symbol and the Symbolic*, 11.

17. John Briggs, *Fire in the Crucible: The Self-Creation of Creativity and Genius* (Los Angeles: Tarcher, 1990), 20.

18. E. A. Wallis Budge, *Book of the Dead* (Secaucus, N.J.: University Books, 1960), 191.

19. Normandi Ellis, *Awakening Osiris* (Grand Rapids, Mich.: Phanes Press, 1988), 189.

20. Bika Reed, *Rebel in the Soul: A Sacred Text of Ancient Egypt* (New York: Inner Traditions International, 1978), 9–10.

21. The phrase first appeared in letters to the Black Mountain poet Charles Olson from his protégé Robert Creeley. All Creeley's poetics, and the subse-

quent school of poetics at Black Mountain, were based on this theory. For more information on the measure of how form is created by the spirit during the process of writing, see Robert Creeley, *Was That a Real Poem and Other Essays* (Bolinas, Calif.: Four Seasons Foundation, 1979).

22. James Joyce, *Ulysses* (New York: Modern Library, 1949), 407.

CHAPTER SIX

1. Lionel Casson, *Ancient Egypt* (Alexandria, Va.: Time-Life Books, 1965), 164.
2. Quoted in Peter Tompkins, *The Magic of Obelisks* (New York: Harper & Row, 1981), 186.
3. Lucius Apuleius, *The Golden Ass*, trans. Robert Graves (New York: Farrar, Straus & Giroux, 1961), 264.
4. Carl Jung, *Memories, Dreams, Reflections* (New York: Vintage Books, 1963), 274.
5. Rainer Maria Rilke, *Letters to a Young Poet*, trans. M. D. Herter Norton (New York: Norton, 1934), 66.
6. For example, see the discussions in John Anthony West, *Serpent in the Sky*, 2d ed. (Wheaton, Ill.: Quest Books, 1993). Many of the ingenious discoveries of Schwaller de Lubicz that seem to have parallels with factors of quantum resonance came from the correlation of his intensive studies of medieval alchemical texts with ancient Egyptian symbology. The study and practice of alchemy itself forms the link between the alchemical gnosis of ancient Egypt and the medieval and Renaissance alchemists, who provided the discoveries and methodology that lie at the heart of modern physics and chemistry.
7. Isha Schwaller de Lubicz, *The Opening of the Way: A Practical Guide to the Wisdom of Ancient Egypt* (New York: Inner Traditions, 1981), 189–197.
8. Literally, "multimindedness." See Appendix B for further information.
9. William Irwin Thompson, *The Time Falling Bodies Take to Light* (New York: St. Martin's Press, 1981), 213.
10. Barbara Mertz, *Red Land, Black Land: Daily Life in Ancient Egypt* (New York: Dodd, Mead, 1978), 253. This book provides a wonderful overview of life during the time of Rameses II.

CHAPTER SEVEN

1. John Anthony West, "Ancient Egypt: The Meaning Behind the Magic," *The Quest* (Winter 1991): 20.
2. For more information on the facts and fictions of the Great Pyramid, see Peter J. Tompkins, *Secrets of the Great Pyramid* (New York: Harper/ Colophon Books, 1981).
3. For more information on the Temple of Luxor, see R. A. Schwaller de Lubicz, *The Temple in Man: Sacred Architecture and the Perfect Man* (New York: Inner Traditions, 1981).
4. John Anthony West, *Serpent in the Sky*, 2d ed. (Wheaton, Ill.: Quest Books, 1993), 104.
5. West, "Ancient Egypt," 20.
6. For more information, see Harold P. Cooke, *Osiris: A Study in Myths, Mysteries and Religion* (1931; reprint, Chicago: Ares Publishers, 1979), 95–110.

7. West, *Serpent in the Sky*, 120.
8. Joseph Campbell, *The Masks of God: Oriental Mythology* (New York: Penguin Books, 1976), 75–76.
9. Colin Ronan, *Lost Discoveries* (New York: MacDonald, 1973), 83.
10. Ibid.
11. For further information, see the documentation of the work of Rupert Sheldrake, a botanist and researcher whose experiments on morphic fields has inspired many experiments. One such experiment on the conduct of rats in mazes provides interesting data that seem to suggest that the offspring of rats who have mastered the maze are more likely to master the maze themselves in a short period of time. For Sheldrake's work, and the experiments it inspired, see Rupert Sheldrake, *The Presence of the Past* (New York: Times Books, 1988).
12. Michael Talbot, *The Holographic Universe* (New York: HarperCollins, 1991), 210.
13. Mircea Eliade, *Shamanism*, trans. Willard R. Trask, Bollingen Series 76 (New York: Bollingen Foundation, 1964), 103.
14. Carl Jung, *Memories, Dreams, Reflections* (New York: Vintage Books, 1963), 202.
15. Erich Neumann, *The Origins and History of Consciousness*, trans. R. F. C. Hull, Bollingen Series 42 (Princeton, N.J.: Princeton University Press, 1954), 284.
16. The Dream Book was first interpreted by the Egyptologist Sir Alan Gardiner. For more information on the Dream Book, see Bob Brier, *Ancient Egyptian Magic* (New York: Quill Books, 1980), 217–220.
17. The Aquarian age is widely expected to begin around the year 2000. However, as with most astrological manifestations of cosmic energy, its influence may be felt earlier. In fact, we are on the cusp of its energy now, a fact that some think may account for the urgency in our transformation as a planet.
18. West, *Serpent in the Sky*, 99.
19. Refer to Chapter 4 for a discussion on mythic and historic time. For more clarification, see Appendix D.

CHAPTER EIGHT

1. Erik Hornung, *Conceptions of God in Ancient Egypt* (Ithaca, N.Y.: Cornell University Press, 1982), 175.
2. Lucie Lamy, *Egyptian Mysteries: New Light on Ancient Spiritual Knowledge* (New York: Crossroads Publishing, 1981), 19.
3. Normandi Ellis, *Awakening Osiris* (Grand Rapids, Mich.: Phanes Press, 1988), 111.
4. Miriam Lichtheim, *Ancient Egyptian Literature*, vol. 1, *The Old and Middle Kingdoms* (Berkeley: University of California Press, 1973), 44.
5. Ibid., 47.
6. Arthur Versluis, *The Egyptian Mysteries* (London: Arkana Books, 1988), 103. A philosopher and scholar, rather than a field Egyptologist, Versluis takes an intuitive approach to much of ancient Egypt's theology. His vision is notable in its attempt to educate our interpretations of ancient Egypt by accessing the tradition of Eastern thought, rather than through Western (Greek) interpretations of Egyptian religion. In reality, both Eastern and Western traditions bear traces of ancient Egyptian mysticism;

therefore, Versluis's comments provide a fuller picture of ancient Egyptian religious life than our purely Western interpretation generally provides.

7. E. A. Wallis Budge, *Egyptian Book of the Dead: The Papyrus of Ani in the British Museum* (New York: Dover, 1967), xiv.

8. Hornung, *Conceptions of God*, 209.

9. Ibid.

10. Ibid., 214–215.

11. Versluis, *Egyptian Mysteries*, 104–105.

12. Herodotus, *The Histories*, vol. 2, trans. A. de Selincourt (London: Penguin Classics), 171.

13. For more information on the ancient healing temples and Asclepios, see my book *The Search for the Beloved*, chaps. 1 and 2.

14. Mircea Eliade, *Myths, Dreams, and Mysteries* (New York: Harper Torchbooks, 1975), 200.

15. John Anthony West, "Ancient Egypt: The Meaning Behind the Magic," *The Quest* (Winter 1991): 21.

16. In an interview with *Quest* editor Ray Grasse, West spoke about the Sphinx and his attempts to prove its antiquity: "I reasoned that if you could prove that the Sphinx had been weathered by water, it would have to mean that the Sphinx was there before the water was there. If that geological dating is correct it would mean that the Sphinx dated from sometime before 10,000 B.C., and probably before 15,000 B.C. Now the actual dating is still at issue, but the scenario is fairly iron-clad. In other words, the sequence of events is fertile savanna, long periods of rains, and then desert.... Absolutely, the Sphinx is weathered by water. It was not built by the pharaoh Chephren around 2500 B.C., and it's a lot older than conventionally argued. Exactly how much older we can't yet determine...." Quoted in an interview with Ray Grasse, *The Quest* (Winter 1991): 23.

17. Ibid., 23–24.

18. Ellis, *Awakening Osiris*, 149.

19. Refer to Michael Talbot, *Holographic Universe* (New York: HarperCollins, 1991), 47. Talbot explains the research that underlies our current understanding of quantum physics. He reports that the physicist David Bohm observed that electrons and other particles are sustained by a constant influx from the implicate order, and when a particle appears to be destroyed, it is not lost, but merely folded back into the deeper order from which it sprang. By implicate he means "enfolded"; by explicate he means "unfolded." "The constant and flowing exchange between the two orders explains how particles [of light], such as the electron in the positronium atom, can shape-shift from one kind of particle to another.... It also explains how a quantum can manifest as either a particle or a wave. According to Bohm, both aspects are always enfolded in a quantum's ensemble, but the way an observer interacts with the ensemble determines which aspect unfolds and which remains hidden."

20. Versluis, *Egyptian Mysteries*, 136.

21. Isha Schwaller de Lubicz, *The Opening of the Way: A Practical Guide to the Wisdom of Ancient Egypt* (New York: Inner Traditions, 1981), 137.

22. Ibid., 130–141.

23. R. A. Schwaller de Lubicz, *The Temple in Man: Sacred Architecture and the Perfect Man* (New York: Inner Traditions, 1981).

24. Robert Masters, *The Goddess Sekhmet: Psycho-Spiritual Exercises of the Fifth Way* (St. Paul, Minn.: Llewellyn, 1991), 47. The Masters material provides even more information on the depth training of the initiates, including not only background material of the work of the magician but also experiential training exercises.

25. Versluis, *Egyptian Mysteries*, 110.

26. Ibid., 138.

27. Joseph Campbell, *The Masks of God: Oriental Mythology* (New York: Penguin Books, 1976), 77.

28. The translation is based on Chapter 44 of The Chapter of Not Dying a Second Time. See E. A. Wallis Budge, *Book of the Dead* (Secaucus, N.J.: University Books, 1960), 459.

29. Hornung, *Conceptions of God*, 95.

30. Campbell, *Masks of God*, 81.

31. Versluis, *Egyptian Mysteries*, 126.

32. Lamy, *New Light*, 29.

33. West, interview with Grasse, 23.

34. Ellis, *Awakening Osiris*, 149.

CHAPTER NINE

1. Joseph Campbell, *The Hero with a Thousand Faces* (Princeton, N.J.: Princeton University Press, 1949), 387.

2. Robert Frost, "Two Tramps in Mud Time," *Complete Poems of Robert Frost* (New York: Henry Holt, 1949), 359.

3. James Hillman, *Loose Ends* (Zurich: Spring Publications, 1975), 167.

4. Quoted in Evelyn Underhill, *Mysticism* (New York: Meridian Books, 1957), 420.

5. Ibid.

6. Miriam Lichtheim, *Ancient Egyptian Literature*, vol. 1, *The Old and Middle Kingdoms* (Berkeley: University of California Press, 1973), 40.

7. A splendid study of the earlier phases of the myth during the Old, Middle, and New Kingdom periods is found in R. T. Rundle Clark, *Myth and Symbol in Ancient Egypt* (London: Thames & Hudson, 1978).

8. For the complete myth and commentary, see Plutarch, "Isis and Osiris," in *Morals*, trans. C. W. King (London: Bell, 1908), 1–71.

9. William Irwin Thompson, *The Time Falling Bodies Take to Light* (New York: St. Martin's Press, 1981), 212.

10. Ibid., 213.

11. Ibid., 215.

CHAPTER TEN

1. In a painting from Pompeii, Saturn is standing, his chest half bare, a sickle in his hand. On certain Roman coins he carries a sickle or ears of corn, indicating his role as the one who cuts to measure.

2. In the development of Christian symbolism thousands of years later, Seth is perceived as linked to Satan, while Osiris is seen as a precursor of the Christ figure. There is a fascinating similarity between the names Seth and Satan. In their most beguiling and deceitful forms, both Seth and Satan appear as serpents. In the Hebrew, *satan* means "he who is the enemy," or the persecutor.

3. Ralph Blum, *The Book of Runes* (New York: St. Martin's Press, 1982), 81.
4. William Wordsworth, *The Selected Poetry and Prose of Wordsworth*, ed. Geoffrey H. Hartman (New York: New American Library, 1970), 163.
5. Ibid., 164.
6. There is also Rumi's great poem, "Who Says Words with My Mouth," which speaks of the malaise of emotional burnout: ". . . I didn't come here of my own accord, and I can't leave that way/Let whoever brought me here take me back. . . ." John Moyne and Coleman Barks, *Open Secrets: Versions of Rumi* (Putney, Vt.: Threshold Books, 1984).
7. *Hamlet*, act 2, scene 2, line 263. In *The Complete Works of William Shakespeare*, vol. 2, ed. W. G. Clark and W. Aldis Wright (Garden City, N.Y.: Doubleday, 1936), 610.
8. William Irwin Thompson, *The Time Falling Bodies Take to Light* (New York: St. Martin's Press, 1981), 217.
9. James Hillman, *Loose Ends* (Zurich: Spring Publications, 1975), 54.
10. See festival calendar in Appendix E. Here you will discover how the holy days of the ancient Egyptian calendar centered on three seasons—winter, spring, and summer, each season relative to the rise of the Nile and the growing period.
11. I quote here the line from the movie *Excalibur*, based on the legend of King Arthur, Launcelot, Guinevere, and Merlin, in which Nicol Williamson makes for us such a marvelous Merlin, a rememberer of the pieces of dream and life.

CHAPTER ELEVEN

1. R. T. Rundle Clark, *Myth and Symbol in Ancient Egypt* (London: Thames & Hudson, 1959), 125–126.
2. Ibid., 132.
3. For in-depth interpretations of Lucius Apuleius's text, see Marie Louise von Franz, A *Psychological Interpretation of the Golden Ass of Apuleius* (Zurich: Spring Publications, 1970).
4. For more precise locations of ancient sites, see Appendix C. As an interesting side note, the majority of the finest early coffins of ancient Egypt were made from imported Lebanon cedar in imitation of the tree that ensnared Osiris. Trees were an uncommon sight in ancient Egypt, and therefore wood was a high-priced commodity.
5. Michael Murphy, in *The Future of the Body* (Los Angeles: Tarcher, 1992), rightly warns that we should not uncritically accept esoteric anatomies, for these usually ancient accounts of chakras, or nadis (energy channels), or kundalini may be imperfect representations of the psychophysical processes that facilitate extraordinary functioning. He writes that

> none of them have been confirmed by modern science, and different schools give different versions of them. In his scholarly *Layayoga*, for example, Shyam Sundara Goswai (1891–1978) catalogued accounts of nadis and chakras in the Vedas, the Upanishads, and Tantra Shastras that differed from such descriptions by other scholars. Satyananda Saraswati, for example, has described seven chakras below the seven traditionally as-

signed to points running from the base of the spine to the top of the head. According to Saraswati, there are 14 major chakras and several minor ones. And how do we reconcile descriptions of different *ochemata*, or subtle bodies, such as the *soma pneumatikon, eidolon, imago, simulacrum, skia,* and *umbra* in the mystical literature of Greco-Roman antiquity? Or the different occult anatomies of Islamic mystics described for example in Henri Corbin's *Spiritual Body and Celestial Earth*? Or the different accounts of Buddha Bodies in Chinese and Tibetan yoga lore? Given the many differences among them, we cannot automatically accept esoteric teachings about metanormal development. (p. 156)

6. Rundle Clark, *Myth and Symbol,* 167.
7. In *The Possible Human* I devoted a chapter to psychophysical work and exercises that activate and harvest the latent genius of earlier evolutionary stages still present in the spine and the brain. See Jean Houston, *The Possible Human* (Los Angeles: Tarcher, 1982), 96–113 passim.
8. Joseph Chilton Pearce, *Evolution's End* (San Francisco: Harper San Francisco, 1992), 46.
9. Houston, *Possible Human,* 100.
10. William Irwin Thompson, *The Time Falling Bodies Take to Light* (New York: St. Martin's Press, 1981), 224–225.

CHAPTER TWELVE

1. The coffin in the tree is also the pillar in the house, the inner sanctuary, the *adytum* or holy of holies, a place so sacred one cannot enter.
2. R. T. Rundle Clark, *Myth and Symbol in Ancient Egypt* (London: Thames & Hudson, 1959), 106.
3. Joseph Campbell, *The Hero with a Thousand Faces* (Princeton, N.J.: Princeton University Press, 1949), 308.
4. Kabir Edmund Helminski, *Living Presence: A Sufi Way to Mindfulness and the Essential Self* (New York: Tarcher/Perigree, 1992), 86.
5. William Irwin Thompson, *The Time Falling Bodies Take to Light* (New York: St. Martin's Press, 1981), 232–233.

CHAPTER THIRTEEN

1. Quoted in Evelyn Fox Keller, *A Feeling for the Organism: The Life and Work of Barbara McClintock* (New York: Freeman, 1983).
2. Michael Murphy, *The Future of the Body* (Los Angeles: Tarcher, 1992), 170.
3. Quoted in Elinor Lenz and Barbara Myerhoff, *The Feminization of America* (Los Angeles: Tarcher, 1985), 5.
4. John Briggs, *Fire in the Crucible: The Self-Creation of Creativity and Genius* (Los Angeles: Tarcher, 1990), 255.
5. I discuss the nature of *kairos* and its relation to Hermes, the god of opportunity, in my work *The Hero and the Goddess:* The Odyssey *as Mystery and Initiation* (New York: Ballantine, 1992), 157–158.

CHAPTER FOURTEEN

1. A discussion of the ancient Egyptian ideas about death and the land of the dead would be too long here. Ample literature exists on this topic. See, for

example, the ancient Egyptian text Book of What Is in Duat, which appears in Wallis Budge's two-volume set *The Gods of the Egyptians* (New York: Dover, 1969), and John Anthony West's *The Traveler's Key to Ancient Egypt* (London: Harrap Columbus, 1987).

2. Scholars like Henri Frankfort and F. M. Cornford related well to Plutarch's rational mode of explanation, for it so closely fit their own.

3. "The Way of the Five Bodies" is both practical and realizable, although mastery required a good deal of discipline and work, much as the initiate of the mysteries must have undergone in ancient Egypt. The methodology and psychology of this way is explored in Robert Masters, *The Goddess Sekhmet: Psycho-Spiritual Exercises of the Fifth Way* (St. Paul, Minn.: Llewellyn, 1991).

4. Ibid., 7.

5. Ibid., 8.

6. Ibid., 8.

Chapter Fifteen

1. Apuleius, *The Golden Ass*, trans. Jack Lindsay (Bloomington: Indiana University Press, 1962), 236–238.

Chapter Sixteen

1. *Nedyt* means, literally, "the fallen state." Whenever and wherever death was found, one was in *Nedyt*.

2. From Utterance 442, Pyramid Text of Unas. Quoted in Miriam Lichtheim, *Ancient Egyptian Literature*, vol. 1, *The Old and Middle Kingdoms* (Berkeley: University of California Press, 1973), 45–46.

3. From E. A. Wallis Budge, *Egyptian Book of the Dead: The Papyrus of Ani in the British Museum* (New York: Dover, 1967), 18–19.

4. Each of the forty-two Assessors is responsible for one of the forty-two crimes listed in the Negative Confession. This was a ritual statement spoken before the god Osiris in the underworld, attesting that the deceased had not committed these crimes. In addition, in the Book of What Is in Duat, there are listed twelve hours of the night. Each of these hours is entered through a pylon guarded by three divine beings: a herald, a guardian, and a messenger.

5. A complete list of the Negative Confessions appears in John Anthony West, *The Traveler's Key to Ancient Egypt: A Guide to the Sacred Places* (London: Harrap Columbus, 1987), 375.

6. Pierre Montet, *Everyday Life in Egypt in the Days of Rameses the Great*, trans. A. R. Maxwell Hyslop and Margaret S. Drower (Philadelphia: University of Pennsylvania Press, 1981), 295.

7. Heliopolis. See Appendix B for further explanation.

8. Miriam Lichtheim, *Ancient Egyptian Literature*, vol. 3, *The Late Period* (Berkeley: University of California Press, 1980), 116.

9. The *heb sed* festival, or rite of renewal, took place during the pharaoh's thirtieth year of reign, whereas the number of years of the Osirian reign was twenty-eight. This may, at first, appear confusing. However, it should be remembered that if the pharaoh did not die before his twenty-eighth year (which was entirely likely, since life expectancy reached into the middle forties in ancient Egypt), then he was not an Osiris; he was still a Horus. Thus the *heb sed* festival was performed to reassure the multitudes that the king

was as much a warrior, protector, and ruler as ever, despite his age. The *heb sed* festival was often repeated after the first occurrence—sometimes once a year—to assure the fertility and strength of the pharaoh.

APPENDIX A

1. For locations of the nomes and cities mentioned in this text, see Appendix C. For more information about these sites, refer to Appendix B.
2. For more information on the weighing of the heart ceremony, see the entry "scales of *ma'at*" in Appendix B.
3. For more information on *uraeus*, see Appendix B.
4. For more information on the epagomenal days, see Appendix B.
5. For more information on the *sa*, see Appendix B.

BIBLIOGRAPHY

Aldred, Cyril. *The Egyptians*. London: Thames & Hudson, 1961.
———. *Egypt to the End of the Old Kingdom*. London: Thames & Hudson, 1965.
"Ancient Egypt: The Meaning Behind the Magic," interview with John Anthony West by Ray Grasse. *The Quest* (Winter 1991): 23–25.
Apuleius, Lucius. *The Golden Ass*, trans. Robert Graves. New York: Farrar, Straus & Giroux, 1961.
———. *The Golden Ass*, trans. Jack Lindsay. Bloomington: Indiana University Press, 1962.
Bachofen, J. J. *Myth, Religion and Mother Right*, trans. Ralph Manheim. Bollingen Series 84. Princeton, N.J.: Princeton University Press, 1967.
Baedeker's Egypt. Englewood Cliffs, N.J.: Prentice-Hall, n.d.
Baldwin, Christina. *Life's Companion: Journal Writing as a Spiritual Quest*. New York: Bantam, 1990.
Berket, Walter. *Ancient Mystery Cults*. Cambridge: Harvard University Press, 1987.
Bernal, Martin. *Black Athena: The Afroasiatic Roots of Classical Civilization*. 2 vols. New Brunswick, N.J.: Rutgers University Press, 1987, 1991.
Berry, Wendell. *Collected Poems: 1957–1982*. San Francisco: North Point Press, 1985.
Blair, Lawrence. *Rhythms of Vision*. New York: Harper & Row, 1976.
Bleeker, C. J. *Egyptian Festivals: Enactments of Religious Renewal*. London: Brill, 1967.
———. *Hathor and Thoth: Two Key Figures of the Ancient Egyptian Religion*. London: Brill, 1973.
Blum, Ralph. *The Book of Runes*. New York: St. Martin's Press, 1982.
Boylan, Patrick. *Thoth: The Hermes of Egypt*. Chicago: Ares, 1987.
Breasted, James H. *Ancient Records of Egypt*. 5 vols. Chicago: University of Chicago Press, 1906.
———. *The Dawn of Conscience*. New York: Scribner's, 1933.
Brier, Bob. *Ancient Egyptian Magic*. New York: Quill Books, 1980.
Briffault, Robert. *The Mothers*. 3 vols. New York: Macmillan, 1927.
Briffault, Robert, and Bronislaw Malinowski. *Marriage: Past and Present*. Boston: Porter Sargent, 1956.
Briggs, John. *Fire in the Crucible: The Self-Creation of Creativity and Genius*. Los Angeles: Tarcher, 1990.

Budge, E. A. Wallis. *The Egyptian Heaven and Hell*. La Salle, Ill.: Open Court, 1925.
———. *Book of the Dead*. Secaucus, N.J.: University Books, 1960.
———. *Egyptian Book of the Dead: The Papyrus of Ani in the British Museum*. New York: Dover, 1967.
———. *The Gods of the Egyptians*. 2 vols. New York: Dover, 1969.
———. *Egyptian Magic*. New York: Dover, 1971.
Bunson, Margaret. *The Encyclopedia of Ancient Egypt*. New York and Oxford: Facts on File, 1991.
Cahoone, Lawrence E. *The Dilemma of Modernity: Philosophy, Culture and Anti-Culture*. Albany: State University of New York Press, 1987.
Campbell, Joseph. *The Masks of God: Creative Mythology*. Rev. ed. New York: Penguin Books, 1969.
———. *Masks of God: Primitive Mythology*. Rev. ed. New York: Penguin Books, 1969.
———. *The Hero with a Thousand Faces*. Princeton, N.J.: Bollingen, 1972.
———. *The Masks of God: Oriental Mythology*. New York: Penguin Books, 1976.
———, ed. *Myths, Dreams, and Religion*. New York: Dutton, 1970.
Casson, Lionel. *Ancient Egypt*. Alexandria, Va.: Time-Life Books, 1965.
Clark, R. T. Rundle. *Myth and Symbol in Ancient Egypt*. London: Thames & Hudson, 1978.
Childe, V. Gordon. *New Light on the Most Ancient East*, 4th ed. London: Routledge & Kegan Paul, 1952.
Cooke, Harold P. *Osiris: A Study in Myths, Mysteries and Religion*. 1931. Reprint. Chicago: Ares Publishers, 1979.
Cornford, F. M. *Principium Sapientia*. New York: Harper Torchbooks, 1965.
Cott, Jonathan. *The Search for Omm Sety*. Garden City, N.Y.: Doubleday, 1987.
Cottrell, Leonard. *Queen of the Pharaohs*. London: Evans Brothers, 1966.
Creeley, Robert. *Was That a Real Poem and Other Essays*. Bolinas, Calif.: Four Seasons Foundation, 1979.
Crowley, Brian and Esther. *Words of Power: Sacred Sounds of East and West*. St. Paul, Minn.: Llewellyn, 1991.
Cumont, Franz. *Astrology and Religion among the Greeks and Romans*. New York: Dover, 1960.
David, A. Rosalie. *The Ancient Egyptians: Religious Beliefs and Practices*. London: Routledge & Kegan Paul, 1982.
The Destruction of the Jaguar: Poems from the Books of Chilam Balam, trans. Christopher Lauçanno-Sawyer. San Francisco: City Lights, 1987.
Durdin-Robertson, Lawrence. *The Year of the Goddess: A Perpetual Calendar of Festivals*. London: The Aquarian Press, 1990.
Egyptian Mysteries. York Beach, Maine: Samuel Weiser, 1988.
Eisley, Loren. *The Immense Journey*. New York: Harcourt Brace Jovanovich, 1957.
———. *The Star Thrower*. New York: Harvest/HBJ, 1978.
Eliade, Mircea. *Shamanism*. trans. Willard R. Trask. Bollingen Series 76. New York: Bollingen Foundation, 1964.
———. *Myths, Dreams, and Mysteries*. New York: Harper Torchbooks, 1975.
Ellis, Normandi. *Awakening Osiris*. Grand Rapids, Mich.: Phanes Press, 1988.
El-Mahdy, Christine. *Mummies, Myth and Magic*. New York: Thames & Hudson, 1989.

Erman, Adolf. *The Ancient Egyptians: A Sourcebook of Their Writings*. New York: Harper & Row, 1966.

Erman, Adolf, and A. Blackman. *Literature of the Ancient Egyptians*. New York: Methuen, 1927.

Foster, John L., trans. *Echoes of Egyptian Voices: An Anthology of Ancient Egyptian Poetry*. Norman: University of Oklahoma Press, 1992.

Frankfort, Henri. *Ancient Egyptian Religion*. New York: Harper Torchbooks, 1948.

Frost, Robert. *Complete Poems of Robert Frost*. New York: Henry Holt, 1949.

Fry, Christopher. *A Sleep of Prisoners*. Oxford: Oxford University Press, 1951.

Gadon, Elinor W. *The Once and Future Goddess*. San Francisco: Harper & Row, 1989.

Gardiner, Sir Alan. *Egyptian Grammar*. 3d ed. Oxford: Griffith Institute, 1957.

Gaster, Theodor H. *Thespis: Ritual, Myth, and Drama in the Ancient Near East*. 2nd rev. ed. New York: Doubleday-Anchor Books, 1961.

Gimbutas, Marija. *The Language of the Goddess*. San Francisco: Harper & Row, 1989.

Goldberg, Natalie. *Writing Down the Bones*. Boston: Shambhala, 1986.

Goodrich, Norma Lorre. *Priestesses*. New York: Franklin Watts, 1989.

Gray, John. *Near Eastern Mythology*. London: Hamlyn, 1963.

Griffith, F. L., and Herbert Thompson. *The Demotic Magical Papyrus of London and Leiden*. London: Grevel, 1904.

Hans, Jenny. *Cymatics*. Basel, Switzerland: Basilius Presse, 1970.

Hart, George. *A Dictionary of Egyptian Gods and Goddesses*. London and New York: Routledge & Kegan Paul, 1986.

Helminski, Kabir Edmund. *Living Presence: A Sufi Way to Mindfulness and the Essential Self*. New York: Tarcher/Perigree, 1992.

Herodotus. *The Histories*, trans. Aubrey de Selincourt. Rev. ed. New York: Penguin Books, 1972.

———. *The Histories*, trans. David Greene. Chicago: University of Chicago Press, 1987.

Heyob, Sharon Kelly. *The Cult of Isis among Women in the Graeco-Roman World*. Leiden, the Netherlands: Brill, 1975.

Hillman, James. *Loose Ends*. Zurich: Spring Publications, 1975.

———. *Healing Fiction*. Barrytown, N.Y.: Station Hill, 1983.

Hillyer, Robert Silliman. *The Coming Forth by Day*. Boston: Brimmer, 1923.

Hoffman, Michael A. *Egypt before the Pharaohs*. New York: Knopf, 1979.

Honor, Alan. *The Man Who Could Read Stones*. New York: Hawthorn Books, 1966.

Hornung, Erik. *Conceptions of God in Ancient Egypt*. Ithaca, N.Y.: Cornell University Press, 1982.

Houston, Jean. *The Possible Human*. Los Angeles: Tarcher, 1982.

———. *The Search for the Beloved*. Los Angeles: Tarcher, 1987.

———. *The Hero and the Goddess: The Odyssey as Mystery and Initiation*. New York: Ballantine, 1992.

Irwin, John T. *American Hieroglyphics: The Symbol of the Egyptian Hieroglyphics in the American Renaissance*. New Haven: Yale University Press, 1980.

Jacobsen, Thorkild, and John A. Wilson, trans. *Most Ancient Verse*. Chicago: The Oriental Institute of the University of Chicago, 1963.

James, E. O. *Myths and Ritual in the Ancient Near East.* New York: Praeger, 1965.
————. *The Tree of Life.* Leiden, the Netherlands: Brill, 1966.
James, T. G. H. *Ancient Egypt.* Austin: University of Texas Press, 1988.
Jochmans, Joseph R. *New Lights along the Nile.* Vols. 1–3. Rock Hill, S.C.: Alma Tara Publishing, 1990.
Johnson, Buffie. *Lady of the Beasts: Ancient Images of the Goddess and Her Sacred Animals.* San Francisco: Harper & Row, 1988.
Joyce, James. *Ulysses.* New York: Modern Library, 1949.
Jung, Carl. *Memories, Dreams, Reflections.* New York: Vintage Books, 1963.
Keller, Evelyn Fox. *A Feeling for the Organism: The Life and Work of Barbara McClintock.* New York and San Francisco: Freeman, 1983.
Lamy, Lucie. *Egyptian Mysteries: New Light on Ancient Spiritual Knowledge.* New York: Crossroads Publishing, 1981.
Lauer, Jean-Phillipe. *Saqqara: The Royal Cemetery of Memphis.* New York: Scribner's, 1976.
Lenz, Elinor, and Barbara Myerhoff. *The Feminization of America.* Los Angeles: Tarcher, 1985.
Lesko, Barbara S. *The Remarkable Women of Ancient Egypt.* Providence, R.I.: B.C. Scribe Productions, 1987.
Lesko, Leonard H. *The Ancient Egyptian Book of Two Ways.* Berkeley: University of California Press, 1972.
Lichtheim, Miriam. *Ancient Egyptian Literature.* 3 vols. Berkeley: University of California Press, 1973–80.
Lurker, Manfred. *The Gods and Symbols of Ancient Egypt.* London: Thames & Hudson, 1974.
MacLean, Paul D. "On the Evolution of Three Mentalities." In *New Dimensions in Psychiatry: A World View,* vol. 2, ed. Silvano Arieti and Gerard Chryanowski. New York: Wiley, 1977.
MacQuitty, William. *Island of Isis: Philae, Temple of the Nile.* New York: Scribner's, 1976.
Maspero, Sir Gaston. *Life in Ancient Egypt and Assyria.* London, 1901.
Masters, Robert. *The Goddess Sekhmet: Psycho-Spiritual Exercises of the Fifth Way.* St. Paul, Minn.: Llewellyn, 1991.
Mertz, Barbara. *Red Land, Black Land: Daily Life in Ancient Egypt.* New York: Dodd, Mead, 1978.
Meyer, Marvin W., ed. *The Ancient Mysteries: Sacred Texts of the Mystery Religions.* San Francisco: Harper & Row, 1987.
Montet, Pierre. *Everyday Life in Egypt in the Days of Rameses the Great,* trans. A. R. Maxwell Hyslop and Margaret S. Drower. Philadelphia: University of Pennsylvania Press, 1981.
Murphy, Michael. *The Future of the Body.* Los Angeles: Tarcher, 1992.
Murray, Margaret. *Egyptian Religious Poetry.* London: John Murray Publishers, 1949.
————. *The Splendour That Was Egypt: A General Survey of Egyptian Culture and Civilization.* New York: Philosophical Library, 1959.
Neumann, Erich. *The Origins and History of Consciousness,* trans. R. F. C. Hull. Bollingen Series 42. Princeton, N.J.: Princeton University Press, 1954.
————. *The Great Mother,* trans. Ralph Manheim, Bollingen Series 47. Princeton, N.J.: Princeton University Press, 1972.

Nicholson, Shirley, ed. *The Goddess Reawakening*. Wheaton, Ill.: The Theosophical Publishing House, 1989.

Otto, Eberhard. *Ancient Egyptian Art: The Cults of Osiris and Amon*. New York: Abrams, n.d.

Patchen, Kenneth. *Selected Poems*. New York: New Directions, 1957.

Paz, Octavio. *The Bow and the Lyre*. 1st ed. Austin: University of Texas Press, 1973.

———. *The Bow and the Lyre*. 2d ed. Austin: University of Texas Press, 1987.

Piankoff, Alexandre. *The Shrines of Tut-Ankh-Amon*, Bollingen Series 40. New York: Harper Torchbooks, 1962.

Plutarch. "Isis and Osiris." In *Morals*, trans. C. W. King. London: Bell, 1908.

Pritchard, J. B. *Ancient Near Eastern Texts*. Princeton, N.J.: Princeton University Press, 1955.

Reed, Bika. *Rebel in the Soul: A Sacred Text of Ancient Egypt*. New York: Inner Traditions International, 1978.

Rilke, Rainer Maria. *Letters to a Young Poet*, trans. M. D. Herter Norton. New York: Norton, 1934.

Robinson, James. *The Nag Hammadi Library*. San Francisco: Harper & Row, 1977.

Romer, John. *Valley of the Kings*. New York: Henry Holt and Co., 1981.

———. *People of the Nile*. London: Michael Joseph, 1982.

Ronan, Colin. *Lost Discoveries*. New York: MacDonald, 1973.

Schwaller de Lubicz, Isha. *Her-Bak: The Living Face of Ancient Egypt and Egyptian Initiate*. 2 vols. New York: Inner Traditions, 1978.

———. *The Opening of the Way: A Practical Guide to the Wisdom of Ancient Egypt*. New York: Inner Traditions, 1981.

Schwaller de Lubicz, R. A. *Symbol and the Symbolic*, trans. Robert and Deborah Lawlor. Brookline, Mass.: Autumn Press, 1978.

———. *The Temple in Man: Sacred Architecture and the Perfect Man*, trans. Robert and Deborah Lawlor. New York: Inner Traditions, 1981.

———. *Nature Word*, trans. Deborah Lawlor. West Stockbridge, Mass.: Lindisfarne Press, 1982.

———. *Sacred Science: The King of Pharaonic Theocracy*, trans. André and Goldian VandenBroeck. Rochester, Vt.: Inner Traditions, 1982.

———. *The Egyptian Miracle: An Introduction to the Wisdom of the Temple*, trans. André VandenBroeck. Rochester, Vt.: Inner Traditions, 1985.

Shakespeare, William. *The Complete Works of William Shakespeare*, 2 vols., ed. W. G. Clark and W. Aldis Wright. Garden City, N.Y.: Doubleday, 1936.

Sheldrake, Rupert. *The Presence of the Past*. New York: Times Books, 1988.

Shorter, Alan W. *The Egyptian Gods*. London: Routledge & Kegan Paul, 1937.

Simpson, William Kelly. *The Literature of Ancient Egypt*. New Haven, Conn.: Yale University Press, 1972.

Steiner, Rudolf. *Eurythmy as Visible Speech*. London: Rudolf Steiner Press, 1984.

Talbot, Michael. *The Holographic Universe*. New York: HarperCollins, 1991.

Thomas, Lewis. *The Lives of a Cell*. New York: Viking, 1975.

Thompson, William Irwin. *The Time Falling Bodies Take to Light*. New York: St. Martin's Press, 1981.

Tompkins, Peter. *Secrets of the Great Pyramid.* New York: Harper/Colophon Books, 1971.

———. *The Magic of Obelisks.* New York: Harper & Row, 1981.

The Triumph of Horus: An Ancient Egyptian Sacred Drama, trans. H. W. Fairman. Berkeley and Los Angeles: University of California Press, 1974.

Underhill, Evelyn. *Mysticism.* New York: Meridian Books, 1957.

VandenBroeck, André. *Al-Kemi: Hermetic, Occult, Political, and Private Aspects of R. A. Schwaller de Lubicz.* Great Barrington, Mass.: Inner Traditions-Lindisfarne Press, 1987.

Versluis, Arthur. *The Egyptian Mysteries.* London: Arkana Books, 1988.

von Franz, Marie Louise. *A Psychological Interpretation of the Golden Ass of Apuleius.* Zurich: Spring Publications, 1970.

Wainwright, G. A. *The Sky Religion in Egypt.* London: Cambridge University Press, 1938.

Walker, Barbara G. *The Woman's Encyclopedia of Myths and Secrets.* San Francisco: Harper & Row, 1983.

West, John Anthony. *The Traveler's Key to Ancient Egypt.* London: Columbus Books, 1987.

———. *Serpent in the Sky: The High Wisdom of Ancient Egypt.* 2d ed. Wheaton, Ill.: Quest Books, 1993.

Whitman, Walt. *Leaves of Grass.* New York: Crowell, 1964.

Whitmont, Edward C. *Return of the Goddess.* New York: Crossroad Publishing, 1986.

Witt, R. E. *Isis in the Graeco-Roman World.* Ithaca, N.Y.: Cornell University Press, 1971.

Woldering, Irmgard. *The Art of Egypt.* New York: Crown, 1967.

Wordsworth, William. *The Selected Poetry and Prose of Wordsworth,* ed. Geoffrey H. Hartman. New York: New American Library, 1970.

Zabkar, Louis V. *Hymns to Isis in Her Temple at Philae.* Hanover, N.H.: University Press of New England, 1988.

Zohar, Danah. *The Quantum Self.* New York: Morrow, 1990.

MUSICAL SELECTIONS

The following list is drawn from music that we have used successfully in the teaching and practice of this work. Readers should feel free to include their own favorites, while trying to keep within the mood of the applicable area. Some selections from one area can be used in the other areas at the guide's discretion.

Area 1 represents background music. The selections are also effective for guided imagery and meditation and during evocation of altered states of consciousness.

Area 2 includes evocative music that is meant to stimulate and enhance the process itself.

Area 3 represents music that has a celebratory character and is often used to accompany the conclusion of exercises and processes.

The music listed below, as well as tapes of the actual Isis and Osiris sessions from which the material in this book was drawn, is available from

Wind Over the Earth, Inc.
1688 Redwood Avenue
Boulder, CO 80304
800-726-0847

AREA 1: BACKGROUND MEDITATIVE MUSIC

Don G. Campbell, *Crystal Meditations* (The Art of Relaxation C-9517).
Coyote Oldman, *Tear of the Moon* (Coyote Oldman).
Constance Denby, *Novus Magnificat* (Hearts of Space HS 11003-4).
Chaitanya Hari Deuter, *Ecstasy* (Kuckuck 11044-4).
Chaitanya Hari Deuter, *Land of Enchantment* (Kuckuck 11081-4).
Kay Gardner, *A Rainbow Path* (Ladyslipper L3C 103).
Gregorian Chants, *Officinum Tenebarum* (Celestial Harmonies 13022-4).
Hildegard of Bingen, A *Feather on the Breath of God, Sequentia and Hymns by Abbess Hildegard of Bingen* (Hyperion Records CDA 66039).

Alan Hovhaness, *Mysterious Mountain* (RCA AGLI-4215).
Keith Jarrett, *Koln Concert* (ECM 810067-4).
Georgia Kelly, *Ancient Echoes* (Heru Records).
Kitaro, *Silk Road* (Canyon 051-052).
Daniel Kobialka, *Dream Passage* (LiSem Enterprises OK 101).
Daniel Kobialka, *Timeless Motion* (LiSem Enterprises OK 102).
Ottmar Liebert, *Borrasca* (Higher Octave HOMC-7036).
Melissa Morgan, *Invocation to Isis* (Kicking Mule KM-414).
R. Carlos Nakai, *Journeys: Native American Flute Music* (Canyon CR-613-C).
Ottorino Respighi, *Ancient Airs and Dances* (Mercury 434304-2).
Mike Rowland, *The Fairy Ring* (Sona Gaia Productions).
Therese Schroeder-Sheker, *In Dulci Jubilo* (Celestial Harmonies 13039-2).
Therese Schroeder-Sheker, *Rosa Mystica* (Celestial Harmonies 13034-2).
Tony Scott, *Music for Zen Meditation* (Verve 817209-4).
John Serrie, *And the Stars Go with You* (Miramar MPC-2001).
Spiritual Environment, *Shamanic Dream* (Nightingale Records 321).
Michael Stearns, *Chronos* (Sonic Atmospheres CD-312).
Michael Stearns, *Planetary Unfolding* (Sonic Atmospheres CD-307).
Eric Tingstad/Nancy Rumbel, *Homeland* (Narada Lotus ND-61026).
Eric Tingstad/Nancy Rumbel, *Legends* (Narada Lotus ND-61022).
Vangelis, *L'Apocalypse Now* (POL 31503).
Rob Whitesides-Woo, *Heart to Crown* (Serenity 005).
Rob Whitesides-Woo, *Miracles* (Serenity 002).
Rob Whitesides-Woo, *Mountain Light* (Serenity 70018-4).
Henry Wolff/Nancy Hemings, *Tibetan Bells II* (Serenity 006).

AREA 2: EVOCATIVE MUSIC

J. S. Bach, *Brandenburg Concertos—Volumes 1 and 2* (COL 42274 and COL 42275).
Samuel Barber, *Adagio for Strings* (RCA AGLI-3790).
Chaitanya Hari Deuter, *Ecstasy* (Kuckuck 11044-4).
Empire of the Sun (soundtrack) (Warner Bros. 25668-4).
Field of Dreams (soundtrack) (Novus 3060-4-N).
Kay Gardner, *A Rainbow Path* (Ladyslipper LRC 103).
Robert Gass and Wings of Song, *Extended Chant Series: Heart of Perfect Wisdom, Kalama, Shri Ram, Om Namah Shivaya, Alleluia* (Spring Hill Music 1005, 1006, 1011, 1012, 1013).
Al Gromer Khan, *Mahogany Nights* (Hearts of Space 11020).
Philip Glass, *Koyaanisqatsi* (Antilles 422-814042-4).
The Gyoto Monks, *Freedom Chants from the Roof of the World* (Rykodisc RACS-20113).
Mickey Hart, *At the Edge* (Rykodisc RACS-10124).
Hildegard of Bingen, *A Feather on the Breath of God, Sequentia and Hymns by Abbess Hildegard of Bingen* (Hyperion CDA 66039).

Jean Michel Jarre, *Equinox* (Polydor 8294556).
Jean Michel Jarre, *Oxygene* (NTI 824746).
Magnum Mysterium, *Collection of Sacred Music* (Celestial Harmonies 18.45012).
Mendelssohn/Bruch, *Violin Concertos* (Capital 69003).
The Mission (soundtrack) (Virgin 905676-2).
Nana Mouskouri, *Libertad* (Mercury 826799-4).
Nana Mouskouri, *Ma Verité* (Philips 826391-4).
Nana Mouskouri, *Passport* (Philips 830764-2).
Nana Mouskouri, *Tierra Viva* (Mercury 832958-4).
Nana Mouskouri, *Why Worry* (Polydor 830492-4).
NASA Voyager II Space Sounds, *Miranda* (Brain/Mind Research).
Olatunji, *Drums of Passion* (COL CK8210).
Carl Orff, *Carmina Burana* (COL 33172).
Francis Poulenc, *Concerto for Organ* (Angel S-35953).
The Rustavi Choir, *Georgian Voices* (Elektra/Nonesuch 79224-4).
Camille Saint-Saëns, *Symphony No. 3* (RCA ATLI-4039).
Jean Sibelius, *Finlandia* (Phillips 9500140).
Bedřich Smetana, *The Moldau* (COL 36716).
Bedřich Smetana, *My Country* (DGG 2707054).
Taize, *Wait for the Lord* (Special Order, Wind Over the Earth).
Pyotr Tchaikovsky, *Violin Concerto in D* (Angel-EMI 32807).
Jeffrey Thompson, *Child of Dream* (Brain/Mind Research).
Vangelis, *L'Apocalypse Des Animaux* (POL 831503-2).
Vangelis, *Chariots of Fire* (Polydor 825384-4).
Vangelis, *Direct* (Arista AC-8545).
Vangelis, *Heaven and Hell* (RCA LPK1-5110).
Vangelis, *Ignacio* (Barclay 813042-2).
Vangelis, *Ode* (POL 1473109).
Vangelis, *Opera Sauvage* (Polydor 829663-4).
Antonio Vivaldi, *Gloria* (Electra 45248).
Paul Winter, *Missa Gaia/Earth Mass* (Living Music LMC-0002).
Zuleikha, *White Pavillion* (Box 9139, Santa Fe, N.M. 87504).

AREA 3: CELEBRATORY MUSIC

Anugama, *Exotic Dance* (Nightingale Records NGH CD-311).
Enya, *Watermark* (Reprise 26774-4).
Hooked on Classics, Vol. 1, 2, and 3 (K-Tel NU 6113, NU 6893, NU 626).
Jean Houston/Howard Jerome, *You Are More* (Wind Over the Earth).
Nusrat Fateh Ali Khan, *Mustt Mustt* (Real World 91630-2).
Nusrat Fateh Ali Khan, *Qawwal and Party* (Real World 991300-2).
Daniel Kobialka, *Timeless Motion* (LiSem Enterprises OK-102).
Eric Kunzel and Cincinnati Pops Orchestra, *Pomp & Pizazz* (Telarc 80122).
La Bamba (soundtrack) (Slash 25605-4).

Brent Lewis, *Earth Tribe Rhythms* (Ikauma COM-3300).
Perles du Baroque (Arion Records ARN 436342).
Bedřich Smetana, *The Moldau* (COL 36716).
Paul Simon, *Graceland* (Warner Bros. 9-25447-4).
Paul Simon, *The Rhythm of the Saints* (Warner Bros. 9-26091-4).

For further information concerning Jean Houston's seminars, books, and tapes, please write to her at Box 3300, Pomona, New York 10970.

PERMISSIONS ACKNOWLEDGMENTS

Grateful acknowledgment is made to the following for permission to reprint previously published material:

City Lights Books: Excerpt from *The Destruction of the Jaguar: Poems from the Book of Chilam Balam,* translated by Christopher Sawyer-Laucanno. Copyright © 1987 by Christopher Sawyer-Laucanno. Reprinted by permission of City Lights Books.

Normandi Ellis: "Song of Isis" reprinted herein in its entirety as Chapters 1–3. Copyright © 1994 by Normandi Ellis. Excerpts from *Awakening Osiris.* Copyright © 1988 by Normandi Ellis. Used by kind permission of the author.

Harcourt Brace & Company: "February 2, 1968" from *Farming: A Hand Book* by Wendell Berry. Copyright © 1970 by Wendell Berry. Reprinted by permission of Harcourt Brace & Company.

Jack Lindsay: Except from *The Golden Ass* by Lucius Apuleius, translated by Jack Lindsay, Indiana University Press, 1962. Reprinted by permission of Jack Lindsay.

New Directions Publishing Corp.: Excerpt from "Be Music, Night" from *The Collected Poems of Kenneth Patchen* by Kenneth Patchen. Copyright © 1943 by New Directions Publishing Corp. Reprinted by permission of New Directions Publishing Corp.

W. W. Norton & Company, Inc.: Excerpt from *Rilke on Love and Other Difficulties* by Rainer Maria Rilke, translated by John J. L. Mood. Copyright © 1975 by W. W. Norton & Company, Inc. Reprinted by permission of the publisher.

Viking Penguin: "When the Ripe Fruit Falls" by D.H. Lawrence, from *The Complete Poems of D.H. Lawrence* by D.H. Lawrence, edited by V. de Sola Pinto and F.W. Roberts. Copyright © 1964, 1971 by Angelo Ravagli and C.M. Weekley, Executors of the Estate of Frieda Lawrence Ravagli. Used by permission of Viking Penguin, a division of Penguin Books USA Inc.

The Quest: Excerpts from an interview with John Anthony West in *The Quest,* Winter 1991. Reprinted by permission of *The Quest.*

PICTURE CREDITS

INDEX

About the Author

JEAN HOUSTON, internationally renowned philospher, human potential expert, and mythologist, is the author of the national bestsellers *The Possible Human* and *Search for the Beloved*, among many other books. Her pioneering work helping the indigenous peoples preserve their cultures while moving into the next millennium has earned her much acclaim. Additionally, Dr. Houston is codirector of the Foundation for Mind Research, and the founder and director of the Mystery School, a thirteen-year-old program of spiritual study and sacred psychology based on the principles of the ancient mystery traditions. Her intensive, high-energy workshops blend lectures and presentations on myth, history, and psychology with music, meditations, and dance.